FL

D1518484

INTERNATIONAL TRACK AND FIELD
COACHING ENCYCLOPEDIA

INTERNATIONAL TRACK AND FIELD COACHING ENCYCLOPEDIA

edited by

FRED WILT and TOM ECKER

PARKER PUBLISHING COMPANY, INC.
West Nyack, New York

PRINTED IN THE UNITED STATES OF AMERICA
13-473645-1   BC

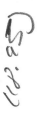

OTHER BOOKS BY THE AUTHORS

Championship Track and Field by Twelve Great Coaches
by Tom Ecker (Prentice-Hall, Inc.)

Championship Football by Twelve Great Coaches
by Tom Ecker with Paul Jones (Prentice-Hall, Inc.)

Illustrated Guide to Olympic Track and Field Techniques
by Tom Ecker and Fred Wilt (Parker Publishing Company, Inc.)

How They Train
by Fred Wilt (Track and Field News)

Run-Run-Run
by Fred Wilt (Track and Field News)

Mechanics Without Tears
by Fred Wilt (U.S. Track and Field Federation)

FOREWORD

One World of Track and Field is gradually but surely becoming a reality. Despite the pessimists who can see only today's chaos in international sports organization and codes of amateurism, despite the great prevalence today of separate nations and self-seeking power groups within those nations, our modern world of sports is evolving a grass-roots unity which, in time, is certain to cover the earth.

Consider the miracle of the Olympic Games with over 100 nations, consider the increasing dual, triangular, and group meets among those nations, consider the growing use of IAAF rules and terminology at all levels of competition, consider the many contacts between coaches and athletes of different countries, and, not least in its effects, consider the growing distribution of international literature on track and field.

Future sportsmen will not judge sportsmen of today by their power to maintain the outworn traditions of the past nor by their ability to dictate the organization of sports today. Service to the realities of the future will be the primary criterion—the sharing of sports knowledge despite competitive differences, the building of mutual respect between competing groups, the restoration of a sense of honor in keeping the essential agreements of amateur sports.

In that sports future, Fred Wilt and Tom Ecker, the co-editors of this *International Track and Field Encyclopedia*, will be given a high ranking. And this book will be regarded as one of the great harbingers of things to come, a landmark in the development of international track and field knowledge.

Through their wide-ranging contacts and through their diligent editing, Fred and Tom have secured a well-balanced high-level product from the 23 coaches of 12 countries who have contributed to this book. Keep in mind that foreign coaches tend to specialize in a few related events, and thus become truly expert. Thus, this is a book that is certain to stimulate your thinking about the techniques of coaching, but equally important, it is also certain to advance the One World of Track and Field so essential to the future of amateur sports.

J. Kenneth Doherty
Former Head Track Coach
University of Pennsylvania
University of Michigan

HOW AND WHY THIS BOOK DEVELOPED

The domain of track and field is basically running, jumping and throwing; yet the sport is filled with many interesting contrasts. Pole vaulting is as unrelated to shot putting as basketball is to swimming, and triple jumping has no more connection with javelin throwing than football with table tennis. The track and field umbrella covers many different sports, and the track coach stands at the crossroads of many divergent skills.

In addition to intimate familiarity with the technique of each individual event, the contemporary coach must have a working knowledge of learning theory, teaching techniques, skill acquisition, administration, cybernetics, physiology, classical mechanics and practical psychology. Yet if a coach travels too far along the path of any one science related to the art of coaching, he soon ceases to play the role of coach and adopts the white smock of the scientist.

Nevertheless, the modern coach can acquire a practical working knowledge of all track and field events and the many related sciences if he will seek out knowledge from those experts from around the world who have each specialized in one particular area of the sport. It is upon such a premise that this volume has been constructed.

Since advanced athletics technology holds no respect for national or language barriers, it was decided that the authors for the individual chapters of such an all-inclusive book should be selected on the exclusive basis of expertise, with no regard for political or cultural boundaries. Thus, the 24 contributing coaches have been chosen from among the best from six continents, making this a book that is truly international in scope. So international and so complete, in fact, that it is not merely a book—it is an encyclopedia!

In this encyclopedia, easy to follow learn-by-doing teaching stages are included whenever they will aid in teaching an event. Each of the events is tackled first from the viewpoint of the beginner, and then the reader is carefully led through the entire range of the event and the related sciences, on up to the absolute limit of current knowledge.

For the coach and the athlete this encyclopedia will afford paragraph after paragraph of useful knowledge. And for the fan it will offer a greater insight into the complicated inner-workings of track and field athletics.

FRED WILT
TOM ECKER

CONTENTS

years. He served as coach of the USA team against the
British Commonwealth in 1966 and in the Pan-American
Games in 1967.

K. O. BOSEN, instructor at India's National Institute of
Sports, has studied track and field coaching methods in the
USA and in East Germany. A former decathlon athlete,
Bosen was coach of India's 1964 Olympic team.

JIM BELLWOOD, one of New Zealand's top track and
field authorities, is a graduate of England's famous Loughborough Training College. He is a teacher of physical education and editor of *Amateur Athletics Coach*, a New Zealand
track and field monthly.

PART II. THE JUMPING EVENTS

G. M. ELLIOTT, a former British Empire champion and
Olympic team member, is Professor of Physical Education at
the University of Alberta. Elliott is Senior Jumping Coach
at the Royal Canadian Legion National Track and Field
Coaching Clinic.

JOHN DOBROTH, himself a consistent seven-foot high
jumper, has devoted much time and energy to the study of
high jump technique. He has been instructor for the advanced
course in high jump at two international coaching clinics.

TOM OLSEN is an internationally recognized authority on

the manufacture and performance of fiberglass materials. He has lectured on the pole vault throughout North America and has written several articles and booklets on the teaching of pole vaulting.

BILL PERRIN, assistant track coach at the University of Wisconsin, has lectured on pole vaulting at two Sports International track and field clinics. He is considered one of the most advanced technical exponents of the fiberglass vaulting era.

DOUGLAS COGHLAN, a graduate of Loughborough College in England, is track and field coach at Rhodes University, South Africa. He spent the 1966–67 school year in the USA, studying for an advanced degree and exchanging ideas with U.S. coaches.

JESS JARVER is a native of Estonia and a naturalized Australian citizen. Jarver, the Senior Coach of the Australian Amateur Athletic Association, is author of a best-selling book on track and field and editor of a monthly coaching magazine.

DR. GEOFF R. GOWAN is one of Great Britain's AAA senior coaches. He was formerly track and field coach of the Loughborough College Athletic Club in England, and is now a professor of physical education at McMaster University in Canada.

PAT TAN ENG YOON, a former triple jump star, has done exhaustive studies of triple jump technique and training. A graduate of Loughborough Training College in England, he is now serving as National Coach of Singapore.

dynamic javelins. An engineer by trade, he has taught javelin throwing at many international track and field coaching clinics.

WILF PAISCH, one of Great Britain's national coaches, has coached numerous British teams in international competition. He has authored a number of technical track and field articles and a best-selling booklet entitled *Javelin Throwing.*

ORLANDO GUAITA, an authority on hammer technique, is a past hammer throwing champion of Chile. He has studied physical education at the Institut National des Sports in Paris, France, and in the USA.

SAM FELTON, Jr., a member of the 1948 and 1952 U.S. Olympic teams, is regarded as a leading hammer authority of the English speaking world. He is credited with doing more for the technical advancement of hammer throwing in the USA than any other person.

INTERNATIONAL TRACK AND FIELD
COACHING ENCYCLOPEDIA

Part I

THE RUNNING EVENTS

Chapter 1

THE SPRINT RACES

by Jim Alford

The dictionary definition of sprinting is "running short distances; running at full speed." In other words, there is no let up, no conservation of energy in any part of the race; every stride demands maximum effort. Strictly speaking, of the standard track events, only the 100-yards and 100-meters races come within this definition, and, even in these events, the effort to apply a maximum possible force at each stride often leads to untimely muscular tension with a consequent loss of range and speed of movement. Skill in avoiding this is often rather vaguely described as the "ability to relax."

In the 220-yards and 200-meters races, this need for a "relaxed" style of full speed running is a little more obvious, but in all these short sprints endurance is entirely local and unaffected by the runner's efficiency in taking up and utilizing oxygen during the race itself.

In the 440-yards and 400-meters races, general endurance enters the picture and there is, however subtle, a definite conservation of energy in order to spread the effort throughout the race to its best effect. But the quarter-miler's pace is so close to his flat-out speed that sheer sprinting ability is the basic requirement for the event and warrants the 440's recognition as the toughest of the sprint races.

The differences between the metric and English sprint races are shown in the following table:

$$100 \text{ m.} = 100 \text{ yds.} + 9.36 \text{ yds.} \ (+.9 \text{ secs.})$$
$$200 \text{ m.} = 220 \text{ yds.} - 1.28 \text{ yds.} \ (-.1 \text{ sec.})$$
$$400 \text{ m.} = 440 \text{ yds.} - 2.56 \text{ yds.} \ (-.3 \text{ sec.})$$

A MECHANICAL ANALYSIS OF THE SPRINT ACTION

The basic movements of running are acquired largely by instinct and partly by imitation at such an early age that the pattern of movement is formed without

3

any conscious learning process. But these naturally acquired movements can, of course, be made more skillful and efficient, and they will become more effective as the athlete gains greater strength and endurance. Improvement in a sprinter's running action is a matter of refining and strengthening instinctively acquired movements—of getting the best possible results from the tools at one's disposal. Running style is the sum total of body build, muscular strength, joint mobility, natural rhythm and coordination, and much of it depends on inherited qualities. But the development of the tremendous sprinting speed needed in modern competition calls for some consciously acquired movements designed to produce such efficiency that all the available power can be used effectively in each stride.

An efficient running action will conform with the basic mechanical principles of movement, and an analysis of these principles will help us determine, always within the limitations of the runner's body build, just what are the most effective movements.

Figure 1.   Figure 2.   Figure 3.   Figure 4.

Figure 5.   Figure 6.   Figure 7.

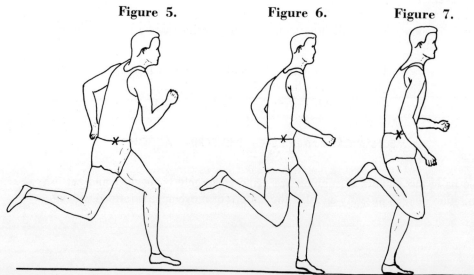

Figures 1–7 show some of the positions a runner passes through during a complete stride. The following terms are convenient to use when analyzing the various phases.

1. The shaded leg is the "driving" leg.
2. The other (free) leg is the recovery leg.
3. Position 1 is the supporting phase.
4. From position 1 to 3 is the driving phase.
5. From position 3 to 6 is the recovery phase.
6. From position 6 to 7 is the transition phase from recovery to drive.
7. X is the approximate position of the runner's center of gravity.

Basically, speed in running is the simple product of rate of striding and length of stride. A sprinter with a stride length of 8 feet and a rate of 4¾ strides per second would develop a speed of 38 feet per second (just under 26 m.p.h.) and would have a potential of about 9.0 seconds for the 100 yards. Sprinters come in all sizes and shapes, and stride length may vary between 7 and 9 feet. An average rate of striding is 4½ strides per second, and, from available statistics, it is unlikely that any top-class sprinter exceeds a rate of 5 strides per second while running at top speed.

Rate of Striding

The rate of striding is concerned with the time taken for the sprinter to move from position 1 to 7. This is governed by—

1. The speed of extension of the driving leg.
2. The speed with which the recovery leg is brought through.
3. The length of time spent in the air.
4. The landing position of the recovery foot relative to the runner's center of gravity.

Extension of the Driving Leg. Provided that the runner's center of gravity is propelled forward the maximum possible distance, the shorter the time spent on the ground the better. Quickening the stride will not necessarily improve sprinting speed, if there is an incomplete extension of the driving leg. The prime consideration here must be the speed of contraction of the extensor muscle groups. Physiological theory is often held back by insufficient data. Hence the term "quality of muscle" is sometimes used to describe a characteristic which is not fully understood. It is certain that some men are born with this "quality of muscle," be it less muscular viscosity, better joint leverage or a more efficient neuro-muscular coordination, which singles them out as natural sprinters. The "quality" is innate, but remarkable improvement can be effected through regular, systematic practice of the proper movements and through a gain in muscular strength.

Obviously, the efficient relaxation of the antagonist muscle groups is also important, and it is reasonable to expect that this, too, will be improved by practice, by an increase in muscular strength and flexibility.

The Recovery Leg. The speed with which the recovery leg is brought through is governed by the strength of the force being applied, and by the moment of inertia of the leg, i.e. its mass and the disposition of that mass. The force available can be increased by a gain in muscular strength. The mass of the leg may be reduced, over the months of training, as superfluous fat is eliminated, and all sprinters recognize the importance of using extremely light running shoes. But the most effective way to reduce the moment of inertia of the leg is to bring some of the mass up closer to the axis of rotation at the hip joint. As the foot leaves the ground the leg begins to flex at the knee, and as the thigh is brought through the leg folds up more and more, often resulting in the sprinter's rear heel lifting as high as his buttocks. (See Fig. 1.) This is a perfectly natural movement, requiring no extra expenditure of energy to carry it out. It is brought about first of all by a natural reaction to the previous powerful leg extension and then assisted by the reversal in direction of the angular velocity of the thigh, coupled with a relaxation of the extensor muscles of the knee. Viewing the runner from his right side as in Figures 1–7, it can be seen that, as the driving leg sweeps back, its angular velocity is in a clockwise direction. Then, as the foot leaves the ground, the angular velocity of the thigh becomes anti-clockwise, but the muscles which had been extending the leg at the knee joint relax and allow the lower leg to continue with its clockwise angular velocity. The more forceful the leg drive, and the more complete the subsequent relaxation of the driving muscles, the higher the heel will rise and the smaller will be the moment of inertia of the leg.

Time Spent in the Air. A sprinter, running at full speed, may spend just under a tenth of a second in contact with the ground and just over a tenth of a second in the air during each complete stride. The time spent in the air depends on the extent of the rise and fall of the runner's center of gravity during that period.

During a complete stride, as in Figures 1–7, there will be a greater rise and fall of the runner's center of gravity than would be indicated by tracing the path of a fixed spot on the runner's hip. Obviously, from the supporting phase to the end of the driving phase the lift of the recovery leg and the arms raises the runner's center of gravity without causing a corresponding rise in the hips. However, once the runner has left the ground the predetermined path of his center of gravity will rise less than that of a fixed spot on the hip, since the lowering of the recovery leg and of the arms now lowers the center of gravity in the body. This low position of the center of gravity in the body as the recovery foot comes to the ground indicates that the path of the runner's center of gravity has risen less but dropped more than that of a fixed spot on his hips. A smooth path of a fixed spot on the hip while the runner is in the air does give a fair indication of the runner's efficiency in cutting down the time spent in the air. In good sprinting, in fact, the rise and fall of a fixed spot on the runner's hip can be as little as one inch and this is essential for the timing of a speedy leg action.

A low trajectory of the path of the runner's center of gravity can be brought about in two ways:

1. By leaning well forward with the trunk, and,
2. by utilizing good flexibility of the hip joint, so that the hips are brought well forward of the foot of the driving leg before the final push from the extension of the knee and ankle joint. Good mobility of the ankle joint will also contribute to this low drive.

The first method is used at the start of a sprint race and is an essential factor in providing balance during a phase of great acceleration. Its drawback is that it limits the height of knee lift, and so cuts down the time available for the recovery foot to develop a backward velocity relative to the ground, before it makes contact. This is not so important while the body is moving fairly slowly over the ground, as in the starting strides, but it becomes increasingly so as the body gains speed. After the accelerating period, therefore, it is more efficient to gain a low trajectory of the center of gravity through hip and ankle mobility.

Landing Position of Recovery Foot. The position of the recovery foot as it lands will also affect the time spent in the air. Reaching out with the foot in an effort to lengthen the stride will increase the time spent in the air and slow up the rate of striding. Moreover this will mean that the foot will be coming down to the ground with insufficient backward velocity. The action of the legs can be compared to that of a wheel insofar as they are continually pushing back at the ground, but this action will be efficient only if there is a drive backward during the complete time that the foot is in contact with the ground. From slow-motion film analysis it would seem that even the best sprinters fail to achieve this ideal since there is a slight check as the foot hits the ground. But the more efficient the sprinting, the faster the foot is moving back as it hits the ground and the less time is spent in this transition from recovery to drive. A good knee lift, good hip mobility, muscular strength and a fast leg cadence all contribute to this. When one watches a slow-motion film it appears that the sprinter is going to bring his foot down well in front of the hips, but, in fact, he uses this position to gain leg speed backwards so that he makes contact with the ground, well up on the sole of the foot, almost under the hips.

Stride Length. Stride length is governed by the velocity and the trajectory of the runner's center of gravity as he leaves the ground, and the position of the recovery foot relative to the center of gravity as he again makes contact. An effort to increase the length of stride by raising the trajectory would be ineffective, as it would lengthen the time spent in the air and decrease forward velocity.

It has already been shown how the landing position of the recovery foot influences the rate of striding. However, if it were possible to exert force over a longer period by bringing the foot down further ahead of the center of gravity it might be worth sacrificing a little of the stride rate. Reference to Figure 8 will show that this is not so. Here the sprinter is exerting a downward-backward force against the ground and the reaction from this drives him forward-upward. This reaction force has been divided into two components—F1 the horizontal

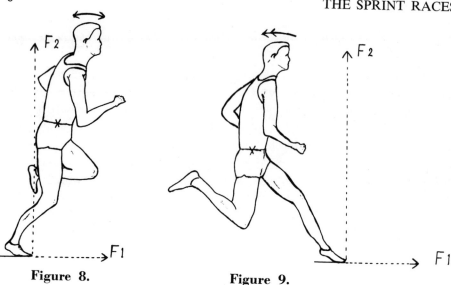

Figure 8.   **Figure 9.**

component and F2 the vertical component. Since the two component forces are applied to the foot of the runner, and the inertia of his body acts at just above hip height, "turning couples" will be formed. F1 will drive the body forward but will also tend to rotate it backward, while F2 will tend to rotate it forward. So there is a form of balance between the rotational effects of the two components, and the thrust of the driving leg presents no problem. In Figure 9, however, where the foot is placed on the ground in front of the runner's center of gravity, both components tend to rotate the body backward and an effort to apply a backward-downward thrust would be ineffective and wasteful of energy; man is not provided with the muscular apparatus necessary for such a movement. Thus the problem of stride length is simply the horizontal velocity the sprinter can impart to his center of gravity by the time he loses contact with the ground. Concerned with this are:

1. The speed with which the sprinter can extend the hip, knee and ankle joint (which we have seen also affect the rate of stride), his muscular strength, joint flexibility and the efficient action of his antagonist and fixator muscle groups.

2. The horizontal distance over which the force is applied. The low position of the hips as in Fig. 3, will affect this, as will the extent of forward movement of the hip and thigh of the recovery leg.

3. The reaction to the force required to give the recovery leg forward velocity. While this leg is accelerating in a forward direction, it will exert a backward thrust to the runner's center of gravity, which will be transmitted through the driving leg to the ground, thus increasing the driving force. A powerful pull through of the recovery leg will increase stride length without decreasing stride frequency, provided that the extensor muscles of the driving leg are strong enough to cope with the additional stress laid upon them. This reaction is

especially valuable to the sprinter as he gains his full speed and is finding it increasingly difficult to move his driving foot back with a velocity greater than his center of gravity is moving forward. The result to this powerful pull through of the recovery leg is the characteristic high knee pickup of good sprinters.

Arm Action. To understand the function of the arms in running it is necessary to analyze further the reactions by the upper part of the body to the forces generated by the thrust of the driving leg and the powerful pull-through of the recovery leg. The thrust of the driving leg is transmitted to the hip bone slightly to the side of the runner's center of gravity. Thus, when the left leg drives, this eccentric thrust will, in the absence of any contrary acting force, set up a turning couple which will rotate the hips (looking downward) in a clockwise direction, pushing the left hip forward. At the same time, the pull-through of the recovery leg will have a similar reaction, tending to push the right hip back. In practice, however, the right hip is thrust forward and so the rotation is in the opposite direction to that prompted by the eccentric thrust of the legs, and the muscular force required to rotate the hips must increase in proportion to the force of leg drive. It is the upper part of the body which absorbs the reaction from the eccentric leg drive. If the arms are kept still, the shoulders will rotate in a contrary direction to the rotation of the hips, and, in distance running, with its slower rate of striding and less forceful drive, it is quite effective to allow the shoulders to absorb most of the reaction in this way. But the shoulders cannot cope with the tremendously speedy and vigorous "stop-start" movements of sprinting and so the more agile arms take over the reaction.

This they can do only if their movement is mainly forward and back. As the left leg drives, the forward swing of the left arm has the effect of thrusting the left shoulder back while the backward swing of the right arm reacts to thrust the right shoulder forward. Thus the shoulders are kept steady and the balance between action and reaction is kept entirely by the arms.

It is true that, as the arms swing forward, there is a slight movement inward towards the mid line of the body. This counterbalances the action of the opposite leg, which also moves slightly inwards so that, viewed from the front, a runner is seen to "knee in" slightly. In this way he is able to bring his foot down very close to the line of running. A sprinter of average build, running along a two-inch wide line, will just touch the line with each foot. An athlete with narrow hips has a certain mechanical advantage in that he can do this and, at the same time, keep the planes of movement of his limbs more nearly parallel with that of the path of his center of gravity.

Although the arms obviously cannot directly propel the runner's body, their action can have either an inhibitory or a liberating effect on the thrust from the legs, and so they can either hinder or assist propulsion. In order to give maximum assistance, their action must match that of the legs both in speed and range of movement.

To facilitate speed of action, the moment of inertia of the arm is decreased by bending the elbow at about 90 degrees. To ensure a forceful arm action the range of movement of the arms must be large. The structure of the shoulder joint is such that there is a natural limit to the extent of the backward swing and consequently no danger of exaggerating range of movement. For this reason alone it is well to emphasize the backward movement.

The backward swing of the arm can also be more useful in encouraging forward thrust from the legs, for while this leg drive tends to pull the shoulders back, the backward swing of the arm at least pushes one shoulder forward. By straightening the arms slightly during the backward swing and bending them again for the forward swing, the backward movement can be made more forceful than the forward one, and the arms can give greater assistance to the leg drive. The straightening of the arm as it swings back is a natural movement which can be seen, in greater or less degree, in all sprinters, skilled and unskilled alike. The sprinter's skill is shown in his ability to utilize this straightening of the arm during the middle (and most effective) part of the backward swing, and yet obtain a good flexion just before the arm begins to swing forward.

THE SPRINT START

The mechanics of the sprint start are concerned primarily with the reactions to the powerful horizontal thrust exerted by the sprinter against the starting blocks. To balance the strong backward rotational effect of this thrust, the sprinter must adopt a starting position with his center of gravity placed low and well forward of the feet. In the standing start position it is impossible to get the center of gravity far enough ahead of the feet and still maintain a motionless position.

Placing the hands on the ground to steady the body, however, is not the perfect solution; the shoulders are now brought too low, even for the great horizontal thrust of the first starting stride, and even the best sprinters show a significant and unavoidable lift of the shoulders during the drive from the blocks. It is essential, therefore, that the hands and arms are placed in such a way as to keep the shoulders as high as possible.

Placing the hands on the track has another disadvantage; to get the required forward position of the center of gravity, the feet must now be placed some distance behind the starting line. A good deal of research has been carried out into the effect of varying the front and back block spacing, but there is no record of any attempt to evaluate the optimum distance of the front block from the starting line. Since Bresnahan and Tuttle stated in 1934 that "a man of 5'8" in height placed the front block 11, 13 and 18 inches behind the starting line for the elongated, medium and bunch starts respectively, and a man of 6'1" in height placed the front block 14, 16 and 21 inches behind the starting line for the same series," these empirical findings seem to have been accepted without question. In theory, the principle would seem to be that the front foot is placed as near to the starting line as possible, as long as it permits the athlete to position his center of gravity, in the "Set" position, the required distance ahead of the front foot.

The earlier experiments on block spacing (Dickenson, Kistler, 1934) were concerned mainly in measuring the differences in the force exerted on the blocks and in the duration of time between the report of the starting gun and the moment the sprinter lost contact with the front block. Taking the three "standard" block spacings of "Bunch" (11″), Medium (16-21″) and Elongated (26″) there was agreement that the sum of the forces exerted by both feet increased as the foot spacing increased. On the other hand, the time taken to clear the blocks also increased as the block spacing increased. Dickenson also claimed that the bunch start got the sprinter to the 2½ yards distance .081 sec. faster than did the elongated start, with intermediate positions giving inter-mediate times. The gain in time taken to clear the blocks for the bunch start was found to average .143 sec., so some of this advantage was lost by the time the runner covered 2½ yards. This might be explained by the fact that the sprinter using a bunch position would start with his front foot some 6–7 inches farther behind the starting line.

The apparent paradox of a block spacing which provided the greatest hori-zontal thrust giving the worst results prompted Henry (1952) to carry his experiments further than those previously made, and he timed his sprinters at 5, 10 and 50 yards. Using block spacings of 11″, 16″, 21″ and 26″, he found that the 11″ spread gave the worst results, the 16″ and 21″ spreads, with no significant difference, gave the best results, and the 26″ spacing was the next best. From Henry's description of his experiments it appears that the runners wore rubber-soled shoes, and that the order of runs was always from 11″ to 16″ to 21″ to 26″. These two factors could possibly have had an unwanted effect on the times of the runs. Sills and Carter (1959) using 9 sprinters timed every 5 yards up to 30 yards claimed that the bunch start gave the best results. Henry's con-clusions agree with the empirical findings of most experienced coaches that a block spacing of between 16″ and 21″ gives the best, balanced position, with the front foot not too far behind the starting line, and presents a good com-promise between speed away from the blocks and force of drive.

No research can be traced into the possible effects of varying the block angles. In theory, the block face should be set at right angles to the desired line of thrust. The thrust of the rear leg should be as nearly horizontal as possible, so the rear block angle should be close to 90 degrees. The line of thrust of the front leg, however, is somewhere between 45 and 30 degrees, depending on the sprinter's ability to accelerate the body mass. A 45-degree block angle is suitable for the beginner, but a 60-degree angle might well be more effective for a strong, experienced sprinter.

Assuming a fixed position of the feet and hands, the height of the hips, in the "Set" position, will depend on the amount of flexion in the legs. The most effective angle of flexion at the knee joint, for power of drive, is one of about 90 degrees. With the front leg flexed at slightly under, and the rear leg slightly over, this angle, the hips will come slightly higher than the shoulders. The important factor is the amount of flexion at the knee; the height of the hips is merely a convenient way of "assessing" the correct angles at the knees. Too low a hip position leads to overflexion of the legs and a consequent weak initial drive, and this in turn leads to a premature lifting of the trunk.

The different characteristics of the starting strides are brought about automatically, simply because this is a stage of great acceleration. The rate of acceleration gradually decreases until, after about 6 seconds, a state of steady speed is reached and maintained as long as possible. Even the fastest sprinters are probably losing speed over the last few yards.

The great horizontal thrust brings about the forward lean of the trunk, which is gradually brought into a more upright position as the rate of acceleration falls off. Since, at the start, the body is traveling over the ground at a comparatively slow speed, the strides are automatically short and gradually increase in length as the runner gains speed. Acceleration depends, in fact, upon the gradual, smooth lengthening of the strides while maintaining a speedy rhythm. Consciously shortening the strides can do nothing but harm.

TECHNIQUE

Good technique, in any event, signifies the rejection of all wasteful movements, and the development, coordination and strengthening of efficient ones. In sprinting the key words are balance and rhythm. Every movement of the athlete's limbs should be coordinated so as to propel his body forward on as smooth and straight a path as possible, and there should be perfect harmony between rate and length of stride.

Too much emphasis on stride speed will lead to *understriding*. The stride will be quickened by being shortened and, although there will be a more frequent contact with the track, less useful work will be done during the moments of contact, and actual speed over the ground will suffer. The iniquitous advice to "cut the strides short" at the start invariably leads to an ineffectual, "pattering" type of running, with a great show of effort for little result.

Too much emphasis on stride length can lead to *overstriding*, if it results in a bounding action or an exaggerated reaching out of the recovery foot just before it comes down to the track. In this case a great deal of effort will be wasted and the rate of stride so impaired that again speed over the ground will suffer.

Both under- and overstriding are obviously faults to avoid. The sprinter would like to improve both the length and the rate of his stride; generally he has to be content with improvement in one without significant harm to the other. In practice, it is very difficult to effect an improvement in leg speed and rate of stride so as to improve actual sprinting speed. The ability to move the limbs rapidly is an innate characteristic of all sprinters. It will improve, naturally, as the athlete becomes stronger and more skillful, but it does not respond well to work directed specifically at its improvement—unless, of course, the sprinter has developed a bad fault of overstriding.

Better results will be obtained by working on strength of drive and range of movement of the limbs. This will slow up the stride during the early stages of practice, but, as the athlete becomes stronger and more accustomed to what are really the correct movements of a full sprinting stride, his rate of striding will again pick up and his sprinting will improve. Provided that he concentrates on a full-blooded drive (with the good range of limb movement essential for this) and also on "running low," he can achieve a good, powerful stride without harm to his proper rate of striding.

Running Low. A word of explanation is necessary here. Many beginners try to achieve this by bringing the feet through low. This is not what is meant at all, and can only lead to bad sprinting. The leg action should be free and uninhibited, with the foot being allowed to swing high at the rear and the knee lifting high in front. It is not the feet or the knees that have to be kept low, but the *hips*, so that however hard the sprinter drives, he still quickly regains contact with the ground and is forced to keep up a good rate of stride.

Stride Length. The fundamental factors that produce a good stride length are as follows:

1. The powerful extension of the driving leg (Figures 1–3).

Whether the hip, knee or ankle joint contributes most to the leg drive is an academic point. The sprinter can afford no weak link in the chain; he must work for a complete, powerful extension in each joint. It may well be that the effective thrust is completed before the leg is fully straightened, but this is immaterial. A thrust of full effort will always result in a full extension of the leg, and good sprinters show an incomplete extension only when they are running at less than full effort.

The proper low direction of thrust will be governed by the flexibility of the athlete's hip and ankle joints in a fore and aft direction. The driving leg should be swept as far behind the body as possible, and both force and direction of thrust will be materially affected by the range of movement of these joints. *Both muscular strength and joint mobility are fundamental to good sprinting.*

2. *Knee Lift* (Figure 3). A high knee lift is characteristic of good sprinting. To the coach it is evidence of a powerful pull through of the recovery leg. It adds to the thrust of the driving leg and, at the same time, gives the recovery leg space in which to move, so that by the time the foot contacts the ground, it is already moving back fast and no time is lost in getting on with the drive.

It often pays to emphasize, and even exaggerate, knee pickup during training, and the sprinter should make sure he has adequate strength in his abdominal and thigh flexor muscles.

Coaches, however, should be wary of giving snap judgments on knee lift. Appearances are often deceptive and depend upon the proportionate lengths of upper and lower leg. Given two athletes of the same height, but with different leg proportions, the runner with the longer thigh will invariably show a lower knee pick up, although the effectiveness of the pull through of the recovery leg may be the same in each case.

3. *Power and range of movement of the arms.* In good sprinting there is no

cumbersome swinging of the shoulders; the powerful, speedy drive of the legs is perfectly matched by an equally powerful and speedy action of the arms. The first essential is muscular strength around the shoulder joint.

Basically, the arms should move straight forward and back, with only a slight inward movement of the forearm during the forward swing, so that the hands never cross the midline of the trunk.

For speed of action two things are important:

1. The arm lever must be kept short by raising the forearm so that there is an angle of about 90 degrees at the elbow.

2. There must be no over-tension in the lower arms and hands, nor around the top of the shoulders and neck.

For the athlete, it is best to think of maintaining an angle of 90 degrees at the elbow throughout the arm swing. The coach, however, will recognize that this angle does not remain constant; the arms tend to open out a little during the backward swing. If the athlete correctly emphasizes the backward swing and avoids over-tension, this will happen quite naturally.

It is essential that the arm lever be kept short throughout the forward swing, and the arm should regain its 90-degree angle by the time it reaches the limit of its backward movement. The athlete will think of a constant 90-degree angle and a powerful, but relaxed pull back of the arms. The coach will watch for a 90-degree angle at the end of the backward swing and throughout the forward swing.

If there is the correct emphasis upon the power of the backward swing, then the range of movement is the maximum possible. The elbows will rise to about shoulder height at the back and the hands to just above chin height in front.

The hands should be kept in a relaxed, cupped position with the thumbs on top. An athlete who is troubled by over-tension will often find improvement if he holds his hands so that the thumb rests lightly on the index finger and the other three fingers are very lightly curled underneath.

Rate of Stride. It has already been stressed that concentrating on the rate of stride seldom produces good results. This is a generalization and, like all generalizations, has its exception. The maintenance of a good rate of striding is mostly a matter of efficient running—that is, of running "low," of bringing the arms and legs forward as short, fast levers, and of getting the recovery leg moving back fast before it contacts the ground under the runner's hips. It is strongly recommended that attention should first of all be paid to the production of a full, powerful stride, and that this should remain the primary goal throughout training. If the coach fears that the sprinter's stride is becoming too slow, he has only to introduce the stimulus of some form of competition to see that the innate leg speed is still there.

While the sprinter is accelerating, a correct body position will ensure that the stride is comparatively short; emphasis on a fast stride here invariably makes it too short. But, when full speed has been gained the stride is automatically at its maximum length and the athlete now enters the most difficult phase of the short sprints. Now the desire to gain even more speed clashes with the physical impossibility of doing so, and the sprinter often "ties up" and fades. There must come a time when it is no longer possible for the runner to move his legs back faster than his body is moving over the ground, so no further increase of speed is possible. But the ability to *maintain* the speed that has been gained must depend, first of all, upon muscular endurance. It goes without saying that a great deal of the sprinter's training should be devoted to improving this quality.

Apart from this, the sprinter must strive to maintain good form and to pour out full effort without any over-tension, and it is here that emphasis on a really fast rhythm of movement, rather than a more vigorous drive is more effective. Nevertheless, the coach should watch to see that this is achieved without restricting the range of movement of the limbs.

Relaxation. When an athlete or coach talks about relaxation he is generally referring to "differential relaxation"; that is, relaxation of tension in those muscles which are not concerned in driving the sprinter forward, and especially in those muscles whose contraction would oppose the required movements.

The beginner will often show crude signs of a lack of this relaxation by tightening the facial and neck muscles, hunching the shoulders or clenching the hands, so that his action becomes stiff and restricted. But even experienced sprinters can feel that they are "tying up" and so losing speed, without showing any obvious signs that they are doing so. Or they may not even be aware of this lack of proper relaxation until, in one particular race, something urges them to stop fighting themselves and they automatically find a new surge of speed.

The problem in full speed running is that all movements are of a "stop and go" nature. The same muscle groups which at one moment have to contract strongly to move the leg backward must immediately relax their tension as the leg shoots forward. When a sprinter, who is already applying full effort, frantically tries to apply still more, he disturbs the correct timing of this switch from tension to relaxation. The "active" muscles stay tensed too long, and so check the flow of the return movement. It must be emphasized that "relaxation" in sprinting is a skill, which can often be mastered only by a great deal of very close to full-speed running.

The self-control and determination of the athlete will also play its part. Extreme concentration is necessary for the sprinter to take advantage of the stimulus of competition without letting it force him into loss of control. He should feel that he is running between two invisible walls which insulate him from all outside distractions and so enable him to run his own race and retain mastery over his movements, whatever the pressure.

Carriage of Head and Trunk. Everybody knows that it is easier to keep good balance during walking or running if the eyes are kept fixed on a spot straight ahead. In sprinting the head should be kept in its natural alignment with the trunk and shoulders; any movement from this position can only hinder balance and weaken concentration. The carriage of the trunk will vary to some extent according to the build of the athlete; for example, a sprinter with poor flexibility in the hip and ankle joints will be forced to adopt a more forward lean of the trunk in order to ensure a low trajectory of drive. The starting strides obviously demand a pronounced forward lean, but once full speed has been gained trunk lean should be very slight. Any exaggeration of it will only hamper knee lift and restrict the movement of the recovery leg.

Foot Action. In sprinting, the runner makes first contact with the ground high up on the outside of the ball of the foot; then the whole of the ball of the foot contacts the ground, and, as the body weight passes over the foot, the heel drops to touch the ground. Then, as the leg drive continues, the area of pressure moves toward the inside of the foot, finishing up under the big toe as the ankle completes its extension. There is generally a slight turning out of the foot as the body weight passes over it, but, in the main, in order to provide the best leverage the foot should be kept pointing straight ahead.

This action should happen quite naturally and instinctively. If it does not, then it is most likely caused by a slight abnormality of joint structure, or by a weakness in the muscles, tendons and ligaments concerned in maintaining proper foot alignment, or perhaps by an incorrect leg action (either not bringing the leg through on a straight path or not making the proper effort to "drive the ground backward"). The remedy for the last two is obvious.

Many successful sprint coaches have emphasized the value of what they call "foot bounce," or sometimes "ankle snap." It must not be inferred from this that they advocate a bounding action. What they are alluding to is the power that comes from a strong and flexible ankle joint and the impression given by the great sprinter of tremendous litheness and elasticity as he completes his drive. The runner who has even a very slight ankle injury quickly realizes how much his speed depends upon the power of his calf muscles and the flexibility of his ankle joints. The sprinter is well advised to devote a good deal of his time to improving these qualities.

Straight Running. In efficient sprinting all of the athlete's movements take place in a vertical plane, which is as nearly parallel to that of the path of his center of gravity as possible. Faults, such as rolling the head, twisting the shoulders or swinging the arms across the body, will dissipate his effort by dragging him from side to side. A good sprinter, running over a two-inch wide line, will just touch the line with the inner edges of his shoes.

A coach, trying to correct the fault of straddling the line of running, will do well to obey the adage "Keep it simple!" A great deal of improvement can be brought about by the simple practice of running at good speed over a straight line. Provided the practice is carried out regularly and with concentration, many slight faults in arm and leg action can be unobtrusively corrected in this way. If this fails, then more specific attention must be paid to correcting the faults in the arm and leg action.

Straddling the line is most often seen in the starting strides. This is often due to over-tension or a conscious shortening of the stride. In either case, the knee lift is weakened and the recovery leg is not allowed to gain its proper position so that the foot can be brought down underneath the runner's center of gravity.

It will take time and patience to correct this fault, but the result will be well worth it.

Figure 10.   Figure 11.   Figure 12.

Figure 13.   Figure 14.   Figure 15.

Figure 16.   Figure 17.   Figure 18.

STARTING TECHNIQUE (Figures 10–18)

The perfect starting position is one which gives
1. The quickest possible response to the gun.
2. The maximum forward velocity from the blocks, and a continuing maximum rate of acceleration for the subsequent strides.

Response to the Gun

The factors which encourage the quickest possible response to the starting signal are:
a) Plenty of practice—but thorough and purposeful practice. Quality is far more important than quantity. Six practice starts carried out with meticulous

concentration are worth far more than 60 performed in a casual, "sloppy" manner, so that the sprinters are encouraged to try to anticipate the starting signal rather than respond to it automatically.

Each start should be treated as a dress rehearsal, and the coach should try to reproduce as faithfully as possible the conditions met in competition. While approximating his holding time between the "Set" and the report of the gun to the "ideal" of two seconds, he should vary it slightly from start to start. A false start should be treated as a serious "offense."

b) The sprinter should build up an identical pattern of movement for every start. The more automatic his preliminary actions become, the better chance he has of building up a "prepared response" to the gun, so that his subsequent movements also become automatic and speedy.

c) He should concentrate on his response to the starting signal, not the signal itself. How he does this is an individual matter, depending upon what he himself finds to be most beneficial. Many sprinters find it best to concentrate on the thrust from the front block; some may find it better to think of "coming out low," or driving the shoulders forward, while others may find that just concentrating on a smooth but strong rhythm of movement will do the trick.

d) Once the sprinter is on the line, he should "withdraw into himself"; his concentration should build up to a peak so that nothing can possibly distract him from his purpose.

Forward Velocity

The factors contributing to maximum acceleration from the blocks and continuity of drive during the ensuing strides are:

a) *Starting blocks.* These should be attached to the track so that there is no play in any direction. The block surface should be firm; the best support is given by a surface which is slotted or holed to take the spikes, so that the sole of the shoe is in contact with the block surface and just the tip of the shoe touches the ground. Extreme care should be taken to line them up with the direction of running.

The front block should be set at an angle of about 45 degrees for the beginner, increasing to about 60 degrees as the sprinter becomes stronger and more skillful. The rear block should be set at an angle of about 80 degrees.

b) *Block Spacing.* The lateral spacing of the blocks will vary a little according to the width of the athlete's hips and the thickness of his thighs. For a sprinter of average build the inner borders of each foot will come about an inch wide of the center line between the two blocks. Some experiment will be necessary here to ensure that the lateral spacing assists straight running.

The fore and aft spacing is not critical to within the nearest inch, but there is a fairly well defined range of spacing, within which the sprinter and his coach can experiment to find the position which gives the best results. A practical method of defining this range is to look at it from the point of view of the sprinter's back knee as it rests on the ground in the "On Your Marks" position. A position of the knee from about 3 inches ahead to about 2 inches behind the toe of the front foot will produce the recommended range of spacing.

The only certain way of ascertaining the one best position for any one sprinter would be to experiment with the use of apparatus which would accurately measure leg thrust and time taken. However, since there is unlikely to be any significant difference in the effectiveness of any block spacing within the recommended range, it can safely be left to the sprinter to adopt the position which he feels most beneficial. Most top sprinters prefer a spacing which brings their rear knee a little ahead of the front foot. The important thing is that the sprinter should settle on a spacing within the recommended range and then stick to it, so that it becomes another "constant" in his pattern of movement.

The distance from the front block to the start line will vary according to the length of the sprinter's trunk and to the block spacing. This is a matter of experiment by the sprinter; he should bear in mind that what he needs is a balanced position which will encourage a powerful leg thrust and a low trajectory, and yet not require the front block to be placed too far behind the start line. As a rough guide, a sprinter about 5' 10" tall will normally place the front block about 15 to 18 inches behind the start line.

A simple way for the beginner to determine his initial block position is as follows:

Ignore the start line for the moment, and take the "On Your Marks" position with your rear knee resting on the ground slightly ahead of the toe of the front foot. Mark the spots where the toes of each foot contact the ground and set the blocks at this spacing. Now stand behind the blocks, step forward over them, place your hands on the ground and look back between your legs as you place your feet firmly on the blocks with just the tips of the feet touching the ground.

Take the "On Your Marks" position again, placing the hands about 12 inches in front of the front foot. Take the "Set" position, raising the hips higher than the head, trying to pitch the body weight well over the hands. The position will probably feel too cramped, so try again, moving the hands an inch forward at a time, until you reach a position which just enables you to lift the hips sufficiently high and pitch the body weight far enough forward to produce a smooth, powerful and low drive out from the blocks.

Measure the distance between the front of the hands and the face of the front block and you will now have your block setting for your preliminary start practice. As you become stronger and more skillful you will be able to pitch the body weight farther forward over the hands, and you may then be able to move the blocks a little nearer the start line.

c) *Position of the Head.* The head should be kept in its natural alignment with the shoulders, and the eyes should be fixed upon a spot about 2–3 feet ahead of the start line. It is a mistake to look too far ahead in the "Set" position, as this cramps the muscles at the back of the neck when the hips are raised to their proper position, and also tends to distract the sprinter's attention. The beginner may feel that he wants to see where he is going, but he will find that the inevitable slight raising of the shoulders as he drives out from his blocks enables him to do this without tilting the head back.

d) Arms and Hands. To keep the shoulders as high as possible and to encourage the correct direction of arm drive, three conditions should be met:

1. The hands should be shoulder width apart.
2. A high bridge should be formed by the fingers and thumb.
3. The arms should be straight.

The hands should be placed with the thumbs and first fingers just behind the start line, and the remaining fingers fairly close to the first finger. This will provide a strong "hinge" over which the arms will pivot.

e) Position of the Hips. The height of the hips in the "Set" position is governed by the amount of flexion in the legs. An angle of about 90 degrees at the front knee and about 120 degrees at the rear knee will produce the most effective combination of speed and force in the leg drive, and this will bring the hips to a position slightly higher than the head and shoulders, as in Fig. 11.

All these points are well illustrated in Figures 10–18. Note that, in the "On Your Marks" position, the shoulders are placed approximately above the hands. Many sprinters find it better still to have the shoulders slightly ahead of the hands as this cuts down the amount of movement necessary in going from the "On Your Marks" to the "Set" position.

Noteworthy here, too, at the completion of each driving phase, are the full extension of the driving leg, the powerful, high knee pickup of the recovery leg and the forceful arm action, with the elbow reaching shoulder height at the end of the backward sweep. The "curling" of the hand at this moment has no significance, except that it does show good "relaxation."

The Starting Strides

There are four simple, basic coaching points here:

1. Run straight! This entails attention to the proper alignment and lateral spacing of the blocks, and the correct position of the hands behind the start line (with the blocks placed in the middle of the lane the hands should be equidistant from the spot where the center bar of the blocks would cut the start line). It helps in training to place the blocks directly over one of the lane lines occasionally, so that the sprinter and coach have a more precise guide to the straightness of the running.

2. Come out low! It is not a good practice for the sprinter to try to keep his trunk low for any set distance, but it is important that he learn to drive really low from the blocks.

The accent is on "drive" because it is the strength of leg drive which controls the amount of trunk lean. There is little point in emphasizing this phase of starting technique unless the starts are made at very close to full speed.

3. Pick the knees up high! If the sprinter tends to stumble when attempting to "come out low," this is generally because of a lazy, incomplete leg and arm action. He is not driving hard enough and, in particular, he is not picking his

knees up high and fast enough to ensure the proper backward drive of the feet as they come to the ground.

4. Drive with legs and arms! Good results will be obtained by emphasizing these basic points. The sprinter will need to take a few "warming-up" starts to prepare his musculature for the stress of full effort, but to perfect the technique required for maximum acceleration from the blocks he will need to run at least 40 yards at full speed, with another 30 yards in which to slow down. This is strenuous practice and will not occupy the whole of a training session, but a reasonably fit sprinter should be able to manage 8–12 full speed starts before fatigue begins to lead to loss of form.

The Finish

Any departure from the running action which has been producing maximum speed can only slow the sprinter down. With this in mind, many champion sprinters have developed an excellent finishing technique simply by concentrating on maintaining effort and good form to a point well past the finishing line.

However, it is possible to gain a few inches at the very end of the race by thrusting the chest forward and downward. The "dip" finish is basically of two kinds. If both arms are pulled back to assist the forward lunge of the chest, the shoulders remain square to the front. However, if the arms continue their normal sprint action there is often a twist of the trunk so that the side of the "torso" is thrust at the finishing line. Whichever method is used, it will be effective only if it takes place during the very last stride so that the slowing up, or complete loss of balance, will take place beyond the finishing line.

Even when the "dip" finish is timed properly there is still the risk of imperceptibly slowing up in preparation for it. The basis of a good finish is the ability to remain "relaxed" while developing full, explosive power. Only when the sprinter has mastered this most difficult technique should he experiment with a "dip" finish.

The general principles mentioned thus far apply to all the sprint events. The 220 yards race brings in the additional problems of curve running and a much greater proportion of sustained full speed running, while the 440 yards introduces the problems of effort distribution, tactics and physical and mental endurance.

220 YARDS AND 200 METERS

A good 220 yards runner must be a good curve runner, since more than half the race takes place around a curve. The smooth, relaxed, efficient style of running which helps a sprinter to excel at the 220 yards also makes bend running easy. The modifications made to the normal running action are just a matter of good balance, and the sprinter is generally not conscious of them. All that is generally needed is plenty of practice aiming to keep to a smooth path within a few inches of the inside of the lane.

When starting on a curve the blocks should be placed near the outside of the lane and pointed slightly inwards so that the first few strides may be made on as straight a path as possible. To line the body up properly the inside hand will now be placed an inch or two behind the start line.

Even when a sprinter finds difficulty in negotiating a bend properly it is best not to confuse him with details, such as leaning in, dropping the inside shoulder or lowering the inside arm. The easiest way to improve his technique is to get him on to a stretch of sand where he can practice making very tight turns, and so acquire the correct movements instinctively.

The real problem of the 220 yards is that of sustaining a full speed action after the initial acceleration of the first 60 yards or so. Much has been made, in the past, of the "coast" or "float." Some coaches have defined this as a very brief and slight relaxation of effort, a sort of freewheeling, for not more than three or four strides, during which no speed is lost. There is still a place for this in running the 220 yards, if the sprinter is inclined to tie up at any particular point.

Other coaches have thought of the coast as occupying the whole of the middle part of the race, between the accelerating first 60 yards and the final effort over the last 40 yards—rather like a car cruising, i.e. maintaining speed with the smallest possible throttle opening. Whether this is called a coast or not is immaterial; it is the cornerstone of 220 yards running.

If the athlete has started properly he will have been running at full speed. It will be impossible to apply more effort. What he has to ensure now is that there will be no weakening of the effort and no misdirected effort. He must keep up the speed and strength of rhythm and yet never lose smoothness and relaxation. Obviously it will be impossible to do this without adequate strength and muscular endurance. The best advice for the sprinter who finds it difficult to relax at top speed is to concentrate on the hands; keeping them loose and relaxed is generally half the battle.

There is often a tendency to slacken off and lose speed just before coming out of the bend, and it is here that the great 220 yards runner often surges past the opposition. This is where the sprinter should rally his forces. No matter how long the finishing straight appears, it will seem no less long if he has "rested" in preparation for it and let his opponents get away.

440 YARDS AND 400 METERS

The quarter miler's running action is basically the same as that used in the shorter sprints; for the first 40 yards or so, it should be exactly the same, for there is no point in anything less than full effort for the start. Even the novice will find it best to start fast and then ease into a fast, relaxed striding action, rather than try to work up to it gradually.

But, in the bulk of the race, when some effort is being conserved in order to spread it evenly over the distance, although the pace is only fractionally below top sprinting speed, this is sufficient to allow the quarter miler to quiet down his movements a little. So, while he settles into a rhythm which will give him the required speed, he should relax and "rest" the arms as much as possible until he needs to bring them into full action again for his finishing effort.

The final effort will start somewhere around the 330-yard mark and, again, there is no question of any great change in the running action. An effort to quicken the stride at this point is unlikely to give good results. The athlete should rather try to strengthen the arm action and leg drive and keep them strong right through the finishing line. Above all, in the final drive for the tape, when fatigue and the proximity of the other runners combine to attack co-ordination and control, there must be a tenacious mental effort to hold on to good form.

Tactics

Accurate judgment of pace and the ability to distribute effort correctly throughout the race are essential for success in quarter miling. Since all top-class races are run in lanes with staggered starts, it will often happen that the athlete sees little or nothing of his opponents, and his pace will depend entirely on his own judgment. Even if he draws one of the inside lanes he should rely upon his knowledge of his own capabilities and not be affected to any great extent by the pace of the other competitors. Certainly nothing should be allowed to interfere with his running of the first 220 yards or so, at what he has found to be his best pace. Effort is a better word to use here than pace, for it may well happen that the stimulus of good competition and perhaps perfect running conditions produce greater speed than intended, although the effort distribution is correct.

Yet there are times when a proper use of tactics is necessary. This applies especially in relay races, when the athlete may be running a leg without lanes. In that case he should keep close to the inside of the track as he rounds the bends. He should not attempt to pass on a bend—with one exception. Toward the end of the last bend he may find a runner in front of him weakening perceptibly. This is the time to strike hard and pass with a rush which will prove demoralizing to his opponent.

If the runner has the lead, he should run his own race at his best possible pace, but it is worth making an extra effort not to be passed in the back straight. He should start his final effort just before coming out of the last bend, so that he makes it difficult for anybody to creep up on his shoulder, and he should hug the inside of the track as he comes out of the bend so that anybody trying to pass will have to go around him.

If an opponent tries to pass him on a bend, or just before entering a bend, he should try to run just fast enough to prevent the other runner from overtaking him. If the opponent can be forced to run wide for a good part of the bend, he will feel the effect of the extra distance he has run at the final dash for the tape.

The most difficult part of the 440 yards race is the third 110 yards, where fatigue is building up and the finishing line still seems a long way off. This is where good tactics are useful even when the race is run in lanes. Although the runner's speed is actually decreasing, it is best for him to think in terms of effort—of "winding up" rather than "winding down." Somewhere around the 220-yard mark he must make a definite effort to keep up the pace. The feeling is one of gradually unleashing more effort—of keeping the running "strong" while still retaining a smooth, relaxed action. If the runner is in an outside lane, there is far greater danger of running too slowly than too fast.

If he has drawn an inside lane, he can adjust his pace slightly to suit the situation. If the others are running strongly, he can use them to pull him along and help him to get within "striking distance" (2–3 yards) as they enter the straightaway. If they appear to be weakening, it will pay him to make an early effort and surge through to the lead. Once in the lead there is only one rule—no letup of effort and no loss of controlled movement.

Even if he has gone a little too fast in the early stages and now feels his strength ebbing away, he must reject any thought of giving up the fight; others are almost certainly in the same boat, or they may have fallen so far back that they have lost confidence in catching him. This is the time for calm, stoical tenacity. If he can hold on to good form with no slackening of effort, he will find that he has more left in him than he thought, and the stimulus of the approaching finishing line will spark off a new burst of energy. It is situations of this type which often produce the breakthrough to best ever performances.

TRAINING

A good coach is receptive to new ideas and eager to make use of any new findings arising out of physiological research into the problems of strength, endurance and speed of muscular contraction. But the little research that has been carried out to date has merely scratched the surface; much of it confirms the correctness of already well-tried methods and much of it complicates rather than simplifies the theoretical background. Consequently, the principles of training are still built on an empirical basis; they are constructed from first- and secondhand experience and discriminate observation, systematized by logical thinking.

In fact, the one firm conclusion to be drawn is that no single factor can be isolated to explain a sprinter's speed—joint leverage, neuro-muscular coordination, strength-weight ratio, gland activity, the bio-chemical properties of blood and muscle, all can be concerned in varying degrees in different athletes. The one thing we do know for certain is that the most effective way to improve these qualities is through sprinting itself.

The good coach is well aware, also, of the individuality of the athlete. It is impossible to lay down a fixed training schedule for any athlete without a full knowledge of his personal circumstances, his experience, performances, physique, temperament, employment and the facilities available to him. Even with a knowledge of all these, a schedule can only be made out on a broad basis, subject to alteration day to day according to the needs of the athlete as his training progresses. Individuals react differently to the same training, and what may be suitable for one may be quite ineffective for another. Certain broad principles, however, apply to all.

1. Training is a way of life. It can be an exciting, challenging and enjoyable way of life. To be sure, if the athlete has set his sights on the top of the ladder, he will have to order his life to provide ample time for his training, but this need not exclude all other interests, nor does it ignore the necessity for earning one's living. It is, in fact, an incentive to healthy living, which is the prerequisite for hard training.

Good training has its psychological effect, and such matters as abstinence from smoking, drinking and unwholesome food, and attention to the keeping of regular hours of sleep become no hardship when they are seen to be an important part of the thorough preparation which produces self confidence.

2. Training should be a gradual buildup. Strength that is gained quickly is lost quickly. The more thorough the preparation, the longer the effects will stay with the athlete and the better he can build up on them in the following years. The top performances are the result of years of training and competition.

We do not know all the answers regarding the intensity of training effort required for best improvement, but certainly continual "exhausting" training will not give the best results. To be sure, there can be no great improvement without real effort on the part of the athlete. Training sessions can be hard and demanding, but, if the buildup is gradual, they will remain within his physical resources, so that by the time he has showered and changed, he is looking forward to his next session.

3. Training should be regular and often—as often as circumstances permit, provided that the athlete is able to feel fully recovered for the next session. This normally means once or twice every day, except during the competitive period.

4. Good training will take the sprinter so far, and then he will meet a psychological barrier to further improvement. The breakthrough will now be provided by the stimulus of competition. This entails a greater expenditure of energy and the athlete should treat his racing as the heaviest part of his training program. He should lighten the remainder of his training schedule accordingly.

The Basic Conditioning Period (Out of Season)

The optimum duration of this period is 3–4 months, but, in practice, it depends on local conditions. In many parts of the world there is virtually no "indoor season," and it is difficult to keep training directed along specific channels, and yet provide sufficient variety and incentive to maintain enthusiasm. In some parts of the U.S.A., where indoor competition is plentiful, the basic conditioning period may be too short to provide the best possible buildup in strength, endurance and technique. This possible disadvantage is outweighed by the opportunity sprinters have of training and racing in proper sprint conditions; that is, on flat, firm surfaces and in reasonably pleasant and warm surroundings.

It is not necessary or wise for the sprinter to carry out all of his training during this period on the track; much of it can be done in more pleasant and invigorating surroundings, especially the slower work which is useful, both to provide relaxation and to improve local endurance in the legs. But good sprinting demands a firm, fast running surface and all training for technique should be carried out on the best surface available.

The basic conditioning period will give the sprinter a rest from the nervous strain of hard competition. It is the time for hard, physical work to build up strength, flexibility, endurance and technique.

Joint flexibility will be improved by emphasizing range of movement of the upper arms and thighs during the running practice. In addition, 10–15 minutes of conscientious exercising to increase the mobility of the shoulder, hip and ankle joints will bring about a big improvement.

Low hurdling is a good practice for developing hip and ankle flexibility. The hurdles need to be no higher than 2'6", since the lateral hip flexibility of the high hurdler is of no value to the sprinter. Half a dozen hurdles can be placed far enough apart to require four strides in between, so that the sprinter alternates his lead leg.

Strength. Much of the strength required by the sprinter can be gained from running practices, especially those in which the resistance is increased in some way. Apart from that, the best form of strength exercise is weight training, which can itself provide some incentive and evidence of progress.

The sprinter is advised to carry out a program of weight training for three days each week during this period. Once he has mastered the skill of handling weights, he should practice with a weight heavy enough to allow him just to manage 3 groups of 6 repetitions of each exercise with 2 minutes rest between each group. Progress can then be made by adding 2½ lbs. extra weight, but cutting the repetitions down to 4, then later gradually increasing the number of groups to 6. When this has been consolidated, he can add another 2½ lbs., but go back to 3 groups of 6 repetitions, and so on. This is by no means the only way to plan a weight-training program, but it is effective and does give some variety to the workouts.

Exaggerated long striding over distances of 50 to 150 yards is a good strengthening and mobilizing exercise. It should be performed at moderate speed and with a pronounced effort made to reach forward with the leading leg. This, of course, is bad sprinting technique, and the athlete will find it a very tiring way to cover the ground, but it will encourage a full range of movement in the limbs. And, provided its use is restricted to the basic period, it need have no lasting effect on technique. When anything like sprinting speed is being used, the emphasis should revert to thrust from the driving leg and pull-through of the leading knee.

This can be alternated with bounding practices in which the sprinter concentrates on drive from the rear leg. Incentive can be provided during these practices by measuring the length of stride, or counting the number of strides needed for a certain distance, or by checking the distance reached in a certain number of strides.

Fast running up fairly steep slopes with maximum use of the arms is also good for leg drive, and fast long striding down gentle slopes is excellent for encouraging a good range of movement.

Harness running is another form of strength training. A "harness" can easily be made from canvas and some rope. The canvas should be placed around the top of the runner's hips and the partner holding the "reins" should apply only enough resistance to make full extension of the hip, knee and ankle of the driving leg just possible, for a distance of about 30 yards.

Endurance. The sprinter's endurance is concerned with some property in or around the muscles themselves. Breathing becomes strenuous and "difficult" only after the race is over. It is the capacity of the muscles to sustain a maximum speed of contraction, and training for endurance must be intensive enough to bring about the appropriate reactions. There must be a great deal of running at such a speed that oxygen debt is being built up very rapidly and also much running under the stress of an oxygen debt, which is close to the athlete's limit. This implies repetitions of speed work with short recovery periods.

Sustained, slow running is useful only in the very early stages of training when the athlete feels that it improves endurance in the legs and encourages mental "toughness" toward fatigue. It is of little value once the athlete is reasonably fit.

For the 440-yard runner, some longer, sustained-effort runs are advisable; runs up to two or three miles with enough effort to create hard breathing for half the distance. Mostly, his extra endurance will be created by increasing the number and length of the fast repetitions.

Forms of "continuous" relays are useful in providing variety and incentive in this "speed-endurance" training.

Technique. Technique is always limited by the runner's strength and endurance; as these improve so should technique, and only then can hard racing apply the finishing touches.

All running is technique work of some sort. The sprinter is always concerned with "running straight," while wasting none of his power and controlling his reactions to the demands of high speed, so that his movements remain well coordinated and "relaxed." During the basic conditioning period much of the work will be just sufficiently below full effort to permit the athlete to produce the sort of "relaxed" running required. As strength and endurance improve, he will be able to do this at higher speeds and over longer distances.

Variety can be given to the practice sessions by using "acceleration runs" over about 300 yards, in which the sprinter starts off slowly, accelerates very gradually for the first 250 yards, and then tries to maintain a fast, relaxed action for the final 50 yards.

"Differential runs" can also be used over distances of 220 to 440 yards for the 100- and 220-yard men, and over 330 and 660 yards for the 440-yard men.

In these the second half of the distance is to be run appreciably faster than the first half.

The following is merely intended as a rough guide to the possible framework of a week's training program during this period:

1st Day.   Fartlek (speed-play) running, amidst the most pleasant and invigorating surroundings available and using suitable slopes for variations in training aims. Weight Training.

2nd Day.   Repetition running on the track, using many, short-distance repetitions, on curves and on straightaways. Acceleration runs. Harness work.

3rd Day.   Fartlek running. Weight Training.

4th Day.   Repetition work on the track, using fewer but longer repetitions. Long striding practice. Bounding practices.

5th Day.   A game, such as squash, badminton, basketball, volleyball, etc. Weight Training.

6th Day.   Fartlek Run.

7th Day.   Differential runs on the track. Repetition runs mixing short and longer repetitions. Long striding practices. Informal relay competitions.

No attempt has been made to suggest the volume or intensity of training for each day, as this will depend on the progress of the athlete. It is best to start off the training on the easy side and then build up the volume in pace with the sprinter's increasing fitness. The volume of training will always be restricted by the athlete's capacity for retaining proper quality in the running.

The intensity of the workouts will also build up quite naturally as the season progresses, but the need for retaining zest and sheer joy in the movements of running will make it necessary to balance the occasional really hard and challenging day's training with one or two lighter days.

The Speeding Up Period (Early Season) 8–12 weeks

The athlete will now aim to maintain what he has built up in strength, and put the final polish on his technique and speed/endurance. The weight-training load will be lightened, either by reducing the number of sessions to two per week or by reducing the number of exercises in each session by 50 percent.

Almost all running will be at racing speed (often faster than racing speed for the quarter miler), and an extra incentive will be supplied by increasing the element of competition in training by means of timed, full speed under-distance runs, or by competition against other athletes. In the latter half of this period the sprinter will meet with his early competitions.

Start and finish practice will form a more important part of the training, and the quarter miler will include plenty of pace work over 220 and 330 yards. Most of the work will be track work, although if some smooth, fast grassland is available, it is worth using it once or twice a week, especially for the speed/endurance work using fast repetitions with a minimum recovery period.

The volume of training will remain about the same, except that there will be a slight easing off a day or two before competitions.

The Competitive Period

This is what the athlete has been building up to. He will now increasingly meet with the strain of nervous excitement prior to importance races, but he should remember that this is the stimulus which produces top performances, and only hard racing can now lift his speed/endurance to a higher level.

Training times will improve as competition lifts performance, but the general aim should be to keep the volume and intensity of training at a level that will maintain the state of fitness that has been built up, and to rely on competition to pull out the athlete's full potential. There is nothing like the conviction that one has trained up to the limits of one's power for producing confidence and determination, but it is now psychologically important that the actual race become the all-important event, for which the athlete "pulls out all the stops." Training should, therefore, be lightened a few days before an important competition, with the day before the event treated as a rest day.

The Warm-up

The competitive warm-up is a necessary mental, as well as physical, preparation for the race. By some experiment in training, the athlete should be able to discover the type of warm-up, under various weather conditions, which gives the best results. He should then use this also as his competitive warm-up, timing it so that it leaves him no more than 20 minutes before his race, just time enough to change his clothing if it has become sweaty, relax for about 5–10 minutes, and then get down to the track and put on his racing shoes and walk and jog and do a few light strides before the race starts. The warm-up should build up gently from slow- to moderate-paced running, and finally to some full-speed running, including two or three fast starts.

Chapter 2

THE MIDDLE-DISTANCE AND DISTANCE RACES

by Gunnar Carlsson

To best understand the complex problem of training the human body to run the middle-distance and distance races, one should oversimplify the process and consider the human body as having two "engines" within it: an aerobic engine, which requires oxygen for fuel, and an anaerobic engine, which functions without a ready supply of oxygen.

Normally, all of the energy needed for everyday activities is received through the workings of the aerobic engine. This aerobic engine, which requires an immediate oxygen supply, is responsible for the combustion of oxygen, which is always directly proportional to the amount of energy which is released in the muscles.

The aerobic engine, therefore, is in use for activities requiring work that lasts "unlimited" periods, such as long running. Its efficiency is limited by the amount of oxygen taken in at the time (oxygen uptake), which is adequate during periods of long, slow running, but which can never be available in sufficient amounts while one runs at high speeds.

When activity is especially high (as in sprinting), the availability of oxygen is not sufficient to provide for the energy requirement. In such cases, some additional energy can be received through the splitting of sugar (glucose), which is stored in the muscles where energy is normally released. This function is the work of the anaerobic engine. It allows activity without a ready oxygen supply and is often referred to as "oxygen debt." Of course, the anaerobic engine supplies most of the energy for fast running, but even while one runs a distance of one mile, the anaerobic engine operates as an auxiliary to the aerobic engine.

The end products of the anaerobic engine's work are energy and lactic acid. Because the collection of lactic acid in the muscles brings about fatigue, energy can be released for only comparatively short periods of time during high-speed running.

The following estimates regarding the use of energy and its release indicate the differences of oxygen uptake and oxygen debt in different length races:

800 meters in 1:45

Absorption of oxygen (uptake)	9.6 liters =	35%
Debt of oxygen	18.0 liters =	65%
Total combustion of oxygen	27.6 liters =	100%

1500 meters in 3:40 (3:58 mile)

Absorption of oxygen (uptake)	20.0 liters =	52.5%
Debt of oxygen	18.0 liters =	47.5%
Total combustion of oxygen	38.0 liters =	100%

5000 meters in 14 minutes

Absorption of oxygen (uptake)	78.0 liters =	81%
Debt of oxygen	18.0 liters =	19%
Total combustion of oxygen	96.0 liters =	100%

10,000 meters in 29 minutes

Absorption of oxygen (uptake)	160.0 liters =	90%
Debt of oxygen	18.0 liters =	10%
Total combustion of oxygen	178.0 liters =	100%

This table is schematic and is estimated with the assumption that a maximum absorption of 5.5 liters of oxygen per minute and a total oxygen debt of 18 liters are all that is possible. A runner with a greater oxygen uptake capacity or a considerably larger capacity to stand oxygen debt will, of course, obtain a better clock time than one who does not have so much ability. The oxygen uptake capacity of the best runners may be as high as 6.0 liters per minute or more. It is very possible also that many runners are able to stand a considerably larger debt of oxygen than the quantities that are shown in these tables.

The figures do indicate the type of training that is the most beneficial in the different running events. The most important consideration for an 800-meter runner is the improvement of his running capacity while maintaining a large debt of oxygen; the 10,000-meter runner, however, should train the capacity of his oxygen absorption. Both properties must be trained, but it is obvious that the main aim of a particular runner's training program must depend on the distance he is to cover during competition.

INCREASING THE CAPACITY OF OXYGEN UPTAKE

To improve the capacity of oxygen uptake, it is necessary for one to run at a speed which requires a great amount of circulation of blood. The best form of training for oxygen uptake is a type of interval running in which the speed of the runs is modest and the rest after each of them is short. It is difficult to estimate exactly how much total distance a runner should log during a training session, but generally an 880-yard runner covers four to five times his race distance, a miler three to four times, a 5,000-meter runner and a 3,000-meter steeplechase runner two to three times, and a 10,000-meter runner one and one-half to two times his race distance.

The speed of these runs must be high enough so that the runner's pulse rate is no more than 15 beats less than his maximum possible pulse rate. For most runners this would require training while the heart is beating at least 185 beats per minute, since most trained athletes have as their maximum heart rate approximately 200 beats per minute.

Interval training belongs to the training complex which we in Sweden call Circulation Training. It merely means training for better utilization of the circulation system. There are other types of training in this complex, but the many different forms of interval training still comprise the backbone of the circulation training system.

To be absolutely sure of getting the best possible training results, one must include all types of interval training in the runner's program. The interval (the recovery period between runs) is very important. It should be taken up with some sort of active exercise such as walking or jogging, and should always be kept as short as possible, especially when short distances are used during the training session. If the interval of rest is too long after 220-yard repetitions, for example, the pulse rate does not remain high enough to provide the best training effect.

If the runner's pulse rate is 185 beats per minute during training, the interval should not be so long that the pulse rate can drop below 120 beats. When one runs repetitions of 110, 220 or 440 yards, 30 to 90 seconds recovery is usually adequate. With interval runs longer than 440 yards, the interval should also be kept short, but the length of the interval is not as important as it is when one runs the shorter distances. In this case, the runs are so long that the pulse rate has time to rise to a higher level during the training runs, and the pulse rate stays at a high level for a long enough time.

The old Swedish training system, Fartlek (speed play), is still useful. This type of training is a type of undisciplined interval training, in that the distances, speeds, number of repetitions, and amounts of rest are dependent upon the train-ing course and the mood of the runner.

CIRCULATION TRAINING BY RUNNING LONG DISTANCES

Distance running is also a type of circulation training. It is known that distance running increases the number of capillaries that are brought into play, which in turn aids in increasing blood circulation. The length of the run shall be between six and twelve miles, and the speed can be as slow as 7:00–7:30 minutes per mile.

IMPROVING THE ABILITY TO WITHSTAND LACTIC ACID (OXYGEN DEBT) THROUGH REPETITION RUNNING

To improve the capacity to stand great amounts of lactic acid in the muscles requires high-speed running during training sessions. At the same time, each of the distances covered must be long enough to insure that a great amount of lactic acid has time to accumulate in the muscles. Practically, then, this means that the running distance cannot be shorter than 330 yards. The number of repetitions will vary from one runner to another, but the basic rule is that the runner must be fairly fatigued at the end of each of these runs.

The period of recovery between these runs will always be longer than in regular interval running. And, each of the succeeding periods of rest, as the workout progresses, will be longer than the previous rest, due to the great amount of fatigue that is inherent in this type of training. The length of the rest period is actually determined by the athlete, who should not be asked to repeat his run until he feels that he can do so at a speed that he feels will be comparable to the previous run.

The types of training which develop the ability to withstand great amounts of lactic acid in the muscles are called Lactic Acid Training. This training can be undertaken during the entire training year, but it is most useful during the three months prior to the opening of the competition season. This type of training should always be done on flat ground, preferably on a regular running track.

During the times of the year when the weather will not allow lactic acid training on the track, a similar effect can be obtained by running on uphill slopes at a very fast rate. When hill running is substituted for running on the track, the distance covered should not be shorter than 220 yards, and the slope should not be so great that it is difficult to complete the 220-yard runs with regular running form.

Along with Lactic Acid Training, we include Tempo Training. Tempo Training is running at racing pace to develop pace consciousness, which can be learned during the regular Lactic Acid Training sessions. A runner who is attempting to run 4:20 for the mile will be able to do so much more easily if he can learn to run 110 yards in 16.2 seconds, 440 in 65, 880 in 2:10, etc. He should learn to do this without having to depend on other runners for pace.

The details of the Swedish training methods can be found on the following chart.

SWEDISH TRAINING SYSTEMS

	CIRCULATION TRAINING	LACTIC ACID TRAINING
General Training Effect	General endurance (condition).	Muscular (special or speed) endurance, pace training, finish strength, spirit.
Characteristics	Low to medium speed, great quantities.	Relatively fast to very fast speeds, less quantity.
Specific Effects of the Training	Increases capacity of the heart and the circulation system, increases oxygen uptake (aerobic function).	Improves oxygen debt capacity, increases alkaline reserves (anaerobic function).

Types of Training	A. Interval Training Systems	A. Interval Training Systems
	1. Short interval (Freiburg method): 110- to 440-yard runs, with the heart rate varying from 15 beats below maximum during the runs to the "warming up pulse rate" between runs. (For example, 185 and 130 beats.) 2. Short interval (Igloi method): 110- to 440-yard runs in 15–22 seconds per 110, with rests of about 15 seconds with little (or no) pulse decreasing. 3. Long interval (Swedish method): Runs lasting 2–3 minutes or 8–10 minutes, for example. 4. Interval sprints (Lydiard method): 20 to 50 50-yard sprints with 60 yards of coasting down. 5. Fartlek. B. Distance Running. (Running without interruption at the same speed.) C. Various other activities (skiing, skating, cycling, swimming, etc.)	1. Repetition running: 1–2 minutes of running at a high speed. 2. Interval pace running: 110–220 yards at pace with 30–90 seconds rest. 3. Interval sprints: (See Circulation Training). 4. Tempo-changing runs: Runs at the competition pace, with a strong finishing spurt. 5. Uphill running: 220 yards or more up a gently sloping hill, finishing with some flat running on the hilltop. 6. Resistance running: Running a distance of 30–100 yards in a harness with resistance (drag, friction device, or even the coach pulling against him) attached. 7. Running in snow, shallow water or sand dunes. B. Special Resistance Training: Barbells, dumbells, iron shoes, springs, stretch rubber, circuit training, short uphill running, etc.

In order to give the proper training for runners of various abilities, the Swedish coaches have devised progressive schedules for interval running and repetition running. See charts 1, 2, and 3.

Beginning the Training Program with a Good Foundation

Warming up (To be done before every training session)
1. 6 to 8 minutes of slow running, landing flat-footed with each step.
2. 10–12 minutes of running at different speeds.
3. 6–8 minutes of bending and stretching exercises.
4. 4–5 acceleration runs of 100–120 yards, the last 40–50 yards at fast speed.

Following is a sample training schedule for a foundation in running, which normally takes up the first two and one-half months of training:

FOUNDATION PROGRAM
FOR MIDDLE-DISTANCE AND DISTANCE RUNNERS
(September to mid-November)

Day 1: Six to ten miles of slow running (about 7–7½ minutes per mile).
20 minutes of weight training (or other strength training), especially for the trunk and back muscles.
10 minutes of "warming down" with jogging, a ball game of some kind, etc.

Day 2: 20–30 x 440 yards interval running, the distance in an easy tempo, with 150 yards of jogging between the runs, making sure that the runner stays in constant motion. Keep the speed of the runs slow enough so that walking between them will not be necessary.
10 minutes of "warming down" with jogging and 4–5 acceleration runs of 100–120 yards.

Day 3: Six to ten miles of slow running (about 7–7½ minutes per mile). (Run on as flat a surface as possible.)

Day 4: 15–22 x 660 yards interval running, the distance in an easy tempo, with 220 yards of jogging between the runs, making sure the runner stays in constant motion.
20 minutes of weight training (or other strength training), especially for the trunk and back muscles.
10 minutes of "warming down" with jogging, a ball game of some kind, etc.

Day 5: 4–6 x 220 yards uphill running, emphasizing a strong leg push and exaggerating the arm action.
10 x 330 yards repetition running, in medium speed (5:20–6:00 per mile).
4–5 x 110-yard acceleration runs in good speed.
10 minutes of jogging.

Day 6: 10–12 miles of slow running over a flat surface (about 7–7½ minutes per mile).

Training Speeds Interval Running	Repetition Running	Sep.	Oct.	Nov.	Dec.	Jan.	Feb.	Mar.	Apr.	Projected Best Result For the Season
220 330 440 660 1100	330 440 660 1320									
32.0 49.0 67.0 1:44.0 2:55.0	38.0 53.0 1:22.0 3:03.0									1:49.0
33.0 50.0 68.5 1:46.0 2:59.0	39.0 54.5 1:24.5 3:08.0									1:52.0
33.5 51.0 70.0 1:48.0 3:03.0	40.5 56.0 1:27.5 3:13.0									1:55.0
34.0 52.0 71.5 1:50.0 3:07.0	41.5 58.0 1:29.0 3:18.0									1:58.0
35.0 53.5 73.0 1:52.0 3:11.0	43.0 59.5 1:31.5 3:23.0									2:01.0
36.0 54.5 74.5 1:54.0 3:15.0	44.0 61.0 1:34.0 3:28.0									2:04.0
36.5 56.0 76.0 1:56.0 3:19.0	45.0 62.5 1:36.5 3:33.0									2:07.0
37.0 57.0 77.5 1:58.0 3:23.0	46.5 64.0 1:39.0 3:38.0									
38.0 58.0 79.0 2:00.0 3:27.0	47.5 66.0 1:41.0 3:43.0									
39.0 59.0 80.5 2:02.0 3:31.0	49.0 67.5 1:43.5 3:48.0									
40.0 60.5 82.0 2:04.0 3:35.0	50.5 69.0 1:46.0 3:53.0									
40.5 62.0 83.5 2:06.0 3:39.0	52.0 70.5 1:48.5 3:58.0									

Chart 1.

PROGRESSIVE TRAINING CHART FOR 1500-METERS RUNNERS

Interval Running	Repetition Running	Sep.	Oct.	Nov.	Dec.	Jan.	Feb.	Mar.	Apr.	Projected Best Result For the Season
220 330 440 660 1100	330/440 660/880 1320/2200									
32.0 49.0 67.0 1:44.0 2:55.0	40.0/ 55.0 1:27.7/2:02.5 3:08 /5:40									3:47.0 (4:05 mile)
33.0 50.0 68.5 1:46.0 2:59.0	41.5/ 56.5 1:30.0/2:05.5 3:13 /5:48									3:52.0 (4:10 mile)
33.5 51.0 70.0 1:48.0 3:03.0	42.5/ 58.0 1:32.5/2:08.5 3:18 /5:56									3:57.0 (4:15 mile)
34.0 52.0 71.5 1:50.0 3:07.0	43.5/ 60.0 1:35.0/2:11.0 3:23 /6:04									4:02.0 (4:20 mile)
35.0 53.5 73.0 1:52.0 3:11.0	44.5/ 61.5 1:37.5/2:15.0 3.28 /6:12									4:07.0 (4:25 mile)
36.0 54.5 74.5 1:54.0 3:15.0	45.5/ 63.0 1:40.0/2:18.0 3:33 /6:20									4:12.0 (4:30 mile)
36.5 56.0 76.0 1:56.0 3:19.0	46.5/ 64.5 1:42.0/2:21.0 3:38 /6:28									4:17.0 (4:35 mile)
37.0 57.0 77.5 1:58.0 3:23.0	47.5/66.0 1:45.0/2:24.0 3:43 /6:36									
38.0 58.0 79.0 2:00.0 3:27.0	49.0/ 68.0 1:47.0/2:27.0 3:48 /6:44									
39.0 59.0 80.5 2:02.0 3:31.0	50.5/ 69.5 1:50.0/2:31.0 3:53 /6:52									
40.0 60.5 82.0 2:04.0 3:35.0	51.5/ 71.0 1:52.0/2:34.0 3:58 /7:00									
40.5 62.0 83.5 2:06.0 3:39.0	52.5/ 72.5 1:55.0/2:37.0 4:03 /7:08									

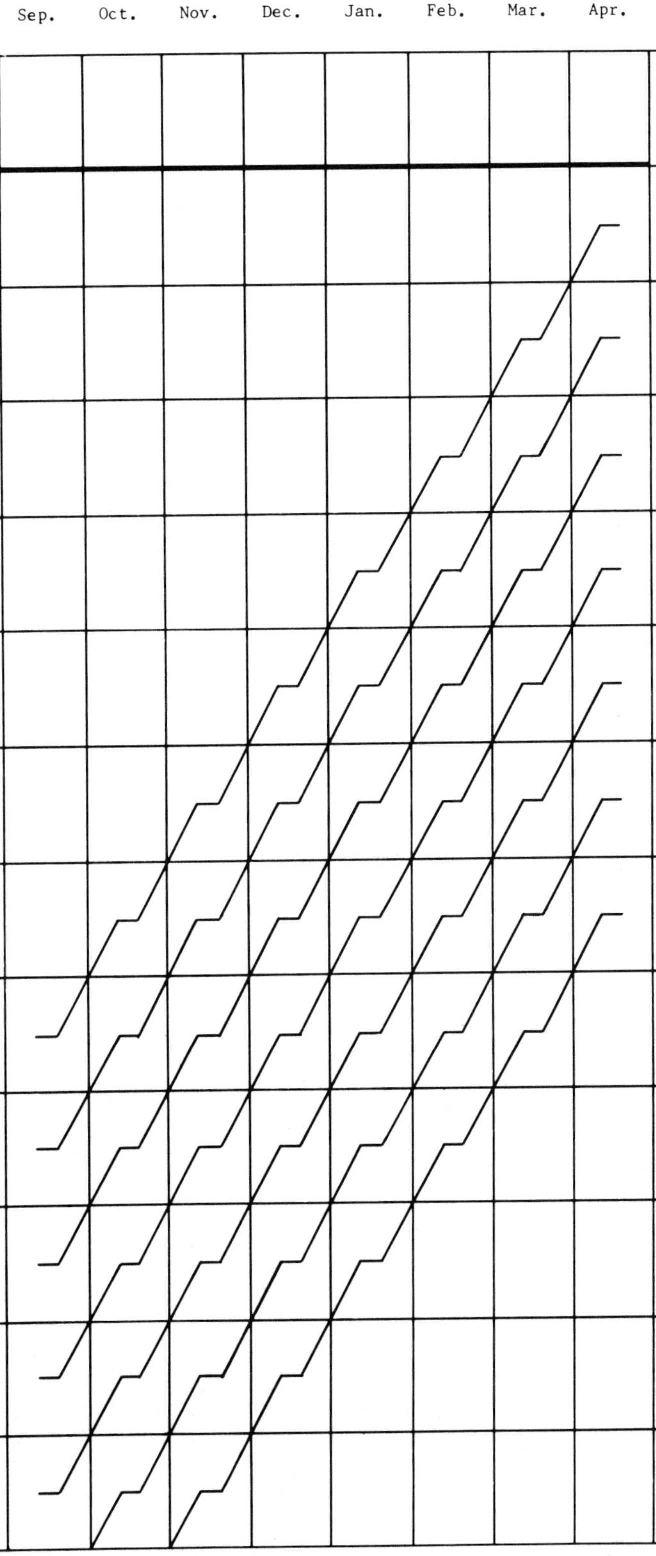

Chart 2.

PROGRESSIVE TRAINING CHART FOR 5,000, 10,000 & STEEPLECHASE RUNNERS

TRAINING SPEEDS

Interval Running	Repetition Running	Sep.	Oct.	Nov.	Dec.	Jan.	Feb.	Mar.	Apr.	Projected Best Result For the Season
220 330 440 660 1100	660/1320 2200/3300									
32.0 49.0 67.0 1:44.0 2:55.0	1:34.0/3:20.0 5:44.0/8:42.0									14:15.0 29:30.0
33.0 50.0 68.5 1:46.0 2:59.0	1:36.5/3:25.0 5:52.0/8:54.0									14:33.0 30:05.0
33.5 51.0 70.0 1:48.0 3:03.0	1:39.0/3:30.0 6:00.0/9:06.0									14:50.0 30:40.0
34.0 52.0 71.5 1:50.0 3:07.0	1:41.5/3:35.0 6:08.0/9:18.0									15:08.0 31:15.0
35.0 53.5 73.0 1:52.0 3:11.0	1:44.0/3:40.0 6:16.0/9:30.0									15:25.0 31:50.0
36.0 54.5 74.5 1:54.0 3:15.0	1:46.5/3:45.0 6:24.0/9:42.0									15:45.0 32:30.0
36.5 56.0 76.0 1:56.0 3:19.0	1:49.0/3:50.0 6:32.0/9:54.0									16:05.0 33:10.0
37.0 57.0 77.5 1:58.0 3:23.0	1:51.5/3:55.0 6:40.0/10:06									
38.0 58.0 79.0 2:00.0 3.27.0	1:54.0/4:00.0 6:48.0/10:18									
39.0 59.0 80.5 2:02.0 3:31.0	1:56.5/4:05.0 6:56.0/10:30									
40.0 60.5 82.0 2:04.0 3:35.0	1:59.0/4:10.0 7:04.0/10:42									
40.5 62.0 83.5 2:06.0 3:39.0	2:02.5/4:15.0 7:12.0/10:54									

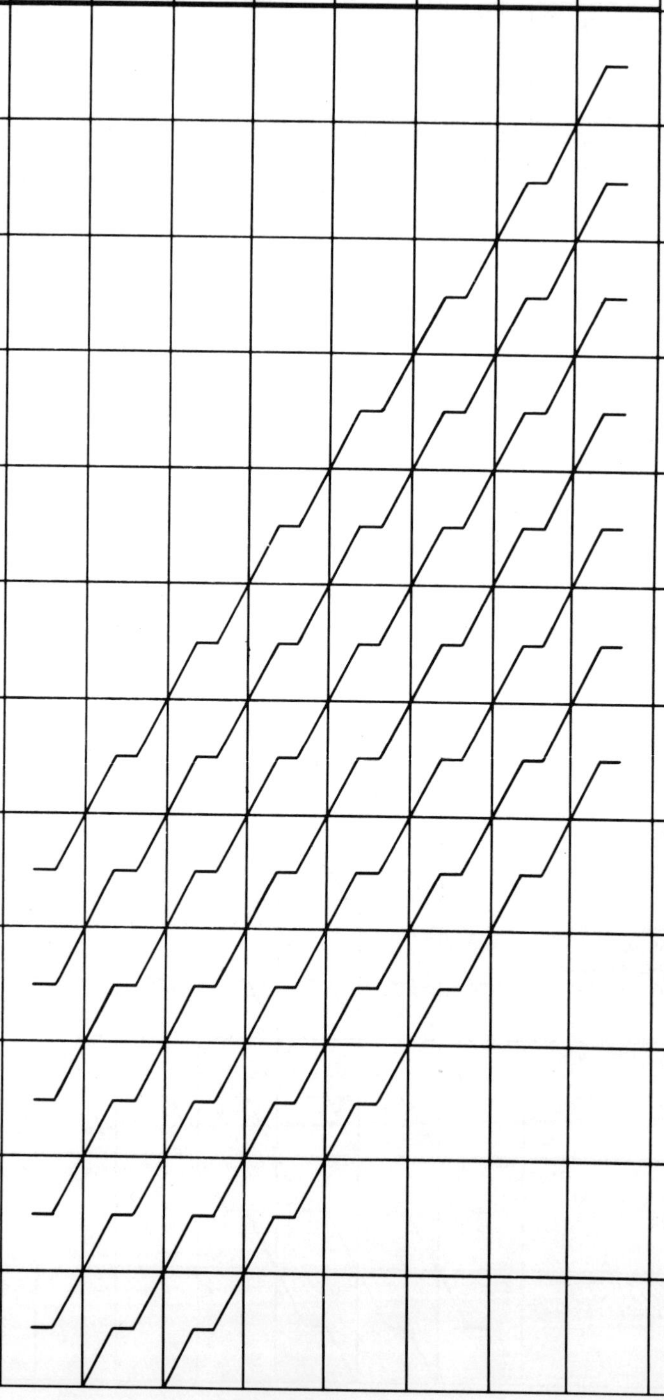

Chart 3.

On the fifth day, during the fall, a long walk can be substituted for the usual program. For the benefit of the mind, it seems to be best to walk in the woods or in some other unpopulated part of the country, mixing occasional runs with the walking. After the walks, some short running should be done to get the feel of running again after having taken a long walk.

The individual coach may want to substitute one day's work for another in the above program, but he should be careful that there is enough variety in the program from day to day so the athlete does not become bored and the workout does not become drudgery.

Although running is the most important part of a runner's training program, there are a number of other exercises which can be integrated into the program in order for the runner to get the foundation necessary to become a top runner, including exercises to develop spring, strength, and flexibility.

The arms and shoulders must be strengthened with weight training or with exercises that tax the arms, such as push-ups and pull-ups. The trunk muscles must be extremely strong, in order to hold the body in place while the leg is exerting its great force against the ground. Long series of sit-ups, and other trunk strengthening exercises, must be done in order to strengthen the trunk adequately. Lying on the back and lifting the legs, from side to side, will also aid in the strengthening of the trunk. Other trunk and back exercises include: (1) Raising the legs while lying, head up, on an inclined bench. (2) Lying face down on a table and raising the trunk while holding the hands behind the neck. (3) Lying on the back and simultaneously raising both arms and legs so that the hands touch the toes.

THE SECOND 2½ MONTHS (Mid-November through January)

880–mile

Following is the second two and one-half months' program for half-milers and milers, to be used after the foundation program on page 35 has been completed. The 5,000 and 10,000 runners and steeplechasers will be treated separately later.

Each day's program should be begun with a good warm-up, bending and stretching exercises, and acceleration runs of 100–150 yards, recovering by walking, springing from the toes while jogging, and more bending and stretching exercises.

Day 1:   4–6 x 60–80 yards uphill with strong strides.
          10–15 x 220 yards interval running, with 30 seconds rest between.
          5–7 x 440 yards interval running, with 30 seconds between.
          1–2 x 165-yard acceleration runs at a fast speed.
          15 minutes warmdown jogging and springing from the toes.
Day 2:   15–25 minutes of long running at half speed (2–3 miles).
          10 minutes of varied slow running, springing from the toes while jogging, and acceleration runs.

20 minutes of weight training and circuit training (three circuits).

10 minutes of easy jogging, a ball game of some kind, etc.

Day 3:   4–6 x 60–80 yards uphill running with strong strides.

4–6 x 1,100 yards interval running, with 1 minute rest between.

15 minutes warmdown jogging and springing from the toes.

Day 4:   6–8 x 660 yards repetition running with 3–6 minutes recovery between runs.

10 minutes of varied slow running, springing from the toes while jogging, and acceleration runs.

20 minutes of weight training or circuit training.

10 minutes of easy jogging, a ball game of some kind, etc.

Day 5:   30–45 minutes of active movement at warm-up speed, followed by a steam bath.

Day 6:   1–1½ hours of running at various speeds through a forest or along roads.

During this training period, include easy running and medium hard runs at distances from 110 to 550 yards, in interval or repetition form. The runs can be made in series of 5–6 x 110 yards, 3–4 x 220, 2–3 x 440 or 550, etc. Include uphill running whenever possible. Finish each day's workout with fast-finishing acceleration runs, easy running, jogging while springing from the toes, and loosening exercises.

5,000, 10,000 and Steeplechase

Day 1:   4–6 x 60–80 yards uphill running with strong strides.

30–40 x 440 yards interval running, with 30 seconds rest between runs.

1–2 x 165-yard acceleration runs at a fast speed.

15 minutes warmdown jogging and springing from the toes.

Day 2:   25–50 minutes of long running at half speed (3–7 miles).

10 minutes of running at various speeds, including easy accelerations every 100–150 yards.

20 minutes of weight training and circuit training (three circuits).

10 minutes of warmdown jogging while springing from the toes, a ball game of some kind, etc.

Day 3:   4–6 x 60–80 yards uphill running.

8–12 x 1,100 yards interval running, with one minute rest between runs.

6–8 x 220 yards interval running, with 15 seconds rest.

15 minutes of warmdown jogging while springing from the toes.

Day 4:   4–6 x 660 yards repetition running, with 2–6 minutes rest between runs.

10 minutes of running at various speed, including easy accelerations every 100–150 yards.

20 minutes of weight training or circuit training.

10 minutes of easy jogging, a ball game of some kind, etc.

Day 5:   One hour of active movement at warm-up speed, followed by a steam bath.

Day 6:   1½–2 hours of running at various speeds along roads or on forest trails. During the workout, include runs at easy and medium hard speeds at distances from 150 to 1,000 yards, and between them include slow jogging. Do them in series of 3–5 x 150 yards, 3–4 x 330 yards, 3–4 x 660 yards, etc. Also do uphill running, and downhill, too, if the slope is very gradual. Finish with fast acceleration runs of 150 yards, easy jogging, and loosening exercises.

THE EARLY COMPETITIVE SEASON (February to mid-March)

880–mile

Training during the early competitive season can be done on the track, on grass, or over a golf course or forest trail. The warm-up is the same, except that the acceleration runs are longer, more frequent and faster. Often, instead of finishing the warm-up with acceleration runs, the runner can substitute a longer, slower type run, 880 yards to one mile in length.

Sunday: 1–1¼ hours of Fartlek. In Fartlek training, include both interval and repetition runs of various distances. The training should be very easy. Include some fast runs down gradual slopes.

Monday: 12–20 x 440 yards interval running, with 30 seconds rest between runs.

15 minutes of warmdown jogging while springing from the toes and easy bending and stretching exercises.

Tuesday: Complete the warm-up with an easy run of one mile.

4–6 x 60–80 yards uphill running, emphasizing a strong leg push and exaggerating the arm action.

8–12 x 330 yards repetition running, with 3–8 minutes recovery.

10 minutes of weight training or circuit training, especially for the trunk and back muscles.

10 minutes of warmdown jogging while springing from the toes and easy bending and stretching exercises.

Wednesday: 2–4 x 1,100 yards repetition running, with 5–10 minutes recovery.

4–6 x 220 yards repetition running, with 2–4 minutes recovery.

15 minutes of warmdown jogging while springing from the toes and easy bending and stretching exercises.

Thursday: 15–25 minutes of slow running (¾ speed) through a forest.

10–15 x 660 yards interval running, with 45 seconds rest between runs.

10 minutes of easy weight training for the arms and the trunk and back muscles.

10 minutes of warmdown jogging while springing from the toes and easy bending and stretching exercises.

Friday: Rest or easy running through the forest, a long walk, or some other light recreation.

Saturday: Pace running (when there is no competition during that week).
For 880 runners, 2–3 x 660 yards, with 15 minutes rest.
For milers, 2–3 x 1,320 yards, with 15 minutes rest.
10–15 x 110 yards in fast, but controlled, speed.
Finish with 10–15 minutes of easy jogging.

5,000, 10,000 and Steeplechase

Sunday: 1–1½ hours of Fartlek in the forest. In Fartlek training, include both interval and repetition runs of various distances. The training should be very easy. Include some fast runs down gradual slopes.

Monday: Complete the warm-up with an easy run of two miles.
12–18 x 660 yards interval running, with 30 seconds rest between runs.
12–18 x 220 yards interval running, with 15 seconds rest between runs.
15 minutes of warmdown jogging while springing from the toes.

Tuesday: 5–7 x 220 yards uphill running with strong strides.
6–10 x 1,100 yards interval running, with one minute rest.
15 minutes of strength training for arm, back and trunk muscles, jogging while springing from the toes, etc.

Wednesday: 2–4 x 2,200 yards repetition running, with 8–12 minutes recovery.
15 minutes of warmdown jogging while springing from the toes.

Thursday: 30–50 minutes of distance running in the forest at ¾ speed.
20–40 x 440 yards interval running, with 30 seconds rest between runs.
10 minutes of weight training or circuit training.
10 minutes of warmdown jogging while springing from the toes.

Friday: Day of rest. A long walk in the forest or other easy activity.

Saturday: Pace running (when there is no competition during that week).
For 5,000 runners, 2 x 3,300 yards, with 15 minutes rest.
For 10,000 runners, 1 x 3,300 yards plus 1 x 5,500 yards, with 15 minutes rest between.
For steeplechasers, 2 x 2,200 yards with hurdles and waterpit. (Steeplechasers must train with hurdles and waterpit 2–3 times a week, always adding one second per 110 yards of workout distance.)

Finish the workout with 10–15 x 110 yards at top speed and a warmdown of 10–15 minutes.

THE COMPETITION SEASON

Following are special 25-day training schedules for middle-distance and distance runners. In each, the athlete need only substitute workout times in the blanks to suit his own ability, as is explained in the Progressive Training Charts on pages 36–38.

The 25 workouts listed should be thought of as an endless cycle of workouts, with #25 followed by #1 again. The only days when the cycle is not followed are those on which there are competitions. If, for example, a competition should fall on day #4, the training program for day #4 will be followed on the day after the competition.

If the runner is able to get plenty of sleep at night, and if his everyday obligations are not physically taxing, then it is recommended that he attempt twice-a-day training three or four days per week. The morning training sessions should consist of either easy running for 45–60 minutes or short interval work, with runs of 110–440 yards, at 17–22 seconds per 110 yards run, with 15–30 seconds rest between runs.

25-Day Training Cycle for 880 Runners

Day

1. 3 x 120 yards acceleration runs
   20–25 x 220 yards interval running, 30–32 seconds, 30 seconds rest.
2. 8 x 100 yards "wind sprints," 30 yards fast and 70 yards coasting, without stopping.
   6 x 330 yards repetition running, with 3–6 minutes recovery.
3. 1 x 330 yards acceleration run.
   10 x 50 yards starts.
   10 x 110 yards near maximum speed, with 3–5 minutes recovery.
4. 3 x 120 yards acceleration runs.
   3 x 1,100 yards repetition running, with 8–12 minutes recovery.
5. 45–60 minutes of continuous running (about 6–7½ miles).
6. 1 x 2,200 yards at an easy speed.
   12 x 100 yards "wind sprints," 40 yards fast and 60 yards coasting, without stopping.
7. One hour of continuous running.
8. 1 x 330 yards acceleration run.
   6–8 x 440 yards repetition running, with 90 seconds rest between runs.
9. 8 x 100 yards "wind sprints," 30 yards fast and 70 yards coasting, without stopping.

220, 330, 440, 330, 220 yards pace running, with 4–8 minutes recovery.

10. 1 x 330 yards acceleration run.
     12 x 440 yards interval running, 62–65 seconds, 45 seconds rest.

11. 3 x 120 yards acceleration runs.
     6 x 440 yards (330 at 880 pace and 110 at top speed), with 3–6 minutes recovery.

12. Fartlek for 1–1½ hours, including 2–3 x 2,200 yards at an easy speed, and various other runs.

13. 2 x 660 yards pace running, with 15 minutes recovery.

14. 3 x 120 yards acceleration runs.
     15–20 x 330 yards interval running, 46–48 seconds, 50 seconds rest.

15. 10 x 100 yards "wind sprints," 30 yards fast and 70 yards coasting, without stopping.
     5 x 440 yards repetition running, with 4–7 minutes recovery.

16. 1 x 330 yards acceleration run.
     10 x 50 yards starts.
     10 x 110 yards near maximum speed, with 4–5 minutes recovery.

17. 3 x 120 yards acceleration runs.
     3 x 1,320 yards repetition running, with 8–12 minutes recovery.

18. 45–60 minutes of continuous running (about 6–7½ miles).

19. 1 x 2,200 yards at an easy speed.
     16 x 100 yards "wind sprints," 40 yards fast and 60 yards coasting, without stopping.

20. One hour of continuous running.

21. 3 x 120 yards acceleration runs.
     8 x 330 yards repetition running, with 2–5 minutes rest.

22. 220, 330, 440, 660, 440, 330 yards pace running, with 5–8 minutes recovery.

23. 3 x 120 yards acceleration runs.
     12 x 440 yards interval running, 63–64 seconds, 60 seconds rest.

24. 3 x 120 yards acceleration runs.
     8 x 330 yards (220 at 880 pace and 110 at top speed), with 4–8 minutes recovery.

25. Fartlek for 1–1½ hours, including 2–3 x 2,200 yards at an easy speed, and various other runs.

25-Day Training Cycle for 1,500-runners and Milers

Day

1. 3 x 120 yards acceleration runs.
    20–25 x 220 yards interval running, 30–32 seconds, 30 seconds rest.

2.   8 x 100 yards "wind sprints," 30 yards fast and 70 yards coasting, without stopping.
      6 x 440 yards repetition running, with 4–6 minutes recovery.
3.   1 x 330 yards acceleration run.
      10 x 60 yards, 10 x 110 yards, 6 x 165 yards at near top speed, with 3–5 minutes recovery.
4.   3 x 120 yards acceleration runs.
      4 x 1,320 yards repetition running, with 8–12 minutes recovery.
5.   1–1¼ hours of continuous running (7–9 miles).
6.   1 x 2,200 yards at a steady speed.
      16 x 100 yards "wind sprints," 40 yards fast and 60 yards coasting, without stopping.
7.   One hour of relaxed running.
8.   1 x 330 yards acceleration run.
      8–10 x 440 yards repetition running, with 4–7 minutes rest.
9.   8 x 100 yards "wind sprints," 30 yards fast and 70 yards coasting, without stopping.
      15 x 440 yards interval running, 63–65 seconds, 45 seconds rest.
10.   440, 660, 880, 660, 440 yards pace running at 1,500-meters (mile) pace, with 5–8 minutes recovery.
11.   3 x 120 acceleration runs.
      8 x 440 yards (330 at mile pace and 110 at top speed), with 4–8 minutes recovery.
12.   Fartlek for 1–1½ hours, including 3–4 x 2,200 yards at an easy speed, and various other runs.
13.   2 x 1,320 yards pace running, with 15 minutes between runs.
14.   3 x 120 yards acceleration runs.
      20 x 330 yards interval running, 46–48 seconds, 50 seconds rest.
15.   8 x 100 yards "wind sprints," 30 yards fast and 70 yards coasting, without stopping.
      4 x 880 yards repetition running, with 6–12 minutes recovery.
16.   1 x 330 yards acceleration run.
      10 x 80, 10 x 110, 6 x 165 yards at near top speed, with 4–8 minutes recovery.
17.   3 x 120 yards acceleration runs.
      3 x 2,200 yards repetition running, with 8–15 minutes recovery.
18.   1–1¼ hours of continuous running (7–9 miles).
19.   1 x 2,200 yards at a steady speed.
      20 x 100 yards "wind sprints," 40 yards fast and 60 yards coasting, without stopping.
20.   One hour of relaxed running.

21. 1 x 330 yards acceleration runs.
     8–10 x 330 yards repetition running, with 2–5 minutes recovery.
22. 10 x 100 yards "wind sprints," 30 yards fast and 70 yards coasting, without stopping.
     20–25 x 220 yards interval running, 30–32 seconds, 30 seconds rest.
23. 440, 660, 880, 660, 440 yards pace running at 1,500 meters (mile) pace, with 5–8 minutes recovery.
24. 5 x 660 yards tempo-changing runs (165 yards at full speed, 330 yards at pace, 165 yards at full speed), with 4–8 minutes recovery.
25. Fartlek for 1–1½ hours, including 2 x 3,300 yards at an easy speed, and various other runs.

25-Day Training Cycle for 5,000 Runners, 10,000 Runners and Steeplechasers

Day

 1. 3 x 150 yards acceleration runs.
     20–25 x 440 yards interval running, 68–70 seconds, 30 seconds rest.
 2. 1 x 440 yards acceleration run.
     6–8 x 1,320 yards repetition running, with 5–12 minutes recovery.
 3. 1½ hours of continuous running (10–12 miles).
 4. 3 x 150 yards acceleration runs.
     10 x 660 yards tempo-changing runs (440 yards at 5,000 pace and 220 yards at top speed), with 5–12 minutes recovery.
 5. 1 x 330 yards acceleration run.
     30 x 220 yards interval training, 32–34 seconds, 30 seconds rest.
 6. 3 x 150 yards acceleration runs.
     10 x 660 yards repetition running, with 2–5 minutes rest.
 7. 1½ hours of relaxed running.
 8. 1 x 3,300 yards easy running.
     20 x 100 yards "wind sprints," 40 yards fast and 60 yards coasting, without stopping.
 9. 3 x 150 yards acceleration runs.
     4–5 x 2,200 yards repetition running, with 5–12 minutes recovery.
10. 1½ hours of continuous running (10–12 miles).
11. 5 x 110, 5 x 220, 5 x 330, 5 x 440, 5 x 330 yards pace running, with 60–90 seconds rest between runs and 3–5 minutes between sets of runs.
12. Fartlek (easy running, with changing speeds) for 1½–2 hours.
13. 2 x 3,300 yards pace running at 5,000 pace, with 15 minutes between runs.
14. 3 x 150 yards acceleration runs.
     25–30 x 330 yards interval running, 46–47 seconds, 30 seconds rest.
15. 1 x 440 yards acceleration run.
     4–5 x 2,200 yards repetition running, with 5–12 minutes recovery.

16. 1½ hours of continuous running (10–12 miles).
17. 1 x 3,300 yards easy running.
    25 x 100 yards "wind sprints," 40 yards fast and 60 yards coasting, without stopping.
18. One hour of relaxed running.
19. 3 x 150 yards acceleration runs.
    10 x 660 yards repetition running, with 2–5 minutes rest.
20. 1 x 330 yards acceleration run.
    3–4 x 3,300 yards repetition running, with 5–12 minutes recovery.
21. 3 x 150 yards acceleration runs.
    8 x 660 yards tempo-changing runs (440 yards at 5,000 pace and 220 yards at top speed), with 5–12 minutes recovery.
22. Two hours of continuous running (15–18 miles).
23. Fartlek for 1½ hours.
24. 1½ hours of relaxed running.
25. 1 x 3,300, 1 x 4,400 yards pace running, with 15 minutes rest between runs.

FORM ANALYSIS

When analyzing middle-distance and distance running form, it is best to talk in generalities, without spending too much time in analyzing any one particular runner's style, since a variety of different (and diverse) styles often fit into "proper" running form.

880–Mile

Figure 19.   Figure 20.   Figure 21.   Figure 22.

Figure 23.   Figure 24.   Figure 25.   Figure 26.

Figure 27.   Figure 28.   Figure 29.   Figure 30.

Figure 31.   Figure 32.

The series of drawings labeled Figures 19–32 shows a good style of running, with relaxed arms, a strong push-off with the feet, a high, driving knee lift, high heel kick, and a good forward lean. Knee lift is particularly important here, since a strong push from one leg while driving over the ground requires a higher knee lift with the opposite leg in order to keep the balance and rhythm of running.

5,000–10,000

Figure 33.   Figure 34.   Figure 35.   Figure 36.

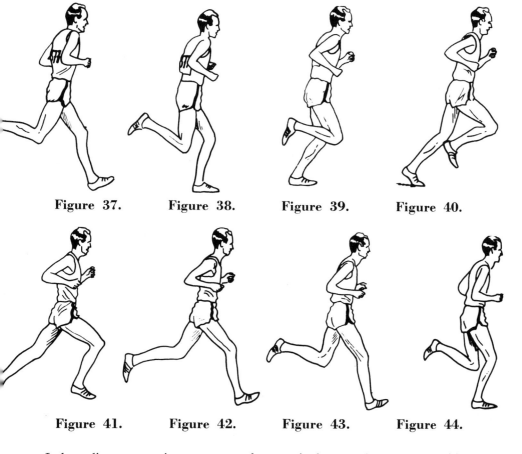

Figure 37.   Figure 38.   Figure 39.   Figure 40.

Figure 41.   Figure 42.   Figure 43.   Figure 44.

In long distance running, economy of energy is the most important considera-tion. In this series of drawings, the runner's arms play a rather passive role and his knee lift is not so high. The leg-push is slower, and, in turn, the stride length is shorter. In this case, the runner is obviously running a 5,000, and his style is more similar to that of a miler than of many 10,000 runners. The 10,000 stride is usually a bit shorter, with less leg stretch and a lower knee lift.

Steeplechase Water Jump

Figure 45.   Figure 46.   Figure 47.   Figure 48.

Figure 49.   Figure 50.   Figure 51.   Figure 52.

Figure 53.   Figure 54.   Figure 55.   Figure 56.

In Figures 45, 46 and 47, the runner concentrates on hitting the top rail of the barrier with the arch of his shoe, which is an absolute necessity to insure that he does not slip. In Figures 48 and 49 he keeps his body low to help conserve energy. The takeoff from the rail in Figures 50, and 51 and 52 is late, as it should be, so that he moves forward rather than up, directly toward the shallow part of the water. Had he attempted to jump sooner, his movement would have been up, and back down, forcing him to land in deeper water. In Figures 53, 54, 55 and 56, his landing is excellent, with one foot in shallow water and his body in position to continue into its normal running stride with the following step.

Chapter 3

RACING TACTICS

by Major Kalevi Rompotti

In order to win, an athlete must not only know how to run, but he must also know how to compete. The competitive capability of a runner is dependent not only upon his physical condition, but to a varying extent upon his tactical ability. Tactical race planning presupposes an ability to predict, at least to some extent, the course of events in actual competition. Executing racing tactics in actual competition presupposes the ability of the runner to take advantage of and profit from the innumerable, unpredictable tactical situations which may develop during the course of any race. In a race among runners of equal physical ability, the winner is usually the athlete who is able to capitalize on the tactical opportunities presented during the competition.

Even the finest tactical plans are useless if the athlete is unable to execute them on the running track. The highest possible degree of physical preparation, endurance, and sprint speed are prerequisites to the most advantageous use of tactics. Only under exceptional circumstances will a runner of inferior physical fitness defeat a much stronger opponent through mere tactics.

The proper use of racing tactics enters the picture only during races run at less than absolute maximum sprinting speed. The 800 meters, 1,500 meters, and one-mile represent the most exacting competitive distances in the use of tactics. In these events, the racing speed is so torrid that often there is not time in which to correct even a minor tactical error.

Racing tactics may be divided into winning tactics and result tactics, depending upon the competitive objectives of the runner.

WINNING TACTICS

Often a runner feels that victory is more important than posting a fast competitive time. This is usually the case in championship competitions and contests between countries. Even in the Olympic Games, victory is more important than posting an outstanding mark.

Winning tactics may be those of any runner who feels he is capable of victory. They depend upon innumerable circumstances and have far more shades of variation than the more impersonal result tactics. Winning tactics are therefore more difficult to execute. For this reason, planning and execution of winning tactics presuppose intelligence, imagination, courage, much competitive experience, the keen eye to judge suddenly developing tactical situations, and excellent physical preparation.

Planning Winning Tactics

The following should be taken into consideration when planning winning tactics:

1. Plan your tactics sufficiently in advance so you will have time enough to practice them in workouts and in minor races.

2. Know yourself. Clearly and accurately recognize your strongest and weakest points. If you are a "stayer," you may win on the basis of your endurance. If you have speed, you may win on this basis. Base your tactical decisions on your best racing assets. Continuously strive to develop these by training, without ignoring improvement of your weaker points.

3. Ascertain the abilities of your chief adversaries. Get acquainted with details of the tactical assets and liabilities of your opponents as much as possible. Determine their strongest and weakest points. Base your tactical solutions on the unscrupulous utilization of the weakest points of your rivals. Estimate also what your opponents know about you and what tactics they think you will use. In this way you may logically decide how to take them by surprise.

4. Check your racing condition a few days prior to major competition, preferably by secret time-trials rather than in competition. Review your tactical plans so as to adapt them to your present physical condition. Neither overestimate nor underestimate your physical capacity and capabilities.

5. Decide as accurately as possible the condition of your chief rivals. Ascertain their latest competitive results. Do not over- or underestimate their capabilities. Study carefully their best marks, the competitive conditions under which these marks were made, the individual lap times, pace variations, length of finishing sprint, and every available aspect of your rivals' racing habits and abilities before drawing your final conclusions as to their fitness and anticipated competitive behavior.

Two weeks before Roger Bannister first met John Landy in competition, he ran a mile race in which he purposely followed an easy pace until the final 440 yards, which he sprinted in 53.8 seconds. In this way he sought to convince Landy that his final sprint was unbeatable. Landy was indeed trapped by Bannister, the world's first sub 4-minute miler. In their mile race, Landy ran the first part at an excessively fast pace, intending to tire Bannister and deaden his final sprint. But Bannister followed at a reasonable speed during the early stages, and according to plan on the final lap overtook Landy, who had paid the price of excessive initial speed.

6. Ascertain the distance of each lap (especially indoors), the quality of the track surface, the number of competitors, and any other factors which may influence intermediate times during the race.

After taking all the above issues into consideration, decide at which phase of the race and exactly how you will strive for victory. There are many possibilities to consider:

a. If you feel you have more speed but less endurance than your most dangerous adversary, you may decide to make your move on the final sprint for the finishing line. You may start this final sprint at the beginning of the last lap, on the backstretch, or during the final hundred meters. Plan the length of your final sprint according to your physical condition. If your chance for victory depends upon your final sprint, you cannot afford to run so fast during the earlier stages that fatigue will rob you of your sprint. Should the initial speed be too fast to suit your plans, you may attempt to dominate the pace by taking the lead for the purpose of reducing the speed as soon as you realize it is too fast for you.

b. If you feel you have more endurance but less speed than your most difficult opponents, it may be to your advantage to make your tactical move at the beginning of the race by leading and maintaining a fast, overall pace. The Russian champion, Vladimir Kutz, won most of his races by "drowning his opponents in a sea of lactic acid" with an extremely fast pace during the first half of the competition. The advantage held by runners who have endurance, compared to faster runners with less endurance, is their capability of holding the initiative from the very beginning of the race in terms of dominating the pace.

c. What tactics should be used against opponents who are superior both in speed and endurance? Is victory possible against such adversaries? Even against these opponents, victory may be possible through use of "surprise" tactics, to be discussed later.

d. A runner who is superior in both speed and endurance should have no tactical worries. In principle, tactical plans should be based upon using to best advantage the runner's best qualities, while preventing the opponent from using his strongest abilities. Because it is often impossible to anticipate tactical developments during the course of a race, one must remain mentally flexible and prepare for surprises. Draw up your racing plans tentatively, so you may alter them accordingly in case of unforeseen tactical situations which arise during the race. Always include an alternative in your plans. Remain open-minded in your thinking, and continually strive for innovations in your tactics.

e. Generally speaking, tactics should be kept as simple as possible. The simplest tactic is, of course, to take the lead at the sound of the gun, and remain ahead throughout the race.

The Execution of Tactics

The execution of tactics may begin even during the warm-up prior to the race. Some athletes boast of their fitness and fast training performances. Do not be deceived or frightened by this. Such talk often comes from a runner seeking to bolster his own confidence. If your strongest adversary were to overhear two of your teammates remarking about your amazing condition and ability, it might be more effective in terms of "gamesmanship."

Position During Competition

If you expect to win, you should run with the leaders from the start. It is most advantageous to be among the first three or four runners during the first lap. Only a very experienced runner at peak fitness can risk remaining behind at the beginning, especially in the 800 and 1500 meters races. However, in longer races when there are many participants and there is a danger of being jostled, lagging behind momentarily may be justified. One method of getting away unscathed at the start of such a crowded race is to run with elbows held high, keeping opponents at a distance.

The shorter the race and the greater the speed, the more important it is to be among the front runners from the very beginning. Always remain reasonably near your most dangerous opponent, and at the crucial phase of the race decisively take the lead (or at least move into second place) with an authoritative increase in speed.

When running in second position, always move behind the right shoulder of the leading runner, somewhat to the side, immediately before turning into the straightaway. On the last lap, keep this position around the turns. From this position you can easily sprint into the lead or respond to the attempts of those behind you who try to pass.

If the pace seems too slow, you may pretend to unsuccessfully take the lead. Thus you may induce the leader to increase his speed according to your preference. If the pace seems too fast, you are in an advantageous position behind the leader's right shoulder from which to rush into the lead and imperceptibly decrease the pace according to your wishes.

When in second position, beware of running directly behind the leader near the curb, because those running third and fourth may easily "box" you to the inside by passing on your right and remaining in an oblique position behind the right shoulder of the leader. You may escape this box only by first slowing your pace, rushing to the second or third lane, and then sprinting past the others. If such a box occurs on the final lap, the winner will have crossed the finish line before an effective escape can be made.

If you run an entire lap of 400 meters in the second lane, you will have run about seven meters farther than an opponent running in the first lane. Generally speaking, run the straightaway about 50 to 60 cm. (20–24″) from the curb. Make certain no one can pass you on your left or "inside." On the bends you may run nearer the curb, since runners generally try to avoid passing there.

Try to follow the runner in front of you in as relaxed a manner as possible, using minimum effort. Run in your own cadence, rhythm, and stride length.

Don't make the mistake of using the same stride as another runner, as this results in excessive fatigue due to individual differences in body structure. It is a mistake to lag behind too long. Tenaciously retain "contact" with the leaders. Avoid thinking of your own fatigue. Comfort yourself with the fact that your opponents are almost certainly more tired than you. Only when the pace of the leader is absolutely suicidal can you safely consider relaxing contact. Pace judgment in such a case is decisively important.

One must not harbor fear of setting the pace or leading. Only a runner who dares to lead can develop into a great runner. It is the leader who is in a position to hold the initiative and dominate the race. By leading you may compel the others to run at a speed which is most disadvantageous to them and advantageous to you. Instead of running in accordance with the plans of the others, you can when leading compel the others to run according to your plans.

Much has been said about the strain and stress of leading a race. Pace-setting is a great strain upon those who lack self-confidence. Nevertheless, in windy weather you will be wise to profit from the pace-setting of others. When the wind is against you, leave the honor of pace-setting to others, if at all possible.

Passing and Breaking Contact

Tactically speaking, "contact" may be described as keeping an opponent within effective striking distance so that he may be caught and passed at will. To improve your position during a race or to "drop" your rivals from contact, it is necessary to make "spurts" of increased pace to pass and break away. These spurts and the time they should be executed can often be planned beforehand. They must be executed suddenly, increasing the pace by surprise, and with energetic authority. To be effective, a spurt must be sustained until your objective is accomplished.

It is most advantageous to pass or break away on the straightaways, but if you want to ensure a surprise, you may spurt on the bends. Avoid beginning the spurt from too far behind, as the sound of your footsteps will reveal your intention. You should be within two meters of the runners you intend to pass before making such a move. When leading and someone attempts to pass, it is often wise to prevent this by rapidly increasing the pace, merely for psychological reasons. If, however, you are passed and you lose your front position, move immediately to the right, behind the right shoulder of the leader, to prevent possible attempts by others to pass.

If you are passed unexpectedly when running in second or third position, and the one who has passed goes into the lead, move immediately to his heels to avoid losing contact.

When running in third or fourth position and your most dangerous rival is directly behind the leader, close on him at a suitable moment as the decisive phase of the race approaches, and position yourself behind the right shoulder of the leader. When you move in the 800 and 1500 meters events, spurt as if stung by a wasp. In longer races the passing spurts may be somewhat "softer." In the final phases of a race, passing should be completely by surprise, because your opponents will most certainly resist relinquishing their positions at this time. Limit the number of passing spurts to a minimum, because they are costly in terms of strength.

Passing efforts are short and sharp. You may be compelled to make such spurts more than once in a race. Spurts to break contact with your opponents must be sustained until you lead by five to ten meters, or even 50 meters from the other competitors. A spurt calculated to break contact is usually limited to one effort and is carefully considered as to where it should be executed and how long it should be sustained. Before making these spurts you should be in the lead or at least in second or third position. Spurts designed to break away and lose contact may be classified as surprise tactics. They should be practiced in training on both the straightaways and bends, running alone and in the company of others.

Observing the Opposition

During the race you should continuously observe your most feared opponents by noting their apparent condition and possible tactical intentions. Those running in front of you may be seen, but you must listen for information about those who follow. The sound of accelerating and sharpening steps indicate tactical danger. Listen to the breathing of your opponents, but do not be deceived by it. A light, quiet breathing or heavy panting may indicate much about the condition of your opponents. On sunny days, you may at times observe those who follow by their shadows.

During the last quarter of the race, it may be wise to make spurts for the purpose of determining the physical condition and tactical intentions of your opponents. Such exploratory spurts presuppose that you are leading. If your most serious rival is "hanging on your heels," make a rapid spurt. If he fails to respond and remains behind, you evidently have the upper hand. But if he still follows closely, you must prepare for a severe final struggle. In this case it may be wise to reduce the speed and conserve strength for the finishing sprint.

If this nearest opponent does not pass you after you have reduced the speed, it means that he too is saving his strength for the final sprint. Prepare yourself accordingly. If you do not have complete confidence in your finishing sprint, there is nothing to do but again increase the speed as much as you can.

If your opponent passes you after you have reduced speed, it evidently signifies that he does not trust his own final sprint and therefore wants to "sap the strength" of your final burst for the finish. In this case the wisest move is to take the lead and reduce the speed—many times, if necessary.

A guiding tactical principle should be to defeat the opponent in his weakest moment. When your strongest rival seems to have succumbed to an attack of fatigue, take unscrupulous advantage of his misfortune by passing and leaving him far behind.

The Finishing Sprint

A race is sometimes won by running a very fast initial pace, gaining an un-assailable lead, and holding it the remainder of the distance without being re-quired to put on a finishing sprint to gain victory. But in most races, victory is won by a finishing sprint during the final lap, or during the last two laps in longer races.

The finishing sprint must begin at the correct moment and at the right place. A sprint which is started too soon deprives you of victory just as surely as one which has been initiated too late and too near the finish.

The length of the finishing sprint depends upon the speed maintained during the race, the type of runner, the runner's condition, and competitive circum-stances. If the pace has been slower than planned, start your final sprint sooner, and vice versa. If the weather is very hot, cold, or windy, shorten your final sprint. A runner who has a fast sprint should develop a short, sudden, irresistible, "rocket" finish. The final sprint of the runner endowed primarily with endurance will be slower but longer and therefore more exhausting to the opposition. The better your physical condition, the longer your finishing sprint can be, regardless of whether you are endowed with more endurance or speed.

Surprise Tactics

During 1931 in Warsaw, Poland, Paavo Nurmi, the lengendary Finn, who was an exemplary tactician, ran *5,000 meters races* on successive days against the 1932 Olympic 10,000 meters champion, Janusz Kusocinski. Since the Pole was very fast (100 meters in 11.5 seconds), Nurmi decided to lead the race from the start. The Pole remained only a step behind Nurmi throughout the first three and one-half kilometers. Nurmi then motioned for Kusocinski to take the lead. The Pole did so indeed, but slowed the pace to almost walking speed, causing Nurmi to again lead and increase his pace. Nurmi expected Kusocinski to begin his kick on the final straightaway, but the Pole completely surprised him by beginning a fierce sprint 250 meters from the finish. A gap of four meters was instantly opened before Nurmi responded with a desperate pursuit, catching Kusocinski on the last turn. At the beginning of the home straightaway, the flying Finn passed the determined Pole, and narrowly won.

Nurmi had noticed that a sprint of 250 meters was too long for Kusocinski and, therefore, in the competition at Katowice the following day began his kick 300 meters from the finish. To Kusocinski's surprise, Nurmi broke contact im-mediately, and won the race due to the lead thus gained.

The final sprint should always come as a surprise to the opponents. Even an insignificant lead thus gained can be decisive in a race among competitors of near equal ability. A lead gained by surprise also has a considerable psychological influence on tired adversaries.

A surprise tactic based primarily on the final sprint is the surest way to victory, if only the runner can execute such a plan. New Zealand's Jack Lovelock, who won the 1,500 meters in the 1936 Olympic Games at Berlin with a world record 3:47.8, had started preparing for a surprise final 300 meters sprint soon after the 1932 Olympic Games, at which time he decided to strive for a gold medal at the next Olympics.

In the 1948 Olympic Games at London, Mal Whitfield of the U.S.A. realized that he was to run against Marcel Hansenne of France, whom he knew to have more endurance than himself. Hansenne had previously achieved 3:47.4 in the 1,500 meters. Another dangerous opponent, Arthur Wint of Jamaica, had won the 400 meters in 46.2 in defeating Whitfield (46.6). How could Whitfield defeat a field which included opponents who were his superiors in both speed and endurance? He chose surprise tactics. After 350 meters, as the others prepared for the last lap, Whitfield unexpectedly "jumped" the field and broke contact by a few meters. This lead was gradually closed, but Whitfield held on for a narrow victory.

In major races today, all who fight through the preliminaries to the final are usually of similar ability. Consequently, the 800 and 1,500 meters events are usually run in close company, making victory considerably more difficult. Some of the competitors may be forced to run wide and thus farther in the second or third lanes. In such cases the ability to maintain contact with the leading runners and fight for position at the front, even on the curves, are prerequisites for victory. In most such cases it is worthwhile to fight to lead or at least to be in second place on the back straightaway before the final bend. It is more advantageous to lead on the last bend than to fight there for position. If you are in first place in lane one coming off the last bend, you have a lead of one meter over the others. Unless you are the leader, when coming off the last bend into the home straight you must be prepared to move to the other lanes to pass your rivals in the sprint for the finish.

Avoid forcing your way between runners in the sprint down the final straightaway. This only breaks your running rhythm and warns your competitors. Use your surprise tactics from the outer lanes.

In the 1956 Olympic Games at Melbourne on the last bend in the 1,500 meters final, Ron Delany of Ireland was running among a mass of ten opponents. He solved this problem in the home straightaway by running the long way around the whole group and sprinting to victory in the fifth lane. In the 1958 European Championships at Stockholm, Brian Hewson of England used the same tactic, but had to move to the sixth lane to find an opening.

Avoid moving too sharply to the right in passing, as this increases the distance to be run. If you move sharply from the inner to the fifth lane, your distance to run increases several meters. If you gradually move the same distance across the track while covering 50 meters, your running distance increases only a few centimeters and your speed suffers little.

Jerking Tactics

Jerking tactics are created by interval training. The purpose of jerking tactics is to tire the opposition by repeated jerks or bursts of speed during the race. This form of tactic suits the thoroughly trained long-distance runner accustomed to leading, when racing competitors known to be strong finishers.

This tactic should be used during the second half of the race. The bursts should be made as unexpectedly as possible once or twice each lap, or always immediately after the follower has again caught up with the leader. Such a burst should be long and fast enough to give a clear lead of at least a few meters.

It is most important to run very relaxed following each such jerk. If possible, use the relaxed "float" on the bends.

The classic example of jerking tactics was seen in the 1956 Olympic Games when Vladimir Kutz thoroughly thrashed the opposition and won the 10,000 meters in 28:45.6. Kutz had practiced this tactic continuously for four months prior to the Games.

The best method of combating jerking tactics is to catch up to the leader gradually by maintaining an even pace, while not permitting the leader to achieve too great a lead.

Obstructive Tactics

Obstructive tactics are a variation of jerking tactics, but they differ in one respect. The object of jerking tactics is to accelerate the pace temporarily, whereas the objective of obstructive tactics is to slow the pace. These tactics are used when a faster runner is up against a competitor with greater staying power or endurance.

By these tactics world-record holder Viljo Heino of Finland tried to defeat Czechoslovakian Emil Zatopek in their first meeting over 5,000 meters at Helsinki in 1947. A week earlier Zatopek ran the distance in the year's best time of 14:08.2, which Heino did not believe himself capable of doing. Heino planned to try to defeat the Czech with a short but fast finish. Zatopek started at a furious pace, which Heino immediately thought much too fast for him. After two laps Heino shot into the lead and imperceptibly attempted to slow the pace. However, Zatopek soon recognized this and again took the lead, increasing the speed at the same time. This Heino vs. Zatopek tactical move was repeated during nearly every lap. The race ended with Zatopek winning by only a stride in 14:15.2, with Heino recording 14:15.4. Zatopek was quite unhappy, and remarked that Heino had ruined a good race. Heino was of the opinion that without these obstructive tactics he would not have had a chance of winning.

Team Tactics

At all levels of competition, including the Olympic Games, it may happen that two or three athletes representing the same team will cooperate in fighting for victory and points. In such cases, tactics are planned so that interests of the team are given preference over those of the individual. Team tactics presuppose unselfish cooperation, because weaker runners must often sacrifice themselves for the benefit of the best member of the team. In addition, the weakest runner must be capable of helping to achieve the highest score possible.

What has been said about individual tactics also applies to the team. However, team tactics are much more complicated and their planning calls for more shrewdness and imagination. Their execution requires even more experience than individual tactics. The responsibility of the coach in regard to planning is very heavy indeed.

Alternation of the lead is the most typical form of team tactics. By changing the leader regularly, a team may take the initiative directly after the start of a race. When changing leaders, the place or places where the changes are to be made, as well as the pace to be maintained, must be carefully planned in advance. The lead is usually changed just before entering a curve. In changing the lead, the pace setter moves to the right just enough to let the runner behind pass him and take the lead on the inside. In 800 and 1,500 meter races, the runner in second position should run just behind the leader's right shoulder on the straightaways. If there are three on the team, the third runner should take a similar position behind the runner in second position. In this way they form a "plow," which is difficult to pass.

When approaching the decisive stage of a race, usually when entering the last bend, the best runner is "played" into the lead. The weaker runners reinforce his attacking position with the "plow" formation by imperceptibly slowing the pace to give their best runner a lead of perhaps two or three meters, which he may be able to lengthen by starting a surprising finishing burst coming off the bend into the final straightaway. By using such tactics the Swedes have on occasion defeated the Finns in 800 and 1,500 meters races in the fiercely fought Finland vs. Sweden matches, even though the Finns are more often expected to win.

In longer distances, such as 5,000 and 10,000 meters, it is easier to support a weak runner by making use of the lead, and perhaps by encouraging shouts to spur him on. The principal aim of team tactics is always to insure victory for the best runner on your own team. To accomplish this, one may even resort to a little bluffing. For example, the next best runner may pretend to be the best by tempting faster opponents into an excessively fast pace from the start or by maintaining a slow pace if his own team's best man is capable of a very fast finishing burst.

A particularly good example of teamwork was given by the two German runners, Bodo Tummler and Harold Norpoth in the 1,500 meters at the 1966 European Championships in Budapest. In the final, all runners relied on their finishing sprint, the first three laps being run at a "funeral" pace. At the start of the last lap, both Germans, by mutual agreement, shot into the lead side by side, keeping this "plow" throughout the turns, with Tummler emerging victorious. Not even the speedy Frenchman Michael Jazy could take the lead during the final lap, despite his furious efforts to do so, thanks to the team effort of the astute Teutons!

Indoor Tactics

Indoor tactics follow the same general principles as those used outdoors. However, since indoor races take place under much more cramped conditions, tactical planning must be done with more precision. The length of the track, particularly the length of the home straightaway, and the number of competitors, must be known in advance. The shorter the race and the greater the number of competitors, the more important it is to be the leader, in second place, or among the leaders from the start. The sharp curves cause the leader to decrease his speed somewhat as he runs the turns, and unintentionally increase his speed as he comes out of the turns and enters the straightaways. The second runner will slow his speed more than the leader, the third runner even more, etc. If one is running in fourth, fifth, or farther behind the leader, a mad dash is required after each bend to regain the same relative distance from the leader as prior to entering the curve. For runners in single file more than three positions behind the leader, it means a series of two "stop and go" rushes each lap throughout the race.

Because the straightaways are short, passing on indoor tracks should take place during the first half of the straights. In preparing to pass, accelerate the pace coming out of the turn, possibly taking advantage of running a bit high on the bank of the curve and gaining downhill speed entering the straightaway, passing just off the leader's right shoulder.

RESULT TACTICS

The competitive objective of the runner is often to achieve his best possible personal result. This is particularly true when seeking to run a certain time in order to qualify for a major event such as the Olympic Games. The best possible result is also important when opposing unquestionably superior rivals. Then the breaking of one's own personal record is a sensible target. In such cases, the runner must resort to result tactics.

When planning winning tactics it is necessary to take into consideration characteristics of the opposition, and their likely tactics. Result tactics are, by contrast, based upon one's own personal abilities. While winning tactics are based on a shorter or longer finishing burst, a condition for successful result tactics is an absolutely correct starting pace, due to the possibility that there will be no finishing sprint at all.

In the planning of result tactics, special attention should be paid to the state of one's physical fitness, the condition of the track, weather conditions, and other variables. Pay special attention to anticipated weather. Result tactics are hardly worth planning if the race is to be run in rainy or windy weather, in torrid heat, or on a soft track.

Success in executing result tactics depends primarily upon a thorough knowledge of pace. One should be able to estimate the lap pace under any conditions within at least two-tenths of a second. For this reason, much training in pace judgment is necessary.

Pace Judgment

Generally speaking, it has always been believed that the best results are achieved by maintaining an even pace throughout a race. A steady pace has been proven by physiologists to be most economical. In actual practice, however, best results have often been achieved by running at uneven speeds. This is not surprising, since man is obviously not a machine which can be mechanically adjusted to ensure a steady pace. The greater part of our world's records and most outstanding performances have been run in the past and will in all probability continue to be run at such a pace that the first half of the race is slightly faster than the last half.

In some cases superb results have been achieved by running the last half faster. There is, of course, always the possibility that still better results might have been accomplished had the first half been run in a somewhat faster time.

It sometimes appears illogical to suggest that during the first half of a race an athlete should be asked to run at less than maximum pace while he still has at his disposal an abundance of physical and mental strength, and that during the second half he should increase his speed after the onset of fatigue.

The 400-meter and 440-yard sprints provide a clear picture of the nature of result tactics. The manifestations of fatigue in all races from 400 to 10,000 meters follow exactly the same laws. The oxygen debt accumulated by good athletes racing over all these distances is approximately identical—18 to 20 liters. The same accumulation of oxygen debt that results from racing six miles or 10,000 meters in 28 to 29 minutes, also takes place in the 400-meter and 440-yard sprints during a period of 45 to 50 seconds! This means that in regard to pace adjustment or relative intermediate timings with which the feeling of fatigue is associated, there should be no difference in principle between 400 and 10,000 meters races, if the question of best results is the one and only issue.

With regard to such branches of sport as marathon, 50-km. track walking, swimming, rowing, cycling, skating, and cross-country skiing, the best results, according to past experience, show that from the viewpoint of the economy of physical and mental strength, best results are achieved by starting at a fast pace and gradually and evenly slowing the speed during the race, except for the finishing sprint. This might be termed a "natural pace."

A faster final half of a race is often somewhat illusionary, due to the runner not being certain of his own condition and starting the race too cautiously, which leads to a slower initial pace. The usual cause of a faster final half is a prolonged finishing effort, often made possible by a slower starting speed.

Tactics for a faster first half are for courageous, well-trained, and determined athletes, aided by a judicious pre-race warm-up. A correct warm-up will facilitate maximum oxygen uptake during the competitive effort.

Effort distribution, which influences the rate at which the athlete runs during competition, is dependent upon individual differences, which include temperament, character, tenacity, experience, motivation, ability, and degree of physical fitness. Every runner should carry out extensive pace trials with a view to determining what starting pace and effort distribution suits him best. No runner should start at such a fast pace that he creates an intolerable oxygen debt during the first half of the race.

When his physical condition is below par, the athlete should run at a conservative pace during the first half of a race. In adverse weather conditions, such as high temperature and humidity, rain, or strong wind, strength should be conserved for the latter half of the race at the expense of a slower pace during the first half. Under these conditions, the advisability of employing result tactics is highly questionable.

The use of an extremely fast pace directly from the start of a race has certain risks. However, the runner who never ventures to take risks will neither achieve good results nor great victories. In a daring, fierce competition, a torrid pace during the first half of the race may well prove to be an inspiration to the runner pursuing athletic immortality in the form of records. Much empirical observation and scientific research is still required in order to identify optimum pace and effort distribution under competitive conditions. It is interesting to note that even pace running seldom involves the even expenditure of effort. Also, mere laboratory experimentation can never reveal the effect of motivation, determination, tenacity, and Finnish "sisu" (the ultimate in fighting courage) upon the degree to which a runner can approach the physiological limit of which he may be capable.

400 METERS AND 440 YARDS

No athlete is ever capable of running the quarter mile from start to finish at his absolute top speed. This is more nearly possible in shorter races. The elements of pace judgment and effort distribution play a decisive role in the one lap event. In this race, the first 200 meters (or 220 yards) is usually run 0.5 to 1.5 seconds slower than the best time the runner is capable of sprinting in a 200 meters race. The second 200 meters of this race is usually 1.5 to three seconds slower than the first 200 meters.

400 Meters Pace Examples

For ready comparison, 440 yards results have been converted hereafter to equivalent 400 meters times by deducting three-tenths of a second. One-tenth second has been deducted from the first 220 yards, and two-tenths from the second. Such converted 440 yards marks have been marked with an asterisk (*). "Time loss" is the difference between the first and second 200 meters in a 400 meters race. "Preservation time" is the runner's best 200 meters time subtracted from the first 200 meters in his 400 meters race.

Name	Year	First 200m	Second 200m	400m time	Time loss	Preservation time
Carr	1932	22.1	24.1	46.2	2.0	0.6
Eastman	1932	21.2	24.9	46.1*	3.7	0.0
Harbig	1939	22.0	24.0	46.0	2.0	0.5
Rhoden	1950	20.9	24.9	45.8	4.0	0.3
McKenley	1948	20.9	24.8	45.7*	3.9	0.3

Name	Year	First 200m	Second 200m	400m time	Time loss	Preservation time
Jones	1956	21.3	23.9	45.2	2.6	0.4
Evans	1967	21.4	23.6	45.0*	2.2	0.5
Davis	1960	21.8	23.1	44.9	1.3	0.7
Kaufmann	1960	21.8	23.1	44.9	1.3	0.9
Plummer	1963	21.6	23.0	44.6*	1.4	1.0
Smith	1967	21.6	22.9	44.5*	1.3	1.7

Even though the second 200 meters is timed with a running start, in all of the world's fastest 400-meter races the second 200 meters has been obviously slower than the first. For example, in all races run under 45 seconds, the actual time difference has been well over one second. The idea that best results over 400 meters can be achieved by even pace running or by covering the first 200 meters slightly slower than the final 200 meters can hardly be considered realistic, despite the fact that in races run under 45 seconds the pace differences show less variation.

If the first 200 meters is more than three seconds faster than the last, it may be assumed that the first half has been run too fast. By contrast, if the first 200 meters is only one second faster, there would be cause for sprinting the first half faster.

Intermediate times for each 100 meters provide a still clearer picture of the character of this competitive event.

Name	Year	First 100m	Second 100m	200m	Third 100m	300m	Fourth 100m	Final time
Carr	1932	10.9	11.2	22.1	11.7	33.8	12.4	46.2
Harbig	1939	11.3	10.7	22.0	11.6	33.6	12.4	46.0
Evans	1967	10.9	10.5	21.4	12.2	33.6	11.4	45.0
Davis	1960	11.1	10.7	21.8	11.1	32.9	12.0	44.9
Smith	1967	11.0	10.6	21.6	11.7	33.3	11.2	44.5

The fact that the second 100 meters is faster than the first is due to its being run on the straightaway with a flying start. In actual fact, the first 100 meters is the fastest, with the pace gradually slowing thereafter. Ideally, the speed should decrease rather evenly on each 100 meters of the one-lap race.

Smith's scorching 100-meter finishing burst reveals he ran the first 200 meters and third 100 meters with unnecessary caution, in consideration of his physical resources. This is also indicated by the exceptionally large difference (1.7 seconds) between his first 200 meters (21.6 seconds) and his world record 200 meters (20.0 seconds). With a faster starting speed, Smith had the ability to run even faster than 44.0 seconds for the 400 meters.

The legendary American advice to quarter milers is, "Run the first half as fast as you can and the last half as hard as possible." This is not far from the truth. The same theory is borne out in 100 yards swimming races, which corresponds to 400 meters and 440 yards track sprints. It is interesting to compare the pacing in record races of these two sports. America's Steve Clark, in swimming his 100 yards world record time of 45.6 seconds (the previous record being 46.5 seconds), had intermediate times of 21.8 seconds for the first 50 yards and 23.8 seconds for the second. Thus the time for the second 50 yards was two seconds slower than for the first. When Gottwaldes won the 100 meters event in the France vs. Finland swimming match with a time of 54.6 seconds, he required 25.7 seconds for the first half and 28.9 for the second, revealing a first half 3.2 seconds faster. Any number of similar examples might be cited in swimming, as well as in other branches of sport.

800 METERS AND 880 YARDS

Tactics for 800 meters and 880 yards are similar to those used in 400 meters races. The best results have generally been achieved when the first 400 meters (440 yards) has been run five to seven seconds slower than the athlete's best time for 400 meters. The second 400 meters is usually two to four seconds slower than the first.

800 Meter Pace Examples

For ready comparison, the 880 yards times hereafter have been altered to equivalent 800 meters results by deducting seven-tenths of a second. Three-tenths of a second has been subtracted from the first 440 yards, and four-tenths from the second lap. Each athlete's best 400 meters is listed, if known. "Time loss" is the difference between the first and second 400 meters of the 800 meters race. "Preservation time" is the runner's best 400 meters subtracted from the time of the first 400 meters in an 800 meters race. The asterisk (*) used after a time in the following examples indicates 880 yards converted to 800 meters time.

Name	Year	First 400m	Second 400m	800m time	Best 400m	Time loss	Preservation time
Eastman	1932	51.7	58.3	1:50.0	46.1	6.6	5.6
Wooderson	1938	52.4	56.0	1:48.4		3.6	
Whitfield	1953	52.5	55.4	1:47.9*	46.1	2.9	6.3
Harbig	1939	52.5	54.1	1:46.6	46.0	1.6	6.5
Courtney	1957	50.6	55.2	1:45.8	45.8	4.6	4.8
Moens	1955	52.0	53.7	1:45.7	47.3	1.7	4.7
Kemper	1966	53.0	51.9	1:44.9		−1.1	
Snell	1962	50.7	53.6	1:44.3		2.9	
Ryun	1966	53.0	51.2	1:44.2*	46.7	−1.8	6.3

As seen in the above examples, in most fast 800 meters races the second 400 meters has been slower than the first, regardless of the advantage of a flying start and finishing burst during the second lap. The fastest second halves by Ryun, and Kemper are interesting exceptions to the general rule.

The intermediate 200-meter times characterize result tactics in 800 meters races, as noted by these examples:

Name	Year	First 200m	Second 200m	Third 200m	Fourth 200m	800m time
Harbig	1939	26.0	26.5	27.1	27.0	1:46.6
Snell	1962	24.7	26.0	25.7	27.9	1:44.3

For a 1:58 800 meters runner, the following pace schedule may be suitable: 28.0; 29.0; 30.0; 31.0 = 1:58.0.

It is interesting to note that the Russian swimmer Illitschev had the following 50 meters intermediate times in establishing a European 200 meters freestyle record: 27.4; 29.7; (100m in 57.1); 30.4; 30.3; (second 100m in 60.7) = 1:57.8. Note that the first half was 3.6 seconds faster than the second.

In 1967, America's Don Schollander swam 27.2; 29.4 (100m in 56.6); 29.5; 29.6; (second 100m in 59.1) for a world record of 1:55.7 and a time difference of 2.5 seconds.

In swimming races it is easier to use a "natural" pace because each competitor has his own lane throughout the race. This avoids interference from the other swimmers and leaves him free to concentrate solely on the task at hand.

As seen from the above examples, the pace pattern followed in competitive swimming closely follows that of track racing over distances of similar duration in terms of time required. However, there are these significant differences between the two sports:

a) Running is a weight-bearing activity, while in swimming the body is buoyed up, thanks to the Archimedes' principle.

b) The legs propel the runner, while the arms are the primary source of propulsion for the swimmer (except in the case of the breaststroke).

c) Swimmers dissipate heat faster than runners, due to the water in contact with the swimmer's skin, thus enabling them to perform at an intense level over a more prolonged period than runners.

1,500 METERS AND ONE MILE

In 1923 when Paavo Nurmi of Finland was training to attack the one-mile world record and to meet the world-class Finnish-Swede, Edvin Wide, he was warned of Wide's fantastic final sprint. Nurmi's answer was simply that he did not expect Wide to have a great finishing kick in their race, because he (Nurmi) would run such a fast third lap that the Swede would be incapable of sprinting at the end. Nurmi had observed that Wide's fast final sprint was always preceded by a slow third lap. What Nurmi had predicted proved perfectly true. He defeated Wide by virtue of a torrid third lap, and established a world record in 4:10.4.

Nurmi's words characterize the pace in 1,500 meters and mile races when top results are the objective. Result tactics make no provision for the luxury of a slow pace to gather strength for the final sprint.

All of the following marks were world records with the exception of those established by Keino, May and Jazy, which were European records. "Time loss" is the difference between the first and second 750 meters in the 1,500 meters race.

Name	Year	First 400m	Second 400m	800m time	Third 400m	Final 300m	1,500m time	First 750m	Second 750m	Time loss
Nurmi	1924	57.3	63.7	2:01.0	65.0	46.6	3:52.6	1:53.1	1:59.5	6.4
Lovelock	1936	61.4	64.1	2:05.5	62.0	40.3	3:47.8	1:57.5	1:50.3	−7.2
Hagg	1944	56.7	59.8	1:56.5	61.5	45.0	3:43.0	1:49.0	1:54.0	5.0
Salsola and										
Salonen	1957	56.8	61.0	1:57.8	60.6	41.8	3:40.2	1:50.2	1:50.0	−0.2
Jungwirth	1957	54.9	59.3	1:54.2	59.2	44.7	3:38.1	1:46.8	1:51.3	4.5
Keino	1967	60.2	55.5	1:55.7	57.7	43.8	3:37.2	1:48.7	1:48.5	−0.2
May	1965	57.0	59.0	1:56.0	57.5	42.9	3:36.4	1:48.6	1:47.8	−0.8
Jazy	1966	58.5	60.0	1:58.5	57.1	40.7	3:36.3	1:51.0	1:45.3	−5.7
Elliott	1958	57.5	60.0	1:57.5	58.0	40.5	3:36.0	1:50.0	1:46.0	−4.0
Elliott	1960	58.2	59.6	1:57.8	56.2	41.6	3:35.6	1:50.4	1:45.2	−5.2
Ryun	1967	60.5	55.5	1:56.0	57.5	39.6	3:33.1	1:49.0	1:44.1	−4.9

The abbreviation WR indicates world record. "Time loss" indicates the difference between the first and second 880 yards in the mile race.

Name	Year	First 440y.	Second 440y.	Third 440y.	Fourth 440y.	Mile time	First 880y.	Second 880y.	Time loss
Nurmi	1923WR	60.3	62.9	63.5	63.7	4:10.4	2:03.2	2:07.2	4.0
Lovelock	1933WR	61.4	62.2	65.1	58.9	4:07.6	2:03.6	2:04.0	0.4
Hagg	1945WR	56.7	62.5	62.2	60.0	4:01.4	1:59.2	2:02.2	3.0
Bannister	1954WR	57.5	60.7	62.3	58.9	3:59.4	1:58.2	2:01.2	3.0
Elliott	1958WR	58.0	60.0	61.0	55.5	3:54.5	1:58.0	1:56.5	−1.5
Snell	1962WR	60.7	59.9	59.0	54.8	3:54.4	2:00.6	1:53.8	−6.8
Snell	1964WR	56.0	58.0	60.0	60.1	3:54.1	1:54.0	2:00.1	6.1
May	1965	58.0	59.1	58.5	58.5	3:54.1	1:57.1	1:57.0	−0.1
May	1965	56.5	59.1	59.4	58.8	3:53.8	1:55.6	1:58.2	2.6
Jazy	1965WR	57.3	59.2	60.9	56.2	3:53.6	1:56.5	1:57.1	0.6
Keino	1967	54.9	62.0	59.2	57.7	3:53.8	1:56.9	1:56.9	0.0
Keino	1966	58.9	59.2	56.9	58.4	3:53.4	1:58.1	1:55.3	−2.8
Ryun	1967	57.6	60.6	59.8	55.2	3:53.2	1:58.2	1:55.0	−3.2
Ryun	1966WR	57.1	58.3	59.6	56.3	3:51.3	1:55.4	1:55.9	0.5
Ryun	1967WR	59.0	59.9	59.7	52.5	3:51.1	1:58.9	1:52.2	−6.7
Anne	Female								
Smith	1967WR	68.0	69.8	70.2	69.0	4:37.0	2:17.8	2:19.2	1.4

Intermediate times in the 400 meters freestyle swimming event, which is the duration equivalent of a mile on the track, presents an interesting pace similarity to the above figures.

Name	Year	First 100m	Second 100m	Third 100m	Fourth 100m	400m time	First 200m	Second 200m	Time Loss
Charlton	1967 WR	58.3	63.1	64.1	62.7	4:08.2	2:01.4	2:06.8	5.4

World records in the 1,500 meters and mile have been established with faster and with slower first halves of the run, but seldom with equal halves. In Lovelock's 1,500 meters world record, the first half was considerably slower than the second, but in his one-mile world record the first half was a little faster. When Gunder Hagg of Sweden ran his first 1,500 meters world record in 3:47.6 (1941), the first 750 meters was 2.8 seconds slower than the second half of the race. But his best 1,500 meters and one-mile races were established with a faster first half of the distance. Peter Snell ran the first half of his second best mile nearly seven seconds slower than the final half, but in his best mile the first 880 yards was more than six seconds faster than the final half. Jazy's best 1,500 meters and mile results, and Ryun's two best mile efforts were also run with reverse speed timings. The athlete with the most consistent times, Jurgen May of East Germany, ran the first half of his 1,500 meters European Record slower than the last, and his second fastest mile at steady pace. But his best mile and 800 meters results were run with a faster first half.

The same runner may return his best results with a variety of intermediate timings in the 1,500 meters and mile. Competitive pace is influenced by many factors, some of which may still be unknown. Nevertheless, common sense must always be the basis of pace planning. It is entirely possible to place too much emphasis on intermediate timings.

It is much less fatiguing and more pleasant to start a race with a relatively slow speed. A slower first half is suitable for younger runners and athletes in less than top physical condition who must race often. However, a runner seeking absolute maximum performance can, if in top physical condition and highly motivated, establish his best results with a "natural pace"—starting at the fastest speed he can maintain and only gradually diminishing the pace throughout the duration of the run. This, of course, produces a slightly faster first half of the race.

Ryun's mile record (3:51.3) in 1966 presents a good example of natural pacing. This result in all probability corresponds closely to his physical condition at the time. He must not have been in such a superb state of fitness when he established his 1967 mile world record (3:51.1), because he might well have broken 3:50 on this occasion with a faster initial speed.

If each lap is about one second slower than the preceding lap in the 1,500 meters and mile events, and the final lap is about the same speed as the first lap, it means the runner has distributed his effort correctly throughout the race, according to a "natural pace."

The time of the final lap will reveal the mistakes of pace judgment. If the

The abbreviations WR and ER indicate world record and European record respectively. "Time loss" is the difference between the first and second 2,500 meters in the 5,000 meters race.

Name	Year	First km	Second km	Third km	Fourth km	Fifth km	5,000 m time	First 2,500 m	Second 2,500 m	Time loss
Maki	1939WR	2:46.0	2:53.0	2:53.5	2:52.0	2:44.3	14:08.8	7:06.0	7:02.8	−3.2
Hagg	1942WR	2:40.5	2:46.5	2:50.5	2:51.5	2:49.2	13:58.2	6:52.0	7:06.2	14.2
Zatopek	1954	2:43.0	2:47.0	2:49.0	2:52.0	2:46.0	13:57.0	6:54.5	7:02.5	8.0
Kutz	1954WR	2:38.4	2:52.4	2:54.8	2:41.9	2:43.7	13:51.2	6:58.2	6:53.0	−5.2
Iharos	1955WR	2:42.0	2:46.0	2:48.0	2:51.0	2:33.6	13:40.6	6:52.0	6:48.6	−3.4
Pirie	1956WR	2:36.0	2:46.0	2:47.0	2:48.0	2:39.8	13:36.8	6:45.5	6:51.3	5.8
Kutz	1957WR	2:37.8	2:46.5	2:44.4	2:44.2	2:42.1	13:35.0	6:46.5	6:48.5	2.0
Keino	1965	2:37.5	2:41.5	2:47.4	2:43.6	2:40.4	13:30.4	6:42.7	6:47.7	5.0
Jazy	1965ER	2:41.2	2:40.2	2:43.8	2:45.0	2:37.4	13:27.6	6:43.3	6:44.3	1.0
Keino	1966	2:38.0	2:44.6	2:41.4	2:47.8	2:34.8	13:26.6	6:43.3	6:43.3	0.0
Clarke	1965WR	2:39.6	2:41.9	2:48.0	2:46.1	2:38.0	13:33.6	6:45.5	6:48.1	2.6
Clarke	1965	2:40.0	2:41.5	2:45.0	2:47.0	2:39.5	13:33.0	6:44.0	6:49.0	5.0
Clarke	1965WR	2:39.1	2:41.2	2:43.5	2:44.7	2:37.3	13:25.8	6:42.0	6:43.8	1.8
Clarke	1967	2:38.5	2:39.0	2:40.5	2:43.6	2:37.2	13:18.8	6:37.7	6:41.1	3.4
Clarke	1966WR	2:40.2	2:36.2	2:41.0	2:41.6	2:37.6	13:16.6	6:36.9	6:39.7	2.8

time of the last lap is slower than the average time for the first three laps, it means the initial speed was too fast. But if the time of the final lap is noticeably (more than three seconds) faster than the average speed of the first three laps, it indicates the initial speed could have been faster. Therefore, it is suggested that according to natural pace running, the 4:20 miler might reasonably consider running his laps in 64; 65; 66; 65.

It is interesting to compare the above intermediate times in the 5,000 meters with Burton's fantastic 1,500 meters freestyle swimming world record, established in 1967, in which he improved the existing world record by more than seven seconds.

Name	First 300m	Second 300m	Third 300m	Fourth 300m	Fifth 300m	1500m time	First 750m	Second 750m
Burton	3:10.9	3:20.0	3:23.0	3:22.4	3:17.8	16:34.1	8:12.4	8:21.7

Burton's time loss between his first and second 750 meters was 9.3 seconds. In this race, his 100 meters intermediate times were: 59.8; 65.2; 65.9; 66.5; 66.8; 66.7; 67.7; 67.7; 67.6; 67.5; 67.5; 67.4; 67.2; 66.6; and 64.0.

As seen from the above examples, practically without exception the world's best 5,000 meters results have been recorded by negotiating the first 2,500 meters two to five seconds faster than the final half of the race. The intermediate times of Iharos, Pirie, and most of those by Clarke are good examples of natural pace running.

When running 5,000 meters against the clock, the speed from the beginning should be sufficiently swift that during at least the first three and preferably four kilometers the pace slows evenly and naturally. A gradual, even, slackening of speed from beginning to end is not the goal, but rather the natural result of an adequately fast initial speed, which is a necessary prerequisite to good final results.

Even if the speed over the first kilometers is only very gradually reduced, the last km. of the race will be the fastest or at least second fastest, due to the final sprint. The speeds of the first and last kilometers are clearly dependent upon each other. If (correctly) the last km. is the fastest and the first km. is the next fastest or vice versa, the fourth km. will in most cases be the slowest, owing to the runner's conserving strength for the final sprint. However, the final result will suffer if too much strength is saved for the finishing sprint. This can be seen from an examination of the above intermediate times of Iharos.

The most economical pace for the second and third km. of the 5,000 meters is the average speed of the race. For example, a 15:00.0 ability runner might ideally run successive km. of: 2:56.0; 3:00; 3:02; 3:04; and 2:58.

Much has been said about running at steady, even speed. However, track races are never run at absolute even pace. An example of apparently even pace running was Clarke's 13:16.6 world record, but even in this race the difference between the fastest and slowest kilometers was 5.4 seconds. Usually in 5,000 meters races the difference is eight to nine seconds between the fastest and slowest km.

We should be more exact in defining "even speed" running. At Stockholm in 1967 when Clarke attacked his 1966, 5,000 meters world record, he planned to run the first 2,000 meters in 5:13, which was three seconds faster than his time at that point when he established his record (5:16.4). However, the time dropped to 5:17.5. His final time was correspondingly about two seconds slower (13:18.8) than his world record (13:16.6). Clarke well knows from what part of the race the seconds may be cut most easily when attempting to establish a record.

10,000 Meters Pace Examples

All of the following marks were world records. "Time loss" indicates the difference between the first and second 5,000 meters of the 10,000 meters race. (The kilometer timings of some of these marks appear on the following page.)

Name	Year	10,000m time	First 5,000m	Final 5,000m	Time loss
Nurmi	1924	30:06.2	14:52.5	15:13.7	21.2
Heino	1949	29:27.2	14:44.0	14:43.2	−0.8
Zatopek	1954	28:54.2	14:27.6	14:26.6	−1.0
Iharos	1956	28:42.8	14:14.0	14:28.8	14.8
Kutz	1956	28:30.4	14:08.0	14:22.4	14.4
Bolotnikov	1960	28:18.8	14:07.0	14:11.8	4.8
Bolotnikov	1962	28:18.2	14:04.0	14:14.2	10.2
Clarke	1963	28:15.6	13:59.0	14:16.6	17.6
Clarke	1965	28:14.0	14:02.0	14:12.0	10.0
Clarke	1965	27:54.0	13:44.0	14:10.0	26.0
Clarke	1965	27:39.4	13:45.0	13:54.4	9.4

It is interesting to compare the pace of the world's fastest 5,000 and 10,000 meters races with those of the world's fastest 1,500 meters and one-mile runs. Finding a pattern of regularity in the 1,500 meters and mile is difficult. Top results are achieved in many different pace patterns in these two shorter events. In the 5,000 and 10,000 meters races there appears a pattern of pace regularity, just as such a pattern appears in the 400 and 800 meters races and their corresponding yard equivalents. In the 5,000 and 10,000 meters events the "natural" pace comes into its own, as can be seen from the above intermediate km timings. This is due to the slower running speed and the entire nature of running longer distances, wherein the disturbing influence of other runners is also less. These longer distances are usually run in single file, whereas 1500 meters and mile races today are often run as a swarming beehive, continually altering places, changing lanes, and using tactical pace changes.

The 5,000 and 10,000 meters runners are usually athletes of more ordinary and uniform ability. By contrast, 1,500 meters and mile runners are usually of two distinct types. One is the "speed merchant," who also makes excellent results

Let us now examine the kilometer timing of some of the above examples.

	Heino	Zatopek	Iharos	Kutz	Bolotnikov	Bolotnikov	Clarke	Clarke
First km:	2:52.2	2:47.5	2:46.8	2:42.5	2:43.0	2:41.5	2:44.0	2:41.5
Second km:	2:54.8	2:56.7	2:50.2	2:51.5	2:48.0	2:48.5	2:45.6	2:43.5
Third km:	3:00.8	2:54.0	2:52.0	2:50.4	2:51.0	2:51.0	2:49.6	2:46.0
Fourth km:	2:56.2	2:55.8	2:51.0	2:50.6	2:51.0	2:51.0	2:51.4	2:47.0
Fifth km:	3:00.0	2:53.6	2:54.0	2:53.0	2:54.0	2:52.0	2:51.4	2:47.0
Sixth km:	2:59.8	2:55.4	2:50.0	2:50.0	2:50.0	2:53.0	2:49.8	2:48.0
Seventh km:	2:56.4	2:53.4	2:53.0	2:57.0	2:52.0	2:53.0	2:53.8	2:50.0
Eighth km:	2:59.8	2:55.2	2:53.0	2:53.5	2:53.0	2:51.5	2:53.8	2:50.0
Ninth km:	2:57.4	2:55.8	2:57.0	2:54.0	2:53.0	2:53.0	2:53.2	2:46.0
Tenth km:	2:49.8	2:46.8	2:55.8	2:47.9	2:43.8	2:43.7	2:41.4	2:40.4
Final time:	29:27.2	28:54.2	28:42.8	28:30.4	28:18.8	28:18.2	28:14.0	27:39.4

Name	Year		First 10,000m	Second 10,000m	Third 10,000m	Fourth 10,000m	Final time	First 20,000m	Second 20,000m	Time loss
Zatopek	1952	OG	32:12	32:15	34:15	36:28	2:23:03.2	1:04:27	1:10:43	6:16
Popov	1958	EC	31:45	30:45	32:05	33:08	2:15:17.0	1:02:30	1:05:13	2:43
Terasawa	1963		32:43	32:52	31:14	31:22	2:15:15.8	1:05:35	1:02:36	−2:59
Bikila	1960	OG	31:07	31:32	31:50	34:01	2:15:16.2	1:02:39	1:05:51	3:12
Bikila	1964	OG	30:14	30:44	31:52	32:20	2:12:11.2	1:00:58	1:04:12	3:14
Clayton	1967		29:57	30:02	30:33	31:44	2:09:36.4	59:59	1:02:17	2:18

The above abbreviations "OG" and "EC" mean Olympic gold and European Championship respectively. "Time loss" indicates the difference between the first and second 20,000 meters of the marathon race.

The 5,000 meters intermediate timings of Zatopek and Clayton are interesting by comparison:

Name	First 5,000m	Second 5,000m	Third 5,000m	Fourth 5,000m	Fifth 5,000m	Sixth 5,000m	Seventh 5,000m	Eighth 5,000m	Final 2,195m	Final time
Zatopek	16:02	16:10	15:48	16:27	17:03	17:12	18:08	18:20	7:53.2	2:23:03.2
Clayton	15:06	14:51	15:00	15:02	15:12	15:21	15:39	16:05	7:20.4	2:09:36.4

In G. Dordoni's 1952 Olympic 50 km. walk victory, (4:28:07.8), his 10,000 meters intermediate times were 51:37; 49:50; 53:37; 55:42; and 57:21. The first 25 km. was nearly 12 minutes faster than the final half.

over the 800 meters and 880 yards distances. The other is the endurance type, who also makes good times in 3,000 and even 5,000 meters races. These two different types tend to create a heterogeneous tactical environment in the mile and its metric equivalent.

The nature of the pace found in 10,000 meters races is quite similar to that of 5,000 meters races. The speed is relatively even with an average difference of 10 to 12 seconds between the fastest and slowest kilometers. The speed gradually declines throughout, until the finishing effort. The best results are made with a 10 to 20 second faster first half of the distance.

THE MARATHON (42,195 meters or 26 miles, 385 yards)

In no other running event does pace judgment play such an important part as in the marathon. More interruptions occur here than in any other running event, due to incorrect estimations of speed and strength. To know the correct initial speed is decisively important. Usually the world's best marathon runners cover the first 10,000 meters with about two or three minutes "preservation time." This means two or three minutes slower than the best time they could produce over the same distance on the track. Beginners should start more cautiously. Five minutes preservation time over the first 10,000 meters would not be unreasonable for a beginner. According to this, if the beginner can run 10,000 meters in 31:00 on the track, his first 10 km. in the marathon should be run in about 36:00. Since the marathon requires the expenditure of considerable energy, it should as a matter of course be run with as even speed as possible without unnecessary bursts and spurts.

Intermediate times in the best marathons and also in other sports such as swimming and skiing with which running may be compared strongly support the hypothesis that best results in running are obtained by use of a natural pace, not only over the shorter distances (400 to 10,000 meters), but also in the longer distances, such as the marathon.

Rhythmic Pace

In the foregoing we have considered various ways of pacing as applied to result tactics. These include even, accelerated, and natural pace. Is there yet another for consideration?

In carrying a heavy travelling bag, one soon becomes tired. By resting for a few steps after every 50 to 100 meters, the bag may be carried almost indefinitely. Rhythmic pace may be accomplished in the same way.

A very fast, continuous pace at even speed soon brings both mental and physical fatigue. By running in a rhythmic speed according to the manner individually most suitable, it is possible to run faster over longer distances. This means only very occasionally inserting short "relaxing intervals" of rest which are of a slightly slower running speed, in order to relieve the boredom, pain, monotony, and fatigue of continuous fast even-pace running. In this way it is possible to run faster for longer distances.

The length and number of these relaxing intervals depends on the length of the running distance, speed, and physical condition of the athlete. While the relaxing intervals in the 200 meters (220 yards) sprint is perhaps only four to six strides and might possibly be repeated once or twice if at all, in the marathon it may have a length of several hundred meters and may be repeated some ten times during the course of the race.

Either consciously or unconsciously, some athletes have clearly established a rhythmic pace in their running. (See Table 1.)

As in the case of winning tactics, best results when using result tactics are obtained by the cooperative efforts of two or more runners in leading and setting the pace.

In the future, world records will be broken more easily if the runners agree in advance to cooperate in alternating the lead to insure the setting of a correct pace as planned in advance, utilizing a natural pace. This may at times necessitate lesser runners occupying the role of "rabbit" in sacrificing their chances of personal best performances by shouldering the responsibility of leading at a record-breaking pace for as far as their abilities permit. It should be noted, however, that such cooperation among athletes for the sake of establishing records is not always accepted by everyone as the purest form of amateur sportsmanship.

THE ROLE OF THE COACH IN PLANNING TACTICS

It is the coach's responsibility to insure that young athletes do not become robots, always running according to the same tactical scheme. A runner must be capable of capitalizing on unexpected competitive tactical situations by quick thinking, perception, and imagination. The sooner the young runner realizes that top results are gained not only by using the feet and lungs, but also by using intelligence and willpower, the quicker he will develop into a seasoned competitor, better capable of achieving his maximum racing potential.

Tactics play an important part in a runner's mental training. Days, weeks or months in advance, depending upon the situation, a runner must concentrate on a proper mental attitude toward the forthcoming race. He must develop the psychological ability to withstand the agony of physical and mental suffering caused by anticipating the next race. In most races the runner must be prepared to struggle from about the beginning of the final quarter of the race against the pain and torture created by fatigue and the onset of feelings of exhaustion. If the runner has not prepared, resolved and dedicated himself in advance to push himself to the limit, then tactical plans are almost useless.

Only after an appropriate background for competition has been established in the form of correct, rigorous training and clean living is it worthwhile for the coach to discuss specific tactics with an athlete. By such simple questions as: "How do you expect your most serious rival to run in your forthcoming race?"; "In what position do you plan to run and at what pace in the race?"; and "At what point do you plan to launch your finishing sprint?" a coach may gradually

Table 1.

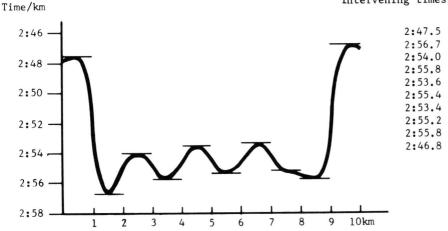

Zatopek 28:54.2   10,000m WR-1954
Intervening times per km:

2:47.5
2:56.7
2:54.0
2:55.8
2:53.6
2:55.4
2:53.4
2:55.2
2:55.8
2:46.8

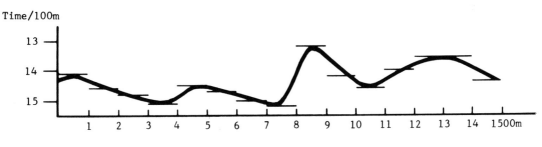

Elliot 3:35.6   1,500m WR-1960

Intervening times per 100m:
14.1   14.6   14.8   15.1   14.5   14.7   15.0   15.2   13.2   14.2   14.6
14.0   13.6   13.6   14.4

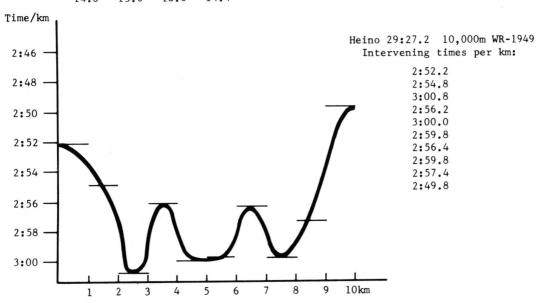

Heino 29:27.2 10,000m WR-1949
Intervening times per km:

2:52.2
2:54.8
3:00.8
2:56.2
3:00.0
2:59.8
2:56.4
2:59.8
2:57.4
2:49.8

and skillfully guide a young runner to consider the tactical aspects of racing. The coach's goal must be to induce the athlete to develop the independent ability to do his own tactical thinking and planning.

The coach should explain to his athletes the fundamentals of winning and result tactics, utilizing suitable examples of notable races by champion runners. The coach should also keep carefully abreast of the era in a tactical sense, remaining familiar with the racing habits of rivals his athletes are likely to meet. This necessitates the recording and study of intermediate timings and various other data of the athletes in question.

Well in advance of a race, the coach should guide his athletes in outlining realistic training and tactical plans. He should arrange tactical training situations individually and in groups, including all types of sudden pace changes, passing, and position changing when running in small and large groups, and sprinting the final 300 meters in cramped, crowded situations where one is apt to be bumped in a wild scramble for the finish line. Additional training at jerking, leading on the turn, pace judgment, final bursts of various length, and use of the "plow" must also be included in tactical training. Such practice makes training for running more interesting.

After each race the coach should make an analysis, examining the tactical mistakes, strong points, and fitness of his own athletes, as well as the more important rivals. Each athlete should record in his daily training and performance diary not only training details, but also tactical comments and intermediate times in all of his races.

The competence of a coach may be judged to some extent by his tactical thinking and teaching of tactics to his athletes, for, after all, a major objective of competition is superior performances in accordance with individual potential.

PSYCHOLOGY AND TACTICS

During the final stage of his career, Paavo Nurmi of Finland was usually content to follow the younger runners and decide the question of victory at the end of the race by a short final sprint, which he had developed into an unusually fast burst. In this way Nurmi established a new world record in the 2-miles in 1931, right from under the noses of his talented and youthful countrymen, Lehtinen and Iso-Hollo. This "lurking" tactic did not please young and ambitious Finnish runners seeking to reach the top in athletics. Thus Lehtinen and Iso-Hollo, who ran world records and gained Olympic medals the following year, afterward criticized Nurmi for not sharing pace-setting responsibilities during the world record 2-miles. To this Nurmi replied that he had spent an athletic lifetime leading the pace for others, and it was now time for the rising younger stars to set their own pace. He also remarked that he would run his own best pace, regardless of the competition, and win by either leading or following, in spite of any tactics used by his opponents.

Nurmi's self-confidence irritated Lehtinen, Iso-Hollo, and other runners of the younger generation, who were worried by Nurmi's words. Nurmi took the world of athletics by surprise in 1933 by winning the Finnish 1,500 meters title using "shadowing" tactics. On this occasion he started his final sprint with 60 meters remaining and gained eight meters on Lehtinen in that short distance. More a marathon than track runner at age 36, Nurmi won this race in a remarkable 3:55.8.

By now the younger Finnish runners had more than enough of defeat at the hands of the wily, cunning Nurmi. In a 3,000 meters race in Helsinki a few weeks later, the younger runners decided to defeat Nurmi by whatever means necessary, and bring about the downfall of the mystic giant of the cinder paths who had become a legend in his own time. Lehtinen, Iso-Hollo, and four others agreed to take turns leading in the race. The eventual winner was to be decided only in the final sprint for the finishing line.

The race was advertised as an attack on the world record, but after the first lap it was apparent the defeat of Nurmi was the real objective of all the master's adversaries. They had but one goal—DEFEAT NURMI!

Three runners took turns leading the race. Olympic Champion and 5,000 meters world record-holder Lauri Lehtinen failed to abide by the pre-race tactical agreement, and followed Nurmi's every stride like a shadow. Nurmi ran mostly at the shoulder of the leader, and refused to drop farther back than third position. After 2,000 meters with Iso-Hollo leading, the speed was still very slow. With 700 meters remaining in the race, Lehtinen attacked with a furious sprint behind Nurmi, took the lead, and at once gained a 30 meters lead. As Lehtinen passed him, the alert Nurmi gave chase, passed Iso-Hollo, and then settled to a steady pace as Lehtinen appeared to be rushing madly away at an insane, suicidal pace. But after a few meters Nurmi realized Lehtinen would not slow his pace, and therefore renewed his pursuit in earnest. After another 200 meters Nurmi was breathing behind Lehtinen's right shoulder, as the others struggled far behind. This order remained until the end of the last curve. Catching Lehtinen had placed a heavy burden on Nurmi's strength. With about 30 meters remaining, Nurmi made a furious attempt to pass, and came abreast of Lehtinen. The younger champion was not to be denied, and summoned his last scrap of "sisu" to break the tape a trifle sooner than the gallant veteran. At last the post-Nurmi runners had realized an athletic ambition of their generation. In spite of the fast final kilometer (2:40), Lehtinen's time was only 8:26.4, which was seven seconds slower than Kusocinsky's world record. Nevertheless, this defeat forecast the sunset of Nurmi's legendary career as a runner.

After this epic tactical race, Iso-Hollo angrily asked Lehtinen why he had not kept his promise to wait until the finishing sprint to decide which of the conspirators to Nurmi's demise would emerge victorious. Lehtinen denied he had broken his promise, and countered with righteous indignation that he had started his "final sprint" 700 meters from the finish.

The final words have not yet been said in the realm of racing tactics, but it can be said on the basis of available evidence at this time that best result tactics involve mutual cooperation among runners, and best winning tactics, from the viewpoint of both spectators and competitors, involve the use of surprise maneuvers.

Table 2.

Some symbolistic pace curves

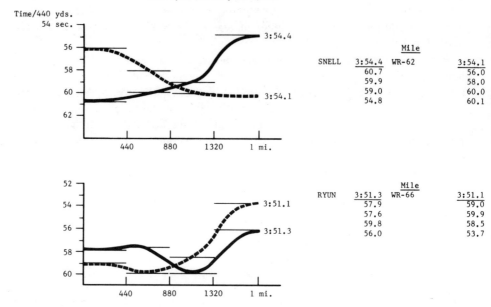

		Mile	
SNELL	3:54.4	WR-62	3:54.1
	60.7		56.0
	59.9		58.0
	59.0		60.0
	54.8		60.1

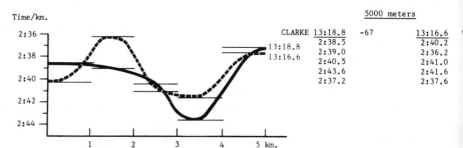

		Mile	
RYUN	3:51.3	WR-66	3:51.1
	57.9		59.0
	57.6		59.9
	59.8		58.5
	56.0		53.7

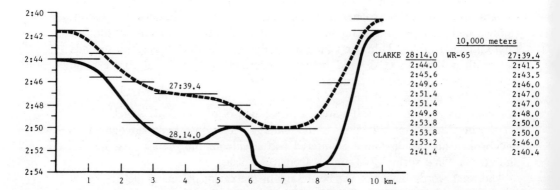

		5000 meters	
CLARKE	13:18.8	-67	13:16.6
	2:38.5		2:40.2
	2:39.0		2:36.2
	2:40.5		2:41.0
	2:43.6		2:41.6
	2:37.2		2:37.6

		10,000 meters	
CLARKE	28:14.0	WR-65	27:39.4
	2:44.0		2:41.5
	2:45.6		2:43.5
	2:49.6		2:46.0
	2:51.4		2:47.0
	2:51.4		2:47.0
	2:49.8		2:48.0
	2:53.8		2:50.0
	2:53.8		2:50.0
	2:53.2		2:46.0
	2:41.4		2:40.4

Chapter 4

TEACHING THE BEGINNING HURDLER

by Stan Wright

Hurdling is sprinting! After establishing this basic philosophy, within a relatively short period of time one can easily teach the beginner hurdling in good style.

1. Divide the beginning hurdlers, according to height, into short, medium and tall groups. Place each group in a separate lane on the track.

2. Start behind a common line crossing all three lanes. Each athlete should sprint three to five repetitions of about 15 strides, in his lane. The standing start should be used, with takeoff foot touching the starting line, and the foot which leads over the hurdle about two and one-half feet behind the line.

3. Then place bamboo sticks (or sticks of any lightweight material) across the lanes, midway between the fourth and fifth strides. Another one should be placed between the eighth and ninth strides. Note that the sticks will be farther apart in the lane of the taller runners.

4. Have the beginners sprint three repetitions over the sticks.

5. Place the flat side of a brick under each end of each stick. Have the runners continue sprinting over the sticks.

6. Turn the bricks to their thin side, raising the sticks to about three inches above the ground. Have the runners sprint over these three times.

7. Turn the bricks on their ends and have the runners sprint over these barriers three times.

8. Add another brick to each side. The sticks should now be about eight inches off the ground. Have the hurdlers continue to sprint over these barriers, and then turn the bricks so that the sticks get progressively higher. The hurdlers should sprint through each increased height at least three times. Continually stress "hurdling is sprinting." As the height of the sticks rises, the athletes will naturally make adjustments in terms of quick pickup of the bent lead leg and higher trail leg recovery.

9. As the sticks reach low hurdle height (30 inches), the athletes will use a

more forward takeoff lean toward the barrier, stretching well forward with the arm opposite the lead leg over the hurdle, and a lateral lift in the trail leg clearance. Since hurdling is sprinting, all these actions should deviate as little as possible from the form used in sprinting.

10. After low hurdle height is reached, place high jump standards beside one set of the "sticks and bricks" barriers, and set the crossbar 18 inches above head height. As the athletes continue sprinting over the sticks, the crossbar should be gradually lowered. The athletes will naturally achieve a clearance lay-out over the barriers as they continue sprinting through. The crossbar need not be lowered much, if any, below head height.

Chapter 5

THE HURDLE RACES

by K. O. Bosen

The most specialized technique in track and field stems from the hurdle races. Apparently, hurdling as a competitive event goes back no further than the early 19th century. But through the ages, this spectacular event has lured the tall and fast-moving athlete with suppleness and mobility of joints to master the skill of hurdle clearance. The hurdle clearance technique of today, as with every other event in track and field, reveals a smoothly graded evolutionary process. Not so long ago, hurdle races were won by running as fast as possible and jumping over the hurdles in the most natural form. Gradually, the technique of clearing the hurdles improved, and with it came better and better performances. Technical development started with a sideward lead-leg hurdle crossing action, and later with the straight front leg clearance, which is the method now employed by hurdlers the world over.

From the early days of Alvin Kraenzlein to the present record-holders, there have been only two important new contributions to accepted hurdling form. The unique, though not much used, two-arm-forward lean of Earl Thomson in the early days was later followed by the exaggerated head-down lean used by Jack Davis and Martin Lauer.

Natural speed has always been important to the success of a hurdler, but not until quite recently has the era of technique consciousness prevailed. The absolute necessity for speed once again came to be appreciated when American supremacy in international competitions experienced a few setbacks. The necessity for speed has been illustrated particularly well during recent years by the champion hurdlers of the world, especially since Harrison Dillard's 1952 Olympic win at Helsinki. Basically it appears that present styles in hurdling are not likely to change much, but improvements in records will continue as perfection in technique, relaxation, and speed become an intrinsic aspect of a hurdler's training program.

High Hurdle Technique

The Starting Position. The most commonly used starting method is the sprinter's crouch start with a "medium" block spacing. In this method of starting the front block is about 38 to 46 centimeters (15 to 18 inches) behind the starting line, with about 40 to 50 centimeters (16 to 20 inches) spacing between the front and rear blocks. When the hurdler has settled down in the blocks for the start, the rear knee should be opposite the toe of the front foot. The face of the front block is set at a 60-degree angle, with the ball of the foot placed flush against the face plate of the block. The rear block is set at an angle of about 80 degrees, with the spikes making comfortable contact and the toe in contact with the ground.

In the "set" position, the front knee is bent at an angle of about 90 degrees, and the rear knee is bent at an angle slightly greater than 110 degrees. In this position the hips will be higher than the shoulders, with most of the body weight on the hands and front foot. The head is held in natural alignment with the body, and the eyes are focused only slightly ahead of the starting line so as to keep the muscles of the neck and shoulders free of tension.

The basic starting position described here may need slight modifications to suit each individual hurdler in order to be able to arrive at a perfect approach to the first hurdle. This modification may take the form of slightly increasing or decreasing the distance from the starting line to the first block, and possibly some adjustment may also be needed in the spacing between blocks.

A fast start is of great importance to the high hurdler. The limited space to the first hurdle makes perfection in the start all the more necessary and difficult to master. Time spent in arriving at the most suitable starting position will therefore pay richly in the final result.

There have been a few cases of hurdlers who have used seven strides to the first hurdle, but most hurdlers use eight. For those using the eight-stride approach, the lead foot is placed on the rear block in the starting position, and the takeoff foot is placed on the front block. If a seven-stride approach is used, the foot position is reversed so that the lead foot is placed on the front block and the takeoff foot on the rear block.

Approach to the First Hurdle. Perfecting the approach to the first hurdle can only be accomplished by trial and error. Experience has shown that any adjustment in the approach stride plan should take place by lengthening or shortening the fourth, fifth, and sixth strides, keeping the first three strides and the last two strides that come before the takeoff normal. The ideal stride length in the approach to the first hurdle might be as follows: (1) 0.60 meters (or 2′); (2) 1.10 (3′7″); (3) 1.35 (4′5″); (4) 1.50 (4′11″); (5) 1.65 (5′5″); (6) 1.80 (5′11″); (7) 1.90 (6′3″); (8) 1.80 (5′11″). The slight shortening of the last stride permits the hurdler to settle into his takeoff for the hurdle clearance with a brief moment of relaxation, bringing his center of gravity slightly ahead and thereby helping in attacking the hurdle in a fast step-over action.

Unlike in the flat sprint races, the presence of the first hurdle at the end of eight strides forces the hurdler to get into normal sprinting angle and sprinting stride rhythm sooner than the sprinter. Coming out of the blocks after the start, no effort must be made to look up at the first hurdle until after the first three or four strides have been taken. Thereafter, the eyes are focused on the crossbar of the hurdle ahead. Though a hurdler reaches his normal sprint action much earlier than the sprinter, the arms function as in sprinting, except during hurdle clearance when the arms counterbalance the extended lead leg position over the hurdle.

It is indeed sound advice to try to reach the first hurdle first in competition. This, of course, necessitates negotiating the approach as fast as possible. The greater the approach speed that the hurdler can handle, the more horizontal his drive will be at the takeoff, resulting in a faster and lower hurdle clearance. The shortened last stride prior to the takeoff, when taken at top speed, will rotate the trunk forward so the drive from the takeoff foot projects the body with an almost horizontal lean or "body-dip" across the hurdle. This exaggerated body lean must start with the takeoff foot in contact with the ground, thereby predetermining the flight path of the center of gravity in a lower, faster hurdle clearance.

The Takeoff. The takeoff distance from the hurdle depends upon the height of the athlete, speed of approach, length of leading leg, and the effective speed of the leading leg action. The actual point of takeoff varies with the individual and the previously mentioned points have a direct influence on the distance of the takeoff. However, on the average the takeoff point is between 2.00 to 2.30 meters (6′6″ to 7′6″) from the hurdle itself. Ninety percent of the effective clearance of the hurdle is determined. An effective takeoff will find the hurdler driving at the takeoff with sufficient body-lean (or dip) to clear the hurdle with a minimum of upward movement. The body-dip makes it possible to raise the seat and lower the trunk in relation to the center of gravity, as the hurdle is crossed.

On reaching the takeoff, with a shortened last stride, the takeoff foot makes contact with the track as in sprinting. The foot leaves the ground in a ball-toe drive with the toes pointing straight ahead. Placing the takeoff foot in a toe-outward position results in a loss of effective driving power. A flat-footed takeoff will result in a "jump" at the takeoff. A good rise up on the toes of the takeoff foot lifts the crotch and places the center of gravity in a sound position to attack the hurdle and reduce the time spent during actual clearance.

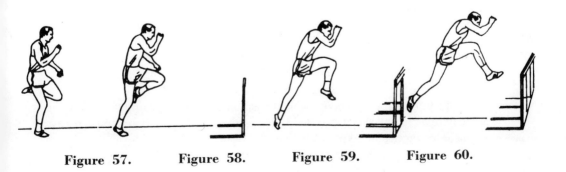

Figure 57.   Figure 58.   Figure 59.   Figure 60.

The body's center of gravity is ahead of the takeoff foot, with the hips and shoulders square to the line of running at all times. In coordination with the actions of the takeoff leg and body-dip, the lead leg is lifted directly forward with the knee well bent as though executing an exaggerated sprint stride. Throughout the actions of the takeoff and hurdle clearance, the hip-shoulder plane must remain constantly square to the direction of running.

The fast bent lift of the lead leg at the takeoff, in a higher than normal sprint knee lift action, encourages continuation of the basic elements of sprinting form. As a result of the fast pickup of the lead leg, there is an increased force of drive off the ground by the takeoff leg. The two actions of the legs working in opposite directions, as it were, has the effect of leaving the takeoff leg behind, causing a good split position of the legs at the crotch. This leg split helps to increase the body-dip in reaction to the fast lead-leg knee pickup, which permits the hurdler to get closer to the hurdle at the takeoff. A straight lead-leg action at the takeoff requires a greater takeoff distance as well as slowing down the takeoff actions considerably. Since the speed of the lead-leg action determines the overall speed of hurdle clearance, it is a point to be stressed in training. Working to move the lead leg so fast that it cannot be seen is sound advice for any hurdler.

As the lead leg is lifted quickly for hurdle clearance at the takeoff, the arm opposite the lead leg is thrust straight ahead and slightly downward to counterbalance the movement of the straight lead leg. This brings the body weight forward and down for the thrust across the hurdle. The trunk dips forward from the hips, with the shoulder going forward in coordination with the opposite arm extension at the takeoff. Ideally, the lead arm should be directed toward the hurdle bar, thereby assisting the body-dip at the takeoff. The arm on the same side as the leading leg remains bent at the elbow in normal sprinting position in readiness to come forward for the first getaway stride after hurdle clearance.

Though there are examples of great hurdlers who have used a head-down method of hurdle clearance, this is not recommended, since such an action is more wasteful than useful. The head should at all times continue facing forward as in normal sprinting alignment. Dipping the head down during hurdle clearance cannot be considered good form, since the basic fundamentals of sprinting are violated by this method.

Hurdle Clearance. The speed of the lead leg and the drive of the takeoff leg thrust the center of gravity low over the hurdle top. As a natural reaction, the takeoff leg, which is left trailing as a result of the wide split at the takeoff, now comes through late, but fast. The trailing heel is brought immediately to the buttocks. Thus the lower leg is folded to the upper leg, permitting the entire trail leg to subsequently clear the hurdle as one unit, with the knee swinging well out to the side and forward to clear the hurdle rail.

The forward dip of the body, which began at the takeoff, continues to produce a flat hurdle clearance. As the body crosses the hurdle, the chin should be over or ahead of the leading knee. This indicates good body-dip into and during the hurdle clearance. The body's center of gravity reaches its zenith before the hurdle, and the foot of the lead leg reaches its highest point some 15 to 30 centimeters (6 to 12 inches) in front of the hurdle bar. From the high point of the path made by the center of gravity, the hurdler comes down and across for the final phase of the hurdle clearance.

Before the buttocks reach the top of the hurdle, the body-dip that thrusts the hurdler low over the hurdle cuts the lead leg over the hurdle rail and down toward the other side. The lead leg is slightly flexed at the knee and not completely locked, even as it crosses the hurdle, but straightens at the knee as the thigh presses the leg downward over the hurdle rail for the landing. Ideally, the heel of the lead foot should be aimed at the top of the hurdle bar to lead the body drive across the hurdle, but it is lifted so fast that it passes over the hurdle rail without touching it.

As the lead leg goes down across the hurdle, the trailing leg should start to come through in a fast lateral sweep. The crotch should be over the hurdle before the trailing leg knee finally reaches the hurdle bar. When the trail leg crosses the hurdle, it should be parallel to the top of the hurdle and at right angles to the lead leg. By this time the lead leg is well on its way to the ground for the landing in a fast step-down action. As the trail leg crosses the hurdle top, care should be taken to cock the foot upward, to avoid striking the hurdle with the toes. To ensure an optimum getaway stride after the landing, the trail leg is lifted up high at the knee, toward the chest.

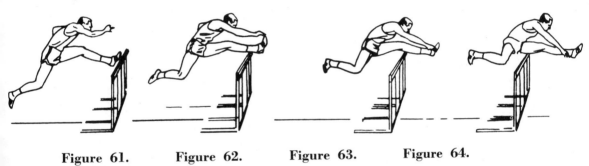

| Figure 61. | Figure 62. | Figure 63. | Figure 64. |

The action of both arms changes with the changing movements of the two legs during the hurdle clearance. The leading arm swings back, bent at the elbow, with the hand carried low. It sweeps backward, outside the knee of the trailing leg, which is moving forward all the time. The arm on the same side of the leading leg swings forward in coordination with the forward movement of the trailing leg on the opposite side. The lead-arm action is controlled by the forward lean of the trunk. A wide sweeping lead-arm action is often seen among hurdlers who are too erect during hurdle clearance. Lack of body-dip over the hurdle leads to hitting the hurdle rail with the ankle of the trailing leg. A good body position will therefore control not only the action of the arms, but also the movements of the two legs.

The key to excellence in hurdle clearance is making sure the legs move continuously throughout the pivoting action of the body over the hurdle. There must be no posed position at any time. Hurdling should be considered a sprint race over obstacles. The action throughout should involve as little interruption as possible in sprinting form. Although for purposes of description and analysis it may be convenient to separate the hurdle clearance into various phases, it is, in reality, a continuous coordinated effort, and not a series of separate parts. Think of hurdling as making room for the obstacles during a sprint race by changing the position of the limbs in relation to the center of gravity of the body, while raising it as little as necessary during clearance, so as to spend the least possible time in the air.

Landing After Hurdle Clearance. The key to a strong landing position after each hurdle clearance is proper balance. The landing of the lead leg after clearance is between 1.15 to 1.40 meters (3'10" to 4'7") beyond the hurdle, almost directly in line with the point of takeoff, although at times the lead leg may cut slightly across the path of the body as it comes down. This landing of the lead leg must be beneath and slightly behind the center of gravity to ensure an immediate return to sprinting action after hurdle clearance. The extreme body lean over the hurdle returns to the body angle in a normal sprint action as the lead leg lands.

Figure 65.   Figure 66.   Figure 67.   Figure 68.

It is sometimes claimed that the lead leg is snapped down as the hurdle clearance is made. Actually the lead leg moves down in reaction to the upward pull-through of the trail leg. Attempting to snap the lead leg down would cause the trunk to rise upright as a result of the reaction. If the lead leg is snapped down and the trunk comes upright, the loss of effective body lean may cause the trail leg to drop, possibly resulting in the foot striking the top of the hurdle rail as it is brought through. Rather than attempting to snap the lead leg down for a fast landing, work on pulling the trail leg through fast and attempt to run away from the hurdle. The faster the trail leg is pulled through, the faster the lead leg will move to the ground. This does not mean that the trail-leg action should be hurried. A fast moving bent lead leg at the takeoff will ensure a proper split between the thighs and the correct position of the trail leg as it is pulled through to assist the grounding of the lead leg.

The recovery of the trail leg's sweeping action across the hurdle may result in the first getaway stride being slightly out of alignment with the other strides. If the lead leg and trail leg do not land directly in line with the takeoff point, this may be remedied in training by sprinting over the hurdles placed along a lane line, and ensuring that each foot lands on this line after clearance.

An Example of Stride Pattern for the High Hurdles:

Start and approach to first hurdle	Strides	Length (m)	Distance (m)
	1st stride	0.60 (2'0")	0.60 (2'0")
	2nd stride	1.10 (3'7")	1.70 (5'7")
	3rd stride	1.35 (4'5")	3.05 (10'0")
	4th stride	1.50 (4'11")	4.55 (14'11")
	5th stride	1.65 (5'5")	6.20 (20'4")
	6th stride	1.80 (5'11")	8.00 (26'3")
	7th stride	1.90 (6'3")	9.90 (32'6")
	8th stride	1.80 (5'11")	11.70 (38'5")
Takeoff distance to first hurdle		2.02 (6'7")	13.72 (45'0")
Landing distance after first hurdle		1.40 (4'7")	1.40 (4'7")
Strides between 1st and 2nd hurdle	1st stride	1.55 (5'1")	2.95 (9'8")
	2nd stride	2.10 (6'11")	5.05 (16'7")
	3rd stride	2.00 (6'7")	7.05 (23'2")
Takeoff distance to the 2nd hurdle		2.09 (6'10")	9.14 (30'0")

Strides Between the Hurdles. As in sprinting, a hurdler must always have a sensation of good leg drive, with the body weight forward, and of concentration upon sheer speed during the three strides between hurdles. The first stride is often the key to proper stride-length between hurdles. This first stride after clearance must be a hard-driving effort of about 150 centimeters (4'11") in length. Examination of the hurdler's spike marks on the track may assist in detecting faults in cutting down or of overstriding.

Beginners usually have a shorter-than-recommended first stride, which causes a loss in the striding and sprint rhythm and in speed between hurdles. The short first stride off the hurdle may also lead to stretching to get to the next hurdle takeoff, resulting in a loss of hurdling form. Top hurdlers come off the hurdle with a full driving stride into normal sprinting action, thereby gaining drive, space covered, and speed, and permitting a shortened last stride before the next hurdle takeoff. This shortened last stride before the next hurdle takeoff places the body weight ahead of the takeoff foot in a good position to attack the next hurdle and reduce the flight time and distance in hurdle clearance.

Young hurdlers often forget that hurdling is sprinting. They must be encouraged to use their arms to aid maintenance of the stride-length and speed between hurdles. An ideal stride pattern between hurdles may be for the first stride to measure about 1.55 meters (5'1"), and the second stride close to 2.10 meters (6'11"), and the third stride about 2.00 meters (6'6") in length. A simple coaching hint to beginners is to avoid striding between hurdles, but drive, lean forward, and sprint. This advice is very valuable, especially once the last hurdle is cleared. The hurdler must drive for the finish tape and maintain body lean into the final sprint to finish. Any lunge or body dip that may then be necessary must come in the last one or two strides, and not be attempted too early. Otherwise there will be a loss of effective sprint action and speed to the tape.

The 100 Meters Hurdles for Women

The 100 meters hurdles for women is the shortest international hurdle event on the track and field program. Technically viewed, the basic technique outlined for the high hurdles is applicable to the women's hurdles as well. There are, however, a few technical differences that are really an adjustment to suit the particular requirements of women hurdlers.

Running Rhythm. Though the approach distance to the first hurdle is 13 meters, the common number of strides to the first hurdle remains unchanged. For women who are excellent sprinters, it may be possible to get to the first hurdle in seven strides, but like the high hurdles for men, this has proved less effective, since the seven longer strides to the first hurdle require a switch over to a quick three-stride rhythm between hurdles. In most cases it has been found that this sudden change of stride rhythm disturbs the development of speed, and has hence been discarded in actual practice.

The distance between hurdles is only 8.5 meters. Therefore, it is not necessary for a woman hurdler to possess any exceptional physical qualities to reach the next hurdle in three strides. But speed between the hurdles and a certain sense of running rhythm is necessary to be able to make use of one's full potential within the confined distance between the hurdles. It has often been the case that a good and tall woman hurdler finds that she has to shorten her strides between the hurdles, since the space is too short for her to be able to make full use of her normal length of strides. An example of the stride plan for the 100m hurdles, included below, shows the progression of eight strides to the first hurdle, as well as the three strides taken between hurdles. On an average, this may be considered a theoretically ideal stride plan for most women hurdlers.

An Example of Stride Pattern for the 100-Meters Hurdles

Start and approach to the first hurdle	Strides	Length (m)	Distance (m)
	1st stride	0.50 (1′8″)	0.50 (1′8″)
	2nd stride	1.10 (3′7″)	1.60 (5′3″)
	3rd stride	1.30 (4′3″)	2.90 (9′6″)
	4th stride	1.45 (4′9″)	4.35 (14′3″)
	5th stride	1.60 (5′3″)	5.95 (19′6″)
	6th stride	1.75 (5′9″)	7.70 (25′3″)
	7th stride	1.85 (6′1″)	9.55 (31′4″)
	8th stride	1.60 (5′3″)	11.15 (36′7″)
Takeoff distance to the first hurdle		1.85 (6′1″)	13.00 (42′7¾″)
Landing distance after the first hurdle		1.15 (3′9″)	1.15 (3′9″)
Strides between 1st and 2nd hurdle	1st stride	1.55 (5′1″)	2.70 (8′10″)
	2nd stride	2.00 (6′7″)	4.70 (15′5″)
	3rd stride	1.85 (6′1″)	6.55 (21′6″)
Takeoff distance to the 2nd hurdle		1.95 (6′5″)	8.50 (27′10¾″)

Hurdle Clearance. While hurdling speed is the single factor that makes the difference between winning or losing a race, the technical particulars of the stride taken over the hurdle depend on the height of the hurdler, her leg length, movements of her leading leg and trailing leg, and the position of her upper body. Natural leg speed is essential to clearing the hurdle with ease and speed, but for the women's hurdles the leg movement is adapted to suit the height of the hurdler, as well as the fact that the hurdle itself is comparatively low in proportion to the natural height of the female hurdler.

Lead-Leg Action. At the takeoff for the hurdle clearance, the thigh of the leading leg is brought up level with the horizontal. The lower leg swings forward-upward only to a point that must be attained for a secure clearance of the hurdle. The difference from high hurdling here is that the woman hurdler has to break the forward swing of the lower leg as soon as the heel has reached the height of the hurdle rail. When this action is mastered for the women's hurdles, it will be seen that there is no complete stretching or locking of the knee joint as the leg swings through for the clearance. For tall women hurdlers, an exaggerated lead-leg action will result in difficulty getting back down quickly. When this restricted lead leg movement has been mastered, the speed of landing behind the hurdle falls in with the rhythm of the three strides between the hurdles.

Tall women find the lead-leg knee slightly bent, even as the leg comes down for the landing on the ball of the foot. For shorter women this will not be possible. Actually, when the lead-leg foot has just passed the top of the hurdle, the thigh accelerates the landing by pressing downward-backward, so that the ball of the lead foot makes contact with the ground at about 1.09 meters (3′6″) from the hurdle.

There are many good women hurdlers who swing their lower leg very vigorously upward so that the knee joint is fully locked during hurdle clearance. This is generally considered less economical because the lower leg goes too high, thereby causing a delayed landing. The principle here is that the type of lead-leg action for a woman hurdler depends, to a large extent, on the size of the woman concerned. Most women hurdlers, however, are quite tall, and this factor makes the locked-knee lead leg action unsuitable for them. For shorter hurdlers, however, the disadvantage of using full locked-knee action is compensated for by a quicker swinging motion of the short leg lever, keeping the rhythm comparatively unbroken.

Trailing-Leg Action. The trailing-leg action is relatively less emphasized in 100m hurdling than in high hurdling. In a rational trailing-leg action, a woman hurdler carries her trailing knee low over the top of the hurdle. Since the hurdle is only 83.8 centimeters (2′9″) in height, the trailing knee of a tall woman hurdler comes through at a slightly downward angle. The shorter hurdler must stretch the trailing leg laterally away, flexed at the knee, so that the degree of downward hang of the trailing leg is far less than is the case with tall women hurdlers.

As the knee of the trailing leg comes over the hurdle rail, the thigh is lifted slightly to bring the flexed leg into position for the follow-up strides after hurdle clearance. As the whole trailing leg begins its ascent, the thigh comes to the horizontal, with the lower leg swinging into place in a high knee-lift position for the first stride after hurdle clearance. To put it simply, the whole action of the two legs in 100m hurdling is more natural, closer to sprinting form, and less vigorous as compared to the action in the high hurdles.

Body Position. The degree of forward lean used by most women hurdlers is practically the same as in normal sprinting. It is not necessary to lean too much, due to the low height of the hurdle. To keep a low trajectory, the tall woman hurdler does not need an exaggerated body-dip as do high hurdlers. An exaggerated body-dip for the tall hurdler is as bad as the head-down type hurdle clearance sometimes found among male hurdlers. The lean used by low hurdlers is mainly for the purpose of getting the center of gravity into a favorable position for the landing behind the hurdle. Again, the degree of forward lean and dip depends on the size of the athlete. Therefore, it is natural and recommended that a short hurdler accentuate the forward lean at the takeoff and above the hurdle, far more than is actually required for the tall hurdler.

The 400-Meters Intermediate Hurdles

As in the other hurdle races, this is an event for the specialist. There have been cases of 400-meters runners who have tried to double in the hurdles and have found it to be quite an ordeal. But a fast time for 400 meters is very necessary to the success of this already-tough sprint race. Because of the degree of fatigue that is inherent in 400-meter hurdling, it is known as the most strenuous sprint event on the track program.

The technique of this event is not quite like that in the high hurdles, and yet not exactly the same as the technique used in the low hurdles either. It may be more accurate to say that 400-meter hurdling is halfway between the high and low hurdle techniques mentioned earlier. The distance of the race, distance to the first hurdle, and spacing between all subsequent hurdles, however, require one to pay special attention to economy of effort and a certain striding rhythm.

One other factor that must be kept in mind is that the 400-meter hurdles race is around two curves, and it is technically preferable to clear the hurdles with a left lead-leg action. This is of importance, since it permits the athlete to maneuver the curves more easily, by running the race close to the inside of the lane without worrying about violating the rules with his trailing-leg action. Then again, due to the left-hand inside direction of running, the left lead-leg action places the center of gravity in a sound position to maintain balance and running rhythm as the hurdler lands, after clearance.

There are several examples of world class 400-meter hurdlers who have used a right lead-leg action. This is, however, not recommended for the beginner, who has the advantage of learning from scratch.

Strides to the First Hurdle. The distance of the approach to the first hurdle is 45 meters (49¼ yards). It is not possible to lay down any hard and fast rule regarding the number of strides to the first hurdle, but most top-class hurdlers seem to prefer 22 strides, with some even trying 21 strides. There are others who recommend 23 strides for the champion and 24 strides for the novice. Whatever the final stride plan selected, remember that an even 22 strides helps one to arrive at the takeoff in a rhythm that is close to the stride rhythm taken between the hurdles. In such a case, the takeoff leg is placed on the front block in the starting position.

The speed of approach to the first hurdle is comparable to the speed of the equivalent flat distance. But in hurdling, due to the presence of the first hurdle 45 meters from the start, the stride rhythm matters a great deal. Therefore, the optimum striding speed is said to be a shade less than the normal all-out sprint for the 400-meters flat race. However, the last four or five strides in the approach to the first hurdle should be of the same rhythm as the strides which will be used between the subsequent hurdles.

Hurdle Clearance. Assuming that the athlete leads with the left leg over the hurdle, at a slower striding rhythm than in the shorter hurdle races, the clearance technique over the 91.4 centimeters (3'0") hurdle is basically the same as the technique described earlier. Since economy of effort and striding rhythm are important factors to keep in mind, the stepping action is less violent and more in keeping with the tempo of the running speed.

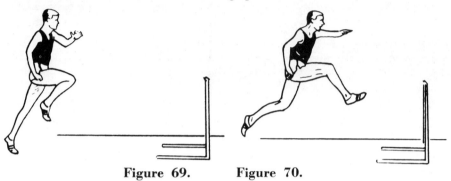

Figure 69.   **Figure 70.**

Learning to hurdle around the curve from a staggered start in lanes, and maneuvering the curve, takes up much time in training. In hurdling around a curve, the main point of difference in technique is to get the right arm across to the left foot, instead of straight ahead as in hurdling on the straight. This will ensure that the natural body lean to the left on the curve is maintained, while the body weight shifts to the left on the curve, enabling the hurdler to land with the body weight in a sound position close to the inner edge of the lane.

The amount of body-dip in 400-meter hurdling is actually a cross between the low and high hurdles. Lean is essential to maintaining form in hurdle clearance, but only enough so that there is no real stress on dipping the body, as in high hurdling. The all-important point to keep in mind is to stay relaxed during the hurdle clearance and to conserve energy.

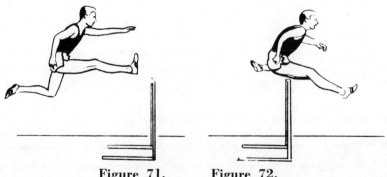

Figure 71.   **Figure 72.**

The length of the stride over the hurdle is about 3.20 meters (10'6"). The takeoff itself is about 2.0 meters (6'7") in front of and the landing about 1.20 meters (3'11") behind the hurdle. These figures indicate a certain amount of float over the hurdle, which is in keeping with the tempo of the striding rhythm.

There must be no attempt made to chop down the lead leg. Rhythm, coordination, and style must be backed up with skilled pace-judgment, in order to produce success in this event. Hurdling style need only be stressed when the technique already in use does not produce an economical means of clearing the hurdles.

Strides Between Hurdles. Fifteen strides between hurdles is recommended for most athletes in this event. However, holding this stride pattern throughout the race is possible for only the best hurdlers, due to the element of fatigue that plagues the 400-meter hurdler during the race. As a result, some hurdlers have to change to a 17-stride rhythm after the fifth or sixth hurdle. Some hurdlers have used 17 strides throughout the race, but this is not conducive to fast times. The additional two strides tend to destroy the stride rhythm during the early part of the race, when the athlete is comparatively fresh.

Using an uneven number of strides between hurdles has the advantage of getting the athlete to the takeoff for the next hurdle without any change in the takeoff leg. Nevertheless, there are hurdlers who, from the very beginning, or after a break in the striding rhythm caused by kicking a hurdle, have changed to an even stride rhythm. Taking 14 or 16 strides between hurdles forces a change in the lead- and trailing-leg actions over every other hurdle. Therefore, using an even stride rhythm makes it necessary to learn hurdling so that the hurdler is able to lead with the left and right legs alternately. In fact, it is recommended that the 400-meter hurdler have a fair degree of hurdling skill with both legs, just in case of such an emergency.

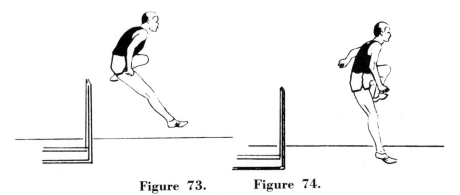

Figure 73.   **Figure 74.**

A few champions have used 13 strides between hurdles. This number is seldom recommended, as it is too exacting for any but the very best to attempt. A 15-stride rhythm gives the athlete an average stride length of about 2.12 meters (7′) in which to cover the 31.80 meters (104′) to the takeoff for the next hurdle. For a 13-stride plan, the average stride length is about 2.45 meters (8′). This is too difficult for the majority of hurdlers to maintain, without leading to premature fatigue.

The Finishing Burst. Having successfully cleared the last hurdle, the athlete has another 40 meters (46½ yards) in which to complete his race. All too many races have been won or lost in this vital finishing sprint to the tape. To be able to hold one's running form at this stage is of great importance. Trying to sprint when one is hardly able to hold on to his running form causes a drastic change in the striding rhythm. This change of rhythm, when the athlete is fast getting fatigued, can cost him the entire race if the opposition is really tough. Only proper speed-endurance training will permit him to increase speed without too much change in the stride frequency over the last 40 meters to the finishing tape.

A Guide to Hurdle Training

After the hurdler solves the problems of stride length between hurdlers, he must concentrate on increasing speed between hurdles. Experience shows that if a hurdler does too much sprinting with the sprinters, or does a considerable amount of sprinting alone, it will interfere with his stride pattern to the first hurdle, as well as his consistency of strides between hurdles. Sprint-hurdling is an attempt to increase the hurdler's speed between hurdles, and yet not interfere with the stride pattern between hurdles. The major preoccupation in hurdle training should therefore be centered around fast hurdling, and not merely sprint training alone.

Hurdling should be considered a sprint race over obstacles, and the action throughout should involve as little interruption as possible in normal sprinting form. Although for purposes of description and analysis it may be convenient to separate hurdle clearance into various phases, it is in reality a continuous coordinated effort, and not a series of separate parts. The best hurdle form is the one that spends the least time in the air during clearance. Think of hurdling as making room for the obstacles during the sprint race by merely changing the position of the limbs in relation to the body's center of gravity, while raising it as little as necessary for clearing the hurdles.

In almost all hurdle races, the race is usually won between the seventh and tenth barriers, thus revealing the importance of speed-endurance in hurdling. Do not make the mistake, therefore, of training over only three to five hurdles. Training should include ample sprinting over three, five, six, eight and also the full ten hurdles, when necessary.

Proper balance after hurdle clearance is a problem with the high hurdler. Unless the hurdler lands in a balanced sprint position as he comes off the hurdle, he will not be able to sprint the three strides to the next hurdle. It is useful to increase the distance between hurdles to a seven-stride distance to correct a bad landing, and still have five strides available for sprinting to the next hurdle. It will be necessary to alter the distance slightly to allow for individual differences between hurdlers, so as to permit the athlete to sprint all out from one hurdle to the next. Since there will be greater speed involved between hurdles now, it may be necessary to lower the hurdles to begin with, and as confidence is gained, they may be raised again to the standard height.

With top-class hurdlers, sprint work may also be done by running between two marks whose distance apart requires a definite number of strides. If available, other athletes may run alongside to provide the stress of competition. By so doing, the hurdler works at sprinting without interfering with the all-important aspect of stride length and stride pattern between the hurdles.

World class high hurdlers sprint the 110 meters over ten, 107-centimeter (3'6") barriers in a time often less than two seconds slower than their best effort over 110 meters flat. The 400-meters hurdlers, going over ten, 91.4-centimeter (3') barriers, are often clocked around three seconds slower than their best 400-meters flat effort. This is proof that "hurdling is sprinting." But to realize the importance of sprint-hurdling, from the point of view of training for the event, it is necessary to understand that hurdling is not merely a pure sprint. For example, some of the many factors that lead to successful hurdling, like racing endurance, time saved between hurdles, time saved in hurdle clearance, etc., can affect the hurdler adversely and produce poor times. To evaluate these points and put them into effective use during training, a look at the accompanying charts for the split times in the 100-, 110- and 400-meter hurdles will prove useful as a coaching aid.

SPLIT TIMES FOR THE 100- AND 110-METERS HURDLES

Unlike the other track events, which are longer than 200 meters, it is not practical to divide the 100- and 110-meters hurdle races into two parts for the purpose of analysis. The distance of the race is far too short and the percentage of time wasted between the starting gun and accelerating to all-out hurdling speed does not make it practical to split the race into two separate halves. Therefore, the best way to compare timings is to clock the hurdler at each hurdle during the course of a race, and then compare the timings.

In clocking hurdlers at various hurdles, the most accurate point to time them is at the instant the lead foot lands after hurdle clearance. Even though the landing distances of the lead foot differ slightly among most hurdlers, the advantages of timing them at the landing rather than when over the hurdle are greater. The numerous individual differences and actual conditions prevalent during a race make it difficult, if not impossible, to derive a clear-cut set of figures and tables for ready reference. Nevertheless, the accompanying charts are a useful guide to the training of hurdlers for pinpointing weaknesses at various stages in a race, so that training may be designed accordingly.

In discussing the chart on the split timings for the 110-meters hurdles, its author, Jagmohan Singh, points out the usefulness of these charts as a device to ascertain the potential scope of improvement of each hurdler, even though these figures are not absolutely applicable to every hurdler, and not always applicable to the same hurdler. The times quoted in these charts are not determined by actual measurement, but rather by calculations. It is suggested that in using these charts as a guide, all times should be made with a gun start. Should times be taken with a running start, 0.2 seconds should be added for the reaction time at the start.

Split Timings for 100-Meters Hurdles
(Times at Landing of Lead-Foot after Each Hurdle Clearance)

	12– 12.5 sec.	12.5– 13 sec.	13– 13.5 sec.	13.5– 14 sec.	14– 14.5 sec.	14.5– 15 sec.
Time at Landing after 1st Hurdle	2.1	2.1	2.2	2.2	2.3	2.3
2nd Hurdle	3.1	3.2	3.3	3.3	3.5	3.5
3rd Hurdle	4.1	4.2	4.4	4.5	4.7	4.8
4th Hurdle	5.1	5.3	5.5	5.6	5.9	6.0
5th Hurdle	6.1	6.3	6.6	6.8	7.1	7.3
6th Hurdle	7.1	7.4	7.7	7.9	8.3	8.5
7th Hurdle	8.1	8.4	8.8	9.1	9.5	9.8
8th Hurdle	9.1	9.5	9.9	10.2	10.7	11.0
9th Hurdle	10.2	10.6	11.0	11.4	11.9	12.3
10th Hurdle	11.3	11.7	12.1–12.2*	12.6–12.7*	13.1	13.5–13.6*
Finish time	12.3	12.8	13.2–13.3*	13.7–13.8*	14.3	14.8–15.0*

*Hurdlers displaying comparatively poor endurance.

The 400-meters hurdles involves a combination of three very important factors that together produce the best results. Technique plays an important role when economy of effort is considered. Speed and pace judgment play a remarkable part when energy distribution is considered. Yet, running rhythm and stride pattern from the start to the finish of the race cannot be overlooked in this speed-endurance event. Accuracy in the stride pattern is very necessary in producing top-class results. Any small change or misjudgment at any stage in the race may result in major losses in time in the latter stages of the race.

There is really no shortcut to the development of proper pace judgment and stride rhythm in the 400-meters hurdles. It is only through hard work and constant repetitions in training that these can finally be accomplished. The 400-meter hurdler should have confidence in his pace judgment and constantly check and verify his pace to and between hurdles. One's best pace is achieved through equal distribution of energy throughout the race.

Normally, the first half of a 400-meters hurdles race is run about two seconds faster than the second half of the race. To develop proper pace judgment throughout the race it is necessary to determine the split timings at each hurdle, at the halfway point, or at the clearance of any particular hurdle as desired in training. Taking it for granted that the stride rhythm and number of strides are well set, the split time reference chart for the 400-meters hurdles shown here

Split Times for the 110-Meters Hurdles

110 M Hurdles recorded in seconds	12.6–12.8	12.9–13.0	13.2–13.5	13.5–14.0	14.0–14.5	14.5–15.0	15.0–15.5	15.5–16.0
Time at 1st Hurdle Landing	2.3	2.3	2.4	2.4	2.5	2.6	2.6	2.7
2nd Hurdle	3.3	3.3	3.4	3.5	3.6	3.7	3.8	3.9
3rd Hurdle	4.3	4.3	4.4–4.5	4.6	4.7–4.8	4.9	5.0	5.1
4th Hurdle	5.2	5.3	5.4–5.5	5.7	5.8–5.9	6.0	6.2	6.4
5th Hurdle	6.2	6.3	6.4–6.6	6.8	6.9–7.1	7.2	7.4	7.6
6th Hurdle	7.2	7.3	7.4–7.6	7.9	8.0–8.3	8.3	8.6	8.8
7th Hurdle	8.2	8.4	8.5–8.7	9.0	9.1–9.4	9.5	9.8	10.1
8th Hurdle	9.3	9.5	9.6–9.8	10.1	10.2–10.6	10.7	11.0	11.3
9th Hurdle	10.3	10.6	10.7–10.9	11.2	11.3–11.8	11.9	12.3	12.6
10th Hurdle	11.4	11.7	11.8–12.1	12.4	12.5–13.0	13.1	13.6	14.0
Finish time	12.7	13.0	13.2–13.5	13.5–14.0	14.0–14.5	14.5–15.0	15.0–15.5	15.5–16.0

Split Timings for 400-Meters Hurdles

Time at Landing after	46.5–47.0	Dif-ference	47.0–47.5	Dif-ference	48.0	Dif-ference	49–50	Dif-ference	50–51	Dif-ference	52.0	Dif-ference	53.0	Dif-ference	54.0	Dif-ference
1st Hurdle		5.7		5.7		5.7		5.9		6.0		6.1		6.3		6.4
2nd Hurdle	9.5	3.8	9.6	3.9	9.7	4.0	10.0	4.1	10.2	4.2	10.4	4.3	10.7	4.4	10.9	4.5
3rd Hurdle	13.4	3.9	13.5	3.9	13.7	4.0	14.1	4.1	14.4	4.2	14.7	4.3	15.1	4.4	15.4	4.5
4th Hurdle	17.2	3.8	17.4	3.9	17.7	4.0	18.2	4.1	18.6	4.2	19.0	4.3	19.5	4.4	19.9	4.5
5th Hurdle	21.1	3.9	21.3	3.9	21.7	4.0	22.3	4.1	22.8	4.2	23.3	4.3	23.9	4.4	24.4	4.5
6th Hurdle	25.0	3.9	25.3	4.0	25.8	4.1	26.5	4.2	27.1	4.3	27.7	4.4	28.4	4.5	29.0	4.6
7th Hurdle	29.0	4.0	29.4	4.1	29.9	4.1	30.8	4.3	31.5	4.4	32.2	4.5	32.9	4.5	33.7	4.7
8th Hurdle	33.1	4.1	33.6	4.2	34.2	4.2	35.2	4.4	35.9	4.4	36.8	4.6	37.6	4.7	38.5	4.8
9th Hurdle	37.4	4.3	37.9	4.3	38.5	4.3	39.7	4.5	40.4	4.5	41.6	4.8	42.5	4.9	43.4	4.9
10th Hurdle	41.8	4.4	42.3	4.4	43.0	4.5	44.3	4.6	45.1	4.7	46.5	4.9	47.5	5.0	48.4	5.0
Total Time	46.7	4.9	47.2	4.9	48.0	5.0	49.6	5.3	50.5	5.4	52.0	5.5	53.0	5.5	54.0	5.6

(Times at landing of lead-foot after each hurdle clearance.)

should prove a useful guide for training, as well as drawing up a pace plan for competitions.

It is no secret that the 400-meters hurdles is one of the most grueling events on the track and field program. Much has been said about the physical require- ments and qualities of a 400-meter hurdler. Besides the qualities such as speed, endurance, technique, and competitive spirit, the most important single factor that makes the difference between a top-class hurdler and a mediocre performer is sense of rhythm and a well-set stride plan.

Training for the 110-Meters Hurdles

The off-season is the best time for the beginner to start learning the event. During this period, a great deal of technical learning can be done to master the basic essentials of hurdling form. Those who are not at the novice stage can use this period to improve their basic physical condition, which will pay rich dividends in the ensuing seasons.

As mid-season approaches, the tempo of training should be intensified. The overall load of training now aims toward greater precision in hurdling skill, better balance, greater speed, and a general maintenance of fitness, strength and endurance.

By the time the competitive season comes around, the hurdler should be technically confident of his hurdling form. His training now depends on the number of races he intends to participate in, and must be regulated accordingly. Generally, training is lighter during this season so that the hurdler maintains a fine competitive edge, and stays comparatively fresh.

General Training Hints. A hurdler's training program must take into account the various factors required to make up a balanced schedule. The five most important aspects to concentrate on follow:

1. *Technique*—This will consist of hurdling over three to five flights for form. The hurdles may be placed at the regulation distance apart or slightly less for the purpose of doing runs at less than top speed. The distance between hurdles may be increased slightly to fit in five strides instead of the usual three taken between the hurdles, with a view to working on running rhythm and speed between the hurdles. Gun starts from blocks over one or two flights of hurdles may be essential to groove in the approach to the first hurdle. Occasional runs over seven flights of hurdles may be necessary as a trial to check on overall hurdling endurance.

2. *Speed*—During the early season, attention will naturally be fixed on develop- ing speed-endurance through Interval Training and repetition work at distances between 100 to 200 meters. The number of intervals is gradually built up over the entire season, thereby producing the desired effect on developing speed. Working with the sprinters for all-out starts and short dashes will take up limited time during the mid-season.

3. *Endurance*—While a certain amount of Circuit training may be attempted

to develop the hard core of general physical fitness, the use of light cross-country running and Fartlek will form the background work for the development of general endurance. As the season progresses, specific speed-endurance will replace most of the work done by way of developing endurance.

4. *Strength*—Weight training and a certain amount of isometric training recommended for the sprinters will form the means of strength development for the hurdler. Besides isotonic and isometric training, the use of sandbags or medicine balls will help develop general strength and at the same time offer a certain amount of variety in the training routine.

5. *Suppleness*—One of the most important requirements in good hurdling is flexibility and mobility of the muscles and joints. Greater natural suppleness is an asset in mastering the complicated aspects of hurdling technique. Besides, it is a positive way of avoiding possible injury. In addition to the usual bending and stretching exercises executed by the sprinters, ground hurdling exercises and exercises for the trail leg and leading leg performed on the side of the hurdle are necessary. There are a number of accepted hurdlers' exercises for this purpose. But for the beginner, it will be necessary to learn them under the guidance of a coach or experienced hurdler. Without this important factor being included in a hurdler's training program, no amount of technique work will develop the required form. General agility and flexibility may be developed to a certain extent in the off-season by playing games that involve quickness of movement and speed, but there is really no substitute for the many complicated hurdle exercises that form the backbone of suppleness training for this event.

Off-season Training. Training will be done on four or five days a week, with two or three active rest days between. This outline program will serve as a guide alone. Training programs depend largely on the hurdler's age, previous experience, time available for training, and the facilities at his disposal. Each aspiring hurdler must take into consideration his own particular requirements and work out a program accordingly.

Monday:	Warm-up, followed by stretching exercises and weight training.
Tuesday:	Warm-up, as if for sprinting, followed by 6–8 x 100 m with 200 m jogging for recovery.
Wednesday:	Some cross-country or Fartlek, followed by weight training.
Thursday:	Warm-up, 8–10 x 5 hurdles for form, followed by 4 x 200 m with 200 m jogging for recovery.
Friday:	Fartlek running, followed by weight training.
Saturday:	Active rest.
Sunday:	Rest.

Pre-competitive Season Training. Training will now be increased to five or six days a week, with only one or two days of active rest between. The hurdler should now attempt more skill work and faster work to sharpen his speed. There will be no drastic changes in the training routine, except that the hurdler should now also participate in other events and run an occasional sprint relay race as a means of keeping sprinting fit.

Monday: Warm-up, stretching exercises and light weight training.

Tuesday: Warm-up, followed by hurdle exercises and stepping over three to five hurdles. Run over the hurdles with five strides between, followed by form hurdling at the regulation spacing with three strides between hurdles, at top speed, from the blocks. This may be done about six to eight times. Finish with 3 x 150 m, jogging 150 m for recovery.

Wednesday: Fartlek, followed by weight training, or, warm-up and some stretching exercises, followed by 10 x 100 m striding fast, ending with Circuit training.

Thursday: As on Tuesday.

Friday: As on Monday.

Saturday: Practice starts with the sprinters, followed by hurdle exercises and 6 x 200 m, with 200 m jogging and walking for recovery.

Sunday: Rest.

Competitive Season Training. As a guide to the aspiring hurdle champion, the pre-competitive and competitive season training of two-time Olympic champion Lee Calhoun has been included. Each program is preceded by the following warm-up:

Jog two laps, followed by bending and stretching exercises to loosen up. Some hurdling at a fast pace over five hurdles for the trail-leg action. 5 x 5 flights of hurdles with five strides between, concentrating on trail-leg pull-through. (Before major competitions, 2 x 5 flights of hurdles all out, and a few starts from the blocks over one hurdle only.) Rest for 5–10 minutes. Five minutes before the actual race, walk and jog alternately and do more stretching exercises.

Pre-competitive Season Training (Lee Calhoun)

Sunday: Rest.

Monday: 4 x 200 m in 25 seconds. Walk 200 m after each.

Tuesday: 10 x 60 m in 6.6 seconds. Walk three minutes between. 5 x gun starts from blocks over two flights of hurdles and a 10 m sprint. Walk two to three minutes after each.

Wednesday: 8 x 4 flights of hurdles plus 15 m sprint. Walk back to start after each. 1 x 300 m in about 34–35 seconds.

Thursday: 10 x gun starts from blocks over two flights of hurdles plus 10 m sprint. Walk back to start for rest after each. 1 x 400 m in about 53 seconds.

Friday: 5 x 110 m hurdles in about 14.1. Walk about 3–4 minutes after each for recovery.

Saturday: Rest.

Competitive Season Training (Lee Calhoun)

This program is identical to the pre-competitive season training outlined earlier, except that Friday's training is eliminated and replaced by complete rest, prior to competition on Saturday. The above workouts require two hours, usually starting at 3:00 P.M. Calhoun's competitive season normally extended from January to June. He rested July, August and September, and began his pre-competitive training in October each year. He trained only once a day, and rested one day before a competition. His last meal was taken four or five hours prior to racing. Calhoun did no cross-country or Fartlek running, nor did he do any type of weight training. He participated in approximately 12 indoor and 18 outdoor competitions annually. He used a right lead leg over the hurdle, with his left leg in the front block about 30 centimeters (12") from the starting line and the right leg in the blocks about 60 centimeters (24") back.

Training for the 200- and 400-Meter Hurdles

The following training plan is a rough guide from a year-round viewpoint, and it is not essentially different from that of the 400-meter flat runners. While the general hints on training for the 100- and 110-meter hurdles apply here, 400-meter hurdle workouts naturally tend to be more intensive than those for the shorter hurdle races. Hurdling rhythm and tactics are important in the longer hurdle races and hence require attention during training, and experience plays a crucial role. The attitude of the athlete toward racing under various conditions can only be developed over a period of time through numerous high-level competitions.

Off-season Training

Sunday: Rest, or active rest.

Monday: Warm-up, followed by hurdling exercises. 12–15 x 200 m interval training. Walk 200 m for recovery after each. Some weight training.

Tuesday: Warm-up, followed by 2–3 timed runs over 300 m and 400 m for pace, with a 300 m walk for recovery, in two sets.

Wednesday: Warm-up, followed by some hurdle technique training and specific hurdle exercises. 5–6 x 3 flights of hurdles at the regulation distance, concentrating on stride rhythm between the hurdles. Weight training or Circuit training as desired.

Thursday: Warm-up, followed by Fartlek running or two sets of 2 x 500 m with 5–7 minutes rest between each run.

Friday: Warm-up, and repeat Wednesday's program.

Saturday: Rest, or active rest.

Pre-competitive Season Training

Sunday: Rest.

Monday: Warm-up, followed by training with sprinters doing short dashes over 30 to 60 meters. 5 x one hurdle working on the approach. A few runs over three flights of hurdles to develop the stride rhythm between hurdles. 10 minutes slow jogging.

Tuesday: Warm-up, followed by specific hurdling exercises with the high hurdlers. 3 x 600 m with 7–8 minutes rest between each, keeping a check on pace. Weight training, if desired.

Wednesday: Warm-up, followed by 5 x 5 flights of hurdles. Rest 10 minutes. 2 x 7 hurdles with 15 minutes of rest between each run. Jog slowly until recovered.

Thursday: Warm-up, followed by sprint starts taken on the curve with the sprinters. 3 x 400 m, with the first 3 hurdles and last 3 hurdles and an intermediate flat run. (The same hurdle placement, and flat run between, is required for the 200 m hurdles, too.) Weight training, if desired.

Friday: Warm-up, followed by Monday's training program.

Saturday: Warm-up, followed by specific hurdle endurance runs. 5 x 200 m flat at an even rhythmic pace and completing the final 200 m with five flights of hurdles. Take 5–7 minutes of rest between each run. 10–15 minutes slow jogging.

Sunday: Rest.

Competitive Season Training

As a guide to the aspiring hurdle champion, the pre-competitive and competitive season training program of Gert Potgieter has been included. Each program is preceded by the following warm-up:

The warm-up is identical for a training session or a competition, and it normally takes between 25 to 30 minutes. On warmer days it may be shortened slightly and on colder days lengthened to about 40 to 45 minutes. It consists of four phases. (1) Two laps slow jogging, with a brief walk after each. Then two laps of slow, continuous jogging. (2) Some light stretching exercises. (3) 4–5 x 150 m wearing spikes, with a 150 m walk after each. The first two repeats are at only half effort, and the rest are at three-quarters effort. (4) Ten minutes rest before the training or race begins.

Pre-competitive Season Training (Gert Potgieter)

Monday: 2 x 500 m very fast, with walking between each until fully recovered, *or* about 5 kilometers (3 miles) cross-country running over a hilly course.

Tuesday:	Rest.
Wednesday:	6–10 x 150 m sprints from starting blocks, with 150 m walk, for recovery, after each.
Thursday:	3 x 3 flights of hurdles with starts from the blocks. This is followed by 2–3 x 300 m at a fast pace, walking between each until completely recovered.
Friday:	Rest.
Saturday:	2 x 400 m in about 52 seconds each. Walk 30 minutes between each for rest.
Sunday:	Rest.

Competitive Season Training (Gert Potgieter)

Monday:	2 x 600 m very fast, with walking between each until fully recovered *or* about 5 kilometers (3 miles) cross-country running over a hilly course.
Tuesday:	4–6 x 150 m sprints. Walk five minutes after each for rest. Then 10 starts from the blocks over the first hurdle.
Wednesday:	2–3 x 300 m or 400 m flat runs according to inclination. Walk between each only until slightly recovered.
Thursday:	2–3 x 5–8 hurdles from the blocks. Walk until fully recovered between each run.
Friday:	Rest.
Saturday:	Competition. If no competition, then time trials of 2 x 400 m, each slightly faster than 50 seconds. On some occasions rest is taken on both Thursday and Friday prior to a Saturday competition, in which case hurdling practice is done on Wednesday.
Sunday:	Rest.

Gert Potgieter cleared the hurdles with alternate leading legs, so that for most of the race he took 14 strides between the hurdles, instead of the orthodox 15 or possibly 13 strides adopted by some champions. He seldom trained more than once daily, although occasionally on Saturdays he put in a 5-kilometer cross-country run in the morning, and did repeated sprints in the afternoon. He spent approximately one hour with each workout, usually beginning at about 4:00 P.M.

Twice a week Potgieter did weight training exercises for the upper body, but he did no weight training for the legs. After his daily track training, described earlier, he did some training on the parallel bars, horse, rope and horizontal bar in the gymnasium. He took part in about ten cross-country races, which did not exceed five kilometers (3 miles), during the pre-season training period, and an equal number of races during the competitive track season. He participated in about 15 to 20 track meets a year.

Chapter 6

THE RELAYS

by Jim Bellwood

Techniques employed in most track and field events are largely dictated by international rules. This is particularly true of the relays. However, within the framework of these specific rules, there has always been tremendous scope for initiative by the astute coach and the methodical athlete.

Until recent years, outgoing runners in all relay teams were confined to a strict 22-yard (20m) take-over zone. This restriction led to the evolution of a great variety of special techniques which all called for imaginative coaching, dedicated training and great precision.

Then, the I.A.A.F. adopted the following new rule: "In races up to 4 x 220 yards (4x200m), members of a team (other than the first runner) may commence running 11 yards (10m) outside the take-over zone, but the baton must be passed only when both runners are in the take-over zone." In other words, the outgoing sprint relay runner now has an extra 11 yards in which to accelerate before receiving the baton. The gross result of changing this rule has been profound and revolutionary. Not only has the traditional character of relay running been changed, but the lot of the poorly trained team has also been made easier.

The Basic Coaching Aims

The successful coach is one who takes measures to ensure the following:
a) Each team member is traveling at his top speed for every inch of the distance he is in possession of the baton.
b) The *relative* sprint speeds of each runner are most effectively employed.
c) A type of baton pass which will facilitate safety and the gain of maximum "free-distance" is practiced to perfection.

Because few athletes can run with full abandon within the confines of the take-over zone, and because most tend to slow down when approaching an outgoing teammate, these objectives provide a never ending challenge. Moreover, because it takes more distance for top-class male sprinters to accelerate to maximum speed than take-over zones even now allow, there is still a great deal of scope for the astute coach and the well drilled team.

Free-Distance

Provided outgoing and incoming sprinters are traveling at top speed at the time, and provided they get no closer to each other, the gap which is bridged by both is known as "free-distance." As prolonged reaching forward by the incoming runner or prolonged reaching back by the outgoing runner must inevitably inhibit sprint speed, both these actions should ideally take place while the athletes concerned are running in step. Then, the reaching forward and reaching back should be timed to occupy only the split second required for slightly exaggerated arm movements by both runners. If this happens, a speed gain of about four feet in zero time can occur at each take-over. This would mean a total gain in zero time for the full race of four yards. It is for this reason that many advocate the type of baton pass illustrated below. (See Fig. 75.) This technique provides the greatest potential "free-distance." Moreover, because the baton is passed to an upturned palm, it is safer.

Figure 75.

The type of change illustrated is recommended at the first and third take-over zones. These are both made on a curve, and it is thus possible to reach back farther with the left hand at these points because of the natural alignment of the shoulders. At the second take-over zone, the change should be made from left hand to right hand. This eliminates the need for changing the baton across to the right hand, with an inevitable check in sprint speed.

Safety Margin

The distance between the point at which the baton changes hands and the end of the take-over zone is known as the "safety margin." If it has done little else, the new I.A.A.F. Rule has provided coaches throughout the world with plenty of scope for the exercise of initiative. In recent discussions with many of the leading coaches in the world, I have found a wide divergence of opinion on how these new sprint-relay rules can be most profitably exploited.

Quite apart from the actual method of exchanging the baton, two very astute and divergent opinions stand out—those of Gabriel Korobkov of the Soviet Union and Geoff Dyson of Great Britain. Korobkov believes that in order to induce the outgoing runner to accelerate with full abandon, the actual baton pass should be planned to take place midway in the take-over zone. This gives 22 yards (20m) in which the outgoing runner can accelerate and an 11-yard (10m) "safety margin."

Dyson argues that no top-class sprinter can accelerate adequately in such a short distance and that baton speed must inevitably suffer. He thinks a four-yard "safety margin" for well-trained athletes is adequate. If we accept this thesis, the outgoing runner has nearly 30 yards in which to accelerate before receiving the baton, plus a four-yard safety margin, which seems to be reasonable. Of course, this is assuming that we are striving for the ultimate and are prepared in the process to accept some risk. We have to bear in mind that top-class sprinters continue to accelerate up to the 60-yard mark.

Relative Order of Running

Contrary to popular belief, only two of the four runners in a sprint-relay team run the same total distance or the same distance with the baton. For instance, assuming that four feet of "free-distance" will be gained at each change and deciding to adopt the Geoff Dyson method, one has the following breakdown:

Runner	Sprints without baton	Sprints with baton	Total sprint
No. 1	0	115 yards, 2 feet	115 yds., 2 ft.
No. 2	28 yards	108 ” 2 ”	136 ” 2 ”
No. 3	28 ”	108 ” 2 ”	136 ” 2 ”
No. 4	28 ”	103 ”	131 ”

As *baton speed* must be the basic objective, the facts in this breakdown speak for themselves. It is perfectly clear that the key runner is No. 1, and that No. 4, the so-called "anchor-man," has the least significant responsibility. Not only does he have the shortest distance to carry the baton, but he also escapes the duty of passing it on.

Ignoring the "human factors," which do not seem to play as important a role as is sometimes afforded them, in order to decide running order, one's logical course to follow is to have each relay candidate regularly run over 136 yards 2 feet and 131 yards, timing each run from the 28-yard mark, and 115 yards 2 feet. If, as has been the case with British teams, these times are analyzed over a long period, selection and order of running can become the product of simple mathematics.

Coaching

Armed with a clear concept of what is involved, the coach must now concentrate on practices aimed at dove-tailing the outgoing and incoming sprinters' speeds. In order to do this he must first select a specific method of baton-pass and then work his runners at top speed, constantly adjusting the check-mark which will indicate to the outgoing runner when to start sprinting.

This sprint-start, if it is to achieve its purpose fully, must take place from a crouch position which will suffer the necessary modification of turning the head to the rear so that the check-mark can be watched. From the moment of starting up to the moment the baton is received, all the normal techniques of sprint-starting should be observed.

The Sprint-Relay Start

The first runner can combine his normal sprint-start position with any one of the comfortable methods of holding the baton. (See Fig. 76.) He should, for reasons which will emerge later, hold it in the right hand.

Figure 76.

The First Change

Crouched in the outside of his lane, ready to accelerate as soon as No. 1 reaches the predetermined check-mark, No. 2 will sprint away, using arms normally for the first 7 to 12 strides. (All changes in sprint relays should be nonvisual.) He then extends the left arm back, as illustrated in Figure 77, in coordination with his stride. At the same instant, the incoming athlete should be near enough to reach forward to place the baton firmly down in the out-stretched palm of No. 2, who will continue sprinting at top speed with the baton in his hand.

Figure 77.

The Second Change

Except that No. 3 takes up a position on the *inside* of his lane and reaches back with his *right* hand, he does precisely what No. 2 has done at the first change.

The Third Change

This change should be identical with the first one. These two right-hand to left-hand changes are used because in traversing a curve, an athlete can reach back farther with the left hand and thus gain more "free-distance."

The function of the fourth runner is the simplest one. He simply has to receive the baton and sprint normally through the finishing tape. Compared with the responsibilities of his three teammates, this is a relatively minor contribution. The fact that it has ever appeared otherwise is due to misconceptions dramatically underlined by unqualified press reporters who have never comprehended that the key runner in a sprint relay is No. 1.

Other Baton-Changing Methods

At least three other methods of changing the baton have enjoyed varying degrees of popularity. In fact, in recent years, the most popular has been the upper-cutting action of the incoming runner into the spread thumb and fingers of the outgoing runner. (See Fig. 78.) Mainly because this action is more natural, there are valid arguments in favor of its use.

Figure 78.

It is simply a matter of individual choice. Although the "Dyson" system seems to provide the possibility of a greater gain in "free-distance," it is of far greater importance to have both athletes traveling at as near top sprint speed as possible when the actual change-over takes place. That is the objective which must largely govern training plans.

4 x 440 yards (400m) and Relays Over This Distance

For top-class sprinters the 4 x 440 yards relay is still a sprint race. Consequently, except that the rules decree that the take-over zone is the only area in which the outgoing runner may start and change the baton, no real deviation from the sprint relay change is necessary or desirable.

For beginners the situation is somewhat different, and several modifications are necessary. First, because the incoming runner may be finishing poorly, a *visual* change should be adopted. This sort of change should be carried out with the same type of baton change as outlined earlier, but the outgoing runner should keep his head turned to the rear until the change takes place. By this means he can carefully judge his acceleration to dove-tail perfectly with whatever speed his incoming teammates may have slowed to.

Secondly, in deciding order of running, the first runner is the key man. It is highly desirable to capture the lead before lanes are broken. It always involves great effort and extra speed to pass an opponent—especially on a curve. For every 12 inches an athlete is forced wide on a curve, he travels a little over one yard of extra distance. Normally, in order to pass, an athlete is forced at least three feet wide or a total extra distance around a full curve of over three yards. For this reason, team members should be conscious of the need for passing opponents on a straightaway, or passing very quickly if forced into making such an effort on a curve. On the other hand, a team with the lead should strongly fight off attempts at passing on the straight and attempt to hold off a passing opponent for the maximum distance possible around a curve.

Finally, for a team containing athletes of very unequal caliber, it can pay dividends to have the best runner or runners carrying the baton for a greater distance than 440 yards (400m). This is possible by having him receive the baton near the rear of his change-over zone and passing it on near the end of his change-over zone.

For distances beyond 4 x 440 yards, all changes should be visual ones. Apart from this, the same tactical and technical considerations apply. It is in these realms that psychology plays a significant role. For example, some athletes like to race in front, while others can only produce their best when coming from the rear. The astute coach weighs the situation carefully and arranges the order of running accordingly. The "fighters" need to be confronted with situations which will demand their pulling back a long lead or warding off repeated challenges on a curve. Placing the right men in the right positions can prove devastating for even the best of opponents. However, the normal practice is to place the best runner last, the second-best first and the slowest third. But this orthodox pattern can be broken by a coach with imagination and initiative who understands his runners and who has inspired them to do better than ever before.

Par Lauf

"Par Lauf," which means pair-running, has been used for many years in Germany to give motivation to "interval training" and for racing. In its true form, pairs of runners race or train against other pairs. They may run full laps or half laps. The important thing is that one must take the baton from his partner and continue until he passes it back. Where this change takes place is immaterial.

Races or training runs are usually decided on a basis which ignores distance and substitutes time in its place. For instance, a race or training run may be predetermined as 10 minutes or 20 minutes. The winning team is that which is in front at the end of that time. This sort of running is excellent interval training, plus good baton-passing practice.

Progressive Relays

"Progressive relays" involve any number of athletes up to 10 or even 15. These are spread evenly around the track, and the baton is passed around for any number of given laps, or for any length of time. The athlete simply receives the baton, passes it on, and then waits until it comes around again. This sort of relay can be used for "warm-ups" of athletic groups, training for sprinters or middle-distance runners, and for teaching correct baton-passing techniques. For purposes of motivation for runners and for coaching baton passing, "progressive relays" are unparalleled. They can also be used to induce greater participation.

If those involved in progressive-relay training are called together frequently to have their general mistakes corrected, very rapid progress in teaching can be achieved. Moreover, this particular activity induces lazy trainees to do a great deal of effective training in a way which is fun.

Shuttle Relays

The only official shuttle relay is the shuttle hurdle relay, with athletes running back and forth over a straight course. The only coaching hint that needs emphasis is that the incoming runner should touch the outgoing runner lightly on the shoulder so as not to impede his forward "explosion."

Sprint Medley Relays

Unfortunately, the sprint medley relays (the most common being 440-220-220-880) usually only decide which team has the best half-miler. All the efforts of the greatest sprinters in the world will be forlorn if the half-miler is not exceptional. Everybody knows this at the outset, so the races are devoid of drama.

What the coach needs to be conscious of in such circumstances is that the sprinter can carry the baton faster than the middle-distance runner. Within the confines of the change-over zone, the sprinter should therefore be allowed to carry the baton for the greatest possible distance and the middle-distance runner for the shortest possible distance. This is simply a matter of carefully defining the actual take-over point when the baton will be passed.

Part II

THE JUMPING EVENTS

Chapter 7

TEACHING THE BEGINNING HIGH JUMPER

by G. M. Elliott

Films of the 1936 Olympic Games in Berlin show a tremendous variety of techniques used in the high jump competition, ranging from the beautifully executed Eastern Cut-off of Kimio Yada from Japan to the rather ungainly back layout of the then European record-holder, Kalevi Kotkas of Finland. For a variety of reasons (including rule changes) most of the different methods used by top-class high jumpers since then can be classified as either a form of Western Roll or Straddle, with the one notable exception of Winter, the winner of the 1948 Olympic High Jump. Over the past few years another transition has taken place in high jumping in that the popular Western Roll has all but disappeared from top-class competition.

From a theoretical viewpoint the straddle type of clearance should give an extremely efficient body position over the bar. When it is performed correctly, it gives near maximum lift at takeoff. A similar argument may be used for the Western Roll, in that near maximum lift may be gained at takeoff, but a not-so-efficient position over the bar is attained.

There have been many reasons for justifying the teaching of the Western Roll to beginners. For example, there are a large variety of so-called lead-up stages. It affords a relatively safe landing position. There is a natural discouragement of leaning into the bar at takeoff.

However, past experience has shown that these so-called advantages may be serious disadvantages at a later stage in the high jumper's career. *If* the aim is to produce efficient high jumpers, then the emphasis should be, at the very start of the jumper's career, on the technique or style that he will be using as an end product—the straddle. This creates a problem immediately for the teacher or coach who has poor jumping facilities for his athletes. It is essential to give a beginning high jumper a landing area which is 100 percent safe in preventing any kind of injury—an area in which he can land flat on his back or upside down on his head, and still come out smiling. It is only by providing a facility of this caliber that the coach can ensure that the jumper will devote his undivided attention to either the takeoff or bar clearance.

For the beginning straddle jumper it is reasonable to assume that the position over the bar should be an easily achieved one—one that is relatively straight in a sort of relaxed position of attention, face downward over the bar. The other details of layout may be encouraged at a later stage in the learning process, remembering that the type of bar clearance is ultimately dependent upon the kind of takeoff performed.

The use of lead-up stages tends to be frowned on by many of today's teachers. Perhaps it is the phrase "lead-up" which gives the wrong impression. It is certainly true to say that the stages should not be isolated learning situations, but rather practices which are designed to give to the performer both confidence and an awareness of the goal he is trying to achieve. With these thoughts in mind, the steps I would follow in encouraging a youngster ultimately to jump high, with the straddle technique, would be:

(*Assume a left leg takeoff and a right leg free-leg swing*)

1.   Standing upright, swing the non-takeoff leg or free leg as straight as possible and as high as possible (without falling over).

2.   Standing with the takeoff leg stretched well forward, foot on the ground, push with the free leg and swing it straight and high, encouraging both arms to swing forward and upward at the same time. Normally it will be difficult for the trunk to achieve an upright position, but the force of the swing should be sufficient to lift the body off the ground.

3.   Stand by the side of a one-inch painted line on the floor, with the outside of the left foot touching the right-hand side of the line. Swing the right leg straight and when it is approximately parallel with the ground, turn the trunk to the left and allow the weight of the body to be transferred to the right foot, which should land on the other side of the line, allowing the left foot to be picked up off the floor and left behind the body. Encouragement of a backward lean of the trunk may be given at this stage, because with the half turn completed, the trunk will be facing the floor, and the hands (if necessary) may be used in assisting in the retaining of balance. Also as the majority of beginners will be transferring from a scissors style of jumping to the straddle, they will be accustomed to swinging a relatively straight free leg with the trunk leaning forward. Therefore, an overemphasis should be placed on the backward lean of the trunk with the free-leg swing.

(The following stages must now be performed with a safe landing area, preferably built up.)

4.   Allow a few wild jumps into the landing area with landings flat on the back and upside down, in order that the jumper's confidence in the landing area may be established.

5.   Try to combine stages two and three with a bar. The left leg is well out in front of the body and on the ground, trunk leaning well back, and the push-off is with the right leg, swinging it straight and high. As the left foot comes off the ground, the trunk should face to the left. This is an important stage for the jumper, because if it is done correctly, the jumper feels that he is being *pulled* off the ground by the force of the free-leg swing. It is essential at this stage that

the bar be placed at a height a few inches above the standing crotch-height of the jumper—thus preventing him from leaning and turning into the bar before he has left the ground.

6. The bar should be raised to maximum height with the athlete still jumping from a standing position (which is different) or with a one-stride approach.

7. The athlete's run should be increased to a three-stride approach, and the bar raised as high as possible.

8. It is important that any future training restrict the length of the run to the equivalent leg strength of the athlete. If his takeoff leg is not strong enough, it will collapse under a faster, longer approach. If his free-leg flexors are not strong enough, they will not move the free leg fast enough for the shortened time available, because of the faster run.

The majority of difficulties that arise from teaching straddle to beginners are well known and are often cited as reasons for teaching the Western Roll. The key, however, lies in three important considerations. (1) The landing area must be perfect, (2) the bar must be placed above crotch-height in the crucial introductory stages, and (3) run-up speed should not be encouraged without the equivalent gain in strength.

Chapter 8

THE HIGH JUMP

by John Dobroth

This chapter will explain the most up-to-date concepts of high jump training and technique. The method of bar clearance discussed will be the straddle. It is recognized that other forms of jumping can be used successfully in negotiating near world class heights, but this is less because of the benefits of other techniques than because the straddle, as described here, is practiced by only a handful of jumpers in the world. When proper straddle technique and training are used more widely, jumps of 7 feet 6 inches will be commonplace.

If a jumper seeks to view jumping as a pastime and doesn't care to spend a great deal of effort in its mastery, other techniques can be used. The western roll, the slow run, locked-kick leg straddle, the dive roll and even the "cut off" or the scissors are adequate for clearing 6 feet 10 inches or more. This chapter will not deal with those methods.

Until recently, the teaching of high jumping has been by out-dated concepts. Such terms as "spring" and "jumping" are not suited to the technical information available on how to clear great heights. This discussion will avoid the traditional approach to the event in order to present fresh mental and emotional attitudes toward a demanding discipline.

TRAINING FOR THE HIGH JUMP

Training will be divided into three segments. The actual length of each segment will depend on the total time the individual expects to devote to becoming a jumper. This particular schedule will assume that the individual is going to work for 12 months. The first segment is termed the Preparatory Phase and lasts about two and one-half months. The second segment is called the Training Phase and constitutes the bulk of the time available, about seven months. The third segment is the Competition Phase and lasts as long as the jumper is engaged in competitive track meets.

PREPARATORY PHASE

During this segment, much effort is spent developing the ability to withstand stress—both cardio-respiratory stress and muscle stress. Simply stated, in order to improve a jumper must be able to do considerable work which can, for our purposes, be called endurance. For this section of training, any enjoyable physical exercise is useful. The more varied the type of work, the more likely the athlete is to remain in training. Swimming, cross-country skiing, and basketball are all better than running. However, they suffer the disadvantage of requiring a great deal of time expenditure to gain results.

During the preparatory period, the jumper does weight-training work and begins to learn the technique of high jumping, but the emphasis is on stamina. The amount of jump training depends on the athlete's level of accomplishment.

If we assume the jumper has mastered the technique, described later in the section, "Technique of the High Jump," his work proceeds toward speeding up reaction time and developing consistency. If the jumper has not yet learned correct technique, some simple drills can be developed to teach correct form during phases I and II.

TRAINING PHASE

The problem of the training phase is to learn or improve correct patterns of takeoff, run-up, and bar clearance while gaining power and flexibility. Some weight-training work helps, and it may be possible to develop routines that include both barbell and pure training exercises to learn patterns of jumping.

Here are some training exercises to help develop jumping ability.

With up to 40 percent of body weight (with barbell or weight-belt apparatus), do short sprints, hops, and skips, alternating legs and speed. The number of repetitions and the distance covered depend on the condition of the athlete.

An exercise of great value in developing the approach is to run short sprints with weights, but without straightening the knee joint on each stride. The function of the run-up is to develop speed and position for takeoff. To do this, the jumper must have control, balance, and power. The run-up is not like sprinting, as greater control is needed. An example of the amount of time and the number of repetitions of these exercises can be found on Chart III, page 134.

The Takeoff

The problem to be considered before tackling bar clearance is to learn the mechanics of leaving the ground (the takeoff). The natural but least effective way to leave the ground is to take short steps, place the takeoff foot in contact with the ground, wait until the center of gravity is over the foot, and then dip down and jump. The lead knee will be bent and tucked under the chest, and the arms may be anywhere, depending on balance requirements.

Mechanically, the natural jumping position is oriented to the quick jumper or the long-levered man. The trouble is that these attributes cannot be developed to the extent that strength can. As in any mechanical problem, if one wishes to gain a particular advantage, he must sacrifice another. In this case, one must try to find ways to increase the amount of force directed against the ground. Since speeding up action can do this, increasing speed should be a partial goal, but not at the expense of power. For example, a bent swing-leg is faster than a straight leg, but the longer radius of a straight leg means more power can be exerted by it. It takes more strength to move the leg, but strength can be developed. Once the leg is moving as a long driving force, it can be bent to speed the action, thus producing advantages in both power and speed.

The best takeoff position yet devised requires the following:

1) Emphasize the advanced position of the plant foot. The more time during which force can be applied, the greater impulse (force x time) can be exerted. "Time" here refers to the time it takes for the jumper's center of gravity to travel from well behind the outstretched takeoff position over the leg.

It is important to remember that the last step is shorter than the next-to-last. This shortening of the last step does two important things: First, it begins the hip rise before the takeoff foot contacts the ground; thus the lift begins sooner. Second, it speeds the takeoff foot in making contact with the ground.

2) Drill on standing and driving the hip, thigh, and then the leg through by pulling forward with the hips and pushing off with the foot. The foot remains pulled up toward the shin. Allow the leg to lock when its speed causes it to, but do not maintain the leg in a stiff state (against its tendency to bend) once it is past a horizontal position with the ground. The free leg (or kick leg) should swing in line with the approach run. If the jumper leans too much or bends excessively, the free leg may "loop" around or kick to the side of the run. The free leg attempts to counterbalance the rest of the body.

3) The arms will drive in an arc along the sides of the body from a position behind the back and parallel with the ground. The arms can be straight until they are in front of the chest on the way up. Then they bend to 90 degrees, thus reducing the radius and speeding the action. The initial backward arm action helps drive the plant foot to quicker contact.

4) Pull with the plant leg until the center of gravity is over the takeoff point; then drive up in phase with the legs and arms.

5) Don't try to rock up with a heel-toe action too quickly. It is not possible to move from heel to toe until all of the jump actions are instituted. That is, it will appear that the foot remains down while many other actions take place, and the takeoff foot is flat almost from its first contact with the ground until the legs and arms are vertical.

Remember, the upward action of the arms and free leg are really causing a reaction, or push, directed at the ground to make the jumper rise. If nothing is in contact with the ground when the action takes place, these actions will neutralize themselves.

Using no steps, this entire motion can be practiced. It can be done while holding ropes, stall bars or gym apparatus for balance. Once the movement is learned, jumps with no "turn" can be done over low objects or at high hanging objects. When jumping for a hanging object, try to hit it with the head and arms as well as the lead leg. When jumping over objects, jump with the torso vertical, emphasizing the push-off.

The Run-Up

Now a run-up can be developed. The takeoff is clearly a function of the run-up. As previously mentioned, the last step is not the longest, as is commonly assumed. Several patterns are found in the last few running steps. All of them emphasize that the longest step is either the second-to-last or third-to-last. One method used by Valeriy Brumel of the U.S.S.R. was to make the last four steps long-short-long-short. At any rate, the objective is to get the body lowest before the last foot-contact is made.

Long strides make for low hip position. If low hip position were the sole determiner of potential lift, the last step would be longest. But it is not. Speed in a vertical direction is what results in height, and by shortening the last step, one's foot contacts are quickened and the lift is begun on the second-to-last foot placement. The hip actually rises from the second-to-last step on. The angle of the second-to-last leg after placement sometimes nears 90 degrees, whereas the last or plant leg seldom forms one of less than 130 degrees. (See Fig. 87.)

The beginning of the run simply puts the jumper in position for the last three or four strides. A run of seven to nine strides is as much as can be used. Using fewer than seven steps poses two problems. First, a short run means that speed must be increased under tension; and second, the position of the body during acceleration is forward of the center of gravity. The hips must get past the torso on the last step, and an excessive forward lean defeats this. Never, however, should the jumper try to lie back. The correct movement is to advance the legs, not to throw back the shoulders.

Two check marks will usually be best. One should be placed two steps from the plant, and another six to eight steps out from the plant. (See Fig. 83.)

The run should be developed with the individual's characteristics in mind. For example, his speed may dictate the distance of the run, while his general ability to effect and use bar clearance methods decide the angle. No matter what results in the end, the run-up should be practiced until it is learned and "grooved." It should be done with vertical takeoffs over objects and over crossbars until the run-up and takeoff are secure. Then a bar clearance method can be learned.

Takeoff and Run-Up Combined

The takeoff work should now have the jumper taking short runs at full stride, combined with a foot plant and takeoff. In the beginning, no more than two or three strides should be used. When full power is applied (with the athlete leaving the ground vertically, using three strides), begin to add steps.

The jumper should not be told to jump straight up, nor should he jump for a target at first. Even if a jumper leaves the ground vertically, he will have to travel some distance forward unless he halts on the last steps.

The jumper should not block, stomp or "pole vault" on the last stride. Instead, he should try to react with all body parts as soon as the foot contacts the ground.

The plant foot should be flat or on the ball of the foot during major movements of lift-off. The jumper should not try to rock up from heel to toe. If he does, he will not be able to apply power with the takeoff foot, but will hurry the body parts trying to accomplish an impossible movement. Develop the idea that the takeoff movement is an active positive movement, not a defensive reaction to an object or situation.

The jumper should never train with more strides than will leave him aggressive and in control on the plant. The best way to think about the high jump takeoff is to relate it to the long jump takeoff. A long jumper, with his step, is trying to grab, pull and explode on his takeoff. He is not "afraid" of hitting an object or worried about being too close or too far from the bar. He drives! Most jumpers never learn to run and take off in the high jump. They learn to be intimidated by the bar and jump to it rather than jumping directly from the run-up. What possible relevance can the bar have to the thrust obtained from the ground?

This technique should be worked on until the jumper feels he can use more speed when he takes off using five or six strides. If a good jumper has a proper takeoff, he should be able to measure an approach of three strides, hit the check-mark, close his eyes and clear six feet time after time. The jumpers who can are confident that at the end of those steps the takeoff patterns will occur. The position of the bar cannot help the jumper leave the ground, and once he has left, he cannot alter the flight path of his center of gravity.

Without question, training for the run-up and the takeoff is the most important part of learning to jump. Coaches who have a jumper leaping at a crossbar before he has learned anything about the principles involved will inevitably be faced with trying to remedy form faults that occur due to faulty takeoff. "He could be great, if only he could get that back leg over. . . ."

Bar Clearance

Bar clearance can be learned best by simple exercise devised by the athlete, with the following principles in mind. The body bends best on the horizontal axis (assuming the man is standing), but the correct type of takeoff favors rotation about the jumper's long axis. Since the torso and free leg are in a nearly vertical position as the body leaves the ground, force is directed through these parts via the hip. (See Fig. 79.) As the torso and free leg fall off from this vertical position (Fig. 80), they are no longer over the point of power application,

Figure 79.

but the hip is and it continues up until the body is generally horizontal. This fact, coupled with the backward rotation developed by the free leg on takeoff, favors a long axis crossing.

Figure 80.

A compromise position called a "dive straddle" seems best. The dive straddle requires that as one part of the body crosses the bar, it must drop toward the ground to permit other parts to rise and cross the bar. The first parts over the bar, assuming correct takeoff, will be the lead or free leg, the right arm, and the head and right shoulder. Generally, these parts will clear without effort if the angle of approach is correct.

If the jumper has some time over the bar (i.e., if he doesn't cross too perpendicularly), the dropping of the lead body parts will lift the trailing parts before they knock off the bar. The trailing parts that are most likely to cause problems are the trailing hip and leg. As you remember, the hip was still over the power source, the push leg, and thus has speed enough in an upward-forward direction to clear the bar.

The clearance of these parts depends on the continued rotation about a long axis, which can be destroyed by common form faults. The most common of these is attempting to maintain the position of a body part in the air after it is over the bar. By failing to allow the lead leg, for example, to drop down, you destroy the natural arc in which the body moves. Once destroyed, this arc cannot be re-created, and the entire body will be subject to gravity at once. The "roll" is advantageous because one part of the body at a time is subject to gravity.

Correct takeoff is made up of two basic movements—forces that cause one-half or one side of the body to lead the jump. These forces are the "thrust forces" of the inside and the "free forces" of the outside. The free or outside section, since it advances first, leads the arc. The speed of rotation depends on the distance of body parts from the axis. The closer to the axis, the faster the rotation. This speed can be controlled by moving the extremities in or out.

The procedure for learning this bar clearance is to begin over a crossbar at 8 or 10 inches. With one step, swing the free leg over the bar, landing on the lead foot—not on the back. Then, raise the bar until it is at two feet, and continue jumping, emphasizing the flow of motion and making sure to land on the lead foot and hand.

When a simple layout has been mastered, attempt to drop the head and torso along with the lead leg, once over the bar. These two body parts can be "jackknifed" (closed again), thus raising the hips. From that point, the trail leg is opened and lifted away from the bar. (See Figs. 81 and 82.) The layout becomes more of a dive as control improves and the bar is raised.

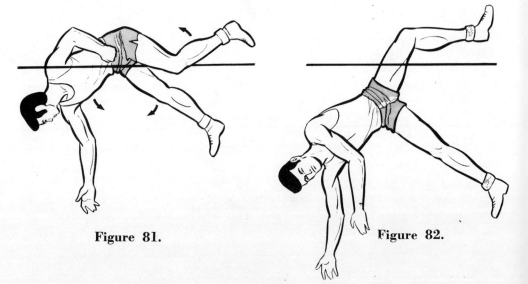

Figure 81.   Figure 82.

The dive is difficult to learn until the bar is above eye level. Otherwise, the jumper will bend at the waist toward the bar before the push-off is complete. This bend is much worse than a "lean" from the ankle, which is unavoidable with a one leg takeoff. Remember, however, that correct takeoff will result in correct position for rotation.

The temptation to try to develop extreme rotation on the plant causes jumpers to make two common run-up and takeoff errors. One is stepping out of the line of run with the second-to-last step (hoping to pivot into and around the bar), and the other is stepping across the line of run with the last stop (trying to angle at the bar with the lead foot).

COMPETITION PHASE

During the competitive season, the training will tend to be lighter and more concentrated. There will be fewer repetitions, and more violent complete movements. The jumps taken will be at higher heights with all effort made to clear each height on the first attempt.

The period needed to bring about a physical peak will vary but may be as much as three weeks of lighter work load. Once the physical peak seems reached—as measured by speed or power indexes—jumping competitions can be held every four days for a period of several weeks. Perhaps an extended competitive season can be broken up, if it is too long, by going back to the training phase for three or four weeks.

Technique cannot be improved greatly at this point, so emphasis is on psychological preparation and tuning activities. Jump sessions which duplicate competitions, with waiting and slow bar progress, can be reproduced. Warm-ups are standardized, rules reviewed, and the jumper's attitudes, strengths and weaknesses discussed.

The potential problems that may occur are covered so that no surprises will develop at meets. Even the competitors should be analyzed so that the jumper will be aware of what to expect.

When in actual competition, the jumper will need to be aware of the rules of the event to decide on strategy. Depending on the particular jumper's ability, he may take certain risks and use the rules to his advantage. *The Jumper should know.*

The basic rules of the high jump competition are these. A jump is any action that breaks the plane of the bar and contacts the pit. If the bar is displaced or if the jumper passes under the bar, it is a miss. Three attempts are given at each height. A time limit of two minutes may be imposed, within which the jumper must jump. Three consecutive misses at any heights eliminate the jumper from competition. The takeoff must be from one foot. The competition may be won in one of four ways. One is to clear a higher height than any other competitor. Another is to clear the same height as another competitor but on an earlier jump. A third is to clear the same height as a competitor on the same jump, but to have fewer cumulative misses throughout the competition. The last is to clear the same height on the same jump, with the same number of misses as another competitor, but to have fewer total attempts (clearances or failures) throughout the competition.

The jumper must know on what jump his best effort seems to occur. This depends to some extent upon how extensive his warm-up has been. If we assume a complete 30-minute warm-up, it seems the best jump will come between the sixth and tenth jumps (including practice jumps). It could be that a jumper's technique and characteristics would cause his best effort to occur around his fifteenth jump. It is important to know, no matter when the jumper seems to have peak effort, what jumps are likely to be superior. With that in mind, the jumper should plan to make his best jumps coincide with the time the bar is raised near and above his best previous effort.

A point often not considered is the benefit of taking practice jumps at higher heights. In this way a jumper may begin his competition at a higher height. If he starts higher than a competitor and clears the remaining heights along with his competitor, he will win. Being able and confident enough to start high can be the difference between winning and losing.

Other considerations regarding choice of starting height and activity between jumps include the number and caliber of the other competitors, weather conditions and the speed of competition. If a large number of competitors must complete their attempts before a jumper has his first attempt (i.e., if his practice jumps were separated from his competitive efforts by some period of time), he may get "cold" or lose rhythm. This rhythm (or cycle of activity) should be checked in practice and proven able to keep the jumper ready for every effort.

Jumpers should determine what rhythm is best for them. Some jumpers will be almost constantly active during a short competition with few competitors. In longer meets, a jumper may do imitative exercises at five-minute intervals while he is not jumping. A jumper must be prepared for periods of up to one and one-half hours without a jump in major competitions, if he is passing heights.

If weather makes it likely that the heights cleared will be low, a jumper's warm-up will have to be more complete; and concern over misses would be of less importance, since consistency will vary. Some jumpers (those with fast approach runs) are affected adversely by loose footing to a greater extent than others, and will have to assume that more jumps will be required to adjust to the surface and to clear the bar.

The run-up that has been developed in practice will not always work on new surfaces. Depending on the texture of the approach surface, adjustments must be made. A jumper must not be afraid to check the run-up between jumps. Using footsteps in lieu of a tape measure can speed up measuring.

Rules allow that the sole of the shoe on the takeoff foot can be built up one-half inch. The heel should be equal in buildup to the sole. The "lever" action used in older built-up shoes is not as useful as a platform type shoe which is all built up. The buildup of the left shoe compared to the right gives the advantage of a leap from a platform, not just a beneficial lever.

The spikes used must be long enough to stop the foot, but not long enough to cause the foot to stick. If the surface is solid, the jumper can use long spikes to get added buildup if the spikes are placed well apart for stability.

Most jumpers do not work out on the day prior to competition. It may be that a jumper could find a light weight workout that will stimulate his system more than taking the day of rest.

The last weeks of training and the period of training during competition should instill a feeling of confidence and faith in a jumper's mind. If the training has proceeded properly, the jumper will not have allowed himself to ever jump at a level beyond his total ability. Jumping at a great height before technique is sound, may, if the height is cleared, cause the jumper to try to reproduce the technique he imagines has made him successful. This may lead him away from sound technique and make him a "luck" jumper who seldom equals his best effort. The best thing that can happen when a jumper attempts this greater height is failure, causing nothing more severe than temporary discouragement. Until form is sound, jumps should remain within limits of total ability.

GENERAL TRAINING INFORMATION

High jumping requires a good understanding of the mechanics of athletics. If the jumper is going to correct mistakes, he must understand what causes the mistakes. Very few mistakes are made after the jumper leaves the ground. Mechanically, nothing can be done to change the flight path of the jumper's center of gravity in the air. The jumper should therefore be concerned with developing technique for run-up and takeoff, before bar clearance is attempted. It may appear to a talented jumper, who seems to get off the ground well naturally, that clearance is the problem. Generally, this is not so. Very few jumpers can consistently clear a height three inches below the vertical height to which they can lift their hips. Those who can have developed correct run-up and takeoff technique.

To clear the crossbar correctly, the jumper needs time over the bar, which seems to be a contradiction of modern-day coaching practices. As one part of the body is over the bar, it should come down to permit other parts to rise, as well as to maintain rotation about the bar. If the jumper tries to cross quickly, he cannot gain these advantages.

In order to combine a fast approach and good clearance technique, a narrow angle (20°–30°) is best.

WEIGHT TRAINING FOR THE HIGH JUMP

Jumping power can best be developed by resistive exercise. These exercises, to be of value to the high jumper, must be heavy, concentrated on certain body parts, and explosively done. Most competitors require fewer than 15 jumps of maximal effort during a competition, so weight training should also follow that pattern.

There are other factors to be considered when developing weight programs which may alter the basic principles of lifting routine. For example, development of the upper body, along with concentrating on the large muscle groups of the leg, will bring the best jumping power increase in the shortest time. It becomes difficult after a time to handle the weight needed to make continued gains in many types of lifts (snatch, jerk, etc.) without more upper-body power. There must be some time devoted to these parts of the body. Since high-weight, low-repetition lifting requires some resting of those body parts directly involved, upper body lifts can be done during periods of lower body recovery.

Another consideration is that many exercises can be learning, as well as power-building, experiences. Thus, in some lifting motions that correlate highly with jumping technique, it may be best to do more repetitions with less weight.

Finally, when dealing with an immature or underweight athlete, one must realize that a well-rounded weight program may be worth more than a jumper's workout. It is possible to change a person's center of gravity by weight training. This will alter jumping patterns, especially if the jumper is young and growing or if he does extensive weight training during an extended non-jumping period. This can be useful to a man who wishes to change his technique from one season to the next. On the other hand, good jumpers will probably be better off if weight distribution stays the same from one season to the next.

For the same reason, jumping over the bar with weights attached to the body can change jumping patterns and should be kept to a minimum. Five percent of body weight, attached at the waist, should be the limit.

Weight training should be done the year around, even during the season with at least a day of rest between workout days. The best method is to divide all training into the three segments already discussed: a preparatory phase, a training phase, and a competitive phase. For the weight-training portion, the fundamental variables of these phases are as follows: amount of weight, types of exercises, number of repetitions and sets, and frequency of exercise.

PREPARATORY PHASE

(Generally, this phase occupies about 20% of the total training period.)

Type of exercise .... basic power lifts (squats, step-ups, leg presses, dead lifts)

Amount of weight .... near maximum

Number of repetitions and sets .... 3–5 repetitions, 3–5 sets

Frequency of exercise .... three times per week

The objective in this segment is to develop power for later use in jumping. The movements are simple power lifts. The amount of work increases as stamina builds. The cardio-respiratory requirements for this period are the highest of the three phases because the amount of work that can be done is limited by stamina. The jumper should not be concerned with anything except lifting heavy weights in simple lifts to build fundamental strength.

TRAINING PHASE

(About 70% of the total training period)

Type of exercise	quick, flexible, smooth
Amount of weight	90% of maximum
Number of repetitions and sets	several systems, but generally 3–8 repetitions, 3–5 sets
Frequency of lifting	three times per week

During the training phase, the jumper is expected to be able to spend more energy on his training. He is strong and has good stamina.

He begins by learning proper technique for handling heavy weights in Olympic and jumping lifts. Proper lifting technique is essential to prevent injury and to have a consistent measure of improvement.

For several weeks of transition, the jumper learns these new lifts. Among the most important are the snatch, the clean (squat and power style), the press and the clean and jerk. These lifts introduce the jumper to the fun of lifting.

Being able to improve his total poundage in the Olympic lifts is a goal in itself and can be important in keeping the athlete involved in power training. Also some of these lifts imitate jumping actions and positions. They build muscle power and tendon flexibility.

COMPETITION

(About 10% of the total training period)

Type of exercise	light, quick jumping exercises
Amount of weight	50%–70% of maximum
Number of repetitions and sets	3–5 repetitions, 3–5 sets
Frequency of lifting	two times per week

During the jumping season, the objective is not to increase power. Hopefully, the jumper's strength will remain even. He may find he can actually increase his best poundages in some lifts, since this period eases off on heavy lifting and allows him to "peak." At any rate, the objective is not to get stronger, but to make use of power previously gained.

The exercises are mostly quick jumping movements such as jump squats, split jumps, etc. The total amount of weight raised should be reduced as the actual competition comes near.

There is no value in cutting out weight training during jumping or com-

Chart I
YEARLY TRAINING OUTLINE

		MONDAY	TUESDAY	WEDNESDAY	THURSDAY	FRIDAY	SATURDAY	SUNDAY
PREPARATORY PHASE	WEIGHT TRAINING	1 hr. 40 min. wt. training (heavy)		1 hr. 40 min. wt. training (heavy)		1 hr. 40 min. wt. training (heavy)		
	GENERAL TRAINING		80 min. stamina training		40 min. stamina training; 40 min. speed & flexibility		20 min. speed & flexibility; 20 min. stamina	40 min. stamina 60 min. speed & flexibility
	TECHNIQUE TRAINING	45 min. of takeoff work		45 min. of takeoff work		45 min. of takeoff work		30 min. of bar clearance; 15 min. of run-up work
TRAINING PHASE	WEIGHT TRAINING	1 hr. 40 min. wt. training (heavy)		1 hr. 40 min. wt. training (heavy)			1 hr. 40 min. wt. training (medium)	
	GENERAL TRAINING		30 min. speed & flexibility; 30 min. stamina		1 hr. speed & flexibility	30 min. stamina; 30 min. speed & flexibility		1 hr. speed & flexibility
	TECHNIQUE TRAINING	15 min. bar clearance; 30 min. takeoff; 15 min. run-up		15 min. bar clearance; 30 min. takeoff; 30 min. run-up			30 min. bar clearance; 30 min. run-up	30 min. takeoff; 15 min. run-up

COMPETITION PHASE

WEIGHT TRAINING	1 hr. 30 min. wt. training (light)	1 hr. 30 min. wt. training (light)
GENERAL TRAINING	1 hr. speed & flexibility	1 hr. speed & flexibility
TECHNIQUE TRAINING	2 hrs. technique training	Compete, 2 hrs.	Compete, 2 hrs.

Chart II
WEEKLY TIME ALLOTMENT

	LIFTING			GENERAL TRAINING			TECHNIQUE TRAINING		
		Heavy	Medium		Stamina	Speed & Flexibility		Take-off	Run-up	Bar clearance
PREPARATORY PERIOD (8–10 wks.)	5 hrs. per wk.	3 hrs. 20 min.	1 hr. 40 min.	5 hrs. per wk.	3 hrs.	2 hrs.	3 hrs. per wk.	1 hr. 30 min.	1 hr.	½ hr.
TRAINING PERIOD (25–30 wks.)	5 hrs. per wk.	3 hrs. 20 min.	1 hr. 40 min.	4 hrs. per wk.	1 hr.	3 hrs.	4 hrs. per wk.	1 hr. 30 min.	1 hr. 30 min.	1 hr.
COMPETITION PERIOD (10 wks.)	3 hrs. per wk.	0	3 hrs. (light)	2 hrs. per wk.	0	2 hrs.	6 hrs. per wk.	2 hrs.	2 hrs.	2 hrs.

petition weeks. The jumper will lose power and muscle tone—the flexibility and resistance to soreness.

The lifts are only briefly described here. It is important to execute these lifts correctly, or at least consistently. If this is not done, the gains cannot be judged validly, and the jumper risks injury to untrained muscles.

Chart III

EXAMPLE OF A TECHNIQUE TRAINING WORKOUT
(Total time: 65 minutes)

1. Jog one-half mile in 4:30.
2. Walk 220.
3. Stretch for 10 minutes, concentration on legs and back.
4. Do bar clearance exercises over a bar set at two feet, or do low standing jumps (15 minutes).
5. Do 30 minutes of takeoff work, beginning with two steps and hopping explosively over the bar (7 minutes). Do hops over objects (in high jump position) with weights (7 minutes). Do three-step approaches, kicking at objects hanging 8–10 feet in the air (16 minutes).
6. Go through the run-up wearing light weights, several times (5 minutes). Do run-ups, with takeoff, reaching for high objects (10 minutes).
   (Alternate to no. 6 above) Run, skip and/or hop with a barbell resting on the shoulders (up to 125 lbs.).
   3 x 110 hops (100 lbs.). Rest two minutes between.
   3 x 110 run, with legs bent (110 lbs.). Rest five minutes.
   3 x 110 leap, four steps, leap, four steps, leap, etc. (110 lbs.). Rest five minutes.
   5 x 50 light sprints (no weight).

TECHNIQUE OF THE HIGH JUMP

Approach

The approach must be fast to provide lift from forward speed. The purpose of the approach run is to reach this speed and get the body into position for the takeoff. The run must be long enough to allow the jumper to reach this speed without tension. When sprinting at good speed for too short a distance, a jumper tends to lean forward, a function of acceleration. Since forward lean must be reversed on takeoff, a short, fast run causes the body to lean excessively from the ankle. Thus the run must be at least seven strides long.

The jumper must start slowly and pick up speed in a relaxed manner. When the last strides are reached, cadence should increase while he is trying to advance the hips and legs ahead of the torso. The approach run can be accomplished in several ways, but one factor remains constant. The run must be continually accelerated. The last two, three or four steps will be the fastest, and the final step, the shortest. Great jumpers exceed seven meters per second (13 m.p.h.) in this phase.

Each step must be in line with the direction of run. One method of approach which is advocated is a three-part run-up. Part one is a walk-up to a check point using slow, short steps to pick up speed. Next, a series of steps, generally three to five, of easy but driving strides five to six feet in length, ending with another check mark. From the last check mark, the final two driving steps are to the foot-plant adjacent to the near standard. Figure 83 shows the run-up and length of stride throughout the approach.

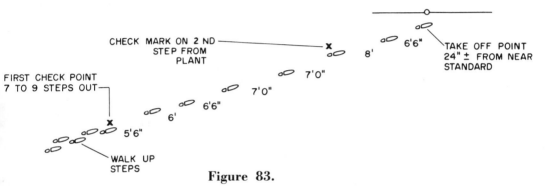

Figure 83.

The position of the legs and feet toward the end of the run is not characteristic of sprinting. The entire foot is in contact with the ground for a longer time, and the knee joints do not straighten after the push-off of the last steps.

Settle

The hips must be lowered prior to the last step, or the push leg will have to overcome both body weight and the compression of the body on the last step. Throughout the next-to-last step, the right knee is bent. To straighten the right leg would lift the hips. In Figures 84 through 88 the hip is rising. The jumper is running up an incline, so to speak. He must develop the ability to reach good speed with this type of hip position. It is not like sprinting. The last three steps before the final stride are over seven feet in length, enabling the hip position to be low.

Takeoff Point and Angle

Notice the takeoff point. (See Fig. 89.) The jumper correctly plants adjacent to the left standard. This (1) prevents lean-in, because one cannot lean without a bar to lean over; and (2) does not allow the jumper to turn, for if he does, he will not reach the bar.

The angle is fairly sharp (about 30°), thus giving him freedom to drive without

Figure 84.   Figure 85.   Figure 86.   Figure 87.

Figure 88.   Figure 89.   Figure 90.   Figure 91.

Figure 92.   Figure 93.   Figure 94.

Figure 95.   Figure 96.   Figure 97.   Figure 98.

fear of kicking the bar. It also gives him time on top to effect his turn. A perpendicular approach makes the jumper stop on the plant to convert speed to height. As a rule, the faster the approach, the narrower the angle. The actual point of takeoff is about 30 inches from the standard and, depending on the angle used, between two and four feet from the point where the jumper's center of gravity crosses the bar.

Takeoff Position

The body at the takeoff should be low and crouched (Fig. 86). But the hip should, at that time, be rising. The plant foot should be forward of the hips with the plant leg flexed (Figs. 85, 86, and 87) as the heel contacts the ground. The chest should not be too far behind the hips—the old "layback" position—but rather should be hunched a bit forward (Fig. 86).

The old concept of layback assumed the function of the plant foot was to "block" and vault up at takeoff. The shoulders were slowed or dropped back to advance the plant leg. This caused the jumper to lose much of the forward speed gained from the run-up and to develop a needless "float" prior to the last steps.

The idea of the takeoff as a driving motion was really discouraged by the early exponents of the straddle. The takeoff seemed, with this style, to depend on the swinging free leg, not on a powerful drive of the push leg.

Arms

Notice the vigorous arm swing that is used. The arms make a circling motion prior to the last step. Figs. 87, 88, and 89 demonstrate upward thrust of both elbows, not just the outside arm. In Fig. 90, the left arm has retreated to help the body rotate. Illustrations 92 through 96 demonstrate the excellent position of the right arm up and around the bar. The right arm has been kept near the body to avoid expanding the moment of inertia at this point.

The early backward thrust of the arms aids in the advance and the fast placement of the plant leg, by reaction. The upward action of the arms creates downward thrust into the ground.

After the lead arm has passed over the bar, it drops away from the body. Because of this, any further rotation of the body will tend not to include the arm, and it will seem to be holding back further rotation, by getting behind the lead shoulder. Actually the arm, being away from the rotating axis, cannot move as quickly as the shoulder. The only useful thing it can do is "retreat" so that by reaction the shoulder will drop.

Free Leg

The illustrations show the position of the jumper's left leg. It is turned in (Figs. 88 and 89). This turn-in can force the right leg to kick to the right of the run. This prevents body rotation on top by directing some force out of the pattern of power. By planting the foot in a turned-in position, the free leg is aided by "opening" the pelvis. This is mechanically sound because of the construction of the hip girdle. It does, however, direct some energy out of line.

It seems obvious that the free leg must move rapidly, and some of the leg speed is generated by the free foot push-off. Still many jumpers do not use spikes on that foot. All free-leg muscles are used to develop free-leg power. The hip pulls the leg, then the thigh and the smaller muscle groups. The foot pulls in and up.

The jumper begins his kick with a bent leg (Figs. 85 and 86), and then the leg locks briefly (Fig. 88) as the foot speed exceeds the thigh speed. The leg again on the way up (Fig. 90) flexes, and then straightens after the leg is over the bar (Fig. 95).

Plant Leg

If the jumper's right leg has been placed out to the side of his run, his left or plant foot will be forced to turn in. This position is not especially bad, in that it helps initiate his turn from the ground. It does, however, work contrary to logical application of force, which would require each step to be directly in line with the run. The rotation benefits are not worth the power loss. Because of the turn-in of the left leg, this leg may drift into the bar too quickly.

Plant Foot

The left foot in the straddle hits heel first (Fig. 84) and then remains flat on the ball of the foot with some heel contact, while the body comes over the foot and the arms and lead leg lift (Figs. 86 and 87). This extended contact of the left foot is one of the prime advantages of the "layback" or, preferably, "advance foot position." The force can be applied for more time, and thus the lift comes from push and strength and not simply from "spring." The foot must be aggressively placed with effort of the hamstring to pull the body across the plant foot (Figs. 84 and 85). If the foot is planted passively, it will block forward momentum.

Turn

Two types of rotation can be used to effect a bar clearance. The first—useful for a slow approach—is to pivot on one's long axis while centered over the bar. If some rotation is done on the ground, the head, shoulders and hips can turn back to face the bar on top. The second takes advantage of the fact that the hips drift across the bar faster than the shoulders.

Note how the hips catch the shoulders from Fig. 92 through Fig. 95. This is because the hips were the last part of the body to receive power. Since the hips and trail leg can gain the advantage of a "teeter-totter" action to get lift, rotation is less useful to aid the last leg clearance. Thus, if the shoulders are not forced to turn back, but are forcefully dropped, especially the right shoulder, the hips can be opened and will come away from the bar. This only works with a fast approach or else the hips will "die" on top. The first type of turn requires a small moment of inertia to get the trail leg out of danger quickly. The second permits the jumper to "reach" for the pit with the right arm and leg, thus releasing the trail hip to rise (Figs. 94 through 97). Note that the jumper lands on his side—not his back—as he uses the second type turn. The body straddles the bar if correct takeoff is made. The right side of his body naturally leads the jump unless the left leg is advanced, as in the hip roll, or if the lead leg is slow or stopped.

Chapter 9

TEACHING THE BEGINNING POLE VAULTER

by Tom Olsen

Assume the beginner is a right-handed vaulter. This means his right hand holds the pole above the left, the left foot leaves the ground last at takeoff, and he swings to the right of the pole.

1. Stand a ten-foot pole vertically in front of the vaulter. Have him place his right hand on the pole at head height and his left hand 18 inches below the right. Both thumbs are up. This is his handhold.

2. Have the vaulter place the "planting" end of the pole on the grass three feet in front of him. Now he springs forward, taking off on the left foot, passing the right side of the pole, using the arms and the pole to give support as he goes forward. He should carry the pole with him as he lands facing the same direction as at takeoff. This should be repeated several times.

3. The vaulter should repeat Step 2 five times, while walking into the takeoff.

4. Have the vaulter jog into the exercise described in Steps 2 and 3, but raise the handhold about two inches each time. He should swing loosely forward, with arms somewhat extended. This should be repeated until he can hold the pole a foot above the highest handhold he can reach. Avoid letting the top (right) hand slide down the pole as he takes off and swings forward.

5. While standing on a chair, the vaulter holds the pole vertically, grasping it as high as he can reach, with hands placed as in Step 1. The pole should be placed one to three feet in front of the chair as the vaulter swings forward to the right of the pole, with arms somewhat extended, taking the pole with him as he lands facing the same direction as at takeoff. This should be repeated several times.

6. Now the vaulter stands the pole vertically in the pole vault box and takes a handhold as high as he can reach. He walks back far enough so that he can take three paces forward to plant the pole and swing forward. With both feet together and the pole nearly horizontal and pointing toward the box, the vaulter begins walking briskly forward, starting with the left foot. As the right foot lands, he slams the pole into the box and brings the arms overhead with an underhand,

forward-upward sweep. He takes off on the left foot, and swings forward past the right side of the pole to land facing the same direction as at takeoff, taking the pole with him. This should be repeated several times.

7. The vaulter repeats Step 6, but he runs into the takeoff instead of walking. He starts with his feet together at a point far enough back so that he can run, using a five-stride approach, taking the first stride with his takeoff or left foot. Each time he repeats this procedure, he should raise his hold one or two inches. Soon the handhold will be one to two feet above the highest height he can reach with the pole standing vertically in the box.

8. With the handhold one or two feet above the highest standing grip he can reach, the vaulter now starts using a seven-stride approach. He begins with the left foot and takes off directly behind the pole with his left foot vertically beneath his right hand. As he improves, he can begin accelerating during the last three strides. He should spring into the takeoff, leading with a vigorously bent right knee, before hanging in an extended position momentarily. As the left side of his chest approaches the pole during the swing-up, he rolls back and brings his knees as close to his handgrip as he can get them. This movement will place his back horizontal to the ground. He should think of getting his hips higher than his shoulders. He permits the arms to remain relatively extended during this roll back. As he improves, he can give himself additional height by pulling downward through the length of the pole as his knees come to his handhold, and as the pole approaches the vertical. He lands facing the same direction as at takeoff, carrying the pole with him. This should be repeated several times.

9. Using a proper pole carry, with the planting end of the pole no higher than eye level and pointed very slightly to the left, hands about 18 inches apart, right hand behind right hip with fingers pointing down, pressing downward on the pole at the fork formed at the thumb, the left hand placed palm down on top of the pole with thumb beneath to support the pole, the vaulter can now practice carrying the pole down the runway. If he finds it more comfortable to carry the pole with a wider handspread, then it will be necessary to shift the left hand toward the right as the pole is planted.

10. Placing the bar at two feet, the vaulter can now begin to vault. As he approaches the bar after takeoff, he should "scissors" the right leg to the left, over the left leg, and the left leg backward-upward to the right, turning his body left so that he crosses the bar face downward. He pushes the pole back toward the runway as he clears the bar. Now he can raise the crossbar three inches each time he clears it, trying for a more pronounced roll-back each time. Soon he will be vaulting well over eight feet and ready to learn refinements of technique and details of fiberglass vaulting.

Chapter 10

THE POLE VAULT

by Bill Perrin

The introduction of the fiberglass vaulting pole caused a great deal of controversy among the vaulters, fans and coaches. It also created the problem of how to coach this seemingly new event. However, through its controversy and complexity, plus its breathtaking big bend and catapult action, the fiberglass pole has added a new, even more exciting spectator event. Also, it has added to the ever growing popularity of track and field throughout the U.S.A., and the world.

PHYSICAL AND PSYCHOLOGICAL ATTRIBUTES OF THE FIBERGLASS POLE VAULTER

Numerous attempts have been made to categorize the attributes needed to be a top-flight vaulter. Generally, these attributes are physical in nature and stress the importance of being over six feet tall and relatively light, with exceptionally good speed, strength, and coordination.

Physical characteristics are important, but many vaulters have succeeded despite supposed physical shortcomings. Fiberglass vaulters seem to come in all physical sizes. Recent 17-foot vaulters have ranged from 5'8" to 6'6" in height. Their weights have been relative to their heights, but have ranged from 140 pounds to over 200 pounds. Their speeds for 100 yards range from 9.5 to near 11 seconds. The one thing they *all* seem to have is outstanding strength and coordination relative to their other physical characteristics.

Immeasurable attributes, such as courage and daring, tremendous desire, resistance to discouragement from defeat and failure, and willingness to undertake endless hours of practice and study, have made them the world's greatest vaulters.

Although much emphasis is placed on the physical, just as important or perhaps more important are the mental, spiritual, and emotional factors. A vaulter may overcome one physical deficiency with another physical attribute, but he must have all the psychological attributes if he is to become successful.

SELECTION AND USE OF A FIBERGLASS VAULTING POLE

Weight Test of Pole

The so-called "weight test" of the pole used should be at least equal to the vaulter's body weight, i.e. a 160-pound vaulter should use a pole that is tested to support 160 pounds at his handhold.

Many factors enter into the selection of the best pole for an individual, such as the vaulter's height, weight, speed, height of top handhold and his skill and experience in using the fiberglass pole. Some pole manufacturing companies do not consider all these factors when designating the weight test of a pole.

Length of Pole

The length of the pole used varies with the age, size and experience of the vaulter. Vaulters holding over 13 feet should use a 16-foot pole. The longer the pole the better the balance, particularly when the pole is gripped near or over 14 feet. Many vaulters feel that poles should be 17 feet long.

Height of Effective Grip on Pole

The height of the "effective grip" on the pole is measured from the top of the top hand, minus the eight inches that are lost when the pole is put in the eight inch deep vaulting box.

Again many factors such as age, height, weight, speed, experience and type of pole used affect the height of the handgrip. However, the following can be used as a general guide. The average vaulter should be able to grip a height equal to twice his own physical height plus 24 inches. Example: A six-foot vaulter's height doubled would be 12 feet, add 24 inches and that would be 14 feet, minus the eight inches lost in the vaulting box, would leave an effective grip of 13 feet four inches.

Methods of Insuring a Good Grip

Most vaulters use one of the following methods of improving grip on the pole—

    a.   Reversed trainer's tape.

    b.   Black friction tape.

    c.   Various liquid and spray adhesives.

    d.   Light coating of cigarette lighter fluid over reversed tape or friction tape.

With all these methods it must be remembered that rules prevent more than two layers of tape.

Coaching and Mechanical Principles Related to the Pole

Many poles have a weak side where the pole will bend more easily. To find it, place a piece of tape around the middle of the pole and number the four sides one through four. Test the pole with each number up and determine where it bends most readily. Start with that number facing upward for all vaults.

THE LANDING PAD AND OTHER FACILITIES

The Landing Pad

The pole-vaulting landing area is of utmost importance in producing good fiberglass vaulters. It should consist of a shock absorbent material such as sponge rubber, air, rubberized fiber, or a combination of these. The recommended dimensions are: three feet high, 16 feet four inches wide and 16 feet four inches in length.

Extensions on each side of the vaulting box are a *must* for safety. Each extension should be the same height as the landing area extended about three feet toward the runway, and four to six feet wide.

The Pole Vault Standards

The vaulting standards should be very sturdy and be high enough to accommodate record vaults relative to the level of competition. They should also be adjustable and have space available to move two feet forward or back. For safety they should be constructed with no sharp edges or extensions that might puncture the vaulter's head or body.

The Vaulting Box

A legal vaulting box must have slanted sides and back as designated by the rules. The vertical walls of the old vaulting boxes damage fiberglass poles where they make contact with the box. A few layers of tape around the pole where it touches the box as it bends will prevent undue wear and tear on the pole at this point.

THE RUN AND POLE CARRY

Length and Speed of Approach

The length of the approach varies from 100 to 150 feet, generally 17 to 21 strides from the start to the takeoff. World class vaulters use an approach of at least 120 feet. The last four strides must be at top controllable speed.

Many outstanding vaulters claim to and actually appear to accelerate during the final four strides to takeoff. This assures a powerful pole plant and the early initial transfer of horizontal energy from the vaulter to the pole.

Check Marks

Generally one or two check marks are used by experienced vaulters. However, beginners may use three or more.

The following is a procedure for placing check marks. The vaulter stands with both feet together on the first check mark which is the start of his approach, steps off with his left foot, gradually accelerating to the next check mark. The second mark should be hit with the left foot at a point 60 to 80 feet from the back of the box.

(Note: It is a good practice to have a "coach's check mark" to the side of the runway at a point four strides—about 30 feet—from the spot where the vaulter's left foot lands at *takeoff*. The distance and accuracy of this check mark should be determined by trial and error in early season practice and competition. Its use by the coach will insure that the vaulter is not losing any valuable momentum at this point by unnoticed shortening or lengthening of his stride in order to hit takeoff marks properly.)

Pole Carry

For clarity, the analysis of the approach and vaulting movements will be described for the right-handed pole vaulter, whose right hand is the top hand and the takeoff is with the left foot.

The distance between the hands on the pole during the approach may vary from 24 to 36 inches. Although an individual matter, hand spread must be comfortable and efficient in order to assist approach speed, a proper pole plant and takeoff.

The position of the pole at the start of the run can be slightly across the body with the tip of the pole at head level or slightly above. The higher the grip, the more it necessitates a high pole carry. The left hand and thumb act as a fulcrum, with the thumb supporting a majority of the pole's weight, while the right hand and thumb apply pressure downward. Do not grip tightly with the hands. This causes tenseness in the arms and shoulders, which is transmitted to the rest of the body.

About five strides from the takeoff the front tip of the pole should be making a gradual descent toward the bottom and back of the box. (Note: The pole should resemble a "magic wand" moving swiftly, smoothly (without jerky movements) from the start of the run to a perfect takeoff angle, with the pole directly above the vaulter's head and takeoff foot. The vaulter's eyes and attention should be focused on the vaulting box from the start of the run until the pole is firmly planted in the box.)

Coaching Points Related to Approach and Pole Carry

1. The speed of the run is about 9/10 full speed, or maximum controlled speed.
2. Carry the pole with the thumbs during approach. During the pole carry, the left elbow is bent 90 degrees and right elbow is bent 100 degrees.
3. Carry the pole so that the planting end is at about head height, and ahead of the left shoulder.
4. Discourage a cross-body pole carriage, because the end of a fiberglass pole whips considerably, and lateral motion should be minimized.
5. The vaulter's trunk should be upright during the last four or five strides before the pole plant.

POLE PLANT

Although the following material is divided into several separate phases, it must be continually stressed that the vaulting action itself is a single movement that takes place in less than one second from the time the vaulter takes off until he clears the crossbar.

The pole plant and takeoff are the two most important phases of vaulting. If one or the other is executed improperly, a good vault is practically impossible. Nearly all problems encountered during bar clearance can be traced back to a mechanically unsound, inefficient combination of actions at the instant of pole plant and takeoff.

The Start of Pole Plant

The pole plant is started about two strides from the takeoff. As the left foot touches the ground in the next-to-last (penultimate) stride, the pole is directed forward and down toward the box. It should be firmly planted and above the head a fraction of a second before the left foot lands again for takeoff.

Action of Arms

During the pole plant, the arms must work relatively close to the body. The right arm starts the pole plant about two strides from the takeoff. Before the left foot makes contact with the ground, the right shoulder and arm are rotated slightly to the right and the pole is brought upward and over the head in a semi-sidearm and to-the-rear curling movement. This keeps the body and pole relation in balance relative to the vaulter's center of gravity. The left hand acts as a support and guide while the top hand is pushing the pole forward and down into the box.

The hand spread at takeoff varies from eight inches to about 24 inches. Most authorities agree that such a hand spread of *at least* eight, to a maximum of 24 inches offers the best mechanical position to control the body and the fiberglass pole.

During takeoff, the left arm is noticeably bent and the elbow is in close to the body, acting as a lever, preventing the body from coming too far forward and losing control of the body and pole.

During the pole plant many vaulters do not shift the hands, but keep the same grip used during the pole carry. Others shift the bottom hand up slightly toward the top hand.

The right arm, at takeoff, should be directly above and in back of the head, and almost fully extended. If the right arm is flexed too much, the transfer of energy from the vaulter to the fiberglass pole is less effective.

The Negative and Positive Bending of the Pole During Pole Plant

There are actually two flexures of the pole taking place during the pole plant. The first is a "negative" bend, and second is the "positive" bend. The negative bend takes place just as the pole makes contact with bottom, before it reaches the back of the vaulting box. The pole bends quickly downward a few inches.

The "positive" bend is the pole's opposite (upward) reaction to the "negative" downward bend. As the pole returns upward and to the side during the positive bend, it continues on into the big bend as the vaulter quickly transfers his body weight to the pole during takeoff.

The fiberglass pole's "negative bend" and "positive bend" are equally important to the success of the vault. A strong and fast over-the-head pole plant produces a good negative bend. A good positive bend is achieved when the vaulter comes onto the pole, before and after the takeoff, with optimum horizontal momentum using the aforementioned arm actions during the pole plant, and arm position during takeoff.

Coaching Points Related to the Pole Plant

1. Start the pole plant two strides before takeoff, as the left foot touches the ground, and complete the plant before the left foot touches again.
2. Have the pole firmly in the box and hands above the head before the left foot touches the ground for takeoff.
3. The last stride before takeoff is usually eight to ten inches shorter than the preceding strides.

THE TAKEOFF, HANG AND SWING-UP

Providing the pole plant has been effective, the remainder of the vaulter's actions and movements will determine the success of the vault.

The bending of the pole also has a direct correlation to the success of the vault. Forces acting in two directions are used by the vaulter to bend and store energy in the pole. These forces act both perpendicularly and parallel to the long axis of the pole.

Perpendicular and Parallel Forces Acting on the Pole

The perpendicular forces applied to the pole at takeoff are most effective as the vaulter's speed and body weight transfer most horizontal forces to the pole. During this brief time, the right hand and arm, near the top of the pole, exert a downward force against the pole, whose bottom end is wedged in the vaulting box. It is doubtful that the left arm exerts any effective upward force in terms of bending the pole.

The action of the legs at takeoff is forward and upward, simulating the dynamics of the take-off in the long jump, thus exerting a parallel force on the pole. Leading the action is the right leg and foot, which are driven forward vigorously in a more horizontal than vertical direction. The right foot should be under the knee or slightly ahead, not under the buttocks.

Simultaneously the left leg and foot extend and the vaulter appears to move forward for an instant in a hanging position. Just after takeoff, and during the hang and swing-up, the right leg is partially extended as the left leg is brought up to and slightly past the right leg. These actions cause the pole to bend away from the vaulter at approximately 45 degrees to his left. The stronger the horizontal forces at takeoff, the more pronounced will be the bend prior to and after takeoff.

Parallel Forces During Roll Back

Parallel force is applied along the long axis of the pole as the vaulter starts his swing upward and roll back actions. During this phase the body is behind the pole and moving upward as the legs, bent only slightly, are brought upward quickly and toward the hands and shoulders. In this action the shoulders become the axis of rotation.

TAKEOFF STYLES

There are three different takeoff styles or variations of these styles, which are used by the world's top vaulters.

First Style

This style closely resembles the takeoff used by the metal-pole vaulters. The body is upright with the chest near the pole, and the left arm ahead of or resting against the pole. The hand spread is around twelve inches. The takeoff foot is directly below the right hand. This takeoff is associated with the dropping of the lead leg during the swing-up.

Second Style

This method is used by many of the Finnish vaulters. The takeoff foot leaves the ground about twelve inches forward of the takeoff point of the first style. The body is in a definite hyper-extended position, with the chest forward toward the pole. The right arm is almost fully extended and the left forearm rests against or along the pole.

Third Style

America's John Pennel used this style. It is characterized by the fixed right angle which the left arm forms with the body during takeoff. The takeoff foot leaves the ground about eight to twelve inches in front of a vertical line drawn downward from the right hand. The right leg is brought forward and up (similar to the long jump takeoff action).

Coaching Points Related to the Takeoff, Hang and Swing-up

1. A takeoff with the left foot directly under the top hand is ideal. However, many good vaults are made twelve inches either forward or back from this point.
2. The takeoff point could be directly below the point where the center of gravity of the body hangs between the wide handspread.
3. The takeoff foot should be directly beneath the pole, not to the right or left.
4. During takeoff, use a long jump takeoff action, driving forward-upward at a 20-degree angle. A vertical jump is undesirable because it does not aid in bending the pole.
5. The vaulter should attempt to run under the bar or through the plane of the uprights at a point four or five feet above the box.
6. The pole always begins to bend before the takeoff foot breaks contact with the ground, providing the pole plant and takeoff mechanics are correct.
7. When observing a vaulter directly from behind at the instant of takeoff, it appears his head and the left upper part of his body are on the left side of the pole and his lower body is on the right side of the pole.
8. The takeoff extension is fully effective if it goes diagonally through the body as a vertical line from the takeoff foot up to the right hand.
9. During the takeoff, the hang and swing-up of the legs play an important part in pole bending and storage of energy in the pole. During the swing-

up, the legs can increase the pole's positive bend if they are extended nearly straight while being lifted quickly toward the top of the pole.

THE ROLL BACK AND VERTICAL BODY EXTENSION

The roll back and vertical body extension can only be effective if preceded by a strong horizontal takeoff and hang position. A premature roll back causes the vaulter to ride too long on his back with legs up, and consequently forces him to turn and come off the pole too soon, in a flat position.

Nevertheless, the roll back, "*properly timed*," must be powerful and very fast. If properly timed, the coupling action can transfer valuable energy and more bend to the pole, while also aiding the vaulter in bringing the legs and hips into position for a good vertical body lift. During the roll back the shoulders are the axis of rotation. (Note: The head and shoulders must be considered as one, and not as separate parts during roll back.)

Action of the Arms, Head and Shoulders

During the roll back the arms aid in keeping the vaulter's center of gravity behind the pole. The right arm remains relatively straight, while the left arm is noticeably flexed, but in a fixed position, thus keeping the vaulter's center of gravity behind the pole. The line passing through the shoulders which forms the axis of rotation during the roll back should remain parallel to the ground until the pull and turn is started. The head *must not* be thrown back separately. This action forces the feet and hips out horizontally toward the crossbar, causing the vaulter to lose control of the vault. The position of the head is relative to the angle of the body as he rotates upward. When the vaulter's back is horizontal, the head is slightly forward, with the chin close to the chest as the vaulter forcefully drives his legs and hips back toward the pole.

Action of the Legs and Hips

Regardless of the takeoff and roll back style used, the legs must be brought powerfully upward and backward in a semi-bent position. The legs should be angled back toward the runway at about a 75- to 80-degree angle until the hips and legs are extended vertically upward just before the pull, turn and push-up action. If the legs are extended toward the crossbar, the vaulter's center of gravity is thrown out away from the pole and into the crossbar when the pull and turn is started.

An imaginary straight line passing through the hips from side to side must be kept parallel to the ground, so the hips may remain square and not be tilted to the right or left during the roll back. Often the hips tilt to the right or left as viewed from the runway. If they tilt to the right, the left leg action is probably too exaggerated, which is the most common fault. However, if the hips are tilted to the left, the left leg is probably not coming forward and up fast enough.

The separate actions of the right and then the left leg during takeoff, hang, swing and roll back are very important, but as the body and legs are extended vertically and slightly back, the legs must be working together to achieve maximum vertical lift.

Coaching and Mechanical Principles Related to the Roll Back and Vertical Extension

1. The head and eyes remain straight ahead from the start of the run until the beginning of the turn, at which time the head and shoulders are back and the eyes are looking vertically up at a point a few feet in front of the crossbar.

2. As the turn is started the head and shoulders rotate together to the left and downward, the eyes are focused on the pole vault box or landing pad.

3. The axis about which the vaulter's body rotates in the roll back is a horizontal axis, passing through the shoulders.

4. Actions initiated by the vaulter with his center of gravity behind the true axis of the pole will increase the pole bend.

5. The pole bend is always maximum during the first one-fourth second after takeoff, before the vaulter's legs and hips swing level with the shoulders. This is because maximum centrifugal force is being developed and transmitted to the pole through the upper hand, as the vaulter is holding his body back.

    Centrifugal force $= MV^2$ or mass multiplied by speed^2 divided by radius.
    $$\overline{R}$$
    Thus energy is stored in the pole during the first one-fourth second after takeoff. All actions after the first one-fourth second following takeoff are designed to receive back the potential energy stored in the pole, at the critical moment during the final phases of the pole's recoil.

6. When the pole bends after takeoff, the center of gravity of the vaulter rises very slowly in a vertical direction. The vaulter moves forward toward the crossbar very rapidly with very little vertical lift of the body. The vaulter must compensate for this great conservation of momentum at the beginning of the takeoff by rolling back, away from the crossbar, as fast as possible. Rolling backward and swinging the legs upward exaggerates the bend of the pole, and keeps the vaulter a greater distance away from the crossbar. The vaulter gains time by this action in which to perform subsequent movements. Remember, this hang, swing-up and roll-back action all takes place in about the first one-fourth second after takeoff.

7. An aggressive roll back will keep the vaulter's center of gravity beneath the handgrip. Movements made with the center of gravity in front of the pole's true axis will throw the vaulter forward into the bar too fast. The

vaulter must concentrate on achieving vertical thrust when the pole recoils.

8. Vertical body extension is a continuation of the roll back, often called the secondary roll back, which takes place as the hips rise above the head and shoulders.

9. This vertical extension of the body upward starts slightly more than one-fourth second after takeoff.

10. The average bend of a fiberglass pole is 39 inches from a straight line.

THE PULL AND TURN

The pull and turn start almost simultaneously, but should be delayed as long as possible in order to achieve maximum vertical lift from the pole as it straightens. Initiating the pull and turn too soon is a common fault. The pole becomes a lifting force as it returns to its normal state. If the vaulter starts the pull and turn too soon, his center of gravity is forced outside of this assisting force and he is thrown toward the crossbar instead of vertically upward. The pull, turn and clearance is therefore a delayed, very quick and powerful movement with the vaulter finally extending his arms almost straight down the vertical axis of the pole. (Note: Generally speaking the turn is started too soon and should not be coached. It will take place quite naturally as the vaulter's hips pass his hands during the roll back and vertical body extension.)

PUSH-UP AND CLEARANCE

Arm Action

As the vaulter's arms are extended quickly down the pole, the left arm reaches its full extension first and is quickly lifted up and away from the crossbar or placed against the abdomen. After reaching maximum extension in its downward thrust, the right arm is also quickly withdrawn and lifted up and away from the crossbar. The pole is released with a quick thrust of the right thumb. After the release of the pole the thumbs are rotated inward, causing the elbows to naturally rotate out and away from the crossbar.

Action of the Head

During the extension of the arms, the head should remain down with eyes on the vaulting box or landing pad until the body clearance is accomplished. The head is thrown back or turned to the left side only when necessary, and then only at the last moment. If the head is thrown back too soon, it forces the chest down, and usually into the crossbar. The above movements aid the vaulter in draping his body around the crossbar in a mechanically efficient arch-flyaway clearance.

Placement of Standards

Standard-placement varies with the weather and with a number of other factors. Normally, standards should be at least twelve to 24 inches deep toward the landing area. The average is about 18 inches behind the back of the vaulting box.

The Landing

The type of landing used is dependent upon the landing facilities. On a good landing pad the vaulter can land on his back, distributing the shock over a wide area of his body. This places less shock and stress on the legs and causes less fatigue in the entire body. In a poor landing facility the vaulter should not land on his back, for obvious reasons. His feet and legs should first make contact, with the legs and body in a flexed position as he rolls backward, making contact with hips and arms, and finally the shoulders in a backward rolling action.

Pre-Season Workout Schedule

Pre-season workouts should start at least three months before the first competition. Training should involve a total range of activity to improve strength, speed, power, timing, coordination, spatial orientation (air-mindedness), endurance, and flexibility.

Pre-season is the most important phase of training and requires more time and physical effort than any of the other periods of training.

Strength and Power Activities

Weight training and other forms of progressive resistance (overload) training is indispensable for most vaulters. Most such work should be done primarily for the arm, shoulder, abdominal and back muscles, and secondarily for the legs.

Some great vaulters do not use weights, but engage in extensive gymnastic training. This in essence is weight training, utilizing the vaulter's own body weight as resistance.

The following is a suggested guide for a weight training program.

1. Weight training should take place on alternate days, i.e. Monday, Wednesday, Friday.
2. Weekly pre-season weight training should include intense, general overall training, lifts for specific related muscles, and one workout devoted to competitive type lifting.
3. During the competitive season, weight training should continue two days weekly to maintain muscle tone. One day should be devoted to general development, and the other to lifting for specific muscle groups. Generally, the weight handled during the competitive season should not exceed pre-season marks.

4. Weight training should follow the regular daily workout. Never use weight training directly before vaulting or performing drills related to vaulting. Weight training may cause muscle injury if directly followed by vaulting.

   Always allow at least two days of rest and recuperation from weight training before vaulting competition.

5. The specific weight lifted and the number of repetitions, sets, and rest intervals used, depend upon individual differences. The vaulter's purpose in using weight training should be to develop strength and power. Strength and power are developed by using few sets, few repetitions, and heavy weights.

   A general guide is to use three or four sets with a weight that can be lifted only four to eight times in succession. If the weight can be easily lifted ten or 15 times, it is too light to develop strength and power.

   The rest interval between sets should be just sufficient to recuperate. Vaulters should stress complete flexion and extension of muscles at moderate speed, and use correct lifting mechanics.

6. To maintain interest and to promote best results in weight training, it should be competitive and have variety. Occasionally change the order and emphasis of the routine, adding new exercises and different variations of basic exercises.

7. The following are suggested weight training exercises for vaulters—
   a. Incline Press. (Shoulder and elbow extensors.)
   b. Leg Curl. (Hamstrings.)
   c. Stiff-Leg Dead Lift with Shoulder Shrug. (Spine extensors, hamstrings, trapezius—also *stretches* hamstrings.)
   d. Hook Lying Sit-Up with Twist. (Abdominal muscles, lateral flexors.)
   e. Quarter Squat with Toe Raise. (Hip, knee and ankle extensors.)
   f. Hanging Leg Raise. (Hip flexors and abdominals.)
   g. Rowing Motion. (Elbow flexors, latissimus dorsi.)
   h. Bend Over Twist. (Back extensors, spinal rotators.)
   i. Lower Arm Triceps Extension. (Elbow extensors.)

8. Running and hopping up stairs is also excellent for the development of strength and power. The best place to do this is in a football stadium, running up the wooden seats rather than the concrete steps. Again, variety is important and various forms of running and hopping up the stadium seats provide a means of development.

9. Sprinting and sprint starts are considered strength and power activities. The distance sprinted can vary from 30 to 50 yards when taking gun starts from the blocks. Sprinting (with and without the vaulting pole) can vary from 50 to 100 yards, and up to 220 yards on occasions. The repetitions vary with the distance and generally range from five to 15, all at near maximum (nine-tenths) speed.

Low hurdling should be done from time to time to develop a constant stride pattern, which is imperative for championship vaulting.

ACTIVITIES FOR IMPROVING REACTIONS

Good reaction time is inherited, but may be improved by some of the following post- and pre-season activities. Post-season activities which may help reaction time are wrestling, boxing, tennis, handball and other related activities. Pre-season and competitive season activities are limited to starts from the blocks, sprinting, hurdling, and gymnastic routines.

ACTIVITIES RELATED TO COORDINATION AND SPATIAL ORIENTATION

Each workout should include some of the following activities: Trampoline, diving, tumbling and free exercise, high bar, parallel bar, walking and balancing on the hands, and rope climbing. Jumping and throwing events may also be included in this category.

Most of these activities and their counterparts can and should be modified to resemble various phases of vaulting techniques.

ENDURANCE ACTIVITIES

Endurance is an important factor, since the pole vault is the first event to start and the last to finish in most track meets. Endurance is acquired through sustained running at moderate speeds for a mile or more, but can also be developed by four to ten repetitions of 220, 440, or 880 yards at one-half or two-thirds maximum speed.

Swimming during the post- and pre-season periods, at moderate distances and speeds is useful in developing endurance, as well as for relaxation.

FLEXIBILITY ACTIVITIES

Gymnastic activities have a definite carry-over to the flexibility useful to vaulting. Exercises such as alternate toe touches, hurdle exercises, trunk twisting and rotations, jumping-jacks and a multitude of other warm-up and stretching exercises, also serve to develop and maintain flexibility.

RELATED VAULTING DRILLS

Related vaulting drills are those activities specifically related to the individual phases of the vault. Their purpose is improving vaulting technique by concentrating on a part rather than on the vault as a whole.

The following are useful related vaulting drills.

1. "Run and pole carry drill." Stress proper form utilizing the overload principle by having the vaulter do several repetitions (ten to 20) at top speed while gripping six to twelve inches higher on the pole than usual, thus placing more stress on the arms and shoulders.

2. "Pole plant drill." Plant the pole with a walking, three or four step, over-the-head pole plant, using the to-the-rear curl, up-over-and-above-the-head action. Repeat forty or more times, stressing a strong, forceful pole plant, starting as the left foot touches the ground (two steps away from takeoff) and completing it before the left foot again lands for takeoff.

3. The "soft pole drill" permits the vaulter to work on the entire vault, using a pole testing ten to 20 pounds under his body weight. The athlete executes the entire vault, using a short approach (50 to 100 feet) and a low grip (one or two feet below his regular grip), simulating the actions and timing of higher vaults. This permits numerous vaults (20 to 40) with minimum fatigue. Thus much work on specific techniques may be done while executing the complete vault. This drill is used by most of the great vaulters in their pre-season and regular season training programs.

4. The "vaulting for height and form drill" should be used at least once a week during pre-season, and occasionally during the competitive season, if the vaulter seems to have reached a performance plateau. The athlete should vault as though in competition, starting at a height a foot or so below his best mark, and working up to a height three or six inches above his previous best vault. During this drill the vaulter may start on a heavier test weight pole, or attempt to raise his grip three or four inches. Vaulting at a height three or six inches above his previous best acquaints the vaulter with the pull-up delay and proper timing needed at higher heights. Setting the standards and crossbar back two feet in practice also aids the vaulter in maintaining proper timing at higher heights in competition.

    (Note: The number of days a week and the number of times a day an athlete vaults is relative to the caliber of the vaulter. The novice should probably vault at least two or three days a week, 15 to 30 times each day. However, vaulting should stop when the vaulter becomes fatigued, as this causes bad habits and poor vaulting techniques.)

5. The "fiberglass pole vault trainer drill" allows the vaulter to practice the takeoff, hang, swing-up, roll back and vertical body extension in parts, or as a whole. Strong and mechanically correct vaulting actions while using the trainer produce a greater elongation of the rubber section of the device and consequently a greater lifting action as the vaulter extends his body vertically upward. Incorrect movements cause little or no elongation of or

lifting forces from the rubber section of the device and make it impossible for the vaulter to extend his body vertically.

Ideally the trainer should be attached to a climbing rope which allows the vaulter to get a few swings for momentum before simulating the vaulting actions. It can also be secured to and effectively used on the cross support of a football goal post.

Three or four sets of five to eight repetitions are usually sufficient for this strenuous vaulting drill.

The following is a general workout schedule for *pre-season, competitive season* and *post-season* training. The previously discussed training activities may be used to construct a personal workout program in accordance with individual circumstances.

PRE-SEASON WORKOUT GUIDE

Monday   Jogging and flexibility activities, the soft pole drill, another vaulting drill, and strength and power (weight training) activities.

Tuesday   Jogging and flexibility activities, four or more coordination and spatial orientation activities, strength and power training (running and hopping stairs), one endurance activity.

Wednesday   Jogging and flexibility activities, vaulting for height, weight training, and endurance activities.

Thursday   Jogging and flexibility activities, coordination and spatial orientation activities, and reaction activities (sprinting).

Friday   Repeat Monday's training.

Saturday   Repeat Tuesday's training.

(Note: At least once a week the coach and vaulter should study films of champion vaulters. If possible, films should be taken in practice and analyzed before each week's training.)

COMPETITIVE SEASON

Monday   Jogging and flexibility activities, vaulting drills related to the problems encountered in Saturday's competition, sprinting, and weight training.

Tuesday   Jogging and flexibility activities, two or three coordination and spatial orientation activities, and one endurance activity.

Wednesday   Jogging and flexibility activities, vaulting for height, one or two strength and power activities, and one endurance activity.

Thursday   Jogging and flexibility activities, one or two coordination and spatial orientation drills, and sprinting.

Friday   The day prior to the meet is generally a day of rest, relaxation and mental preparation for Saturday's competition.

Saturday   Competition. (Note: Following competition on Saturday or Sunday is an ideal time for one of the two weight training days recommended during the competitive season. Also, an ideal time to study and analyze film taken in training and competition is on Sunday or before practice on Monday.

Then the vaulter can work on techniques that films show need more emphasis.)

POST-SEASON TRAINING

This is the ideal time to emphasize the development of strength and power through an intensive weight training program and the other recommended strength and power activities. This is also a time for changing to other activities which offer a variety, challenge, and competition. Some sports which develop good reactions and other related skills are wrestling, handball, tennis, and most of the team sports.

FIBERGLASS VAULTING ANALYSIS

Figures 99 and 100:   The vaulter is in an upright position, starting his pole plant on his left foot, two strides from the takeoff. Notice the pole angling downward into the vaulting box as it is brought upward and to the vaulter's right side for an over-the-head pole plant.

Figure 99.   **Figure 100.**

Figure 101:   This illustrates an excellent takeoff position, with the right arm nearly extended and the left foot under and slightly ahead of the top hand. The right knee is driving forward and the left arm is flexed but fixed, keeping the vaulter behind the pole.

Figure 101.

Figure 102: An excellent takeoff and hang action is shown as the right knee and foot continue forward, with the left leg extending back. Notice the wide spread of the legs as he attempts to drive straight ahead briefly (more horizontally than vertically, in a hanging position).

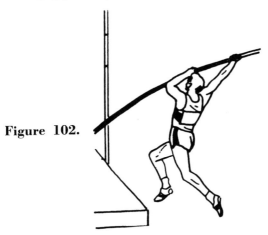

Figure 102.

Figures 103 and 104: The end of the hang and the start of the swing-up are shown as the semiflexed left leg is now coming forward very fast toward the semiflexed right leg. The body passes the true vertical axis of the pole prior to the swing-up and roll back.

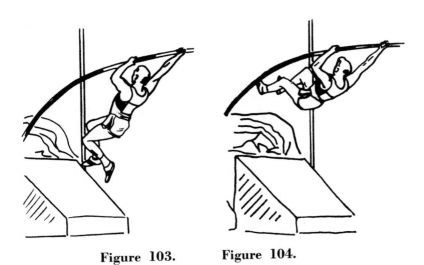

Figure 103. **Figure 104.**

Figure 105:   Notice that the legs are noticeably flexed and the left leg has caught up with the right leg, with the hips starting to pass the shoulders. The pole has reached its maximum bend at this point and will begin recoiling as the vaulter continues upward. The shoulders remain as the axis of rotation while the arms remain unchanged until the hips nearly reach the top hand.

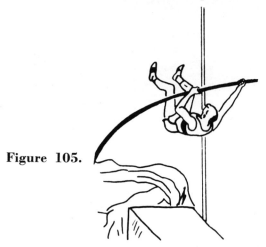

Figure 105.

Figures 106, 107 and 108:   At this point the legs are extending upward and back as the vaulter attempts to stay on his back and extend his body upward along the vertical axis of the pole.

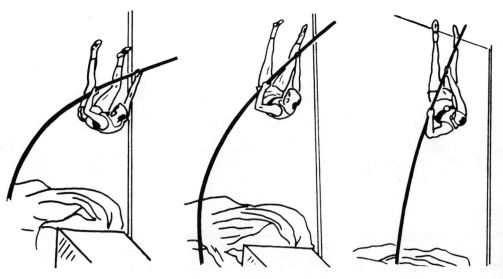

Figure 106.   **Figure 107.**   **Figure 108.**

Figures 109, 110, 111, 112 and 113:   The pull, turn, push-up and clearance are well executed in these final phases. Note that the vaulter has remained on his back as long as possible to achieve maximum vertical lift. The pull, turn and push-up occur very quickly and powerfully with the vaulter's eyes looking down and back toward the landing pad. This aids in vertical lift off the pole and keeps the body concaved as the vaulter drapes his body around the crossbar in an arch-flyaway clearance.

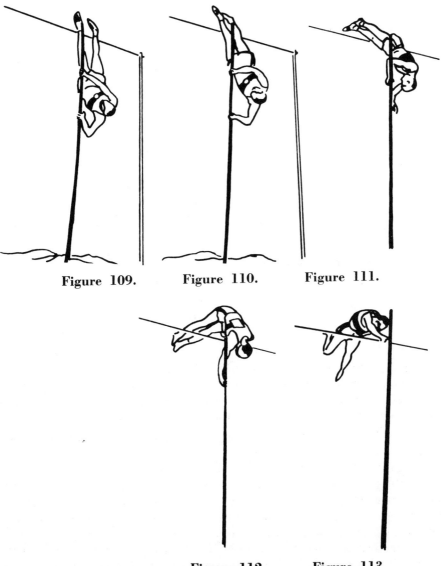

Figure 109.   **Figure 110.**   **Figure 111.**

Figure 112.   **Figure 113.**

Chapter 11

TEACHING THE BEGINNING LONG JUMPER

by Douglas Coghlan

When teaching the long jump, many coaches apparently believe that once they have given their pupils a run-up, and have told them to run fast, to jump high, and not to sit back at the landing, they have done all that is necessary. There is no reason, however, why the fundamentals of balance in the air cannot also be developed in children—even at the early age of 11 or 12 years.

The traditional method of teaching long jump has been to teach a running-in-air or hitch-kick style by means of a series of leading-up stages, as follows:

1) Using a short run and a deeply dug, soft sand pit, the athlete runs forward to land in a semi-split leg position in the sand, with the takeoff leg trailing. As the feet touch, the athlete sinks into the sand with the hands used to help break the fall.

2) The athlete runs forward two or three strides, jumps, and changes legs in the air so that he lands in the same manner as before, but with the takeoff leg now in front.

3) In the third stage, the athlete runs forward as before, changes legs in the air, and brings the rear leg through so that the feet are together for the landing. A springboard is valuable at this point to give sufficient height and time for the athlete to perform the movements with a short run-up.

Then, combining this action with a long run-up, the athlete should be doing something similar to a one and one-half stride hitch-kick in the air.

In actual practice it often happens that beginners fail to achieve success with this method, since they have difficulty in mastering the technique of swinging back an extended leg, which is the key to the whole movement. Most novices simply reverse legs with both of them bent, a movement which has no beneficial effect on mid-air body posture and balance.

Other disadvantages are that only one athlete can perform at a time, unless the sand pit is particularly large, and that the sand quickly becomes packed and difficult to land in. Triple jumping technique, then, can be taught more quickly and effectively to a large group of people by the following alternative method:

162

1) The athletes run freely, hopping into the air every four or six strides, landing on the takeoff foot, and continue to run on landing. A quick demonstration is the easiest way to teach this.

2) The athletes soon develop balance, and some will develop a free swing action with the non-hopping leg. This movement is emphasized. (Again a quick demonstration is effective.)

3) The free movement of the non-hopping leg should be guided into an extended leg swing backwards in the air. Points to stress at this stage are as follows:

1. High knee lift at takeoff,

2. Extended leg swing of the non-hopping leg,

3. Maintenance of an upright, balanced posture,

4. Landing with control, and with the free leg coming through flexed for the next running stride,

5. Relaxation of the hopping leg during the flight, and

6. Extension of the hip joint during the sweep-back of the non-hopping leg.

Practice at this stage should continue over several periods with various aspects of technique receiving attention, until the athlete has developed a respectable hitch-kick during the hop with the non-hopping leg.

Equal time should be spent hopping on the right foot and the left foot, to develop the hitch-kick action in both legs.

The most important part of the movement is the swing-back of the free leg past the hip line, since it is this movement that gives the desired reaction in the trunk. To achieve this, it helps to have the athletes stand on the hopping leg, leaning against a wall, supported on the outstretched arm. The complete swinging action of the free leg can then be practiced.

At the Pit

When athletes are first brought to the pit to practice, let them jump for height, using the "pop-up" exercise in developing the takeoff. Holding up a target to reach is also valuable, especially if the athletes are encouraged to touch it with their chests. High knee lift and explosive takeoff should be emphasized.

The athletes should also learn the "hang" position. Many athletes fail to achieve this "hang," but "pike" at the hips instead. To overcome this tendency, or to teach the "hang" from scratch, the instructor will find that the standing broad jump is valuable. If possible, have the athletes jump from both feet off a bank or other raised surface into sand. While in flight, the arched position is attempted.

This movement can also be used to teach the correct landing position. Following the hang, the athlete bends his legs, pulls them through quickly and lifts them high for the landing. As the athlete lands, he should "give" at the knee, coming into a squat position, and sit back in the sand. Forward momentum will not normally be great enough to allow the athlete to pivot over the feet to a standing position. Those that manage to do this are bringing the feet down to the sand too soon.

The athletes next attempt to get the "hang" position during the "pop-up," but some will not manage this immediately, as it is difficult to emphasize the leading-leg knee lift and then to drop into the hang position. A springboard is useful at this point, but even using it, many athletes will sit back in the sand as they land.

Once the athletes are beginning to achieve a respectable "hang" during the "pop-ups," a revision of the hopping skills should be made. The hitch-kick action must be added during the "pop-up." Emphasis on the leading-leg swing should give the desired result.

The Run-up

Up to this point, only the takeoff, flight and landing have been covered. The other important consideration is the development of a consistently reliable run-up.

Beginners could start with a 15-stride approach. They may work in pairs so that several people can learn at one time. No. 1 stands with his feet on the board, then sprints along the run-up, taking the first stride with the jumping foot. No. 2 counts the strides and marks the fifteenth. Stride counting is done by counting only the jumping leg, 1, 3, 5, 7, 9, 11, 13, 15. No. 1 runs through six times, and then has a group of six marks where the fifteenth stride landed each time. The average of these marks is then taken as the athlete's starting point. He uses this starting mark and practices until he is able to run from it and place the jumping foot close to or on the board at every run. When he has developed a consistent run, slight adjustments in the mark can be made.

If a cinder track is available, athletes can work out their run-ups in pairs, using the lanes on the track so that a large number can work at the same time. The distances are then measured off and transferred to the run-up.

Each athlete's run-up should be measured so that it is not necessary to work it out each time. Many times an athlete can judge his mark by some permanent indicator, such as a marking on the side of the runway.

As the athlete becomes older and improves in skill and speed, the run-up can be extended to 17, 19, or 21 strides. Suggested distances for run-up length are as follows:

Age	Boys	Girls
Under 19 years	100′–120′	90′–120′
Under 17 years	80′–120′	80′–120′
Under 15 years	80′–120′	70′–100′
Under 13 years	60′–90′	50′–80′

General Points

1. Shoes should always be worn. Bare feet greatly reduce efficiency and are easily bruised. Even when shoes are worn, extra heel protection in the form of sponge rubber or a plastic heel cup is advisable.

2. Long spikes in the sole dorsi-flex the ankle as the foot is planted at takeoff and give greater range of movement.

3. The ground immediately next to the takeoff board, on the run-up side, should be kept flush with the takeoff board. There is often wearing at this spot, and the edge of the takeoff board may be left sharp, causing severe injuries to the soles of the feet.

4. Athletes should never be made to jump over something in an effort to encourage height at takeoff. This will cause them to draw up the legs into a tucked position, the exact opposite of the "hang" position they should be learning.

5. Little or no explanation of takeoff theory should be given, especially about the length of the last three or four strides. Avoid remarks about "slamming the foot down hard." Similarly, it is doubtful if advice on "coasting" or "settling at the hips" will help the novice. There now appears to be some doubt about the value of these actions.

6. Sand pits should be regularly dug over. Sand should be raked from the sides of the pit toward the center to avoid banks building up around the pit.

7. A wooden distance indicator board beside the pit is much appreciated by all athletes.

8. Do not attempt to teach everything at once. Allow frequent opportunity for jumping with a full run-up, right from the start.

9. Remember that a good run-up, takeoff, and landing are the essential features. Improving the balance in the air will improve the landing and enable the athlete to land with the heels well out ahead of him.

10. Encourage long jumpers to sprint and hurdle.

Chapter 12

THE LONG JUMP

by Jess Jarver

The primary objective in all competitive jumping is to project the athlete's center of gravity through the air at the maximum velocity in the required direction. If the direction is upward only, the result is the high jump; if the direction is forward and upward, the long jump results.

The long jump starts with a run-up aiming to accumulate maximum horizontal speed. The jumper attempts to approach the takeoff board with extreme accuracy before becoming airborne with a minimum loss of momentum.

The takeoff action, responsible to project the jumper at the optimum angle into the air, takes a little over a tenth of a second. During this short period, the takeoff foot is actively planted onto the board; the shock is absorbed by a slight flexion of the ankle, knee and hip joints, and is followed by a vigorous extension of all these joints.

The explosive extension which lifts the jumper off the board is assisted by the swinging movements of the free leg and arms. The center of gravity (C of G) of the jumper now leaves the board at an angle of about 20 degrees, and as contact is lost with the ground, the forces developed during the run-up and takeoff become effective. To counteract adverse forces, retain balance and attain a most economical landing position, the jumper employs a movement pattern while in flight.

The distance achieved in the long jump depends mainly on the velocity and direction of forces applied at the takeoff, when horizontal speed is transferred at the desirable angle. Once contact has been lost with the ground, the jumper's center of gravity will follow a predetermined flight curve which cannot be altered by any action on the part of the jumper. However, in order to obtain the maximum possible distance, the jumper can adjust his limbs and body relative to his center of gravity at any given time to obtain a more economical landing position.

It is therefore generally accepted that the primary aim in the long jump is to obtain maximum takeoff velocity and project the jumper through the air at the best possible trajectory. Hence the most important phases in the long jump are the approach run and the takeoff.

The sequence of movements in the air, depending largely on the forces developed at the takeoff which become effective once the body has left the ground, are of minor value and are regarded as the secondary aim in the long jump, and should not be overestimated.

Even though speed and spring are the major factors in deciding the distance jumped, and no action can alter the parabola of the jumper's center of gravity, the jump should still be regarded as a complete unit from the start of the approach run to the final movements of the landing. It is essential not to overlook the fact that the efficiency of the landing is dependent upon the mid-air movements, which in turn are closely related to the effectiveness of a properly executed takeoff and run-up. The landing itself actually epitomizes all that has gone before, and in most cases cannot be improved or corrected without changing the actions preceding it. The jump must be regarded as a whole, even though it is usually divided into separate phases for analysis and learning.

It is apparently the simplicity of long jumping, depending so much on the horizontal velocity of the approach run and the forces applied at the takeoff, that has kept improvements relatively small. With speed being the biggest factor, Powell points out that "It is a basic principle of dynamics, that other factors being equal, the greatest horizontal distance is achieved by the body having the greatest horizontal velocity at the takeoff." Thus, progress in long jumping has closely followed the pattern of sprinting. It took 35 years (from Al Kraenzlein to Jesse Owens) to add less than two feet to the world mark, and in the following 30 years only another few inches have been accumulated. Even in depth there has been nothing comparable to the tremendous upward surge registered in most other track and field events. The only exception was Bob Beamon's fantastic 29'2½" (8.90 meters) leap at the 1968 Olympic Games in Mexico City.

There has also been very little development in the actual techniques employed. In the early 1920's, the "hitch-kick" or a modified "running in the air" action started to take over from the so-called "sail" jump, and toward the end of the decade, the latter had virtually disappeared among leading exponents.

A better version of the sail—the step technique—which kept a wide striding position until the actual landing when the trailing leg was brought forward, still continued. But it was used mainly by beginners, learners, or those who possessed excellent sprinting speed but regarded long jumping as a side event.

Although the event, for obvious reasons, was still dominated by first-class sprinters, emphasis on the takeoff and a better movement pattern in the flight soon allowed fewer fast athletes to enjoy success. Better understanding of the mechanics involved in the jumping increased the depth of the performances until the general acceptance of the hitch-kick virtually forced the development of long jump technique to a standstill. Further improvements have been due mainly to the increased participation in track and field, better facilities, and improved physical conditioning methods.

It is therefore apparent that due to the inherited characteristics of speed and the already rather thoroughly exploited methods of increasing strength, the future improvements in the long jump can be expected mainly through improved technique in the transfer of run-up speed.

It has been clearly shown that speed and spring are the two most important single factors deciding the distance jumped. At the same time it is true that neither speed nor spring can be at its maximum, as it is impossible to integrate maximum speed with a maximum takeoff effort.

THE RUN-UP

The run-up, responsible for accumulation of maximum horizontal velocity without inhibiting the takeoff, is the most important single phase in the long jump. It must be sufficiently long to enable the athlete to reach the board at close to maximum speed; it must be controlled to permit an effective takeoff; it must be precise to bring the takeoff foot square on the board.

Length

To reach what can be called the "peak-controlled velocity" is perhaps the greatest single problem in long jumping. Available research data, although limited, indicates that regardless of his sprinting ability, the human being reaches maximum speed in about six seconds. This means that if a jumper is to reach top speed, he requires a run-up of more than 60 yards. However, the same research shows that at about 50 yards the athlete is within one percent of his maximum speed. As the additional speed gained between 50 and 60 yards is apparently imperceptible, it appears that a run-up close to 150 feet is sufficient for most athletes.

Geoffrey Dyson has observed that long jumpers attain no more than approximately 95 percent of their maximum sprint speed in the approach run. Thus, according to Fred Wilt, a jumper whose best 100-yard time is 10.0 seconds will average 30 feet per second, and his run-up speed prior to the takeoff will be 28.5 feet per second (95 percent of the maximum). He will cover the final 20 yards in 2.1 seconds. By the same token, a long jumper capable of 9.6 for the 100 yards will clock 2.02 seconds over the last 20 yards, moving at a speed of 29.7 feet per second.

The exact length of approach is obviously an individual matter and depends mainly on the ability to accelerate, the age of the jumper and the stage of training he has reached. The latter is perhaps the most important, because to increase the length of the run-up, the jumper must have gained sufficient strength through training to enable him to have the required control and energy for the takeoff lift.

The approximate length of the run-up can be established by a series of 50- to 60-yard sprints on a cinder track, or on a similar surface where foot marks can be observed. Stride length will become constant when the athlete reaches his maximum speed, thus allowing the most suitable length of approach to be determined.

It can be generally said that the run-up for experienced long jumpers is somewhere between 130 to 150 feet, involving 17 to 23 running strides. The possibility of a slightly longer approach should not be overlooked when dealing with well conditioned top-rate jumpers.

Uniformity

Although the approach in the long jump should be an accumulation of speed right from the first stride, it differs from a sprint acceleration because of the urgent necessity of bringing the jumper's takeoff foot at maximum controlled velocity accurately to the takeoff board. This requires careful precision in the stride pattern and a consistent rate of acceleration.

To achieve uniformity in the stride length and consistency in acceleration, the approach run must begin from the same position with the same rate of acceleration (obviously maximum) and no variations whatsoever.

The most common starting position is a stand-up start with feet parallel, but a crouch start, even with the use of starting blocks, might add to the precision. Experience has shown that the most erratic steps are the first one or two, so every effort is needed to standardize these through body angle and the length of the first stride. It is also usual that the last few strides before the takeoff cause upsets in the exactness of the approach if the jumper attempts to make last-second adjustments. This can be avoided through constant practice.

Although many jumpers use check marks, their practical value is rather doubtful. Check marks (usually two are used in addition to the starting mark) are only helpful in the stages when the run-up is in the process of being established. Once this has been achieved, they serve, at the most, only as a psychological aid.

The first check mark can be eliminated immediately after the beginning of the approach has been standardized. The second, often placed eight strides from the board, is useless right from the start, as it can consciously be hit only at the expense of concentration. And it is obvious that adjustments during the last few strides will only mean loss of forward speed. It is interesting to note how experienced jumpers, who by habit keep on using check marks, regularly miss them without noticing it.

Last Strides

Just before the takeoff point, all the jumper's movements should be coordinated to allow for an effective takeoff, to rocket him into the air along the desired path. This can only be achieved if the action is well under control during the last few strides of the approach run. "Control" is perhaps the key word here, as no horizontal velocity should be sacrificed, but any attempt to accelerate should also be avoided. The so-called "gather" or coast is perhaps best described as maintaining the previously attained sprinting speed while mental and physical preparations are made for the actual takeoff. Although the mental concentration necessary to exclude everything from the mind except the forthcoming leap has already started with the first stride, it reaches its peak just before the takeoff.

The physical preparations include some adjustments in adopting a more upright position of the trunk, and sometimes also slight alterations in the length of the last two strides. The straightening of the body permits the takeoff foot to reach slightly ahead of the jumper's C of G (center of gravity) for a better forward-upward drive from the board.

A shorter last stride, although different views exist about it, seems helpful to get a slight bend of the takeoff leg, described as "compressing the spring" by Geoffrey Dyson. It also permits the jumper's C of G to be directly over the board as the takeoff foot strikes, and slightly in advance of it when leaving the board.

The pattern of good long jumping is by no means consistent, but either chopping the last stride or stretching it is disadvantageous. A too short and chopped last stride would place the jumper's C of G too far ahead of his takeoff foot, making an effective lift impossible and causing an increased forward rotation. An over-stretched last stride would bring the jumper's body weight directly over the takeoff foot at the moment of the lift, or even leave it behind. In both cases the lift will be upward, resembling a high jump takeoff, and valuable forward speed will be lost.

The word "gather" should be interpreted with extreme care. As the loss of horizontal velocity must be kept to a minimum, and proper sprinting action requires relaxation anyway, the preparations for the lift are hardly noticeable in good jumpers.

Actually, many first-class jumpers apparently ignore the idea of a coast, and either sprint to the takeoff, maintaining the speed accumulated in the approach, or, in extreme cases, even attempt to accelerate. The last, however, could be dangerous, as an attempt to accelerate when moving at top speed causes tension and can have adverse influence on the actual takeoff.

There seem to be great individual differences in final stride patterns prior to takeoff. Jumpers who are very fast sprinters usually have less "gather" at the board, while those with little sprinting ability prefer to place more emphasis on the takeoff and prepare themselves, accordingly, by lowering the C of G during the final strides for a better lift from the board. Schmolinsky has recorded the following contrasting examples:

	Jumper A (Best 100m: 10.4)	*Jumper B* Best 100m: 11.0)
Third from last stride	6'10½"	6'4½"
Second from last stride	7'6½"	7'11½"
Last stride	6'10½"	6'7½"

Although there were apparently no standard changes in the length of the last strides because they vary according to the type of the jumper and his speed, an obvious change in the rhythm of the stride pattern is noticeable in most top-class jumpers. The rhythm changes occur during the last three strides, which are performed at a higher cadence than the previous sprinting strides. The changes are influenced by the C of G dropping slightly during the final strides before the takeoff, and being caught on the rise when the takeoff foot hits the board, without being allowed to drop again. The cause of the lowering of the body's C of G is the lengthening of the strides.

THE TAKEOFF

At the takeoff the jumper is concerned with two important tasks:
1. Obtaining a vertical lift
2. Maintaining as much of his horizontal speed as possible.

Thus the takeoff phase is responsible for attaining the best vertical velocity without reducing essential horizontal speed.

The action at the takeoff allows only a fraction of a second to change from horizontal speed to vertical momentum. It is achieved by the application of maximum force from the takeoff leg. The magnitude of the vertical lift depends on the time this force is applied, or the impulse. Although the duration of time over which the force can be applied is important, it is the intensity of force (maximum power) that decides the effectiveness of the takeoff.

The takeoff is usually divided into three major phases:
1. The foot plant.
2. The absorption of the impact.
3. The active lift.

In planting the takeoff foot, the action is similar to the actual movement in running. The jumper does not wait until the foot has touched the track, but he places the leg on the board in an active backward and downward movement. The knee is only fractionally bent as the foot touches the board.

As the takeoff foot is planted, the forces of active placement and transfer of the body weight onto the takeoff leg are absorbed by a slight flexion in the ankle, knee and hip joints. The knee starts to bend as the jumper's C of G continues to move forward and reaches 145 to 150 degrees at the moment when the jumper's C of G is directly over the takeoff foot. During the flexing of the knee joint, the extensors in the takeoff leg are pre-tensed for the following explosive stretching action.

As the C of G moves forward, the takeoff leg starts to extend until the toes leave the board, approximately 12 to 16 inches behind the jumper's C of G, with the takeoff leg forming an angle of about 80 degrees with the track. As the jumper's takeoff leg moves over the ball of the foot, pre-tension of the foot extensors is created to conclude the lift off the board. Finally, the jumper is projected into the air with the trunk upright, strongly assisted by the upward-forward swinging movements of the free leg and arms.

The whole action from the moment the takeoff foot touches the board until it leaves, takes, according to Schmolinsky, only 0.12 seconds. During this short time the theoretical length of the jump will be determined by the takeoff velocity, takeoff angle and forces created by the jumper.

Velocity at the Takeoff

It is impossible to perform the takeoff without reduction of speed, because the takeoff foot, which must lift the jumper, must therefore dwell on the board longer than would be the case during the supporting phase in sprinting. As the takeoff foot contacts the board, a further loss occurs, because the thrust checks the jumper's forward speed. Research data from the U.S.S.R. indicates that about 6 percent of forward velocity is lost during the next-to-last stride when the jumper is preparing for takeoff. A further 10 to 15 percent is lost during the takeoff itself.

To cut this deceleration to a minimum, the jumper is forced to compromise between run-up speed and takeoff force. As neither speed nor spring can be at maximum, Geoffrey Dyson suggests that the proportion should be approximately two to one in favor of horizontal velocity. This means that more explosive power must be developed during the takeoff to avoid sacrificing forward momentum attempting to obtain a better lift.

The force developed at the takeoff in a vertical jump from a squat position ranges from about 180 to 1000 pounds. Therefore, at the end of the takeoff it becomes obvious that the deciding force is applied during the last phase of the extension of the knee joint. This makes over-bending of the knee and a reaching

Figure 114.   Takeoff Action. Note the path of C of G as it travels through a distance of about 3 ft. 6 in. and is continually rising.

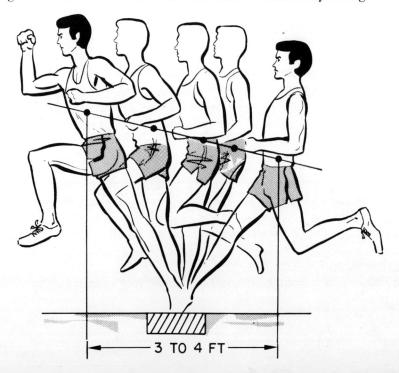

3 TO 4 FT

last stride dangerous, as both will reduce forward speed without adding much to the lifting force. (See Fig. 114.) Normally the lower leg makes an angle of approximately 120 degrees with the ground as it hits the takeoff board.

Takeoff Action

The takeoff action must be executed so that it ensures full continuity of changing the run-up into a jump. The takeoff foot must strike the board just in front of the jumper's C of G which is directly over the board when the foot has "settled." The heel hits first, but a full heel-to-ball-to-toes roll is not practical in the long jump, since it would mean a loss of forward speed. The flat of the foot is put down fast and firm with the knee slightly flexed. The body weight passes over the takeoff leg which is extended, powerfully driving the jumper forward-upward with the maximum vertical impulse directed through the jump-er's C of G. The C of G has meanwhile been caught on a slight rise as it has traveled through a distance of three to four feet while the takeoff foot has been in contact with the board. (See Fig. 114.)

Simultaneously the free leg, shoulders and arms are accelerated upward to add to the impulse of the lift. The proper use of the swinging movements of the free leg and arms is important. Provided the momentum achieved through the swinging movements coincides with the force achieved by the extension of the takeoff leg and is directed in the right direction (through the jumper's C of G), it adds considerably to the vertical impulse of the jumper.

According to Korenberg, the swinging movements also lead to an increase in the distance between the jumper's C of G and the point of support. Thus the instant the takeoff is completed, the body's C of G is more displaced in the direction of the swing. (See Fig. 115.)

Figure 115.   Movement of jumper's C of G's at the takeoff. C—C of G of the body. C_A—C of G of the arm. C_L—C of G of the leg.

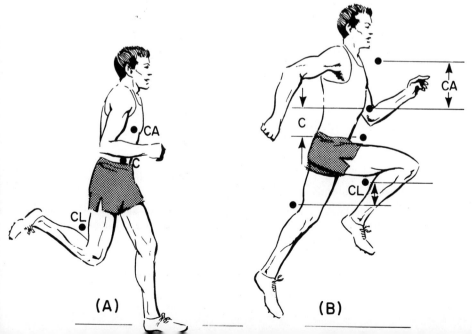

(A)   (B)

It is noticeable, according to Yuri Verhoshanski, that at the start of the takeoff the mass of the swinging parts of the body has a negative acceleration compared with the jumper's C of G. As the C of G of the swinging parts shifts forward, the vertical acceleration changes to positive. The supporting force is now directed downward, the load on the supporting force is increased, and the vertical acceleration once again changes to negative. In experienced jumpers the maximum force of the swing precedes the straightening action of the supporting leg, as the forces acting on the point of support are reduced with the final effort of the takeoff leg.

As the swinging movements are most effective toward the end of the supporting phase, the importance of the second part of the takeoff is once more emphasized. It is here that by making full use of the free leg and arm power, a more vigorous transference of momentum is created without sacrificing speed. (See Fig. 116.)

TYPICAL EXAMPLES OF THE RELATIONSHIP BETWEEN
SWINGING MOVEMENTS AND THE SUPPORTING LEG.

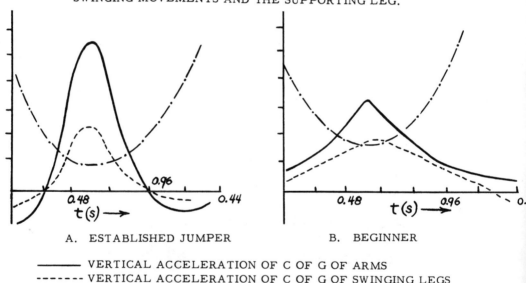

A. ESTABLISHED JUMPER   B. BEGINNER

───────── VERTICAL ACCELERATION OF C OF G OF ARMS
- - - - - - - VERTICAL ACCELERATION OF C OF G OF SWINGING LEGS
—·—·— ANGLE OF BEND OF SUPPORTING LEG

Figure 116.

Only when all movements at the takeoff are coordinated and the jumper's C of G is directly over the line of forces exerted, will the body be driven at the maximum possible speed in the required direction. This is achieved by coordinating the free leg and arm swing so that it starts with the takeoff drive. A simultaneous increase of the force and duration of this action leads to an increase in the force impulse.

The importance of developing speed in all takeoff movements should be obvious as the faster the body is projected into the air the higher it will rise, and the greater the distance of C of G will travel. However, to ensure that the takeoff is allowed to exert its full force, there must be no attempt to introduce other movements before it has been completed. An attempt to rush into the movements of only secondary importance (the action in the air) affects the efficiency of the takeoff.

Takeoff Angle

The optimum angle of 45 degrees for the projection of a missile is not suitable for the long jump takeoff. To avoid losses in horizontal velocity a much lower angle is necessary. A projection of the C of G at a 45 degree angle would require slowing down on the board (or a takeoff thrust backwards)—both achieved only through considerable loss of horizontal velocity.

It should be mentioned, too, that 45 degrees is the optimum angle only when the C of G would be at the same level at the takeoff and landing points. In the long jump it is higher at the instant of the takeoff. (See Fig. 117.)

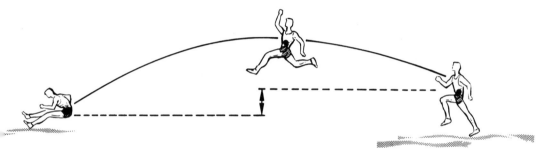

Figure 117.   Flight path of C of G. Note that C of G is lower at landing.

It has been generally recommended that the takeoff angle (the angle between a vertical line and the line from the takeoff foot through the jumper's C of G) should be below 30 degrees. (See Fig. 118.) In fact, film studies of first-class performers show a wide variety of takeoff angles with the majority falling between 15 and 25 degrees. The exact angle of projection apparently depends on the jumper's sprinting and jumping abilities and how he compromises between the horizontal and vertical takeoff velocities.

Rotation

The reaction to the forces created at the takeoff initiate certain rotations. The turning effects in these rotations depend on the magnitude of the force and on the length of the lever-arm. Theoretically, a jumper can leave the board with forward or backward or no rotation at all.

In practice, however, the forward rotation is most common. It occurs through the pivoting action over the takeoff foot while it is momentarily at rest on the board, and the vertical component of the jumper's leg thrust is behind his C of G. This causes the athlete to leave the board with not only linear acceleration but also with forward rotation around his C of G.

25°

Figure 118.   A typical takeoff angle.

Fortunately, the jumper may control this rotation in the air to a certain degree. Since he is unable to change his total angular momentum in flight, reversing or slowing forward rotation must be achieved by creating sufficient forward rotation in his legs to exceed his total angular momentum.

The Landing

The landing depends very much on the previous phases, especially the takeoff and the action in the flight. The aim in the landing is to achieve a position with the feet far forward of the jumper's C of G without falling back in the pit. Though there is nothing the athlete can do to change the path of his C of G once the body is in flight, he can rotate his limbs around it to achieve a more efficient landing position. Thus, while the arc traveled by the C of G has a predetermined distance, the actual distance jumped can be lessened or increased by the position of the body and legs at the moment of the landing.

The best position for landing is described by Geoffrey Dyson as one which continues the flight trajectory of the C of G as far as possible and provides the greatest possible distance between the jumper's heels and his C of G without causing him to fall back. (See Fig. 119.)

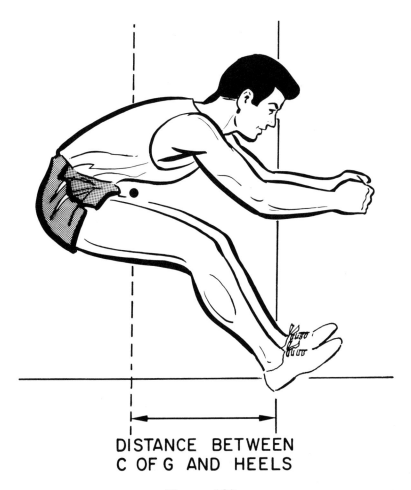

DISTANCE BETWEEN
C OF G AND HEELS

Figure 119.

Rajko Miler suggests that the jumper's feet should touch the pit at the point where the tangent to the flight path of the C of G, drawn at the moment of making contact, crosses the plane of the pit. (See Figs. 120 and 121.) In practice, however, it seems unlikely that the jumper's heels will contact the pit beyond or even in the line of the flight curve of his C of G. Investigations by McIntosh and Hayley at the Birmingham University found that, despite the position of the trunk, the feet of the jumpers always cut the sand nearer to the takeoff board than the trajectory of the C of G.

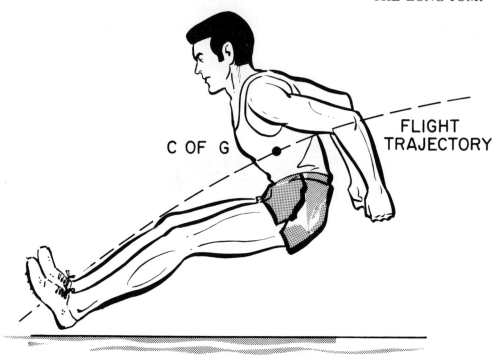

Figure 120.

Although the landing action depends on the jump itself and on the flight technique employed, the legs are brought forward, with the knees slightly bent and the trunk as far upright as possible. Ideally the arms should be pointing backwards just before the landing to assist in keeping the trunk erect. At the moment the heels cut the sand, the arms are brought forward to pivot the body over the heels with knees now well bent to absorb the shock and shorten the

Figure 121.

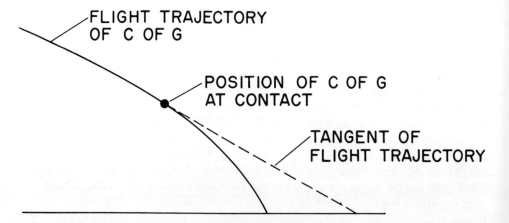

FLIGHT TRAJECTORY
OF C OF G

POSITION OF C OF G
AT CONTACT

TANGENT OF
FLIGHT TRAJECTORY

a. b. c.

Figure 122. Compromise in Landing Positions (a.) Trunk well back lowers the hips in relation to C of G and causes falling back. (b.) Trunk well forward forces the hips and legs prematurely down. (c.) Compromised position.

"body" lever pivoting over the fulcrum of the feet. The farther back the trunk in landing, the greater the distance achieved, as it allows the legs to be stretched out well ahead of the jumper's C of G. However, this has its limits because a backward-leaning trunk will lower the hips in relation to the jumper's C of G and will force him to fall back in the pit. At the same time it must be remembered that the farther forward the position of the trunk, the shorter the distance jumped. With the head, shoulders and arms forward and downward, the hips and legs in relation to the jumper's C of G are also forced down. This necessitates a compromise position at landing. (See Fig. 122.)

It is obvious that a good landing position is achieved in different ways, depending on the technique employed during the flight and the amount of rotation created at takeoff. In the sail type mid-air action where the jumper takes the landing position immediately after the takeoff and is unable to reverse or reduce forward rotation during the flight, the landing position can only be poor. The forward position of the trunk forces the hips and legs back and the heels prematurely into the pit.

In the hang technique the trunk is erect during flight and the jumper is in a good position to fold from the hips immediately before the landing. The folding or "jacking" movement increases angular velocity, although it is necessary in raising and extending the heels just before they cut the sand.

In the hitch-kick, if correctly executed, the trunk should be erect with one leg forward when approaching the landing. The trailing leg is brought forward to join the leading leg just before the actual landing takes place. It is important to reach this position late, as when it is attained too soon the jumper will be rotating forward again. At the moment the jumper makes contact with the ground in the hitch-kick landing, he has the choice of two different procedures. He can land in an elongated position over bent knees, or over the bent trailing leg which has caught up in the last moment.

Although all long jumpers are aware of the need to keep the legs up as high as possible on landing and the trunk leaning backward, it is noticeable that this position is never achieved. In an attempt to avoid sitting back (and because of the forward rotation originated at the takeoff), a compromise is reached, with

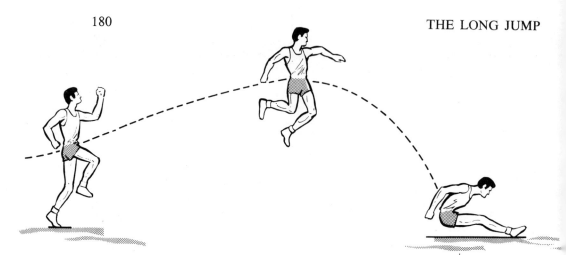

Figure 123.   The pre-set vertical parabola in the long jump. Note that air resistance slows down horizontal motion and blunts the flight path slightly. In jumping it is very negligible and the path can be considered as parabolic.

the trunk leaning slightly forward and the legs dropping below horizontal immediately before the landing.

The Flight

As the result of the impulses derived during the run-up and takeoff, the jumper leaves the board with a certain amount of horizontal and vertical momentum and, in most cases, also with some forward rotation. Once he has left the ground, he can do nothing to change the path of his C of G nor his total angular momentum. The jumper's C of G will travel along a pre-set parabola. (See Fig. 123.)

While the run-up, takeoff, and perhaps the landing are the important factors in deciding the distance jumped, the actual movements in the flight are only of secondary value. Their main purpose is to counteract any rotation developed at the takeoff, and to adjust the jumper's limbs around his C of G for the most efficient landing position. For this, three basic techniques—the sail, the hang and the hitch-kick—have been used.

The Sail

The Sail is a very natural jump with little demand in the learning stages. After leaving the board, the jumper bunches up with his feet and legs assuming the landing position immediately after takeoff. By bunching into the sail position, the body mass is brought closer to the C of G. This does nothing to counteract forward rotation developed at the takeoff. On the contrary, the angular velocity is increased and forward rotation is sped up. Further, the trunk comes forward to meet the legs, causing the hips and legs to move back. This forces the heels prematurely into the pit, making an efficient landing a virtual impossibility. It is a technique used only by beginners and is not recommended.

The Hang

In the hang technique (Fig. 124) the jumper, after executing the takeoff movements, extends his body in the flight. Once the free leg has completed its drive, it is dropped and moved backward. It joins the takeoff leg, both trailing the now extended body with the arms raised and pointing vertically upward. The moment of inertia about the horizontal axis of momentum is increased, and any forward rotation developed at the takeoff is therefore slowed. But as the legs are passive in the flight, insufficient angular momentum is developed to exceed the total angular momentum of the jumper to completely counteract the forward rotation. At the instant the movements in the air are completed and the legs are brought forward for landing, the original body rotation will again reveal itself.

This makes it necessary for the jumper to move his arms vigorously forward, down, and backward from their position above the head, before the landing. The arm swing coincides with the forward movement of the legs, which are bent at the knees. If the legs are brought through straight, the trunk will be dragged forward and down. If only the arms are swung downward and forward, it would shift the hips and legs farther back, as in the sail technique. Either action will bring about a poor landing.

Figure 124. The Hang.

Because the action in the air is passive, there is risk of assuming an early landing position. This will permit a return to the original forward rotation and must be avoided. The arm and leg movements in the hang should be completed only immediately prior to the actual landing.

The pure hang technique, mainly because it lacks sufficient leg movement to absorb and counteract forward rotation, has lost its previous popularity. However, some athletes successfully combine the hang with the hitch-kick action. This can best be achieved by hanging during the first part of the jump and, after having reached the highest point in flight, continuing with the hitch-kick into the pit. It keeps the already erect trunk in an advantageous position, and by the added leg movement it will, if properly executed, avoid the re-occurrence of the original forward rotation before the landing.

The Hitch-Kick

To counteract any forward rotation developed at the takeoff, and to achieve the most economical position for the landing, the most commonly employed mid-air action is the hitch-kick (Figure 125), sometimes also called "running in the air." The benefits of the hitch-kick might be exaggerated, because the action in the air is only of secondary importance. However, the hitch-kick permits a smooth takeoff, balance in the flight, and makes possible an excellent landing position. The angular momentum created by the forward rotation of the legs and vigorous action of the arms develops sufficient angular momentum to absorb the forward rotation and assists in turning the trunk and hips backward. This, in turn, permits a most efficient landing procedure, provided the legs are not brought forward too early.

Figure 125.   The Hitch-Kick.

In the hitch-kick, the jumper, on leaving the board, lifts the thigh of the free leg through a vigorous knee pick-up and leaves the takeoff leg dragging behind. The free leg is then moved downward and backward as a long lever while the takeoff leg, having flexed after the takeoff drive has finished, comes forward well bent, forming a short lever. The angular momentum generated by the straight leg moving downward-backward is balanced by the reaction of an equal angular momentum in the trunk in the opposite direction. Some of this momentum is reduced by the other leg moving forward. But as it comes through as a short lever, it produces much less angular momentum, allowing the trunk to rotate backward. The angular velocity of both legs is the same, but the angular momentum due to the different length of the leg-levers differs.

The rotation of the legs is assisted by synchronized arm action. The arm opposite to the takeoff leg helps the swinging movements at the takeoff by moving through a downward-backward direction, and the other arm continues in a backward circle.

A possible second stride follows the first, after the position of the legs has been reversed. At this stage, when the free leg is pulled through to join the relatively high leading leg, the danger of the original forward rotation, just prior to landing, is again imminent. This is because further backward rotation of the trunk is lost once the leg movement in the flight has been completed. This problem can be partially counteracted by a more efficient use of the arms and, even better, by adding another stride in the air. The additional stride, provided the jump is long enough to allow its completion, will not only add to the backward turning of the trunk, but will also prevent the trunk from rotating forward again during the brief passive wait for the landing.

Detailed Analysis of the Hitch-Kick

Before studying this detailed analysis of "proper" technique, remember it is advisable to keep in mind that it is wrong to accept every champion as a representative of "perfect" technique. It is also incorrect to copy the technique of a champion without fully understanding his good and bad points, and the reasons why he employs certain actions.

Without a clear picture of sound mechanics of an event, there is also danger of copying the unimportant—the individual and manneristic parts of the action—and overlooking the deciding factors of technique, which are sometimes hidden in a deceptive way.

First, it must be kept in mind that what appears to be perfect technique for one athlete may not necessarily be sound for another. Several individual characteristics, such as natural speed, mobility, flexibility, range of movements, strength, etc., make different approaches to technique necessary. It is impossible to describe a standard technique suitable for all athletes.

Also there is always the question, often remaining unanswered, of whether the athlete succeeded because of the technique he employed, or in spite of it. Without details of the jumper's individual characteristics, his training background and many other personal factors, it is often impossible to give an answer, because even some glaringly obvious shortcomings in technique can have a cause unknown to the analyzer.

However, generally speaking, all champions employ sound basic mechanics in their jumping technique. It might sometimes be hidden behind some impressive refinements, sometimes behind a clumsy sequence of movements, but at a closer look it is always there. It is the ability, consciously or unconsciously, to separate the decisive basic mechanical factors from the unimportant that distinguishes the champion from the average competitor.

The Run-up (Objective: Accumulate Horizontal Velocity)

Figure 127.

Figure 128.

Figure 126.

Figure 129.

Figure 130.

Figure 131.

Figure 132.

Figure 133.

Figure 134.

Figure 135.

Figure 136.

Figure 137.

Figure 138.

Figure 139.

Figure 140.

Figure 126:   The jumper is approaching the board and is showing a slight "gather" to prepare for the jump. He has lowered his hips to drop his C of G during the supporting phase of the stride before the takeoff. This enables him to catch the C of G moving forward and up as the takeoff foot strikes (Fig. 126). If used, this "gather" must be executed with extreme care to avoid any loss of horizontal speed.

Figure 127:   The jumper demonstrates relaxed sprint form just before the takeoff leg starts moving forward, ahead of the body.

The Takeoff (Objective: Achieve Maximum Vertical Lift)

Figure 128:   The jumper is about to complete his last stride, with body erect and eyes looking straight forward, indicating confidence in his well executed run-up. The takeoff foot has moved well ahead of the C of G as it is ready to strike the board.

Figure 129:   The takeoff foot hits the board almost flat. The swinging leg is left well behind, with the heel high as it is swung through, perfectly relaxed, and is now ready to assist in the creation of vertical impulse as it starts a fast short-lever action forward and up.

Figure 130:   As the jumper's C of G passes the vertical plane of the foot in contact with the board, the takeoff leg, slightly flexed to reduce resistance to forward motion, starts to drive.

Figure 131:   The drive is strongly assisted by the free leg swing, which forms a pendulum with a short radius and moves at remarkable speed. (Compare the driving leg's knee joint extension and the jumper's arm movement with the great speed of the swinging leg.) The free leg swing has been well coordinated with the takeoff leg and precedes its final extension.

Figure 132:   The vigorous extension of the takeoff leg, having used every available force to propel the athlete forward and upward, has been completed. The jumper has lost contact with the ground, and the flight path and the velocity of the C of G have been determined.

The Flight (Objective: Absorb Any Rotation which Occurred at the Takeoff, and Prepare for an Efficient Landing)

Figure 133:   The jumper has left the ground with a slight forward rotation and starts to absorb it by creating local rotations around his C of G through the hitch-kick movements.

The free leg starts moving down and backward in a long lever action while the takeoff leg, flexed in reaction to the drive, is brought forward as a short lever. The arms, supporting the action vigorously, help with balance and also contribute slightly toward efforts to create a backward rotation.

Figure 134:   The second stride in the air has commenced with the body erect and the trunk taking a slight backward lean. The arm and leg work is well coordinated as the left leg begins to move downward in a long lever while the right starts to flex.

Figure 135:   With the long extended body, the hitch-kick movement continues as the backward-moving leg sweeps through a long lever motion and the forward-moving leg travels, well bent, as a short lever.

Figure 136:   Preparations for the landing start as another stride begins with the right leg moving forward once more.

The Landing (Objective: Place Feet Well Ahead of the Jumper's Center of Gravity)

Figure 137:   The jumper is reaching a good landing position with the right leg high and well extended, while the left leg has started its recovery to join the right leg. The right arm moves forward and downward.

Figure 138:   The jumper has arrived in the landing position just before his heels are ready to break the sand. It is through the delayed arrival in the landing position that very little of the original forward rotation is evident. An early completion of the hitch-kick action would have permitted the original forward rotation generated at takeoff to again reveal itself, causing the feet to drop prematurely before landing.

Figure 139:   The heels break the sand well in advance of the jumper's trunk. The knees have started to flex to enable the body to pivot over the fulcrum of the feet in an effort to avoid falling back. Since the arms have been kept forward during this phase, they contribute very little toward the forward motion which is achieved mainly by the thrust of head and shoulders.

Figure 140:   The landing has been successfully completed as the body has pivoted over the relaxed and flexed knees.

TRAINING

General

Training is usually defined as "bringing a person to a desired state or standard of efficiency." In the long jump, as in all track and field events, the desired efficiency is extremely high. A successful approach to long jump training must therefore carefully cover all aspects to achieve the highest possible level of physiological, psychological and technical fitness. The key word here is "careful," as all phases in training must take their place in proportion to the demands made by the event, as well as the individual's mental and physical characteristics.

The long jumper's training program is based on two accepted factors: progressive loading and the interval principle. This means that whatever the methods used, the progressive increase in the intensity of work should be adapted in a form of rhythmical pattern of efforts and recoveries. The intensity of the work is not fixed, although targets of fitness and skill are constantly moved higher. It includes harder and easier phases as well as full recoveries, with each phase having its own interval arrangement.

A specific event like the long jump needs its own specific type of training and physical fitness. Maximum performances can result only from a broad and complex training program which, besides the training for the event itself, includes a certain amount of work to improve both the hard core of basic fitness and specific fitness. However, care must be taken that the supplementary training is not overemphasized so as to exclude practicing the event itself. Both conditioning and the perfection of jumping technique must be kept in their proper proportion and conducted in close unity.

Since the predominant factors for quality performance in the long jump are speed, power, mobility, coordination and neuro-muscular skill, the best results are obtained by emphasizing these factors in training with the end product constantly in mind.

Speed

Mechanically speaking, speed is the distance covered in a time unit. In long jumping the main concern is the speed in the approach run and the speed of the takeoff. Both depend largely on an apparently inherited ability to contract muscle fibers fast and on efficient neuro-muscular coordination.

Nothing can be done to alter the inherited structure of muscle fiber. However, by improving the collaborative effort of muscles and nerves and the related qualities, such as strength, power and skill, both run-up and takeoff speeds can be improved. This is achieved by continuous high speed repetitions of the movements concerned until all components form a more rational pattern of the overall action and the disturbing and hindering movements are eliminated by the nervous system.

Since speed contributes at least two-thirds toward the final long jump result, its place in training obviously must take an important position. In the early stages of his career, the long jumper benefits by training with sprinters. But as soon as his basic sprinting skill has been established, the speed work must become specific for long jumping. The jumper is still involved in the development of muscular power, mobility and neuro-muscular coordination in order to improve his speed, but most other aspects of sprinting are relatively unimportant. There is no need for reaction speed to the starter's gun, and no demand for local muscular endurance to maintain speed. A certain amount of toleration to oxygen debt and general endurance, measured by the efficiency of the cardio-respiratory system, are required in an indirect way. Although both of these qualities are of no direct value in competition, because there is usually enough time to recover between competitive jumps, they are nevertheless needed in training to enable the athlete to perform more work in the time available.

The speed training of the long jumper, except in the general conditioning phases, should therefore concentrate mainly on full speed sprinting at distances of about 50 yards, numerous repetitions of the actual run-up with sufficiently long recoveries, and takeoff practice at full speed. Full speed must be emphasized for all these training routines. It is only through high-speed repetitions that the nervous system becomes accustomed to coordinating the muscles needed for the particular movements and eliminating superfluous and antagonistic muscle action.

Power

Mechanically, power is the rate of doing work. In human performances it is speed and strength combined to develop fast, explosive movements against resistance. Power depends upon the tension muscles can develop in moving the body levers, the range through which muscles act upon levers, and the rate at which this action occurs. Development of power is closely related to strength and speed as, within certain limits, an increase of strength will bring an increase in velocity. It is also closely allied to skill training through the force-velocity relationship, employment of the best lever system, and coordination of movement.

In long jump training the power is developed through improving both strength and technique. It applies for the power required in the run-up as well as the power needed for an explosive takeoff. If the skill training is performed as closely as possible to the precise velocity-resistance relationship, and the best lever system is employed in the running and jumping techniques, the remaining important factor for developing power in long jumping is strength.

Muscular strength, the capacity to exert maximum force to overcome resistance, is developed through progressive resistance exercises, mainly weight training and self-resistance exercises. Isometric, and combined isometric-isotonic exercises, lacking motivation and dynamic action, seem to have little value for long jumpers with the exception of perhaps being used for the treatment of injuries.

Although the degree of strength required in all phases of long jumping is very high, strength training should not become an end in itself. As in speed training, the training for strength must be specific. After an all-around training program has developed a satisfactory standard of strength, the exercises chosen must be closely related to the "real" action. This means emphasis on exercises to develop ankle, leg and abdominal muscles, with weights and without. When an artificial load, such as the barbell is used, it is important to analyze the exercises thoroughly to assure that they have direct value to a particularly important phase in the long jump.

Development of power for the execution of a particular skill, such as the long jump, cannot be attained only by development of the components of power in isolation. The exercises for the development of these components must be closely related to the movements in the skill and accompanied by repetitive practice of the skill itself.

Other Factors

There seems to be no need to emphasize the importance of mobility and suppleness in long jumping, as this applies to all track and field events and there are numerous exercises to choose from. However, the neuro-muscular coordination, an area much in need of more research, should be mentioned.

It is obvious that a great deal of significance must be attached to technique, too, especially in dealing with young jumpers. The structure of the movements in the run-up and takeoff, the execution of the movements in the air, and the rhythm of the jump as a whole nccd considerable attention.

While training with a full-length and full speed approach is ideal to establish the whole jumping action, it is often more practical to work on only one phase of the event at a time, in practice. First, the jumper does not have sufficient endurance to execute the number of "total" jumps required in the time available for his training. Second, it has been indicated that the central nervous system suffers from fatigue when under constant demand to put together a series of complicated movements at great speed.

To overcome these difficulties, the jumper must compromise and combine short run-up jumps with specialized conditioning exercises, such as jumping with and without weights to imitate the jumping action.

TRAINING IN DETAIL

The training of the long jumper, according to his individual inherited characteristics and his athletic age, is based on the following:
1. General conditioning
2. Specific conditioning
3. Technique training

These three basic factors are responsible for the following:
1. Development of general endurance and good all-around strength.
2. Development of power, spring and specific endurance.
3. Development of the movement pattern and rhythm of all phases of the jump.

Individual differences between the jumpers and their stages of training make it impossible to establish a pattern of distribution of each of the three elements in the training plan, but usually general conditioning is emphasized in the early stages of the jumper's career, with specific conditioning gradually taking over as the jumper becomes established. (See Fig. 141.)

Figure 141.

DISTRIBUTION OF GENERAL AND SPECIFIC CONDITIONING

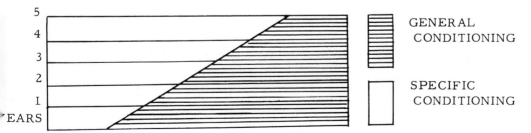

The Technique training follows a slightly different pattern and, while the beginner will spend much of his training time in learning the various aspects of long jump technique, the established jumper will be more concerned with the elimination or improvement of the particularly weak links in his technique.

The Yearly Plan

In general, a year's training plan in the long jump follows the same trend as in other track and field events. It could be divided into four major parts:

1. Active rest
2. The foundation phase
3. The preparation phase
4. The competitive phase

The four phases vary in duration and overlap each other. There are no distinct changes from one phase to another, nor is the work planned for each phase restricted to one particular training method. They can and should be adjusted to the needs of different individuals in different ways. (See Fig. 142.)

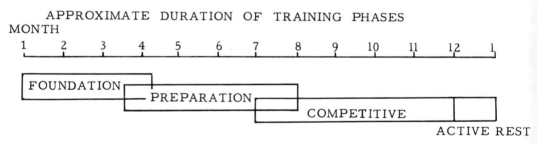

Figure 142.

Active Rest

Active rest follows the competitive season and is used as the major recovery phase from the physical and mental strains of regular training and competition. The working load is dropped considerably, but a passive rest is avoided as it would reduce the achieved level of efficiency, especially that of physical fitness. For a full mental recovery it is advisable for the jumpers to find other types of physical activities or sports. It would keep them away from the environment of familiar places and persons, the same jumping pits, dressing rooms and lockers. However, jumpers who find it difficult to pursue another sport for a short time only can participate in carefree jumping and running, or they can tackle the skills of other athletic events. These activities should be treated as fun without following a set training plan.

The duration of active rest varies from individual to individual and can last from a few weeks to a few months. Provided there is no drastic drop in the physical fitness level, a longer rest is advisable in many cases.

Foundation Phase

Immediately following the active rest, the foundation phase begins. Hard, all-around conditioning, in an attempt to lay a solid foundation of general fitness, takes priority. The work load is gradually increased with emphasis on strength, power and general endurance upon which skill and specific conditioning can be built in the following stages of training.

Training methods used in the foundation phase vary from jumper to jumper, but, in general, they include some cross-country running, Fartlek, and repetition running for improvement of the cardio-respiratory efficiency. The cross-country runs and Fartlek training should be conducted over hilly terrain with creeks and fences, to offer some jumping and bouncing activity as an added incentive.

The relative value of the general endurance training must always be kept in mind. A long jumper is not interested in becoming a first class cross-country runner. His aim is to jump farther than before. Thus his endurance work is designed to improve his cardio-respiratory efficiency to enable him to increase the amount of work in training. Improved general endurance will allow him to perform more sprinting and to execute more jumps with shorter recoveries. He can simply produce far more work in a shorter time—an important factor to most athletes in training.

Cross-country runs and Fartlek, ranging from 15 to 30 minutes in duration, are ample for the long jumper. His track work during the foundation period usually resembles that of a sprinter and is dominated by several repetitions over distances ranging from 100 to 330 yards with walking or jogging recoveries.

In addition to the attention given to the improvement of general endurance, resistance exercises to develop all-around strength, as well as specific power, are important in the foundation phase. How much of this resistance work should be directed toward all-around strength development and how much toward more specific tasks depends largely on the athletic age of the jumper. A long jumper who has reached a satisfactory level of all-around strength would be wasting his time on prototype weight training.

Basic strength training involves large muscle groups primarily and does not have to be identical to the actual long jumping itself, although exercises more directly concerned with jumping or sprinting should always be preferred. Depending on the individual (it must always be remembered how each jumper differs in his inherited characteristics and stage of development), the resistance exercises for all-around conditioning could be chosen from the following:

1. *Bouncing Exercises.* Hopping on the spot, knee-lift jumps, jack-knife jumps, jumps from squat position, skipping, etc.

2. *Jumping Exercises.* Repetition hops on both legs, repetition jumps similar to triple jump's second phase, repetition combinations of hops and steps—such as hop, hop, step, step, step, hop, hop—jumps over and on boxes and vaulting horses in a gymnasium, standing long jumps, repetition double-legged hops, standing triple jumps, etc.

3. *General Resistance Exercises.* Abdominal curls, leg raises, push-ups, leg lifts on wall bars, running in deep sand or snow, uphill sprints, sandhill sprints, etc.

4. *Resistance Exercises with Weights.* If general all-around development is desirable, the choice should come from accepted all-around weight training exercises. However, if a slightly more specific approach is required, here are some suggestions: Cleans, step-ups, half-squats, snatches, front squats, inclined sit-ups —with and without weights; leg raises—with and without iron shoes; jump squats, bouncing split squats, calf raises, resistance running, hamstring curls, split jumps with dumbbells on the bench, etc.

It must be kept in mind that the relative value of weight training for long jumpers is still an area requiring further research. Weight-trained athletes, as well as jumpers who have never touched a barbell, have been successful. It is not known whether they have succeeded because of or despite the methods employed. Generally, however, it seems that the supplement of weight training, whether it emphasizes heavy loads and limited repetitions or lighter loads and more repetitions, must be used in long jump training. However, if any doubt exists, bouncing, hopping and general resistance exercises should take priority.

The amount of skill training and actual long jumping during the foundation period depends largely on climatic conditions and available facilities. If favorable, there is no reason why they should not be included in the training programs. Provided time allows for the work on jumping technique without sacrificing an improvement in strength, endurance, and power, it is strongly recommended to include this type of work. After all, looking at the examples set in professional fields of art, one finds that the time that athletes spend on skill work is far behind that of ballet dancers.

Preparation Phase

After the change from the foundation phase to the preparation phase, the total training load starts to decrease. However, the intensity in training is still increasing, as the focus starts to shift toward specific conditioning and the completions to come. This is done gradually, ensuring that the jumper can take full advantage of the new level of physical fitness by the introduction of more skill training and specific conditioning, without allowing the hard core of fitness to drop.

During the preparation phase the emphasis from all-around resistance exercises changes to specific exercises in order to improve power under conditions as close as possible to the real movements in the long jump. The emphasis is also focused on muscle groups responsible for the major work in the actual jumping itself. Jumping in all forms, including numerous short run-up long jumps, sprinting, and a large volume of specific resistance exercises emphasizing speed-strength, form the bulk of work during the preparation phase.

The basic fitness work should always be only supplementary to the specific fitness required in long jumping. The emphasis during the preparation phase gradually shifts to aspects directly concerned with the event. At the same time it must be kept in mind that it takes years to develop the basic core of fitness, and according to the training stage of the athlete, a certain amount of conditioning work is carried out right through this phase into the competitive season.

Although it is extremely difficult to draw a distinct line between basic and specific conditioning, the following changes take place in the long jumper's work during the preparation phase:

1. Training to improve the cardio-respiratory system through cross-country runs and Fartlek is gradually dropped from the training program.
2. Emphasis on track running shifts from development of general endurance to running rhythm and direct improvement of speed.
3. Resistance exercises are gradually changed until those designed to improve leg power are predominant.
4. The amount of skill work increases from about 15 percent to 40 percent of the total.

It is during the preparation phase that the sprint training of the long jumper becomes separated from that of the sprinters. The foundation phase should be sufficient to reach basic speed endurance, and the long jumper, concerned only with explosive acceleration over a relatively short distance, changes his training accordingly. This does not mean that the long jumper is not running distances over the run-up length. He would need a certain amount of tolerance to oxygen debt in training, and the longer sprint distances are also beneficial to develop rhythm and relaxation. But besides 100-, 150- and 220-yard repetitions, the number of accelerations of distances up to 60 yards, and of the actual run-up distance, take an increasingly important part. Toward the end of the preparation phase, up to 20 repetitions of actual run-ups should regularly be included in several training sessions each week.

While jumping during the foundation phase was mainly concerned with keeping in touch with the skill and using a variation of jumps as part of the conditioning program, the preparation phase is used to improve all aspects of the actual long jump technique. For this reason, skill training is increased until at the end of this training phase it takes nearly half of the jumper's training time.

The skill practice is usually adjusted so that each phase is given separate attention in short run-up jumps. This applies for the actual long jumping as well as the specific conditioning exercises initiating a certain phase of the jump. The takeoff training employs jumps with emphasis on the full extension of the takeoff leg, forward-upward drive, and the explosive movements of the swinging leg. Landing training concentrates on getting the heels well ahead, on improvement of trunk position, and on the correct arm action.

Although takeoff action should take priority over the movements of the flight in training, both are successfully combined in jumps using three, five, seven and nine stride run-ups. Emphasis is naturally on height and correct movement sequence and not distance. Often the board is avoided in short run-up jumps to prevent injuries, but generally it is not advisable when emphasizing the whole jumping sequence, as the takeoff board increases spring and affects the timing accordingly.

Opinions differ about the advisability of full scale jumping in training. However, as skills deteriorate badly under maximum effort, it seems important to include a reasonable amount of full speed run-up jumps into the preparation phase. These assist in eliminating shortcomings, both in the jumping technique and in the run-up itself. Naturally, the full-scale jumps are not aiming for distance, but occasional jumps measured serve as an indication of training progress. After all, jumping for distance is the best test to measure the effectiveness of the preceding training.

The value of separate fitness tests should not be underestimated, and tests must regularly be included in the foundation and preparation phases. They have enormous psychological value and also help to discover weak links in the conditioning work. These tests could include maximum efforts in resistance exercises, and in activities closely allied to long jumping, such as short dashes, standing long jumps, vertical jumps, standing triple jumps, and the like.

The amount of barbell exercises to be included in the preparation period should be approached with care. The weight exercises should by no means be the main item among the wide range of resistance exercises. The jumper must have enough time and energy left to develop his specific jumping power. The interest is in developing better long jumpers, not in developing better weight lifters. Six inches gained in the long jump has more value than a 50-pound squat increase.

In deciding the weight exercises, preference should be given to rapid movements. It is also wise to avoid planning for too many weight training workouts and aiming for high poundages. Short and vigorous sessions with relatively light weights, ranging from about 50 percent up to 80 percent of the maximum should make up the bulk of the program. The maximum weight, arrived at through tests at the start of the foundation phase, should, of course, be regularly checked. This will allow for progressive increase in the weights handled by the athlete.

The choice of exercises in the early part of the preparation phase could include some leg presses and step-ups, but as the competitive season approaches, these vanish from the program, leaving only springy-type exercises with weights. Here the choice must include a variety of angles in the knee bend and in speed, to prevent a rapid adaption of the jumper to one single type of movement.

Competitive Phase

The first part of the competitive phase usually overlaps the preparation period, as competitions in the early stages should not be allowed to interfere with training. During the early part of this phase the training becomes very specific, aiming for maximum speed, an accurate run-up, and the most efficient jumping technique. Certain resistance exercises are still in the program, but the need to continue with all-around conditioning is debatable.

After the change to the competitive phase has been completed, the training load and intensity are gradually eased, allowing for longer recoveries before competitions and emphasizing quality rather than quantity.

Sprint training in the competitive phase becomes very specific and is dominated by short explosive dashes and repetitions of the actual approach runs. Longer sprint distances are in the program once or twice a week, to assure that speed endurance is kept up to the required level.

Numerous repetitions of the run-up, aiming to improve speed and accuracy, are a must. Knowing the relative value of horizontal velocity, it is advisable to conduct regular checks to assure that the jumper is moving as closely as possible to maximum speed at takeoff. The first guide is a comparison of the run-up speed in actual jumping with the speed achieved while sprinting over the approach-run distance. This will indicate approximately how much horizontal velocity is lost by the jumper when preparing for the takeoff movements. It can be checked by simply timing the athlete from the start of his run-up to the moment the takeoff foot contacts the board, and comparing it with the time over the same sequence when an actual jump is executed. Regular checks in this manner are advisable during the competitive season.

Another method of checking velocity losses at takeoff is to time the jumper over the last two, five-yard stretches before the takeoff. Comparison of the times indicates not only how much speed is lost in preparation for the takeoff but is also helpful to decide whether the run-up has been sufficiently long to allow the jumper to reach his maximum speed. The timer must stand well back from the run-up to reduce the angle of vision. (See Fig. 143.)

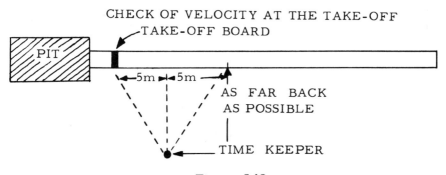

CHECK OF VELOCITY AT THE TAKE-OFF

Figure 143.

The exactness of the run-up requires more than just casual attention. After the maximum speed has been established, the work should concentrate on assuring that the jumper can cope with the direct and indirect factors influencing his run-up in competition. Among the factors to be considered are track and weather conditions, outside disturbances, physical well-being on the day, and many others. Wind conditions can change during the competition, or even during a single jump, with a sudden gust. Adjustments made according to the previous effort may be valueless. The jumper therefore has to alter his run-up practice to allow for different track and wind conditions. He also needs numerous full speed repetitions of the run-up to develop an extra sense, allowing him to make adjustments even when moving at close to maximum speed.

In order to achieve an uninhibited takeoff, the jumper must work on his run-up all the time. Hence, constant run-up practice, not only over the set approach but also in short sprints and in judgment of distances, takes priority in the competitive training phase. The jumper must have confidence in his approach, knowing that when he starts at a set point he will take off at a set point. The confidence engendered by this knowledge is measured, not in inches, but in feet, because instinctive action is always much faster than conscious movement.

There seem to be somewhat different views on the amount of jumping to be used in training during the competitive phase. It has been advised that little or no jumping is recommended during the middle and late season, as the effort of long jumping takes a great deal of the elasticity from the muscles of the jumping leg. Often champions are reported to confine their training only to sprinting and maintaining leg strength. However, it must not be overlooked that the champions usually have established a satisfactory technique and can afford to cease jumping practice at some stage during the competitive season or continue with occasional form jumping at half-effort. The champions are also competing with regular monotony, often several times a week at the height of the season. They must therefore make adjustments according to their competitive calendar and, while reducing the number of jumps executed in the preparation phase, still continue to polish the shortcomings in technique.

In actual jumping during the training sessions, the jumper is also faced with the problem of finding a suitable distribution between jumps executed at full speed with a full length run-up, and jumps with short and medium approaches (five, seven, nine or eleven strides).

It is obvious that in order to master the long jump technique, the jumping action must be divided into several parts and each part practiced by special exercises. After the execution of each phase has been mastered, the separate elements are gradually brought together to complete the action. Using a full or medium length run-up is usually unsatisfactory, and only tackling it with a five- or seven-stride approach usually proves adequate. This means that a certain amount of work, depending on the development stage of the athlete and the number of shortcomings in his technique, must be done by using repetition jumps with a short run-up until undesirable habits are broken and a desirable movement pattern has been established.

After each phase has been perfected and combined in harmony with each other into a complete jump, it must be practiced with different degrees of effort. Daily jumps using the same movement pattern, with the same degree of effort, would be useless. It is possible to execute perfect movements at a medium effort only to find them deteriorating under pressure. Hence the degree of effort must be varied when using short or medium length run-ups, and maximum speed efforts with a full run-up must also be included.

Although there has been some reluctancy about using full effort jumps in training, it must be emphasized that recent studies have demonstrated the specific nature of each skill, showing that skilled movements performed at different speeds are really quite different from each other. These studies have shown how skills deteriorate when performed under pressure at full effort.

Distribution of Work in Each Phase

The distribution of work between general conditioning, specific conditioning, technique and speed during the three major training phases (overlooking active rest), depends largely on the athletic age of the jumper, his individual characteristics and his general level of fitness. These factors also guide the approximate duration of the foundation and preparation phases, the change to competitive period and the distribution of work during the competitive season.

The training of an athlete is a continuous experimentation. Each athlete has his own individual approach to training, load and intensity during the whole year. No training plan can tell the number of repetitions to be performed of a certain exercise on a certain day in a certain phase. However, in general, the distribution of work could follow this approximate pattern:

Foundation Phase

First month:	1. All-around conditioning, including general strength and endurance.	85 percent
	2. Keeping up the level of technique achieved.	15 percent
Second month:	As in the first month, but with an increase in both training load and intensity.	
Third month:	1. All-around conditioning, including strength and endurance.	50 percent
	2. Specific conditioning.	35 percent
	3. Keeping up the level of technique.	15 percent

Preparation Phase

First month:	1. Specific conditioning.	50 percent
	2. All-around conditioning.	35 percent
	3. Keeping the level of technique.	15 percent
Second month:	1. Specific conditioning.	60 percent
	2. Technique improvement.	20 percent
	3. Speed improvement.	10 percent
	4. General conditioning.	10 percent
Third month:	1. Specific conditioning.	40 percent
	2. Technique improvement.	40 percent
	3. Speed improvement.	20 percent

Fourth month:	1. Technique improvement.	40 percent
	2. Speed improvement.	35 percent
	3. Specific conditioning.	25 percent

Competitive Phase

First month:	1. Speed improvement.	50 percent
	2. Technique improvement.	30 percent
	3. Specific conditioning.	20 percent

The following months are adjusted according to needs in the development of the jumper and according to the competitive calendar.

Chapter 13

TEACHING THE BEGINNING TRIPLE JUMPER

by Geoff R. Gowan

Stage 1: Station the students in a suitable position for good observation and demonstrate a standing triple jump, emphasizing the even rhythm of the three phases. Analyze briefly but clearly the work of each "active" leg and demonstrate. Stress the necessity for even rhythm in the jumping and demonstrate. Let the students practice standing triple jump concentrating on even rhythm. A large multi-purpose landing area enables many participants to work at one time. It is suggested here that the initial demonstration and brief explanation should not exceed two minutes.

Almost immediately there are two opportunities for successful participation. First, the mastery of the correct leg sequence, and secondly, the establishment of even rhythm. In addition, the first simple competition can occur. A fellow group member can be challenged for distance, or a personal best performance can be measured for comparison with later efforts.

Marker flags or tape measures already laid out in the landing areas make early knowledge of results possible. The criterion for acceptance of a distance at this stage will be an even rhythm jump.

An attempt should be made immediately to eliminate the following problems and faults, which will save much time in unlearning bad habits at a later stage.

a. Encourage a starting position with one foot forward. This is the takeoff foot, usually that used for long jump and high jump, although it must be mentioned that there are notable exceptions to this rule among world class jumpers.

b. Encourage flat-footed landings. Some students will attempt to land on their toes, losing effectiveness in subsequent takeoffs.

c. Encourage bending of the active leg at the knee during the recovery following each jump. This helps in overcoming a tendency in beginners to reach for distance with a straight leg, causing a checking of horizontal momentum, and also increasing the possibility of a heel bruise.

d. Ensure even rhythm by encouraging a gradual buildup of height over the three phases of the jump—low–higher–higher. Lack of rhythm usually results from a first phase which is too high and consequently too long. This leads to partial collapse of the unconditioned leg on landing which in turn results in a very short recovery "step."

Introducing the standing triple jump eliminates most of the problems associated with rhythm, as the performer is not asked to cope with run-up speed which he has neither the strength nor skill to manage effectively. The elimination of an approach run in the introductory phase of the event enables the teacher to indicate the need for active use of the legs throughout the three phases as an important means of producing distance.

Stage 2:   After establishing rhythm and recognizable technique, the active use of the jumping legs can receive attention. Demonstration will highlight this. The jumpers can attempt to gain increased help from their leg movements. Some additional practices may be of value here, and the following are recommended. They would seem to have the advantage of offering conditioning as well as skill improvement. They are:

a) continuous hopping on the takeoff leg, concentrating on forward progress with good knee flexion;

b) continuous hopping and stepping, left, right, left, right, etc., concentrating on forward progress with good knee flexion;

c) continuous stepping with the other leg, concentrating on forward progress with good knee flexion.

These activities have to be taught, of course, and can be made interesting by being made competitive. The coach can record personal best distances for a certain number of repetitions, or he can time each athlete for certain distances.

Of course, some conditioning activities will be taking place, too, since it is quite false to think of technique in isolation. Following skill practicing with the use of available teaching aids, a second competition can be introduced. By retaining the even rhythm of the first competition and now augmenting it with more active and skillful use of the legs, more effective takeoffs should result. This will produce an increase in total standing triple-jump distance and improvement on the recently achieved personal best.

Stage 3:   Assuming recognizable technique, even rhythm and active use of the legs, there must now follow a slight speeding up of the entire jump, *without* loss of rhythm or range of movement. An attacking attitude must be developed, leading to a faster execution of movements. Provided this can be achieved without loss of rhythm and range, the more explosive execution of performance will produce further gain in distance, thus aiding motivation.

Simple competition should follow this stage. A new personal best can be attempted, or jumping relays can be quickly organized with teams of three vs. three or two vs. two—standing triple jump, plus standing step, step, jump.

The teacher must realize that efficient performance may require more or less time depending upon individual ability. Therefore, it is unwise to suggest time allocations for each stage.

Some reference should be made to body position and the use of the arms at this time. Their earlier neglect was intentional because concentration on rhythm, leg work, and buildup of height from phase to phase, and the development of urgency in moving *forward* and upward in the quick execution of the performance are of prime importance in the initial teaching stages. Additionally, it has been found that body position usually requires little attention, provided the previously listed progressions are developed steadily. In fact, at the standing triple jump stage there will be a certain amount of forward lean of the trunk due to the need to overcome inertia at the start of the performance, and also in partial reaction to the forward movement of the flexed recovery leg.

The major problem to be faced concerning body position is associated with the final (jump) phase. Here the athlete frequently finds himself in an unfavorable takeoff position due to problems encountered at previous stages of the performance. This problem is accentuated by the folding of the body in the air (sail style), so producing a mediocre landing position. As a means of countering this difficulty, the jumper should be encouraged to produce an open, long, body position after the final takeoff (hang style).

The head plays an important role. In the first two phases the head should be in normal alignment with the body, with eyes looking forward. In the final phase, the head should be lifted slightly with the eyes looking forward-upward. At this stage of the jump the performer adopts the role of long jumper and strives mentally and physically for height.

It is frequently useful to suspend a flag or marker above the landing area and encourage the performer to look up to this flag at takeoff for his jump phase. Correct positioning of this visual aid will also encourage the development of the long body position in the air (great moment of inertia) discussed earlier.

The arms are used in orthodox manner. They are synchronized with the legs and their movement is therefore essentially natural, though some increased lateral movement is visible. In addition, there is the normal forward and backward movement because of the part the legs play in retaining balance during takeoff and in flight.

Because this teaching is geared toward the "Polish" or "flat" type of technique, where conservation of momentum is of paramount importance, emphasis on the power and range of arm movements will show an increase from phase to phase. After the final takeoff, they will, synchronized with the legs, blend together and work in an orthodox "hang" arm action.

It is strongly recommended that any necessary teaching of arm action be left to a late stage of development, since much of the arm movement involved is natural to running and balance, and attention to detail at an early stage is detrimental to the total performance.

Stage 4:   The successful marriage of technique and conditioning activities, coupled with numerous and suitably designed competitions, make the addition of an approach run possible. It is at this stage that the thoroughness of the earlier teaching is put to the test. Because approach speed brings with it problems related to balance, timing and landing shock, it would be very unwise to attempt too much too soon. Therefore, a three-stride approach is taught. Regardless of the athletic future of the performers—inter-squad, interscholastic, intercollegiate, or international—basic fundamentals will apply.

A starting position either with feet together or one foot in advance of the other is advocated and demonstrated. The ability to reproduce this identical position on endless occasions is the prime aim. Because three strides are being used, the jumper takes his first stride with his *takeoff foot* and consequently makes his third stride with the same foot.

An attacking, balanced, fast cadence run is demonstrated, culminating in a *running takeoff* resulting in a low, fast first phase. This is crucial to further effective progress. The run must blend into the first phase. This demands considerable skill, and the teacher must use every appropriate, available teaching aid to establish this concept.

The performers practice, starting correctly and running three strides into the triple jump, emphasizing the run into the takeoff, keeping the first phase low and fast, and retaining rhythm, leg action, and buildup of height as before.

If the jumpers have mastered the ability to hop skillfully in the earlier stages, the addition of an approach run will be achieved in less time and with greater success. At this stage in progression, too much height in the first phase following the short approach run will not only prove detrimental to conservation of momentum but may lead to destruction of rhythm. Great stress must therefore be laid on the low and relatively short first phase.

There are those who advocate the marking of ratios of distances on the ground as a means of ensuring rhythm. While it is agreed that in individual cases the marking of lines will help to overcome problems of this kind, ratios should be used as a last resort. An externally imposed set of distances is essentially false and somewhat of a distraction. An attempt to strike marks on the ground while in the act of jumping can influence the head position with consequent potential loss of control. It can also produce a reaching action with the legs, so causing a checking action on landing, in addition to possible heel bruising.

It is preferred to inspect the ratios of the jumper after his performance and, assuming suitable rhythm, leg action and speed of execution, to draw inferences from these as to possible areas for addition or reduction of distances from phase to phase. The use of a stopwatch in timing performance from takeoff to landing can be a useful source of information.

Certainly worthy of mention is the use of plastic heel cups which protect the heel from bruising and, as such, help in avoiding loss of confidence through injury.

Competitions can be reintroduced along the lines indicated previously. A new personal best, now with a three-stride approach, can be attempted, with distance being scored, provided the technique passes the scrutiny of the teacher. Critical observation of peer performances is also recommended as this tends to develop understanding of requirements, particularly when performances are commented upon by the teacher. The retention of good technique and the linking of a three-stride approach should enable a performer to add approximately 3–6 feet to his previous performance.

Stage 5: As the performers become capable of handling a longer approach run, and consequently more approach speed, the three strides are extended to 5, 7, 9, 11, etc. The addition of two strides each time ensures an odd-numbered total, so retaining the same starting position and the same takeoff foot. The same emphasis is laid on the running flat takeoff, with balanced body position and active, well-flexed jumping legs.

In time the run-up length is extended according to individual abilities, always remembering that while the fastest possible approach is the ideal to be striven for, approach speed is worthless if it cannot be used positively by the athlete.

Throughout this increasing approach, no account has been taken of a takeoff board. This again is deliberate policy. Takeoff boards create havoc if they are placed in the path of a jumper before he has the necessary skill or established movement patterns for successful jumping.

Ideally, the jumper must be taught to transfer the measured distance of his current run-up to the competition runway. (This approach technique is established as a result of many, many runs with a *full jump.*)

Reproduction of the familiar approach pattern in terms of starting position, sprinting run, balanced attacking run onto the *takeoff stride*, (a better concept than takeoff board), will ensure optimum performance. Check marks are frequently useful in stabilizing the early strides, but two should be a maximum. It is a sound idea to establish a check mark after three or five strides during the gradual extension of the approach run detailed earlier.

As the run-up increases to say 15 or more strides, it is sound, particularly for jumpers who are highly motivated and talented performers, to establish a check mark some five strides from the takeoff spot, and to encourage a mentally and physically controlled attack from that point to the running takeoff. This requires much practice, but it is advocated because it aids the quick execution of the three phases, thus ensuring conservation of momentum and efficient successive takeoffs.

The importance of the approach run should never be underestimated. Much more time must be spent on the skill associated with the approach run than is spent by the majority of jumpers. The run-up must conclude with a full jump, or at least with the hop phase, with a controlled landing in sand, but in a balanced position ready to proceed into the remaining two phases. The landing in sand from the first phase is a safety factor and increases the number of quality repetitions possible in a training session.

In Summary:

1. Introduce the event. Talk little. Give the best possible demonstration. Use appropriate, available visual aids.
2. Retain what is good. Augment this as learning continues.
3. Technique and conditioning should not be kept separate.
4. Introduce suitably designed competitions.
5. Progress according to individual ability.
6. Never neglect approach skills.

Chapter 14

THE TRIPLE JUMP

by Pat Tan Eng Yoon

The triple jump, or as it is sometimes called, the hop, step and jump, dates back to ancient Grecian times. The Greeks competed against one another regularly in a form of jumping similar to triple jumping as we know it today. It is reported that Phylos jumped 16.31m (53'8") and 16.66m (54'8"), but that he took off from the ground four of five times, instead of only three.

From this early form of triple jumping was developed the style which is used all over the world today. At first the jumps were performed by using the legs alternately, L-R-L or R-L-R, but later the Irish athletes changed the method of jumping by hopping twice and jumping once, L-L-L or R-R-R. The present style of triple jumping, L-L-R or R-R-L, developed in England around the turn of the century.

Speed seems to be a very important factor in the triple jump, but of even more importance is tremendous leg strength and muscular coordination. This is borne out by the fact that many Japanese jumpers who were not exceptionally fast have managed to surpass 48 feet. Of the world famous Japanese jumpers of the past, only Chuhei Nambu, the 1932 Olympic champion, possessed great sprinting ability, having run 10.5 for 100 meters. His compatriots, Oda, Tajima and Harada, were unable to break 11 seconds, yet all these men bettered 51 feet in the triple jump. What these men, and others who lack speed, have in common is terrific leg strength. They are able to spring back up each time they land on the ground. Moreover, they are good technicians. First the Japanese, and now the Russians, have taken the lead in this event. Their triple jumpers do not possess exceptional sprinting ability, but they have developed tremendous leg strength through their training methods and research into the event.

From an historical survey of the triple jump an idea can be obtained as to its development. The first 50-footer, Dan Ahearne of the USA, when recording 50 feet and 11 inches back in 1909, had these phases: 20', 11'3", and 19'8". It seems that the jumpers of his time were trying for a big hop and a big jump, with the step as a linking phase. The development appeared to be in the direction of getting the maximum distance in the first phase, with the second phase suffering from the overreaching first. In 1931 when Mikio Oda of Japan jumped 51'1⅜", his phases were 21'4", 11'6", and 18'3⅜".

Then came a swing over to an emphasis on the jump phase. This appeared to have come from the Australians, with men like A. W. Winter and Jack Metcalfe putting emphasis on the final phase. When Metcalfe jumped 51'9¼" (15.78 meters) in 1935, his three phases were 18'6", 13'6" and 19'9¼".

From the record books it looks like the attempt to achieve a longer second phase, the step, was first made by Luis Brunetto of Argentina in 1924. When jumping 50'7¼" for second place in the Olympic Games, Brunetto hopped 20'4", stepped 15'7", and jumped 14'8¼". He thus appears to have been the first athlete to increase the length of the step phase, but he, like so many others before and after him, overdid one phase, forgetting about maintaining balance in all three phases.

The lengthening of the step phase was really carried to an extreme during the mid-1950's, this time by a Russian—Leonid Shcherbakov. When Shcherbakov triple jumped 51'6⅛", his three phases were 18'6", 17'3", and 15'9⅛". His 17'3" middle phase is believed to be the longest step ever by a top-flight triple jumper in competition.

It was soon realized that it is unwise to overdo any particular phase in triple jumping at the expense of the other phases, because the total effort then suffers. Balance is very important in all three phases. Shcherbakov appears to have learned this through experience. Three years after recording his 17'3" step, he modified his jumping style and had phases of 19'8½", 16'3½", and 17'2½" for a total of 53'2½".

The present methods employed by the Russian jumpers appear to get the most out of each of the three phases, but with a little more emphasis on the first two phases. On the other hand, Josef Schmidt of Poland, the great exponent of the "flat" technique with a combination of spring and speed, has brought a new medium and style into triple jumping. His exceptional speed and technique, which call for a lower jumping trajectory for the first two phases, enable him to conserve much of his horizontal momentum for the final phase. Russia's Viktor Saneyev, winner of the Mexico City Olympic crown with 57'0¾" (17.39 meters), diverged only marginally from the Shcherbakov technique by sharpening the cadence of the final three or four approach strides and using a flatter hop.

When comparing the Russian and the "flat" technique, one can see that the Russian method tends to have a longer hop, while the "flat" technique emphasizes the jump phase. This brings us back to the era of the long hoppers and the big jumpers; the only difference between the present and the past is that the present jumpers have reasonably long steps. In other words, the jumpers of today have balanced phases.

It can be seen that a swing from one phase to the other, often to an extreme, has been beneficial, as it has enabled the various exponents and their coaches to see the results of their theories. The success or failure of any new trend results in a development, either in the same direction or in a different one. The balance between the three phases in triple jumping has taken this forward step. It is only by getting the maximum out of each of the three phases that one can obtain the maximum distance in the total effort.

RATIOS—RELATIVE JUMPING VALUES OF THE JUMPING PHASES

The use of ratios in triple jumping is a result of the theoretical and practical analyses made on the event. It is related to the actual distance covered in each of the three phases, which, in turn, is governed by triple jumping technique. Ratios should be used as a guide toward better jumping results.

The aim behind the use of ratios is to obtain balanced efforts in all the three jumps. An unbalanced phase will upset one of the other two phases and this will, in turn, affect the overall jumping performance.

Ratios which have been put forward by different authors have been:

3:2:3   F.A.M. Webster (Great Britain)
6:5:6   Mikio Oda (Japan)
10:8:9   Pat Tan Eng Yoon (Singapore)
7:6:7   Toni Nett (Germany)
10:8:9   Dietrich Gerner (Brazil)
10:7.2:8.1   Yuri Verhoshanski (U.S.S.R.)

3:2:3—This was the result of a study carried out by F.A.M. Webster, who observed the Japanese training methods during the 1936 Olympic Games. The Japanese were the best triple jumpers in those days and had been dominating the event for the previous eight years.

6:5:6—This was put forward by the Japanese Olympic champion, Mikio Oda, who had observed that the step phase in all the jumps by the Japanese was rather weak and unbalanced in comparison with the other phases, and with the overall jump. He pointed out that with the 6:5:6 ratio a longer step would result, and the whole jump would be more balanced.

10:8:9—In a study undertaken in 1957, the author noted that Oda's 6:5:6 ratio permitted an increase in the step phase, but that it would result in an unnatural reduction of the hop phase, which might prove detrimental to the entire jump. It was suggested that a 10:7:10 ratio was ideal for beginners learning the event, but that there was too much loss in the step phase, thereby making it unbalanced for the top performers. The 10:8:9 ratio was advocated as a sound ratio for top performers. This places relative emphasis, first on the step phase, which is normally the weakest, and then on the hop phase, and finally on the jump phase.

7:6:7—Toni Nett, after measuring 30 competitive jumps by Josef Schmidt and V. Einarsson, discovered that on an average, the ratio arrived at was 7:6:7. This was in connection with the "flat" technique, of which the two were accomplished exponents. Nett suggested that the most economical ratio is 35%, 30% and 35%.

10:8:9—Dietrich Gerner, who for several years was the coach of Adhemar F. da Silva of Brazil, the 1952 and 1956 Olympic champion, pointed out that the best ratio should be that in which the hop and step total are double that of the jump, and that the difference between the hop and the step should be in the ratio of 5:4. He put forward certain percentages for each of the three efforts: 37%, 30%, 33%. When worked out according to his pattern of ratios, this results in a 10:8:9 ratio.

10:7.2:8.1—This ratio was the result of a conversion from the original percentage of efforts put forward by the Russians: 38½%, 29½%, 32%. However, according to their coach, Yuri Verhoshanski, to obtain the maximum out of each phase, the jumps should follow these percentages in the three efforts: 37.8%, 28.9%, 33.3%.

It is interesting to note the different ways that some world class jumpers have triple jumped, with each following a particular ratio:

Einarsson (Iceland)	18′2″	−17′0	−18′6″	53′8″
Schmidt (Poland)	18′5″	−15′3″	−19′11″	53′7″
Michailov (U.S.S.R.)	21′4″	−16′5″	−16′0½″	53′9½″
Boase (Australia)	19′6¼″	−15′9″	−18′3″	53′6¼″
Fedosseyev (U.S.S.R.)	20′6″	−15′9″	−16′11″	53′2″
da Silva (Brazil)	20′4″	−15′7″	−17′4″	53′3″
Tomlinson (Australia)	19′3″	−15′10″	−18′2″	53′3″
Shcherbakov (U.S.S.R.)	19′8½″	−16′3½″	−17′2¼″	53′2¾″

Without a doubt, each jumper had a respectable step phase, thereby ensuring that the jump on the whole was a balanced one. The question that quickly springs to one's mind is, would each of these jumpers have jumped just as well using another ratio? Jumpers use a particular rhythm because of the way they have been jumping in their training. Therefore, each jumper follows a predetermined jumping pattern. This means that the jumper has to adopt a certain ratio pattern, and this must suit his mental and physical makeup. The ratio *must* fit the athlete. The determining factors are such variables as leg strength, mental attitude, experience in the event, and speed of approach.

THE THREE BASIC STYLES OF JUMPING

A survey of modern-day triple jumping reveals that there are three basic styles of jumping (Figure 144). The basic technique is the same in all three, but there are variations. Knowing which style to use depends to a certain extent on the qualities of the jumper himself.

The three basic styles of jumping can be termed:
a. The normal or natural method,
b. The double-arm shift method, and
c. The "flat" method.

The normal or natural method. This style of jumping is suited to the springy type of athlete who does not possess exceptional speed. The jumper attempts to jump higher with each succeeding phase. He therefore tries not to have too high a trajectory in the hop phase.

The arms are used as balancers, working in opposition to the vigorous leg movements. During takeoff and in flight, the arms are kept "long" for added impulse.

The hop phase is shorter than the hop phase of the double-arm shift method, but longer than the hop phase of the "flat" method. On the other hand, the jump phase is considerably shorter than the final phase of the "flat" technique, but it appears to be of the same length as the jump phase of the double-arm shift method.

The double-arm shift method. This style of jumping appears to be exclusively Russian and put to good effect by their jumpers, who have set world marks with it.

The jumper must possess tremendous leg strength, achieved only after many months of conditioning the legs. Compared with the other two styles of jumping, the hop phase in the double-arm shift method is not only higher in flight trajectory but longer in distance. Thus, in order to be able to rebound again after such a long, high hop, the jumper must possess great resilience, agility and strength.

Besides the hop phase being higher than normal, the other two phases are also of considerable height. However, the jump phase has the lowest trajectory of all the three styles.

The main characteristic of this style is the double-arm shift, from which the

Figure 144.

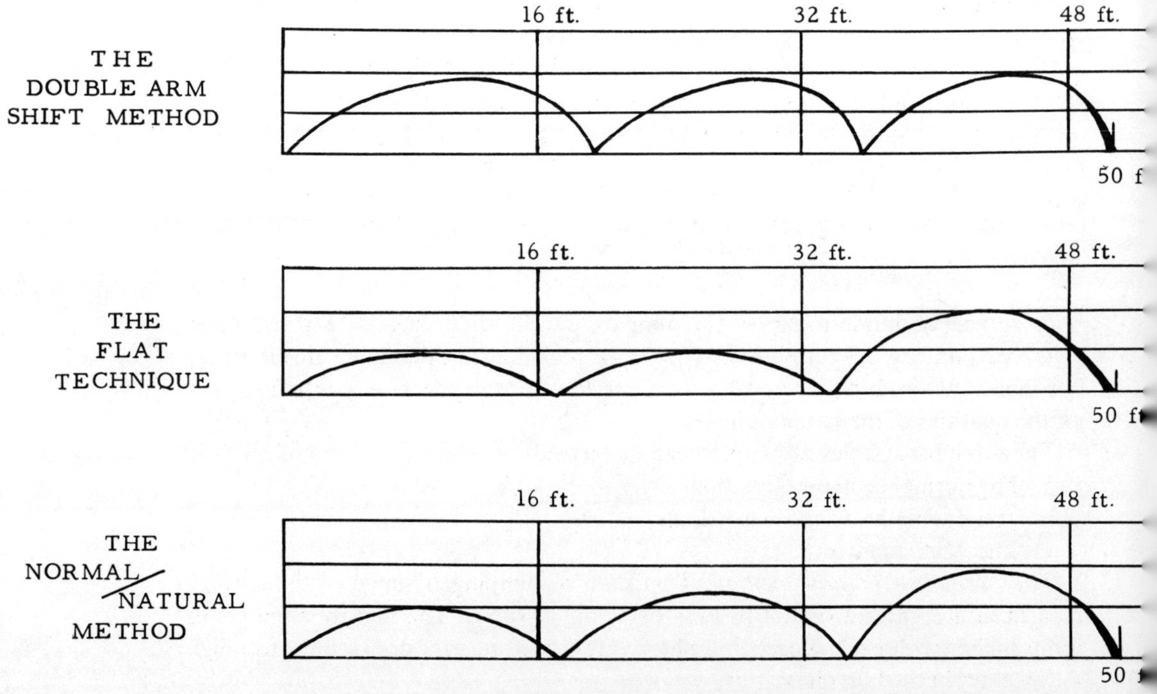

A DIAGRAMMATIC COMPARISON OF THE THREE TYPES OF JUMPS.

name is derived. Both arms are shifted to the rear during the hop flight and also after the jumper has taken off for the step phase. Both arms are then swung forward and upward from behind the trunk, coinciding with the spring up for the step and the jump.

The "flat" method. Although there were other jumpers who had used the "flat" method of jumping, it was not until Josef Schmidt of Poland created a new world mark of 55 feet 10¼ inches that it became well known.

In this method of jumping, the athlete tries to keep the flight trajectory of both the hop and the step phases comparatively low, conserving his horizontal momentum for the final phase. The hop phase is shorter than in the other two methods, and appears "flat." Hence the name. It is in the jump phase that the trajectory is higher and, therefore, the jump is the longest of all the three phases.

The "flat" method of jumping requires a very fast approach. Perhaps it is the extremely fast approach and the great horizontal momentum attained that prevent the "flat type" of triple jumper from going so high in the hop phase.

Basic Principles and Technique

Since momentum is so important, speed, therefore, is one of the basic principles underlying the triple jump. The faster one can run, the farther he can jump, of course, but in the triple jump other factors are important. A very efficiently coordinated neuro-muscular system is necessary, too, because the athlete has to perform certain movements in the air and on three takeoffs.

Balance, which is very essential in so many physical activities, is also a prerequisite here. A loss of balance in the hop landing forces the athlete to make a small and hurried step, and thereafter all form is completely lost because of the loss of balance.

A high knee pickup is one of the most essential movements that can be mastered in the triple jump. When the knee is picked up in the correct manner during the hop, the step, and finally the jump phase, the jumper will begin to notice a decided improvement in overall performance. The beginner picks up his hopping leg straight, causing him to land in an unbalanced position, unable to utilize the power to rebound into the air again.

A good landing position from the hop and the step is necessary to get the maximum drive into the air for the succeeding phase. The body weight must be behind the landing leg, and yet not back so far that it creates difficulties in the landing position. In these landings, the knee must "give" and at the same time be ready to straighten vigorously, forcing the body upward and forward.

Arm action is important in triple jumping, just as it is in sprinting. The arms help to counterbalance the leg movements in the air and into the air. In the step and jump phases, they help to give some impetus from the ground, besides acting as balancers.

The question of proportion between the three phases of the triple jump deserves a place as one of triple jumping's basic problems, although it is discussed in more detail in an earlier section of this chapter. It is difficult to state dogmatically the best ratio to be used because of individual differences which make this impossible, except, perhaps, in the case of beginners. Even the champions themselves jump differently at times, but they all have one thing in common—a big step. Whatever ratio is used, emphasis must be on the step phase and its proportion with the other two phases. The modern conception of triple jumping is to make the step as big as possible, thus turning the event into three jumps.

The height of the hop phase depends on the style of jumping, but in no circumstances should it be higher than the jump phase. It was once thought that if the hop phase was high, then the jumper would never be able to regain his balance after the shock of landing from a high hop. However, it has been proved that the jumper can have a reasonably high hop phase, provided his legs and body have been conditioned to deal with the extra height. Examples of jumpers who can manage high and long hops are the Russian jumpers with their double-arm shift technique. What is vital, however, is that the hop knee is brought through, flexed.

A smooth approach run is necessary so that the transfer from the speedy approach to the hop will also be smooth. Since the athlete is trying to get his hopping knee through, flexed, he should approach the board with a high knee pickup. This approach run must be long enough so that at the end of the run, the jumper can get the feel that he is running off the board.

The head is the rudder in most physical movements, including the triple jump. The athlete must try to keep his head up and look forward throughout the entire jump, except in the jump phase, when he should attempt to look skyward. As a result of the correct head position, the trunk remains upright during the hop and step phases, giving the athlete the feeling of moving forward. If he does not get this feeling, then he is probably leaning too far back, thus losing momentum.

The Hop Phase (*Left leg is assumed here.*)

The speed of the run-up is transferred to the whole jump through the hop takeoff. In order to preserve this momentum, the jumper has to keep his takeoff movements on a forward-upward plane, using the flexed free leg and opposite arm to good effect to balance the powerful leg drive of the takeoff leg.

The takeoff in the hop is a flat-footed one, with the athlete keeping his body upright throughout. Some coaches recommend that the triple jumper counteract forward rotation in the hop by swinging the free leg back in a hitchkick-like movement, and at the same time bringing the hopping leg forward in a flexed position. This action tends to destroy the balance and cause an awkward landing position, with the weight of the body too far behind the landing leg. The swinging of the free leg back, straightened, is not necessary. If the takeoff is correct and the jumper looks straight ahead, keeping his head up, he will not have much forward rotation to upset his balance.

As soon as the jumper leaves the board, he strives consciously to maintain an upright trunk, relaxes his body, and tries to float through the air. He brings his hop leg forward and through, in a flexed position. The free leg should be relaxed and allowed to swing back slightly flexed, to counterbalance the action of the takeoff leg. The hop leg is kept in this forward position, with the thigh parallel to the ground and the lower leg relaxed. The athlete waits for the ground to "come up" before stretching the hop leg to make contact with it.

If the landing is anticipated, it will cause one of the following to occur:

1.   The hopping leg will move down too soon, resulting in the contact with the ground being achieved too early. Then, instead of the body weight being behind the hopping leg on landing, it will have passed beyond it already. A hurried and small step will result.

2.   The hopping leg will straighten and extend too soon. Thus, it will be impossible to achieve an ideal landing where the hopping leg contacts the ground, flexed, to reduce the shock of landing and then extends in the driving action of the step takeoff. The eventual takeoff has to be made too hurriedly, due to the premature straightening of the hopping leg. Just as in No. 1, the resultant step is small and very low and balance is thus upset.

The arms play an important part in triple jumping, because they act as balancers and they can be used to help gain height in the takeoffs for the step and jump phases. The tendency is for the jumper to land from the hop with his arms wide of his body. Instead, the arms should travel in the same plane as the legs, straight forward and backward. If one of the arms swings too far to the rear on landing, then it will tend to pull the shoulder to the rear also, causing an upset in the balance of the jumper.

Thus, in the hop landing, just before contact with the ground is made, the right leg will be trailing, relaxed and slightly flexed at the knee. The left leg is in front of the body, flexed at the knee, too. The thigh has been parallel to the ground, but the knee which was brought sharply through, has been gradually dropping as the lower leg starts to extend and stretch out slightly. The body is upright all the time. Landing from the hop can be either flat footed or on the heel.

In the actual landing position, the left leg is slightly in front of the body with the body weight just behind it. The right leg which has trailed has moved close to the body, still flexed at the knee. The athlete is now in a compact position and a powerful one from which to thrust.

The two arms are close to the body. The right arm has moved down and back and the left arm down and forward.

The body is upright. In this compact position, no unnecessary or excessive strain is placed on any particular section of the body, other than on the hopping leg.

The left leg "gives" at the knee and so do the hips. This "giving" or flexion of the hopping leg is very important because it is the ultimate straightening of this leg with an explosive extension that provides the spring for the step phase. The ankle helps provide this spring with an additional drive after the knee has been fully extended.

The Step Phase

Just prior to the hop landing, the athlete gathers himself for an explosive spring into the air for the step. This means that there is a flowing continuity from the first phase to the second. Although the left leg provides the "spring" for the step, it is aided by the hip extending and the trailing right leg being swung through and upward powerfully. The lower leg is kept close to the thigh, so that the foot does not precede the knee. The left arm is "hooked" forward and up, bent at the elbow, so that it rotates outward, while the right arm is driven back. Both arm movements are vigorous. The spring from the left ankle adds the finishing touch.

While some athletes drive the left arm forward and the right arm to the rear, others use both arms in a forward direction, thus concentrating on the lift, which is so necessary in the step phase. Both arms are swung forward, flexed, and then they straighten. The Russian double-arm shift method is a further modification of this technique in that both arms have already been swung back to the rear of the trunk just prior to landing and from their behind-the-trunk position can be swung forward and upward into the step takeoff.

The jumper then "floats" through the air. He relaxes and tries to maintain this for as long as he can. Just before the landing occurs, the athlete swings both arms to a point behind his body laterally. They remain there, flexed slightly, until the landing is about to take place for the step phase. Then they move down and forward so as to coincide with the upward drive for the jump.

Just after the step takeoff, the left leg trails behind the body. However, the leg does not remain in this trailing position throughout the step flight, because of the difficulty in maintaining this position. It imposes a severe strain on the "direct" load muscles, which cannot support this heavy load. This partly explains why athletes who try to trail the step takeoff leg in the air away from the body are soon forced to cut down their step length and make a premature landing.

The correct position of the trailing leg is forward, in a flexed position, where it will remain just under the body. There is then little or no strain because this leg is directly below the body. It can be seen that this position is more compact and balanced.

Just before the landing in the step phase, the trailing leg commences to move back. This is merely a reaction to the front (right) leg's moving forward and "opening" at the lower leg. To an observer, the jumper appears to stretch more for the step at this late stage, because the rear leg moves up, and then the two legs "open" out, one going forward and the other traveling back.

Due to the difference in the arm action between the one arm forward and the two arms forward variations, this difference is carried over into the jump takeoff. In the one arm forward style, the left arm is forward to balance the right stepping leg and the right arm is back. The two arms move down to a position at the side of the body as the step landing takes place. This helps to keep the body in a compact position and also assists in helping to "cushion" the shock of landing.

As in the hop, the landing leg "gives" at the knee and ankle with a slight flexion, assisted by the hips and the entire body. The jumper's main aim now is to get as much height as he can, because he has little momentum left. Thus he can now afford to have his body weight a little farther back than it was in the previous landing. Nevertheless, the jumper still strives to get his center of gravity forward when he leaves the ground.

Some jumpers commit the fault of jumping when still leaning back and thus obtain good height but poor distance. Others are so anxious to jump that they land with the body weight too far forward, and they experience considerable difficulty in keeping the body up, with an eventual premature landing in the pit.

The Jump

The jumper uses his arms and trailing leg to help obtain drive and height for the jump. The trailing leg is swung through, flexed at the knee, as high as the knee will go, in an effort to get the hips up as high as possible. The lower leg is kept close to the thigh in this vicious swing-through, so that a fast movement can occur. The body is not kept upright but is "pushed" up to get height. Once the athlete has left the ground, he strives to keep a good body balance in the air as long as he can, fighting off the tendency of the upper body to rotate forward and downward.

To help the body attain a good balance in the air during the jump phase, one of the long jump styles (the sail, the hang or the hitch-kick) is used. Either the hitch-kick or the hang will put the upper body in a more upright position, but it is usually not possible to perform a full hitch-kick action because there is not the same momentum nor time that an athlete possesses at the takeoff for the long jump.

Some triple jumpers have used the hang technique quite successfully, but most resort to the sail method. In the sail style, the jumper brings his left leg through, knee leading the movement very sharply, just as the long jumper does at takeoff. The right arm is swung forward and up with a vicious uppercut action to coincide with the driving action of the left knee. Then the takeoff leg springs up and forward to join the leading leg, while the left arm, which has moved back, flexed, to a point just behind the body, now moves forward, and the right arm moves down. The jumper is now holding a position with his body leaning forward slightly, legs extended in front, flexed at the knees, and arms held in front of the shoulders.

Landing is then made in this manner with the legs, which have been flexed, being extended at the very last moment. At the same time, both the arms are also swung down and back to assist. The legs are, however, dropping lower all the time and usually a poor landing position results.

With the double-arm shift method, both arms are in a better position to coordinate with giving lift to the jump and to coincide more with the hang technique. Both arms are behind the body as the step landing is about to be accomplished. The arms are already moving forward simultaneously as the landing is made. This forward driving movement is cooperative with the entire body action at landing. As the arms move down to travel forward, the shoulder girdles are depressed and relaxed, and this wave of relaxation continues to the hips. The body is relaxed, with the right knee at its deepest flexion as the arms reach a position by the side of the body.

As the arms start to move up and forward, slightly flexed at the elbow, the explosive extension of the right leg occurs, and the knee straightens, driving the body forward and up. The left knee has, of course, been swung up. The arms move up until they reach a position behind the head. They are still slightly flexed. The takeoff leg moves forward and up, and flexes on the way up, while the left leg which was forward with the thigh parallel to the ground, moves down to meet the other leg. They both arrive at a position directly below the body, which is upright, and the lower legs are flexed. Thus, the thighs are almost in vertical alignment with the body in this type of hang style.

There is an interesting variation of the hang style. Instead of the arms being swung to a position above the head in the manner just described, they are swung to that point by raising them from behind and not from the front, as the jumper attempts to look upward. This is supposed to have the effect of bending the upper trunk backward, which in turn helps to give a backward displacement to the trunk.

Landing in the Pit

The aim should be to land with the legs as far in front of the body as is possible without falling back. As much as nine inches may be gained from an efficient landing. In the sail style nothing much can be done to obtain a good landing position, because the jumper is already in the landing position when he travels through the air. With the hang and hitch-kick styles, a better landing position may be achieved.

The jack-knife landing position appears to be the one most commonly used. A landing position in which the whole body is extended slightly seems more advantageous, but this type of landing has two very big disadvantages: (1) When landing in such a position, the upper body is too far back, behind the knees and feet, causing the jumper to fall backward into the pit. (2) In order not to fall back into the pit, the jumper must touch down earlier than with the jack-knife style, therefore nullifying the advantage of getting the feet farther in front of the center of gravity.

DOUBLE-ARM SHIFT TECHNIQUE

Hop Takeoff (Figs. 145 and 146)

The jumper shows fine form in Fig. 145 where his hop leg is about to move down and back. His hips are also about to "flex" slightly in preparation for the takeoff, which is demonstrated clearly in Fig. 146. He has driven forward and upward with a strong supporting action by the knee lift of the free leg. From the action of the right arm, it can be seen that his drive is more upward than normal, a characteristic of this style of jumping. This is confirmed in Fig. 148, where the height of the hips has risen considerably when compared with that shown in Fig. 147.

Figure 145.

Figure 146.

Figure 147.

Figure 148.

Figure 149.

Figure 150.

Figure 151.

Figure 153.

Figure 154.

Figure 152.

Figure 155.

Figure 156.

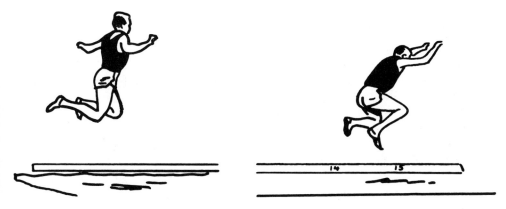

Figure 157.   **Figure 158.**

Figure 159.

Hop Flight (Figs. 147–148)

Immediately after the takeoff, the hop leg is about to be brought forward while the free leg is moving backward. However, the jumper has taken it back flexed, rather than permitting it to move back and down with a slight extension. This might mean a slight lack of relaxation by the jumper. In Fig. 148, the hop knee has completed its movement forward, and it appears that the knee has been taken a little too high. This could mean a slight upset in the balance of the body, and hence the trunk is a little more inclined forward than upright.

Fig. 149 shows the jumper extending his hopping leg for the ground while the free leg has moved back and away from the body. Notice the head of the jumper and how stable it has remained throughout the hop phase.

Hop Landing and Step Takeoff (Figs. 150 and 151)

The landing has just occurred and the jumper is about to flex his hips and legs while the arms are moving down to the side of the body. The landing is flat footed and if anything, the jumper appears to lack the relaxed posture so necessary at this stage. However, in Fig. 151 he displays a sound takeoff action with a powerful extension of the hips, knee and ankle. Note especially the lift of the thigh of the free leg.

Step Flight (Figs. 152–154)

The jumper's position indicates how successful he has been in his takeoff. The knee of the free leg continues to move upward from its powerful swing from the rear, while the trail leg is gradually moving forward to compact position directly below the body. The trunk position in Fig. 153 is again a little too inclined forward at this stage of the flight.

The jumper now prepares for the landing, and his arms are moving behind his body while his legs "open" out. The free leg extends for the landing and jump takeoff, while the trail leg moves back and away from the body "in sympathy." Fig. 154 also indicates that the jumper has anticipated his landing instead of waiting for the ground to come up. This has no doubt caused his trunk to lose its upright position and to rotate forward too soon.

Step Landing and Jump Takeoff (Figs. 155 and 156)

In Fig. 155, the step landing is just about to take place, with the landing leg on its way down and back. In the meantime, the arms and the trail leg are also about to move in a forward-upward action. The forward inclination of the trunk is still noticeable, whereas it should have been a little more upright. This has resulted in the trunk position being more forward in Fig. 156 for the jump takeoff. Here, the jumper has attempted to get his hips as high as possible and has made good use of his takeoff leg, knee lift of the free leg, and the upward swing of both arms.

Jump Flight and Landing (Figs. 157–159)

The jumper has adopted a sail-style flight. His body has continued to rotate forward, offering no opportunity to do anything to offset the forward rotation. He has brought his legs through well with the knees leading the movement. From the height of the hips in Fig. 158, the jumper appears to have succeeded in employing a powerful spring into his takeoff action. However, in spite of the forward rotation of the trunk, the jumper has managed to adopt a good landing position with his feet well ahead of the body, and with a long powerful swing of the arms to assist.

Throughout the entire jump, the athlete has kept his head up. Both the arms have been fully employed in all the phases to help obtain maximal lift for the step and jump takeoffs, a characteristic of this style of jumping. In comparison with the other styles of jumping, this one is "power" jumping, with the athlete striving to obtain maximum distance for the first two phases and going all out for the final phase.

TRAINING

The triple jumper must follow a specialized training program which contains the items he requires to enable him to perform with success. Unlike the long jumper who is usually very strong in his jumping leg only, the triple jumper must be strong in both legs, and he must condition his entire body, especially the legs, to stand up to the punishment and strain of the landing phases. At the same time, the legs have to be so resilient that the jumper can spring up again each time without much loss of horizontal momentum.

A fast approach run is vital. The momentum that can be generated during the run-up is transferred to the entire jump via the first phase. Clearly the faster this run-up is, the greater the body speed will be, and the more momentum there will be for the final phase.

While strength training and speed training are important, there must also be skill and rhythm jumping in the training schedule. Their importance cannot be overstressed. The strength and speed must be merged into a coordinated unit, along with jumping rhythm. Hence the need for the athlete to perform many jumping activities which will impose strains and stresses on the body. For example, in jumping 50 feet, he will need a hop of around 18 feet, followed up with a step of at least 15 feet, and a 17-foot final phase. This requires maximum effort in each phase, and so the entire body and the all-important legs must experience and undergo the same kind of jumping rhythm and pressure during training sessions.

Another factor in the development of the triple jumper is the time it takes to achieve the total jump. In a way this is tied up with rhythm and ratio, but nevertheless the result is a combination of both speed and power. It is one thing to be fast, and one thing to have power, but when the two are combined, satisfying results can be achieved.

Basically, the triple jumper's training program should consist of the following:

a. Strength training
b. Speed and endurance training (running)
c. Special speed-power training
d. Rhythmical jump training
e. Special conditioning training
f. Technique training

Strength Training

There is no doubt as to the need for strong and powerful muscles in triple jumping, and one of the easiest ways of gaining this needed strength is through training with weights and barbells using the overload principle. Of course, the muscles can also be developed and strengthened by a variety of other exercises, such as hopping continuously on one foot, jumping over obstacles with both feet and performing continuous giant steps, etc.

The weight training exercises which are recommended are as follows:
1. Two hands press.
2. Two hands snatch.
3. Two hands clean and jerk.
4. Half squats with barbell.
5. Leg extension exercises with boots (weights added).
6. Sit ups with weights held behind the head.
7. Ankle extension exercises (heel raises).
8. Hops on one leg with weights.
9. Hanging from wallbars with weighted boots and lifting knee.
10. Squat hops on the floor with weights.
11. Hip raises with weights attached to hips (body supported in supine position by hands on floor and feet resting on chair).

Since the aim is to obtain power, there should be a minimum of repetitions for each exercise—no more than five for each exercise. With certain exercises, such as the two hands snatch, the athlete may be able to lift the load only once, especially when he is near his maximum.

Speed and Endurance Training

It is recommended that the training program be similar to that of a sprinter, with modifications. The training program should consist of the following:
1. Cross-country running through forests and over hilly ground. It is advantageous if the course includes obstacles which necessitate the athlete's having to jump over them.
2. Wind sprints over 1000m, with alternate 40m sprinting and 160m jogging.
3. 200m and 300m repetition runs.
4. 150m repetition runs at one-half to three-fourths speed with a constant resting interval.
5. Sets of 100m at one-half speed, followed by 60m at three-fourths speed.
6. Repetition 40m sprints.
7. Practice runs over the full length of the run-up.
8. Starting with sprinters, using blocks.

Special Speed-Power Training

The basic aim in this type of training is to coordinate the jumping power with that of the jumping speed. This means that the athlete will have to use his legs repeatedly for a series of repetition jumps to cover a certain distance in a predetermined time.

The following types of jumps are recommended:
1. Hops with single leg.
2. Combination jumps, such as Right, Right, Left, Left.
3. Successive jumps with alternating legs ("giant" steps).

It is also recommended that there be two types of training jumps—one with the athlete taking five rebounds and the other, ten rebounds.

Five successive rebounds, using giant steps, R., R., L., L. or R., R., L.

a. 46'–49' in 3.8 secs. progressing to:

b. 49'–55' in 3.5 secs. progressing to:

c. 55'–62' in 3.0 secs. progressing to:

d. 62'–75' in 2.8 secs.

Five successive hops, with either leg.

a. 43'–46' in 4.0 secs. progressing to:

b. 46'–52' in 3.8 secs. progressing to:

c. 52'–59' in 3.3 secs. progressing to:

d. 59'–69' in 2.8 secs.

Ten successive rebounds, using giant steps, R., R., L., L. or R., R., L.

a. 105'–108' in 7.0 secs. progressing to:

b. 108'–115' in 6.0 secs. progressing to:

c. 115'–124' in 5.7 secs. progressing to:

d. 124'–138' in 5.5 secs.

Ten successive hops, with either leg.

a. 99'–105' in 7.5 secs. progressing to:

b. 105'–111' in 6.3 secs. progressing to:

c. 111'–121' in 6.0 secs. progressing to:

d. 121'–131' in 5.6 secs.

The above training schedules should be used with an approach run of seven strides. Since the jumper will have to accomplish each distance within a certain time, his approach will have to be fast.

Rhythmical Jump Training

The jumper will be able to give full concentration to the movement and action of his legs in this type of training. Rebound is essential, and at the same time the athlete should be able to feel the "down pressing" action of each landing leg.

1) Hopping on one leg (50m–200m) with emphasis on the hop knee being pulled through to the front. Repeat with the other leg.

2) Giant steps (50m–200m), trying to float and to "let the ground come up."

3) Hopping with the same leg over obstacles which are placed about 20 inches above the ground.

4) With both legs, jumping over low hurdles (2'6") placed on the ground. Knees to be pulled into the chest during flight.

Special-Conditioning Training

This is an activity which will help give the legs and body even more conditioning. If the jumper is on top of a box 3–4 sections high, and he has to hop down and rebound again to the top of another box, his leg, hips and body have to absorb the shock of landing from such a height and still be in a position to extend powerfully upward. This type of training, which can also be made progressively difficult, can provide the athlete with the necessary conditioning for his legs, hips and body.

The following exercises are recommended:

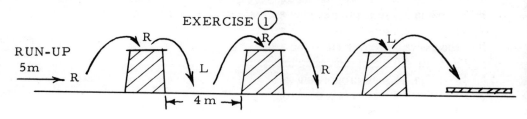

Figure 160.

1. (Fig. 160) Hop onto the first box, using the right leg, and step to the floor, landing with the left leg; rebound onto the second box, landing with the right leg, then hop to the floor, landing with the right. Carry onto the top of the third box, landing on the left, with the final takeoff to land with both feet on a mat. The sequence is R., R., L.; R., R., L. Always strive for height off the last box. Progress to increase the distance between the boxes from 13′ to 14′10″. Also change to L., L., R.; L., L., R.

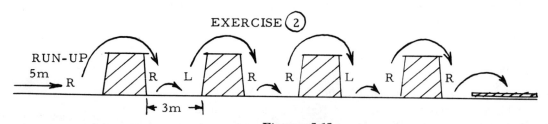

Figure 161.

2. (Fig. 161) Jump over boxes with this pattern: R., R., L.; R., R., L.; R., R. This time four boxes are used with the distance between them 10′. Progress to 11′6″ and also change to L., L., R.; L., L., R.; L., L.

Figure 162.

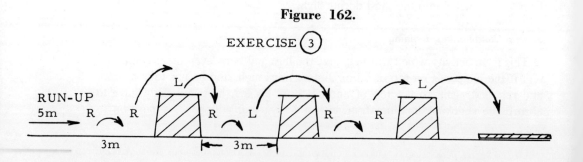

3. (Fig. 162) With this exercise, three boxes are used. The pattern of jumping is two hops, R., R. followed by L., landing on top of the first box. Then
change to R., L. between boxes one and two. Clear the second box with the
takeoff from L., landing on R., etc. The complete pattern is R., R., L.; R., L.;
R., R., L. The distance from the first takeoff to the first box is 16'5" while the
distance between the boxes is 10'. As the jumper improves, progress to an
increase of 1'6" between boxes.

EXERCISE ④

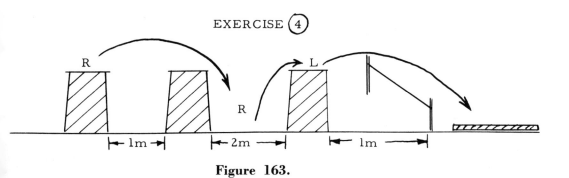

Figure 163.

4. (Fig. 163) Three 1½' boxes are used, with a distance of 3' between one
and two, 6' between two and three, and 3' to the high jump bar. The pattern of
jumping is hop from one over two and then bound to land on three with the
other leg, jumping into the air and over the bar to land on a net. The sequence is
R., R., L. or L., L., R.

EXERCISE ⑤

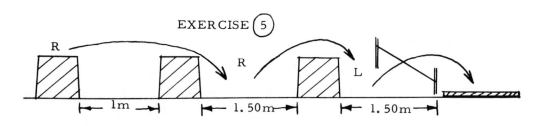

Figure 164.

5. (Fig. 164) This exercise is a variation of No. 4, but the emphasis is now
more on the "step" phase. Three boxes are used with 3' between one and two,
4'6" between two and three, and 4'6" to the bar.

The jumper hops with the right leg from box one clearing the second box,
and then he bounds up again with the right to clear the third box and land on the
left. The third spring is now from the left leg and over the bar to land on the mat.
Progress to an increase of 8" between boxes.

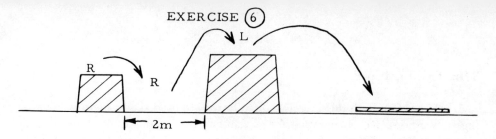

Figure 165.

6. (Fig. 165) Two boxes are used, with box one lower than box two. The heights are 1′8″ and 2′4″, and the distance between them is 6′6″. Hop down from the low box, then spring up to land on the high box with the opposite leg, and take off, landing on the mat. The sequence is R., R., L. The distance between the boxes is increased 1′6″ each time until the maximum is attained.

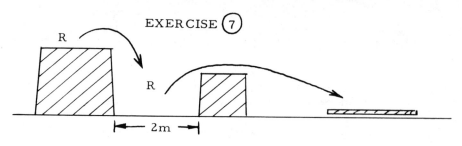

Figure 166.

7. (Fig. 166) Two boxes are used, but this time the placing of the boxes is reversed from that of No. 6. The jumper hops down from the higher box and springs up to clear the second box, landing on the mat. The distance between the boxes is 6′6″, and this is increased 1′6″ each time.

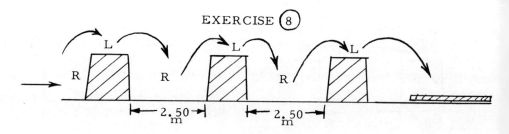

Figure 167.

8. (Fig. 167) Three boxes, each 1′6″ high, are used. The distance between each box is 8′. Alternate legs are used, with the sequence being R., L., R., L., R., L. The jumper runs and springs up, landing on top of the boxes with the left leg while landing on the ground with the right. The final landing is on the mat. Progress to an increase of up to 3′ in height and 20′ between boxes. Naturally, with an increase in height and the distance between boxes, the length of the approach run must be increased also.

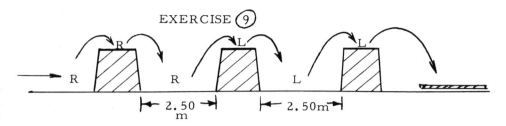

Figure 168.

9. (Fig. 168) The number of boxes, the height of each box, and the distance between boxes are the same as in No. 8. This time, however, the sequence is R., R., R.; L., L., L. The jumper takes off with the right from the ground, lands with the right on top of box one, bounds off to land with the right on the floor between one and two, and then changes to his left to land on top of box two. Progress to an increase of up to 3′ in height and 20′ between boxes.

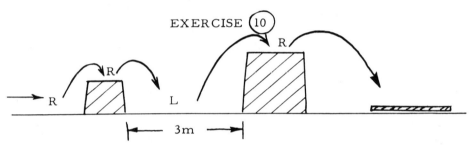

Figure 169.

10. (Fig. 169) Two boxes, 1′ and 1′8″ high, are used. The distance between the boxes is 10′. The jumper hops with his right leg from the floor, lands on box one with the right, bounds off, landing on the ground between boxes one and two with his left, springs up to land on box two with his right, and takes off to land on the mat. The sequence is R., R., L.; R. As the jumper improves, increase the height of box one to 1′8″ and box two to 4′. The distance between boxes is also increased up to a maximum of 20′.

Technique Training

While it is very necessary for the athlete to undergo a rigorous training program to provide him with essential strength, conditioning, speed and endurance, he must also be sure that he is sound in his technique. It is therefore imperative that the athlete perform the actual triple jump during training, but from a modified approach. His run to the board, no matter how short it is, should always be at full speed. Jumping at anything other than full effort can have a detrimental effect on rhythm and balance.

The athlete must work on technique much of the time, doing the same complex movements over and over again until he can perform them automatically. He must "groove" the muscle-nerve paths which are being utilized, so that they have no difficulty in traveling back and forth from the central nervous system to the muscle groups in use. In order to do this, the athlete must not be content to go out onto the track and merely triple jump until he is tired. He must, instead, think in terms of perfection and work on a particular point in his technique every time he makes a jump.

In practicing the triple jump from a shortened approach run, the athlete is performing the skill as a whole, which is very desirable. But since the triple jump is made up of a complicated series of movements, it is also necessary to practice the event in parts, as follows:

Hop and Step. This will enable the athlete to concentrate on the hop landing and step takeoff, and also help him to obtain a bigger step effort. The approach run is the same as that used in the triple jump practice. The athlete hops, and then he steps into the pit, trying to hold the step for as long as he can. It is a good idea to have the jumper attempt a much bigger step phase than he would normally use in the whole triple jump effort.

Step and Jump. This is a transition from the previous activity and is an aid in getting the body to react more quickly and vigorously from the step landing into the jump phase.

Approach Run. The athlete must spend time practicing his run-up over the full distance so that he can hit the board almost every time without overstepping the board. By constant practice, his stride length will become more regular and consistent. He should also attempt to increase the length of his approach run from season to season, as a longer approach run will add to his horizontal speed.

Approach Speed. As the athlete improves, he must gradually increase the length of his run-up until he is capable of jumping with the extra speed that comes with a full approach run. Too often there is no increase in the distance recorded when a jumper switches from a shortened approach run to a full-length run. This might indicate that he has not been able to cope with the extra speed resulting from the longer approach run, and so speed must be increased progressively.

Seasonal Training

The year can be divided into three different training periods, each with a specific purpose. The period during which the athletes do the most work is the period after the competitive season is over. This has often been called the "off-season" period. There is, however, a gradual transition from the competitive season to the off-season training period so that the muscles can gradually get used to the hard work involved.

Off Season. The jumper uses this period to build up his reserves of strength. He tries to increase his power, especially in his legs, and his endurance capacity.

Based on the different aspects of training, and using a six-day week of training, the athlete can indulge in:

First day: Rhythmical jump training and triple jumping (technique)
Second day: Strength training
Third day: Speed and endurance training
Fourth day: Special conditioning training
Fifth day: Strength training
Sixth day: Special speed-power training.

The two sessions of strength training are a very important part of the training. Acquisition of strength through weight training cannot be overemphasized.

Pre-competitive Season. As the season approaches, the character of the training period begins to undergo a gradual change. Speed training runs begin to appear more often in the training schedule.

First day: Speed endurance training/special speed-power training
Second day: Strength training
Third day: Special-conditioning training
Fourth day: Speed and endurance training
Fifth day: Strength training
Sixth day: Technique training.

Although the speed and endurance training session appears twice, the emphasis is now more on speed to prepare the jumper for the speedy approach runs that will be necessary when the season is underway. Strength training is still an important part of the program.

Competitive Season. The amount of training the athlete does during this period depends on the amount of competition he gets. As a rule, the intensity of the workouts decreases, although the athlete still does some weight training. He also performs some jumps during the training periods, but the number of jumps is rationed. The jumper should also begin to train with the sprinters, performing starts with them occasionally.

First day: Speed training
Second day: Strength training (modified)
Third day: Special speed-power training
Fourth day: Technique training
Fifth day: Speed training
Sixth day: Speed training.

If the athlete has a competition at the end of the week, it is important that he avoid jumping hard during that week, so that his legs will feel "springy."

Part III

THE THROWING EVENTS

Chapter 15

TEACHING THE BEGINNING SHOT PUTTER

by Friedrich Hess

Former world record-holder Parry O'Brien developed a putting form in 1951 which has set the pattern of technique. Others have refined and improved O'Brien's basic form, but the general pattern of movement remains essentially the same.

Shift and lift! These simple words describe the major movements used in shot putting—the simplest of the four throwing events. The putter initiates movement of the shot by shifting backward in the direction of the put. During this backward shift the trunk is somewhat horizontal. Upon arrival at the center of the circle, crouched in a strong, compact putting position, the shot is lifted explosively upward-forward, with the putter turning his hips and shoulders to the front. He imparts a final impulse to the missile after the body weight is off the rear foot by striking with the arm, wrist, and fingers. This action is characterized by sequential movement to produce continuous acceleration of the shot and preserve continuity of momentum.

1. Draw an official size shot circle on concrete with chalk. Draw a straight "line of direction" through the center of the circle, pointing in the direction of the put, and indicate this direction with an arrowhead at the end of the line. Draw a cross line dividing the circle into front and rear halves. The sidewalk bordering a playing field is an excellent surface from which to put.

2. The putter should stand erect at the back of the circle, facing away from the direction of put, with hands on hips. The right-handed putter should place his right foot on the line of direction with the right toes touching the circle where it intersects with this line.

3. He bends forward at the hips until the trunk is horizontal, bending the knees naturally. Now he straightens the trunk and legs, coming to the original erect standing position. This "lifting" movement should be repeated several times. Note that this action does not cause the shoulders to turn as he lifts.

4. The putter stands in the front half of the circle, with hands on hips, both

feet to the left of the line of direction, legs spread comfortably, about two feet apart, with toes almost touching the line of direction. The left side now faces the direction of put. The putter moves his right foot six inches directly forward, and turns it 45 degrees to his right. Now he should turn his trunk 90 degrees to his right and bend forward at the waist over a bent right knee until his trunk is horizontal. Now he should lift directly up until his trunk is erect. Have him repeat this until it feels natural to lift directly upward to an erect position.

5. Have the athlete repeat No. 4, lifting faster. The hips and shoulders now turn naturally to the left as he reaches the erect position. This is caused by the position of the left foot.

6. Have him repeat No. 4 again, lifting even faster, introducing a slight jump as he lifts. This will cause the weight to be lifted forward over the left leg, along the line of direction of put.

7. Have him repeat No. 4, lifting more powerfully. As the body weight moves forward in the direction of the put and both feet break contact with the circle, he will find it necessary to reverse the position of his feet to avoid going out the front of the circle. The left foot flashes back and the right foot speeds forward, passing in mid-air. The body weight settles over the well-bent right leg, on the line of direction at the front of the circle, when he has lifted really fast and powerfully. This is the reverse.

8. The putter places the shot in the palm of his left hand and supports it at about chest height. He lays the right hand loosely on top. He turns the hands over, reversing their position, so that the right hand is now on the bottom, supporting the weight of the shot on the fleshy pads at the "roots" of the three large fingers. The little finger and thumb support it away from the palm. The elbow is directly beneath the shot. Now he places the shot against the right side of his neck, in the hollow above the right collarbone, below the right jaw. The right elbow is below the shot in front of the body, and the right wrist is bent. He should permit the shoulders to slump forward. He holds his left arm straight and extends it in front of his body, pointing at the ground at an angle of 45 degrees.

9. While holding the shot as described in No. 8, the putter takes a position in the circle as described in No. 4. The left foot is near the front of the circle, about six inches to the left of the line of direction. The right foot is spread two to two-and-one-half feet to the right of the left foot, on the line of direction pointed back at a 45-degree angle. The trunk is horizontal over a bent right knee. The shoulders are pointed opposite to the direction of the put. The putter focuses his eye on his right toe, and extends his left arm toward the back of the circle at an angle of about 45 degrees.

10. From the position described in No. 9, the shot is lifted upward and forward and is delivered a short distance outside the circle along the line of direction. The arm should *not* be used at this stage. As experience is gained, the shot can be lifted more powerfully and faster, still not using the arm. The right elbow comes through very high as the shot is delivered. Remember that lifting is done *before* turning the hips, shoulders, and trunk to the left. This

should be repeated often to gain the ability to get the shot moving really fast during the lifting action. As the putter lifts faster and more powerfully, he will find it necessary to reverse the feet as described in No. 7 in order to remain in the circle.

11. Have the athlete repeat No. 10, but as the shoulders come square to the front after the lifting action, he should now strike powerfully with the right arm, with right elbow high, adding a final impulse after the arm extends by "flicking" the wrist and fingers. As the right arm strikes, the left arm moves back with elbow bent. During the arm strike, the left shoulder should be as high as possible, the right shoulder should be still higher, and the right elbow even higher. Both shoulders must keep moving forward during the arm strike.

12. Practice putting at a 45-degree angle over a low crossbar, supported by pole vault standards.

13. To teach the shift (or glide), make a long straight line with chalk on concrete. A sidewalk is excellent for this purpose. Have the putter stand on his right foot. He lifts his left leg behind and hops backward for a distance of 20 yards along the straight line, using short, easy hops.

14. Have the putter bend forward at the waist until the trunk is almost horizontal. He then extends the left leg straight behind and lifts it about 18 inches off the ground. Both arms are extended in front, pointed at an angle of 45 degrees toward the ground. He then hops backward 20 yards along the straight line. The putter next takes five backward hops for distance; then one for distance, trying to keep the trunk horizontal while hopping.

15. Have the athlete repeat No. 13, but instead of extending both arms in front, have him clasp both hands to the right knee. This will assist in keeping the trunk horizontal. Now he should practice taking long, powerful backward hops, keeping the trunk horizontal.

16. Returning to the circle drawn in No. 1, the putter holds the shot as described in No. 8 and stands in the back of the circle, facing opposite the direction of the put. He places the right foot on the line of direction, toes touching the inside of the circle at the back, supporting the weight of the body and the shot on the right leg. He moves the left leg, relaxed, backward toward the front of the circle, along the line of direction, tapping the circle with the left toe to retain balance. As the left leg moves backward, he bends the trunk forward and bends his right knee.

Have him focus his eyes on the rim or a short distance behind the circle. As his left leg extends fully with left toe resting on the ground for balance, the trunk will be nearly horizontal. He should lift the left leg directly upward, with heel approaching hip height. This lifts him on his right toes. Now he bends the left knee and brings it forward toward his right leg. While the left knee moves toward the right leg, the right knee bends, placing him in a crouched position at the back of the circle. As the left knee approaches the bent right knee, he tips his body weight toward the front of the circle. Now, with the bent knees nearly together, he shifts directly backward by simultaneously lifting and kicking the left leg toward the front of the circle, along the line of direction, and thrusting powerfully backward by extending the right knee. As the right leg is extended, thus moving him backward, he snatches the right leg under himself to catch the full weight of his body. The right foot grounds well underneath so that the shot would not hit the knee or foot but would fall to the ground well beyond the right foot and knee if he were to drop the shot as the right leg is planted. In this position, the right foot is on the line of direction, but has turned left from the starting position, and now points between 45 and 90 degrees to the line of direction. The left foot is grounded only momentarily after the right, landing not more than six inches to the left of the line of direction. In this, the putting position, the shoulders remain 90 degrees to the line of direction of the put, the left arm remains stretched to the rear, the trunk is still essentially horizontal, and the body is now in a position for a powerful upward and forward lift. This movement should be repeated often without putting, making no effort to gain distance across the circle in the shift, but keeping the right foot low to the ground as it is snatched under the body.

Draw a "graph" 10 feet long with chalk on cement. Lines B and C are parallel, three and one-half feet apart. Line A runs beside line B, but is not parallel to it. Line A is 12 inches from B at one end and four feet from B at the opposite end. Draw parallel "lines of direction" across A, B and C, perpendicular to B and C, one foot apart.

17. Have the athlete repeat No. 15, gliding across the graph drawn in No. 16. He starts on the "line of direction" which has only 12 inches between A and B. The right foot glides from A to B, and immediately the left foot positions itself near C. This movement is repeated on all the "lines of direction," with concentration on keeping the trunk horizontal and the shoulders square to the rear throughout the glide.

18. Combining the glide with the putting action in No. 11, the putter shifts, lifts and puts from each of the parallel lines of direction described in No. 17. As he improves, the powerful, explosive forward-upward lifting action will necessitate a reverse.

19. If the putter arrives at the putting position with the left foot "in the bucket" (well to the left of the line of direction), have him keep the right foot flat on the ground in the movements prior to driving backward across the circle, not lifting the heel from the ground until the last possible moment.

As a general rule, the shift across the circle should add approximately one-seventh of the standing putting distance. To demonstrate the value of the correct sequence of movements in the standing put, have the putter try this drill:

a) With toes to the board, stand square to the direction of the put, holding the shot as in No. 8. Hold the left arm horizontal, straight ahead. Keep the head up and, using only the arm, push the shot as far as possible. Put three times and mark the best effort.

b) Stand as in (a), but this time, instead of simply pushing with the arm, bend the knees and twist the trunk around to the right as far as possible without shifting the feet. In order to put, straighten the legs, unwind the trunk and drive with the right arm. Mark the best of three efforts, which should be three or four feet farther than in (a).

c) Stand with the left side facing the direction of put, with feet 18 inches apart, left foot up close behind the stop board. Turn the right foot 45 degrees to the right, with trunk turned back, and head facing back. Lift all the body weight back over the right foot. Drop into the putting position by bending both knees, and carrying the shot outside the base formed by the distance between the feet. The left arm is pointed toward the back of the circle. From this position, lift the shot straight upward, extending the right leg to lift the body weight over the left leg. As the weight moves forward, off the right leg, and as the chest turns to the front, strike powerfully with the right arm. This adds another two to four feet to the put.

d) Repeat (c), but this time lift the shot well out beyond the stopboard with such a powerful sustained effort that it is necessary to reverse the feet to remain in the circle.

Think of shot putting as SHOT LIFTING, and remember that the SHIFT and LIFT are the essence of shot putting.

Viel Glück!

Chapter 16

THE SHOT PUT

by John A. Savidge

The shot put is the simplest of all the throws because of the absence of full rotation (as in hammer and discus) and the lack of aerodynamic factors (as in discus and javelin). Shot-putting movements have become even more simplified with the inception of the O'Brien technique in the early 1950's.

Jim Fuchs was, in fact, the first athlete to emphasize the injection of speed in the preliminary movements of shot putting and the contribution that the body could make if properly positioned.

These basic aims were not fully explored, however, and it was left to O'Brien to capitalize on the advantages that Fuchs had indicated were present, and to overcome, through his starting position, the disadvantages that Fuchs had exhibited. This Parry O'Brien did in a magnificent manner, and he was thus clearly responsible for the terrific (no other superlative is adequate) upsurge in shot put performances.

A Precision Event

Relatively simple though the technique may be, it is a precision event with little tolerance allowed for substandard execution. Overcoming the inertia of the body mass and missile by driving across the ring and landing in the crouched position, the athlete uses the powerful, but relatively slow, muscles of the legs and trunk to accelerate the missile and place it on its ultimate path. The putter further accelerates it by using the weaker but much faster muscles of the arm.

While the circle of seven feet in diameter is limiting and decides to a great extent the technique of the event, the athlete operates outside the ring by applying effective force both outside the back of the ring and beyond the toe board.

Mechanically speaking, the shot-putter aims for a long line, a straight line and acceleration throughout, although the latter two aims are never fully accomplished.

Finger and Arm Positions and Movements

The putter holds the shot in the right hand with the weight supported on the "webbing" of the three middle fingers. The thumb and little finger act as wedges since they have a purely passive role and are not used in the final "finger flick" phase.

The three middle fingers should be behind the shot. If they are splayed out too much, only the longest finger is able to apply its full force and, in all probability, it would be subjected to stresses beyond its capacity. However, the placing of the three fingers close together results in bad stability of the missile, and therefore a compromise position is necessary.

The shot is then placed so that it almost "rests" in a position formed by the "cellar" of the collarbone and the jaw. The right elbow at this stage is underneath the shot in a supporting role.

Resting in this position, any movement of the body is imparted to the shot, while the low elbow position ensures that a considerable relaxation of the arm and shoulder girdle is achieved. If the elbow is kept high and the shot thrust into the neck, tension in these two muscle groups is at once apparent, and this is detrimental to later movements. (See Fig. 185.) The athlete takes up a position at the back of the ring with his right foot turned directly to the rear and his back facing the toe board. (See Fig. 170.) The left leg acts as a support, with little or no weight on it. The left arm is raised so that, viewed from the rear, the left hand and the shot are in one line. This important aspect of the starting position is essential if a premature uncocking of the body position is to be avoided and a flat-backed throwing position is to be achieved in the front half of the circle.

The athlete in Fig. 185 would have done better to have achieved, at that stage, the excellent left arm position he later adopts in Fig. 188. Any additional unnecessary movement only serves to complicate technique.

Figure 170.   **Figure 171.**

Figure 172.

Figure 173.

Figure 174.

Figure 175.

Figure 176.

Figure 177.

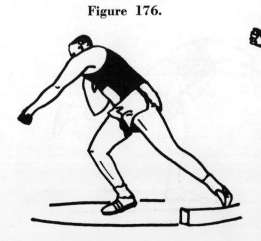

Figure 178.

Figure 179.

Figure 180.

Figure 181.

Figure 182.

Figure 183.

Figure 184.

Body Positions and Movements

The body is allowed to drop over a well-flexed right leg so that in its lowest position, the shot, if dropped, would fall at a position outside the ring. This is essential if the range of movement is to be extended. (See Fig. 172.)

The movement across the ring is initiated by allowing the hips to overbalance toward the toe board, and then the body is driven across the circle by a violent strike of the right leg, assisted in a scissoring movement (somewhat like the free leg movement in high jumping) by the left leg, which moves down and backward toward the toe board and its final position. (See Fig. 174.)

During this time the body must be kept in its down-and-back position and must not be allowed to come upright, since the low down-and-back position is fundamental to the next phase.

The movement is more commonly termed the "shift" or "glide" rather than the "hop," and indeed good shot-putters are always slightly in contact with the ground during this movement.

Figure 185.   **Figure 186.**

Figure 187.   Figure 188.

Figure 189.   Figure 190.

Figure 191.   Figure 192.

Figure 193.   Figure 194.

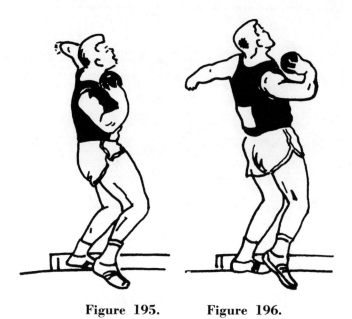

Figure 195.   Figure 196.

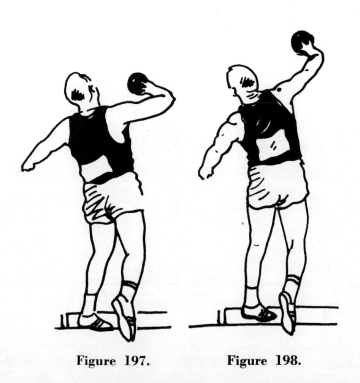

Figure 197.   Figure 198.

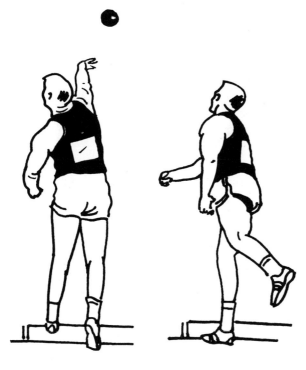

Figure 199.   **Figure 200.**

Leg and Foot Positions and Movements

In quick succession, following the drive of the right leg, it is recovered and placed under the body, still strongly flexed and with the body still in a low down-and-back position. (See Fig. 175.)

Almost immediately the left leg drops into a position slightly off center to the right leg so as to offer a point of resistance to the subsequent movements.

Several most important points arise at this stage. (See Fig. 194.) It has been essential to adopt a complete toe-back position in the rear of the ring so that the rear leg could be adequately flexed and the body put into its low starting position. The lower the position adopted, the further back the right toe must point.

During the shift, however, the body tends to adopt a higher position due to the action of the legs in movements executing the shift. This does not mean that the athlete should adopt a high position. A high position is a bad position! Since the body does tend to raise in the movement in the ring (See Figs. 173–176), the extreme backward pointing of the right foot is diminished, and the foot lands at an angle of 45 degrees to the center line of the circle. The distance between the two feet will vary, being determined by the height of the athlete and the angle of his backward body lean. If the athlete displays a narrow throwing base, he will be in a cramped position, shortening the range of movement. Most first class shot-putters take a base of about 3'9", i.e., the right foot just in the back half of the circle.

When Fuchs adopted his very extreme low-back position, it was at the expense of a backward right foot which, while advantageous to the subsequent lifting movement, is detrimental to the forward motion that accompanied it. The result was that with the retracted right hip position, he was never able to finalize the movement quickly enough over his front leg, and therefore he became a "back leg" putter, with the effect of shortening the range of movement.

The left leg position here is a very important factor. Should the left foot land on the same direction line as the right foot, many obvious faults will instantly appear. If it were possible to inject extreme high speeds into the shift, there would be no real problem. However, since the movement across the ring takes up less than 3'6" (less than half the diameter of the ring), such desirable speeds are unattainable.

Should the putter place his left foot on the center line, he will attain a position, which while very powerful, he will not be able to use. He will fail to bring his body to a vertical and forward position, or he will tend to prematurely rotate his shoulders around his left foot in an effort to operate beyond the toe board. He will therefore (1) never get over his left foot, or (2) drop his left shoulder, and almost certainly withdraw it, consequently shortening the range of movement and diminishing effective force.

At the other end of the scale, should the athlete place his left foot too far to the left of the direction line, he will (1) lose height at release, (2) have a tendency to open out to a side-on position, (3) produce a premature right hip movement, leaving himself on his back foot, (4) reduce the effectiveness of his left foot position in relation to a point of resistance.

"In the bucket" is an illustrative phrase that coaches have used since the 1930's to describe the old "sideways on" position. As the illustrations show, the employment of an O'Brien technique can lead to a left foot position at the extreme point of the toe board. (See Figs. 194 and 197.) This is not an "in the bucket" position since the athlete has traversed the circle in that desirable straight line, but at a tangent. If from the rear the straight line is maintained, the fault is a minimal one. Of course, if the shot is swung back along the orthodox direction line with a resultant loss of energy, this is a basic error.

Many athletes find it difficult to obtain a good left foot position and at the same time traverse directly across the ring. A modified toe-back starting position, which results in a modified left hip starting position, is often helpful. Additionally, in the shift the athlete not only tends to rise, but tends to uncock. (See Fig. 193.) This is also a result of the right foot landing at a more square-on position, pulling the right shoulder around. It could be argued that both the opening-out and rising body movements are desirable, since the final throwing position then accentuates the movements rather than initiates them, and acceleration is better maintained.

After landing in this position, one must not merely maintain acceleration, but increase it. While the violent lifting movement produces the greatest acceleration in the event, there is a dwelling period between the right and left foot landings when acceleration almost always lessens. Our aim, therefore, is never really accomplished with reference to our "acceleration throughout" principle.

This "rock-over" movement between the right and left foot landings is desirable since it ensures continuity. If the left leg lands before the right leg, this causes a pause and reduces body position over the right leg. Fuchs had this trouble in a different way. Due to his sideways-on position, his very high left hip position prevented his left leg from coming down quickly enough—a mistake that does not occur in the O'Brien technique since the left hip is low, and the natural flexion of the knee allows the left leg to come down quickly.

Immediately the left foot lands, and only then, as the left foot offers a point of resistance, do the right leg and trunk extend in a violent upward movement. No premature shoulder rotation is desirable at this point. The athlete stresses the vertical movement which blends with the forward movement initiated by the shift, resulting in a forward and upward flight path of the shot. (See Figs. 177 and 178.)

Position at the lifting stage is all-important. If the shot is allowed to continue in its forward movement and drift into a position in front of the right knee, the throwing position deteriorates very quickly. Rotation, which must be the only saving grace for the athlete, must of necessity occur, since the fundamental lifting position has eluded the athlete and short-circuited his movements. Rotation, plus the arm, will be his only salvation, and his performances will mirror his positional shortcomings.

The good athlete will delay the rotation until the body is well over a strongly flexed left leg, and then, with the right leg and body extensions complete, will rotate the shoulders, further accelerating the shot along its predetermined flight path. (See Figs. 179 and 180.) The shoulders should continue to move forward, because the arm has yet to strike. At this juncture the left shoulder is not allowed to fall away or retract. The athlete must put into the shot and not *away* from it—a very common novice error. The correct position is beautifully shown in Fig. 196.

In this illustration, one can see the wisdom of the placing of the shot in the starting position. If it is incorrectly placed or is allowed to fall away from the neck during the lifting phase, it will either fall behind the plane of the shoulders when they are rotated and result in a throw, or induce a premature arm strike and lessen effective force.

Naturally, during the lifting movement, the shot will be lifted from its original position (See Fig. 180.), but the period between this point and the forward rotation of the shoulders is marginal.

Final Movements

The athlete then enters into the final arm strike phase. With the body weight over a flexed left leg, the right arm moves into a high right elbow position. Having started with a low, right elbow position, the lifting movement has put this relaxed arm into a position where the right hand, elbow and shoulder are in one plane, thus utilizing the strongest operating position. (See Fig. 197.) The right leg, having done its work, has now been dragged forward (Fig. 197) by the forward and upward action of the right side of the body, particularly in the right hip area.

With the left side of the body still moving forward and upward, but with the right side catching up and going beyond, the left leg is extended to further increase vertical movement, and the right arm is violently forced away, with the right wrist and fingers imparting the missile's final acceleration. (See Figs. 198 and 199.)

The left arm has played a passive role throughout, following the left shoulder and folding away in the final stages to allow the right arm to strike. (See Figs. 194 and 199.)

Overzealous use of the nonactive left arm can lead to withdrawal and buckling of the left side. The reverse which follows is a movement which adds nothing to the distance, but enables the athlete to stay in the ring. (See Figs. 199 and 200.) It cannot be stressed too much that the reverse is the product of the correct throwing movements.

It is essential to maintain contact with the ground during the period when force is being applied, and the shot-putter will observe this by remaining in contact with the ground with his left foot during the final stages. However, the violent upheaval of the body both forward and upward in the throwing position seems to indicate to an athlete of the 60-foot class that while appreciating the mechanical wisdom of contact, the practical reason of staying in the ring must over-ride this. The majority of athletes in this range show a position as in Fig. 198 where left foot ground contact is broken just, but only just, before the shot leaves the hand. To delay the reverse even a fraction later would possibly result in fouling.

Since it is impossible to increase the acceleration of the shot without a point of contact with the ground, any premature reverse is not only undersirable, but is unpermissible.

Any premature straightening of the left leg will tend to interrupt the flowing forward and upward movement and reduce the range of movement by blocking the athlete's forward motion.

The problems and the technical equations are apparent. Thus, the coach must know what will be necessary to overcome these problems and lead to a mastery of the technique.

Muscular Strength Comes First

A novice primarily will be concerned with the acquisition of a technique, and yet many aspects of this technique will be very dependent on pure muscular strength. In fact, the novice's main basic errors can be traced directly to lack of muscular strength. Should an athlete be insufficiently strong to master technical movements, it would appear therefore to be "putting the cart before the horse." Quite obviously an athlete in this category will better further his ambitions by forsaking the circle and shot for the gymnasium and weights, remedying his strength defects before tackling the technical problems.

Assuming, however, for the moment that an athlete's immediate strength level is sufficiently high, and the competitive season is finished, the training program will go along these lines:

It is necessary to familiarize oneself with the actual throwing position in the front of the ring, and here the standing put plays an important part.

Be cautious, however, since the standing put is not really the event. It is possible to adopt a superb throwing position in the standing put which is impossible to duplicate after the glide with its forward movement. The consequence is that the novice athlete finds little difference in distance between the standing put and the complete movement. This is because at this stage in his development, the glide has not been sufficiently "married" to the final throwing position, and continuity has suffered. In addition to this the athlete has adopted a much more powerful standing put position than he could arrive at following the shift.

Athletes can, of course, achieve continuity by sacrificing the low position. Most novice athletes, and even seasoned campaigners, often produce low angled puts of considerable distance. This is because the release speed of the implement is high, and its flight path is straighter than if a low throwing position had been achieved. For the really long throws, however, it is essential that the shot be lifted at a high release speed and at a proper angle, and not made into a "line drive."

At one time it was felt that the glide would add approximately one-seventh of the standing put, e.g. an increase from 49 feet with a standing put to 56 feet with the glide. Nowadays one feels that a rather smaller percentage is added to the standing put—around one-tenth.

After familiarizing himself with the final throwing position, the athlete must now work on the shift. This again is not the event proper, and continual repetition of the glide without the actual throwing movement can lead to "posing" difficulties and movement consciousness. "Self-analysis leads to paralysis."

Since no novice shot-putters fail to use the arm, the accent should be on properly using the legs and trunk. It might be helpful at this stage to use an overweight shot in an effort to remind the athlete of the importance of proper leg and trunk action. Care should be taken not to use this too often, since the fine shades of timing can be affected if too much use is made of an overweight missile.

As timing is all important, the athlete should endeavor to throw all-out all of the time and have measured marks out to satisfy his appetite regarding distance. This does not mean that aimless all-out throwing is being recommended. But the habits and timing in training should be as in competition, so that the athlete adjusts very easily from the training ground to the competition stadium.

In the athlete's early stages it will be possible for him to take a maximum quantity of actual throwing, but as time goes by and the quality of his performance improves, he will find it not only injudicious but also impossible to get quality *and* quantity. If he is in a temporary fatigued state through too much quantity putting, he will find that his technique will be unconsciously adjusted in an effort to maintain distances. A series of modified techniques will then be successively employed with disastrous effects.

Few novices after the glide will be able to adopt a fine throwing position, as in Fig. 176, because of a number of factors. The very low starting position is fundamental, since the leg will be under strong flexion and must be able to propel the athlete and the shot at the necessary desirable speed across the ring. In addition the drive of a strongly flexed right leg will assist in the fast recovery of it (as with the recovery stride in sprinting), enabling the athlete to get the flexed right leg under the body, or, more important, *in front* of the moving body weight.

There is a tendency for the body to rise during the execution of the shift. Should the athlete start with a high body position and then rise, the inevitable higher body position will place him in a throwing position with the weight on the left leg, and a slightly flexed right leg will then be able to make a minor contribution to the subsequent throwing movement.

Another novice error at this point will be that the "tail" will be sticking out, robbing the athlete of the highly important flat-back position. Then the maintenance of a "stretched left shoulder position" is often the remedy. (See Fig. 176.)

The ultra fast right-leg action (Figs. 177 and 178) makes use of the correct position. It is not enough to land in a correct position, one must also use it. This position (Fig. 177) is not static as in standing putting. It is only briefly available due to the athlete's forward motion.

The accent then will be to VERTICALLY lift the shot as soon as the left leg lands. In driving upward with the right leg, one finds a slight flexion of the left leg is highly necessary. Fig. 182 shows the athlete has almost halted his forward motion by prematurely straightening his left leg. This has shortened the range of movement, since he has been unable to "chase" the shot beyond the toe board. The right side, therefore, has not been allowed to follow through. The action of the right hand illustrates this admirably.

The desirable "wave it goodbye" forward action of the athlete's hand, properly illustrated in Fig. 198, does not come about because the athlete has dropped the right elbow in the arm strike phase, but because he has been reluctant to allow the shot to be released. He has used the mobile launching pad of the shoulders to operate a fast arm. Now, and only now, are the shoulders almost square to the front. The shoulders should never be a relatively static platform with the arm "stabbing" the shot. One can appreciate from Fig. 194 that the athlete has delayed the rotation of his shoulders until the last moment, i.e., until the body weight is almost over the left foot. While for the coach it is a question of UP and *then* OUT, the athlete will interpret this as UP *and* OUT.

The final force imparted to the shot, called the "finger flick," performs another useful purpose. The action of this force sets up a reaction which travels down the arm and body and has the effect of driving the body back toward the ground, thus helping the athlete to remain in the circle. If the athlete has rotated too early and has scorned the lifting motion, he will in all probability get an excellent finger flick due to that rotation. But the reaction will not help to cancel out the body's strong forward movement, and he will then foul by going beyond the toe board.

The rising of the body and the uncocking of the shoulders start during the initial drive across the ring. The flight path is then almost in a straight line. This is much more than could be achieved with the old sideways-on position where the path of the shot from a high standing position to a low middle-of-the-ring position (from where it was accelerated) formed a V-like path.

Mechanical forces used should be along a straight line, i.e., between the shot's low starting position and its point of release. This is never quite achieved as the left leg tends to disturb the rising flow.

Much can be learned from the landing position of the shot after release. Should it go to the left of the direction line, either the movement across the circle has been incorrectly too far to the left, i.e., at a tangent of the circle, or the left shoulder has been dropped and withdrawn, perhaps because of a badly executed left arm movement, which "hooks" the shot away from its forward direction line.

If the shot lands to the right of the direction line, the left leg has either landed too much in front of the athlete, thus blocking his forward movement, or the athlete has prematurely straightened his left leg and has gone around it, rather than "over the top" of it. Also, the flat-back position in the front of the ring may not have been achieved, therefore allowing only partial lift and premature rotation around the left foot.

As we said, many technical errors will disappear as the strength level rises, and when a reasonable degree of competence is achieved, the athlete's workout will resemble the outlines of this program.

Off-Season Workouts

During the winter the athlete will devote his energies to raising his strength levels by weight lifting. Without going too deeply into schedules, we state that heavy poundages and low repetitions will form the bulk of the athlete's work since muscular strength will be the aim and not muscular endurance. General fitness and mobility must be catered for. A nonbody contact sport, such as basketball, handball, squash, etc., offers the shot-putter much help in this area.

During this period, the occasional throwing sessions will be used to stress the progress of gymnasium work, but the real technique sessions should start around March/April when weight-lifting schedules will be curtailed in favor of such sessions. Preceded by correct warm-up and followed by some sprinting work (preferably from blocks, since the static starting position in this event can be likened to the "set" position in the dashes), the athlete's workout sessions should be six days a week with 30 puts per session. Naturally, once the season starts, the problem of remaining fresh for competition disturbs this routine, and so no violent exercise will be undertaken during the two days prior to a competition.

It is reasonable to assume that if one hasn't got "it" on Thursday, nothing is likely to produce "it" between Thursday and Saturday! As the athlete gets more proficient, it will still be necessary to throw a considerable amount during workout sessions to retain the fine shades of timing the event demands.

Jim Fuchs was once asked what his coach told him to concentrate on during competition. I, with my ears wide open, listened for these words of wisdom. Words of wisdom they were indeed, but not what I had expected. Fuchs said that his coach always said the same thing to him prior to a competition: "Jimmy, put that damned thing out of the stadium!"

That is what competition is all about! The great American pole vault coach, Dick Ganslen, once remarked that during one of his athlete's temporary low-point performances, "I corrected him by giving him a Diet of Fundamentals."

If something goes wrong during competition, it cannot be attributed to that lucky uniform, or to that crooked left finger, or that extra half cup of coffee that you had on the day when the long one appeared, but to some fundamental factor in the technique which has gone awry and must be traced. Many are traced directly from the starting position.

I think it apt for an athlete of my size to quote the great poet Longfellow, who said (and this applies to shot putting no less than to any other aspect of life), "Not in the shouts and plaudits of the throng, but in ourselves, are triumph and defeat."

Chapter 17

TEACHING THE BEGINNING DISCUS THROWER

by Bill Huyck

1. Stand with feet one yard apart, hands on hips, and knees bent.

2. While standing in this position, turn the right foot 90 degrees to the right and turn the body and head to the right as far as possible. The left heel will lift and turn out naturally.

3. Now turn strongly to the left, spinning around the left shoulder and left foot as if they were hinges of a door. At the start of the turn, get more power by spinning the right heel away from you, pivoting on the right toes. During the turn, drive the right hip forward and up by straightening the right leg. After straightening the right leg, drive straight up with the left leg. The right foot will drag forward and off the ground as your body moves upward and around to the left. Repeat this movement until it can be done smoothly.

4. Again stand in the position with feet one yard apart, knees bent, right foot turned 90 degrees to the right, and body and head turned as far to the right as possible. However, this time wrap the left arm loosely around your chest. The left arm remains wrapped in this position throughout the throw. Now drop the right arm and permit it to hang loosely by your side, like a piece of rope.

5. Turn strongly to the left, first straightening the right leg, and then driving the left leg straight up. As you turn to the left, the right arm swings out of its own accord, and the right foot drags forward on the ground. Repeat this until the movement comes smoothly.

6. Pick up the discus. It rests on the first joints from the ends of the fingers. Relax the thumb. If you turn the palm down, the discus will fall out. With thumb up, roll the discus off the forefinger along the ground. Soon it can be rolled as much as 30 yards in a straight line. The discus always leaves the first finger last, whether it is rolled or thrown. To insure that the discus always leaves the first finger last, make certain that the elbow is never bent when throwing. Now practice throwing the discus ten feet straight up in the air. Again, do not bend the elbow; make certain the discus leaves the first finger last.

7. Stand in a preliminary throwing stance, feet one yard apart, knees bent,

right foot turned 90 degrees to the right, head and body turned to the right, left arm wrapped loosely across the chest, and right arm hanging loosely by the right side, holding the discus. Turn fully to the left, straighten the right leg, and drive the left leg straight up, in that order. The right arm will swing loosely up, and the discus will leave the hand spinning in a clockwise direction. Throw gently and often from this preliminary throwing stance, but not farther than 30 feet. Make the discus fly flat or parallel to the ground as it leaves the first finger last. It may be necessary to press down on the discus with the right thumb, palm to the ground, to make it fly flat.

8. As you continue to throw from a preliminary throwing stance, gradually become accustomed to holding the discus farther out from the right side as you start the throw. Continue to throw in this manner without adding additional movements. A week of throwing from a preliminary throwing stance will result in a stronger leg, more body drive, and a cleaner throw. Do not use preliminary swings at this time.

9. After a week of throwing from a preliminary throwing stance, learn the preliminary swing. Hold the discus at your side as described in No. 6 above. Without bending the elbow, swing the discus about hip height close to the body, across to the left side. As it reaches the left side, place the left hand flat against the side of the discus to keep it from falling from the right hand. Now swing it back to the right side, removing the left hand as it starts to the right. Repeat this again and again, but lift the discus a bit higher each time it passes in front of you. Soon you will be swinging the discus at arm's length parallel to the ground at shoulder level. Centrifugal force will keep the discus from dropping as it passes in front of you. "Catch" the discus as it comes to your left side with the left palm facing up, held at shoulder level. As it swings back to the right at shoulder level behind the right shoulder, the discus may be turned up somewhat in the hand to prevent it from falling. This exercise aids in executing preliminary swings properly.

10. The preliminary swing. Place the discus flat on the upturned left palm, held at left shoulder height. Cover the discus with the right palm, overlapping the edge of the discus with the first joints of the forefingers on the right hand in a normal discus hold. Swing the discus at shoulder level parallel to the ground, to the rear behind the right shoulder, at arm's length, and return it to the original position on the left palm. Keep the right palm down through this movement. Centrifugal force will prevent the discus from falling. One preliminary swing is enough before throwing. Too many, or fierce preliminary swings may cause a loss of balance.

11. The turn. Draw an official size discus circle on concrete with chalk. The sidewalk bordering a playing field is an excellent surface from which to throw. Draw a straight line through the center of the circle, pointed in the direction of the throw. Draw a cross line dividing the circle into front and rear halves.

12. Draw chalk footprints in the circle. Left (1) and Right (1) will straddle the line of direction about shoulder width apart at the rear of the circle, pointing opposite to the direction of the throw. Draw a six-inch cross as footprint Right (2) at the center of the circle. Draw footprint Left (2) at the front of the circle,

slightly to the left of the line of direction, pointing a bit toward the right of the direction of the throw.

13. Walk through the turn. Stand on footprints Left (1) and Right (1) without the discus, at the rear of the circle, facing opposite to the direction of throw. Lift the left heel, pivot on the ball of the left foot, and turn as far to the left as is comfortable. The right heel will now rise, and you will also pivot left on the ball of the right foot. For better balance, keep the balls of both feet in contact with the concrete as long as possible while turning. Keep your back erect, and the left shoulder up. Continue turning left on the ball of the left foot, pivoting on footprint Left (1). You will now tend to face toward the direction of the throw. As you continue turning left, the right foot will leave the concrete. Now pick up the right knee high and drive the right foot down on the cross at Right (2) at the center of the circle. Continue turning left or counterclockwise by pivoting on the ball of the right foot, which is now on the cross at Right (2) at the center of the circle. The left foot now leaves footprint Left (1) and is driven in a straight line to footprint Left (2) at the front of the circle. Left and right knees pass close together as the left foot travels directly from footprint Left (1) to Left (2). Walk through the full turn often to gain balance. Keep the left arm wrapped across the chest, and the right arm hanging down near the right side like a rope. At the end of the turn, the right arm will swing out of its own accord. Gradually increase the speed.

14. As balance improves and proficiency increases, introduce a slight jump as you turn around the left foot. Both feet will be off the ground momentarily during the slight jump from the left foot on footprint Left (1) to the right foot, landing on the cross marking Right (2) at the center of the circle. Repeat this often. This movement is known as "running rotation" across the circle. If you have a tendency to fall backward as the left foot reaches footprint Left (2), this can be avoided by making certain all the weight of your body is on the left leg at Left (1) as you start moving into the turn.

15. The complete throw. Repeat the movement described in Nos. 13 and 14 above, but with the discus in the right hand. After completing one preliminary swing, again swing the discus to the right as though executing another preliminary swing. Start the turn just as the right arm completes its path to the rear. The throwing arm should trail relaxed, wide of the body at shoulder level, throughout the turn. Start the turn in a slight "sitting down" position. The trunk remains erect and shoulders level throughout. In the throwing position, with feet on Right (2) and Left (2), the body weight moves from the rear (right) leg forward, over, and beyond the front (left) leg. The longer you can resist the temptation to throw for distance, the better the throwing will be. Get most of your weight over the left leg as you start the turn to avoid falling backward when you arrive at the throwing position in the front half of the circle.

16. The reverse. As your weight moves forward, over, and beyond the front (left) leg, the discus leaves your hand opposite the right shoulder and the right foot comes forward. Drop your weight on the right leg as it reaches the front of the circle. Let the body turn left, shift the left leg quickly to the rear, and bounce on the right leg, producing a simple reverse.

Chapter 18

THE DISCUS THROW

by David Pryor and H. H. Lockwood

Myron's famous sculpture, "Discobolus," reflects the discus style characterized by the ancient Greeks. (See Fig. 201.) At that time there was very little standardization of the event. The discus was hewn from wood or stone and thrown with an underarm bowling action, for accuracy as well as for distance.

Discus throwing as it is now known began as a "classical revival" in the late nineteenth century. At that time there were strong attempts to recreate the ancient style of throwing, and this restricted the development of technique as we know it today. In the 1908 Olympic Games in London there were competitions for both "free-style" and "Greek-style" discus throwing, but soon after this the "Greek-style" faded out.

In the period prior to 1930 the evolution of modern discus throwing was very slow, with little coaching available and not much written on the event. The most usual style was one which involved a "side-toward-the-direction-of-throw" start and a rotating, stepping action into the actual throwing position. The footwork was along the line of the direction of throw.

A significant change in the event during this early period was the substitution of the 8′2½″ circle (2.5 meters) for the 7′ circle which was originally used for both shot and discus. This change came about in 1911, and immediately J. H. Duncan of the United States improved his own world record to 156′1⅜″, an increase of nearly 11 feet. The added distance available for movement in the circle was to have great bearing on the technical evolution to come.

Duncan's record stood until 1924, but the early thirties saw the adoption of improved techniques enabling more speed, greater range of movement, and stronger throwing positions. Two athletes at Stanford University—Eric Krenz and Phil Fox—were among the pioneers of the "back-to-direction-of-throw" technique, which was the direct forerunner of the technique that is recognized as orthodox today. Starting at the back of the circle, with the thrower facing the opposite direction of the intended throw, the style is characterized by a spinning action on the left foot, and, as Fox himself described it, "You move almost

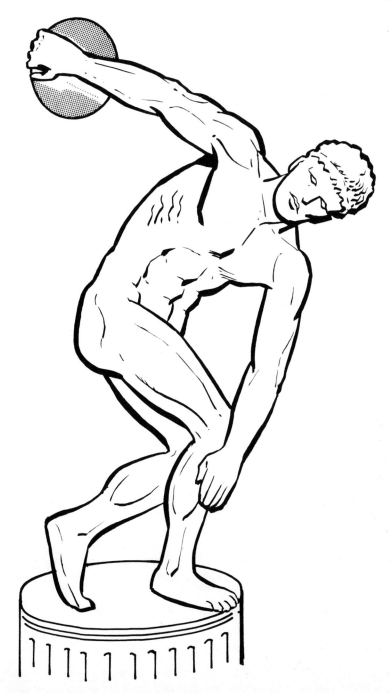

Figure 201. Myron's *Discobolus*. Bronze statue from about 450 B.C. illustrating Greek style of discus throwing. The posture of the thrower indicates an under-arm bowling action.

backwards, letting your back lead the action." These words remind one of Al Oerter, the four-time Olympic champion, who manages to achieve throws in excess of 200 feet with a form of this technique.

Adolfo Consolini of Italy, who dominated world discus throwing immediately before and after the Second World War, employed a "back-to-direction-of-throw" start, but tended to waste some of the available width of the circle by dropping his left foot back just as he was about to pivot on it at the beginning of the throw.

The years following the Second World War saw the birth of the style of throwing that is widely used today. Robert Fitch of the U.S.A. experimented with setting the left foot around until it was pointing in the direction of the throw, and then driving *forward* across the circle. This initial part of the action, intrinsically different from the phase of the style it replaced, resembled the action of a sprinter. It enabled more forward momentum and a stronger throwing position at the front of the circle. The increased efficiency of the style was soon proved when Fitch set a new world record of 180'2¾". His previous best had been 166'10".

Fitch's success in 1946 was viewed by coaches with a wary eye, but other throwers were impressed. Further modifying Fitch's technique, Sim Iness won the 1952 Olympic title and in 1953 became the first man to surpass 190'. The same year his great rival, Fortune Gordien, threw 194'6" for a new world record, which stood for six years. Gordien and Iness are regarded as classical exponents of the "running-rotation" style, innovated by Fitch.

"Running rotation" is still the style most widely used today. The only main variation is in the type of release employed. Throwers have tended to fall into two main groups: those who release while still in contact with the ground and those who release in the air after an upward springing movement at the end of the turn.

Throwers who release while in contact with the ground lay more stress on driving the hips and upper body up and over a bracing left leg (relying on the leg's hinging action) to provide lift for the discus. This type of action depends on a comparatively wide throwing base.

The other main group of throwers rely more on the upward drive of both legs. This upward drive begins earlier and tends to utilize a narrower throwing base. The bracing action of the left leg still occurs vigorously, but it is shorter in duration. This type of action culminates in an off-the-ground release, and the reverse becomes an essential part of the throwing action.

"Running Rotation" Discus Technique

The Start. The thrower adopts a position at the back of the circle, facing opposite the direction of throw. The feet are shoulder width apart and parallel. The body weight is evenly distributed over the balls of both feet. Two or three preliminary swings are usual to "get the feel of the discus." The preliminary swings should be easy and controlled and accompanied by the transference of

Figure 202. **Figure 203.**

Figure 204. **Figure 205.**

Figure 206.   Figure 207.

Figure 208.   Figure 209.

Figure 210.   **Figure 211.**

Figure 212.   **Figure 213.**

Figure 214.   **Figure 215.**

Figure 216.   **Figure 217.**

Figure 218.   Figure 219.

Figure 220.

the body weight from the ball of the left foot to the ball of the right as the discus is swung from left to right. During the preliminary swings, the discus comes to the left and is caught on the upturned palm of the left hand just in front of the left shoulder. As it comes to the right, it is checked by a slight supination of the right hand. (See Fig. 202.)

During the last preliminary swing when the discus is moving around to the right, the thrower adopts a lower position by bending his knees, but at the same time keeping his head upright, back straight and seat in. (See Fig. 203.) While the discus is still back to the right and the weight is on the right foot, the thrower begins to set the left foot around to the direction of the throw by turning out the left heel. (See Fig. 204.) As he pivots on the ball of the left foot, his legs assume a "bandy" position with both knees pointing outward (Figs. 204 and 205), and he now transfers his weight completely over the ball of the left foot. Good balance, with the body weight right over the ball of the left foot at this stage is essential, and any deviation will lead to faults later on. As the "setting" action is taking place, the right foot must be kept down as long as possible. (See Fig. 204.) It must also be stressed that this initial phase of the throw (Figs. 202–205) must be executed slowly in relation to what follows it.

Drive Across the Circle. When in the "set" position (Fig. 205), the thrower begins his straight line drive across the circle. The right foot and leg are brought as close to the left leg as possible (Figs. 206 and 207), and the right knee should be lifted high. (See Fig. 208.) Notice here the strong resemblance to sprinting action. (See Figs. 206–208.) Hence the term "running rotation."

This phase of the throw is relatively faster, with the emphasis on a powerful driving action from the left leg to take the thrower to the front of the circle. As he nears the front, the thrower performs a scissoring action with his legs (Figs. 210 and 211) to bring himself into the throwing position. (See Figs. 212–214.) The thrower leads the turn with his legs, while holding back the right shoulder and discus. To assist this, the left arm is kept curled across the chest. (See Figs. 207 and 208.)

The Throwing Action. The effectiveness of the throwing position, or lack of it, depends directly on the movements which have preceded it at the back of the circle and during the drive forward. Points to look for in a good thrower in the throwing position (Figs. 211–213) are as follows:

1. The body's weight well over a bent right leg. (Good balance in the starting position and a high knee pickup in the drive across the circle will facilitate this.)

2. A strong throwing position with the discus kept well back to enable maximum length of pull. (Keeping the legs together in the drive across the circle will speed up their turning or scissoring action and allow them to move ahead of the upper body and arms, thus creating torque or "wind-up" in the throwing position.)

3. A landing facing the *rear* of the circle. (In order to avoid turning too far before the actual throw has begun, the thrower should avoid spinning on the

left foot at the rear of the circle. This can result from going too fast at the back of the circle during the setting action.)

4. The left foot should be down and in contact with the ground as soon as possible at the front of the circle. (Here it looks as though the foot could be down sooner—see Figs. 211–213. This enables the thrower to fully utilize his strong "wound-up" position as soon as possible. While waiting for the left foot to come down, the strong throwing position can be wasted if the thrower starts to unwind before fully effective force can be applied to the discus. Referring to the thrower's movement at the back of the circle, one can see how he can get his left foot down quickly at the front.)

The drive across the circle from the left foot must be a powerful one. As the other movements described above take place, the left leg and foot move in a straight line, with heel leading from the back of the circle to the front.

The Release. Once in the throwing position there must be no hesitation. Ideally it is a position the thrower moves through, not to. Simultaneously, the right side of the body is driven around into the throw, and the body weight is driven forward and upward from the bent right leg. The turning of the right side is initiated by screwing the right foot around, followed by the turning of the right knee, right hip, right shoulder, right arm, and finally the discus. The release is completed by a powerful forward movement of the shoulders. (See Figs. 214–218.)

The Reverse. Basically the reverse consists of leaving the ground, either during or immediately after the release, and changing the position of the feet with a scissoring movement. The right foot is stamped down, with the toe turned inward, close to the rim, in a position approximate to that of the left foot in the actual throwing position. Equilibrium and control are then achieved by poising the body weight over the right leg. Any dangerous forward lurch may be checked by bending the right knee and bending the body well over it. Bringing the left leg up to a position parallel to the ground also helps to gain control. (See Fig. 220.)

Rhythm and Timing. A fine sense of rhythm and timing is essential to good discus throwing. The accepted general time-sequence or rhythm of the throw can be represented as follows:

S. . . . E. . . . T . . ., Bang, Bang.

The "setting" action represented by "S. . . . E. . . . T" begins at the end of the last preliminary swing. It is marked by the steady turning action and pivoting on the ball of the left foot, at the back of the circle, until it points to the direction of the drive and eventual throw. This phase of the throw is comparatively slow and controlled.

The "Bang, Bang" should follow very closely after the "T," and correspond with the placing of the feet in the throwing position. First, the right foot lands in the center of the circle. Second, very shortly afterward, the left foot lands at the front of the circle.

The second "bang" marks the beginning of the final phase of the throw,

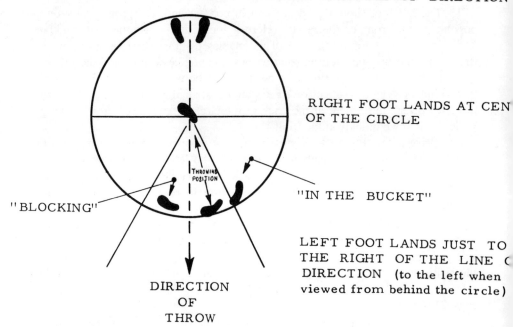

START WITH FEET SHOULDER WIDTH
APART ASTRIDE THE LINE OF DIRECTION

RIGHT FOOT LANDS AT CEN
OF THE CIRCLE

THROWING POSITION

"IN THE BUCKET"

"BLOCKING"

LEFT FOOT LANDS JUST TO
THE RIGHT OF THE LINE (
DIRECTION (to the left when
viewed from behind the circle)

DIRECTION
OF
THROW

Figure 221. If the left foot lands on or to the left side of the line of direction, it will "block" the thrower at release, preventing him from getting "squared up" to the throw. If the left foot lands too far around to the right, "in the bucket," this will detract from the strength of the throwing position.

namely the unwinding action initiated by the driving in of the right side of the body. It is the essential explosive climax to all the movements that have preceded it. (See Fig. 221.)

Theory of Technique

All accepted ideas of good discus technique have been formed as a result of athletes actually throwing and developing efficient and successful styles. This development has been accompanied by critical analyses by coaches, leading to acceptable theoretical bases of technique.

Ultimately, the factors which determine the length of the throw can be classified into three groups:

1. The speed at which the discus leaves the hand,
2. The upward inclination from the horizontal at which the discus leaves the hand, and
3. Various aerodynamic factors affecting the flight of the discus.

The aim of all coaching is to make these factors optimum.

Release Velocity. By far the most important factor contributing to the length of the throw is the speed at which the discus leaves the athlete's hand. A small variation in the release velocity will cause a considerable difference to the length of the throw. Throwing with a full turn was an improvement over the standing throw because of the increase in release velocity, making it possible to apply force to the discus over a longer distance.

Adoption of a "back-to-direction-of-throw" start greatly increased the amount of forward drive possible and increased the range of turning by another 90 degrees.

During the turn, the steady application of force to the discus causes acceleration culminating in the final release velocity. However, overhead motion picture analysis of discus throwers has shown that during the discus turn, the acceleration from start to finish is by no means constant. (See Fig. 222.)

Figure 222.

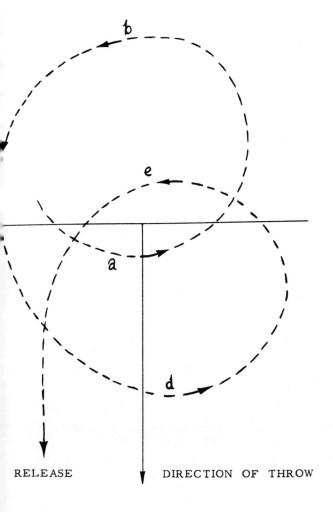

INITIAL ACCELERATION
a AFTER END OF LAST
   PRELIMINARY SWING

b CONSTANT SPEED
   DURING "SETTING" ACTION

c ACCELERATION AT DRIVE OFF
   LEFT FOOT ACROSS CIRCLE

DECELERATION DURING
d DRIVE WHILE WAITING FOR
   RIGHT FOOT TO COME DOWN

e GREAT ACCELERATION
   DURING THROWING ACTION

RELEASE   DIRECTION OF THROW

The beginning of the turn is marked by gradual acceleration, from the end of the last preliminary swing until the point where the left foot is set around to the direction of the drive across the circle. (See Figs. 202–206.) The drive across the circle from the left foot initiates a phase of increased acceleration which lasts until the thrower has taken off. Deceleration then continues until the right foot has landed in the center of the circle and initiated the throwing action. The actual throwing action is accomplished with great acceleration. (See Figs. 214–220.)

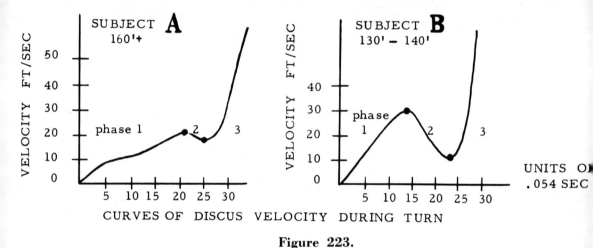

CURVES OF DISCUS VELOCITY DURING TURN

Figure 223.

Although the 130′–140′ thrower represented by Graph 2 in Fig. 223 attains a greater velocity of the discus in the early part of the throw, his final release velocity is less, and consequently the distance of his throw suffers. The rapid acceleration shown during phase one is probably due to spinning on the ball of the left foot at the back of the circle. This, as has already been pointed out, can lead to a weak throwing position in which the thrower lands at the front of the circle too far around into the direction of the throw. The consequent decreased pull available to the thrower cuts down the eventual release velocity.

All throwers exhibit three phases in terms of discus velocity:

1. Acceleration	Turn	Turn and drive off
2. Deceleration— briefer period	Turn	In air and landing in throwing position
3. Great acceleration— brief period	Throwing action	

A better thrower whose discus velocity during the turn is represented by Graph 1 in Fig. 223 shows more gradual buildup and lower discus velocity in phase one but much less deceleration during phase two. Thus, better throwers actually commence phase three with greater discus velocity which enables them to attain a greater eventual release velocity. It must be stressed, however, that about 75 percent of the release velocity is not obtained until phase three. This underlines the importance of holding the shoulders, right arm, and discus well back. (See Figs. 213 and 214.) The thrower makes this possible by his movement at the back of the circle when he is ready to drive off the left foot. (See Fig. 206.) The aim must be to keep the right leg as close to the left as possible. As the thrower then drives across the circle, his legs, being close to one another, will have a small radius of turning. This increases their speed of turning proportionally and, as they come to the front of the circle, allows the lower half of the body to get into position as soon as possible.

Virtually inseparable from this matter is the subject of torque between legs, hips, shoulders, and right arm. Torque, which may be likened to the potential power of a coiled spring, is an essential ingredient of the throwing position. The bodily movements described above may well help to achieve it by allowing the legs to move ahead of the upper body.

At the front of the circle, the unwinding action or release of torque takes place, beginning with the driving in of the right foot, knee, and hip. (See Figs. 211–213.) There is very little doubt that, contrary to the formerly held belief, the thrower can start driving the right side of his body into the throw before the left foot alights. What is still in dispute is, how powerful and effective is any such turning in of the right side that takes place before the left foot lands, and how much of it is merely induced by the angular momentum of the legs coming into position?

The turning in of the right side of the body is completed by the driving in of the right shoulder and arm to effect the release. In this unwinding action the force engendered by the stronger muscle groups of the legs, especially the right leg, and the trunk, is transmitted to the discus via the arm.

The actual contribution of the arm is very limited as an applicator of its own muscular force. It is rather the link between the stronger muscle groups of the legs and trunk and the discus. Any contribution made by the arm to the throwing action comes under the category of what physiologists term "ballistic action." It is characterized by a preliminary stretching of the prime movers, followed by a very rapid contraction (accompanied by a relaxation of the antagonists), and often a relaxation of all muscles involved when peak velocity has been reached, so that the movement is completed under its own momentum. Prime movers, of course, are those muscles directly responsible for a movement, and the antagonists are those which, when contracted, oppose it. In flexing the arm the biceps are the prime movers and the triceps are the antagonists.

On-Ground and Off-Ground Release

On landing at the front of the circle, as well as driving the right side of the body into the throw to precede the strike of the arm, it is also necessary to start extending the legs and lifting the trunk. The evolution of discus technique in the last 20 years has given rise to two distinct types of release, both of which have achieved throws in excess of 200 feet. Both styles involve factors common to all good throwers; the difference in the two methods is essentially a difference in emphasis.

Throwers who release on-ground use a relatively longer throwing base and are mechanically justified in throwing while in contact with the surface of the circle, on the basis that no effective force can be transmitted to the discus unless the thrower is firmly in contact with the ground. This is a direct corollary to Newton's third law of motion, which states that "to every action there is an equal and opposite reaction." With reference to all the throwing events, this means that a thrower by being in contact with the ground at release is able to exert downward pressure by pushing with his legs and in so doing causes an equal and opposite reaction which is imparted to the missile he is throwing. The immediate implication is that if he is not in contact with the ground at release, the thrower will not be able to make use of such an obviously valuable reactive force. However, in the case of the throwing events, the body applying the force to the missile at release, namely the thrower, already possesses momentum built up from previous movements while still in contact with the ground.

Further justification for throwing in contact with the ground is provided by the "hinged moment" principle. The right leg and foot in the center of the circle and the braced left leg at the front of the circle provide a turning couple, and the left leg, applying a brake to the already fast-moving body of the thrower across the circle, has the effect of speeding up the top half of the body (and of giving the discus a greater velocity at release). To what extent this is possible is difficult to determine.

In actual fact, the number of world class performers in both discus and shot who release off-ground has increased considerably in recent years. Toni Nett, putting many of them forward as examples in an article in *Die Lehre Der Liechtathletik*, asks if trying to release on-ground might be as bad as applying a brake to the whole effort.

One further argument in favor of releasing off-ground is that in achieving the wide throwing base necessary for the on-ground release, the time spent in getting the left foot down well forward, at the front of the circle, may be time wasted. During this time lag, the valuable "wound-up" effect of the upper body and discus may be partly lost before a fully effective pull is exerted on the discus.

The Reverse (Figs. 218–220)

At the end of the throw, the thrower must leave the circle, under control, from the rear half. At the climax of the turn, the thrower is at the front of the circle, and, ideally, he has performed a combination of bodily movements that have enabled him, at release, to give the discus a maximum forward velocity. Therefore, immediately after the discus has left his hand, the thrower's first priority is to prevent himself from fouling at the front of the circle. However, any attempt to check himself must not detract from the effort he has put into the throw. Thus the reverse has two aims:

1. To obtain a strong follow through to the throwing action, and
2. To avoid fouling after delivering at maximum velocity.

The reverse appears to be a far more integral part of the type of discus technique which employs an off-ground release, although it does not take place until after the discus has been launched. It is probably essential to the upward and forward springing action, as well as serving as an eventual check to forward movement to prevent fouling. In the on-ground type of release the reverse occurs well after release and as such contributes very little to the actual throwing action, but almost entirely to the prevention of fouling.

Release Angle

The release angle is the angle between the horizontal and the flight path of the center of gravity of the discus at release.

The discus is an aerofoil, and as such it is subject to forces of lift and drag similar to an airplane wing. Complicating the issue further, the action of the discus in the air is gyroscopic due to its rotation and symmetry. These two factors are helpful to the discus thrower; the shape helps to resist the force of gravity for part of the flight, and the gyroscopic action gives the discus stability.

To theorize on this matter is really pointless as the factors affecting one throw will vary from those affecting the previous and the next. Tests conducted in wind tunnels have substantiated what has already been said. As Dr. Richard Ganslen of the U.S.A. put it, "With a complete photographic record of a given discus flight, when the angle of the discus at all times would be ascertainable, it would be possible to plot the path of the implement and to write a formula for this particular flight, but it would be useless for any other throw." Fortunately, this matter does not affect the thrower unduly. The technique of a particular thrower develops more from trial and error and from imitation, not from reading detailed accounts of discus theory. Minor adjustments at launching will give the required angle of release and, unlike the case of discus velocity, small variations in the release angle will not cause drastic differences to the length of the throw.

Studies of slow-motion films of ten throwers made by H. H. Lockwood and referred to in the chapter on discus throwing in the British publication, *Athletics*, showed that all had angles of release between 30 and 45 degrees and six of these were between 34 and 37 degrees. The factors contributing to the angle of release are:

1. The lift given to the discus by the bodily movements of the thrower (not including the arm), and
2. The plane in which the throwing arm moves as it strikes.

The general movement of the thrower across the circle is in a horizontal direction. The slinging action of the arm succeeding the unwinding action is nearer the horizontal than the vertical. Upward force, or lift, must be provided by the action of the trunk and legs. The resultant angle of release is somewhere between the horizontal movement of the thrower across the circle and the vertical contribution of trunk and legs together, with minor adjustments in the arm action. Training and practice produce the optimum angle of about 37 degrees.

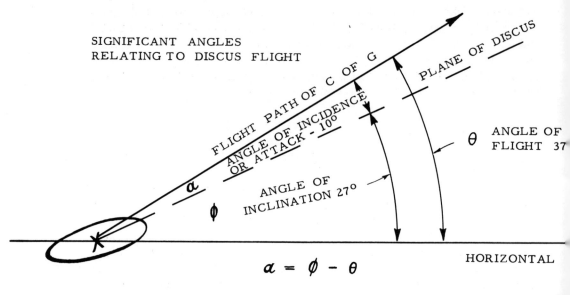

SIGNIFICANT ANGLES
RELATING TO DISCUS FLIGHT

FLIGHT PATH OF C OF G

PLANE OF DISCUS

ANGLE OF INCIDENCE
OR ATTACK - 10°

ANGLE OF
INCLINATION 27°

θ ANGLE OF
FLIGHT 37

α

ϕ

$$\alpha = \phi - \theta$$

HORIZONTAL

Figure 224.

The angles of incidence and inclination are different ways of measuring the position of the discus at release. (See Fig. 224.) If the discus is launched with its nose too high, forces of drag will affect the discus too early. This will cause the discus to stall and produce a poor throw. The ideal angle of incidence is between —5 and —10 degrees, which will postpone the stall of the discus for as long as possible. Therefore, at release the thrower must keep the nose of the discus reasonably well down. This is achieved by a medial rotation of the wrist which presses the base of the thumb down on the discus.

In addition, as the discus leaves the hand, the thrower should try to impart as strong a rotation to the discus as possible by wrist action and a strong tangential pull with the index finger. (Some throwers tend to release from their second fingers.) A strong rotation will utilize the gyroscopic potential of the discus and prolong its stability in the air. This will delay its subjection to forces of drag.

Wind Effect on Flight

Because a head wind increases the velocity of air flow past the discus, its aerodynamic effects are very similar to an increase in release velocity. Both lift and drag are increased. Increased lift keeps the discus in the air longer, but increased drag reduces ground speed. However, at first the lift increases more than the drag so that at moderate wind speeds the overall effect can be advantageous to the thrower. To take full advantage of a head wind, the nose of the discus should be kept down at release to increase the negative angle of incidence, and thus to minimize drag for as long as possible.

A cross wind from the right can have a stabilizing effect on the discus. The opposite is true of a wind from the left. In such cases, the thrower should adjust his starting position at the back of the circle to make the direction of his throw one which is advantageously affected by the wind, provided he still keeps within the limits of the 45-degree sector.

Training for Discus Throwing

Improvements in discus throwing during the last half-century have occurred not only as a result of the evolution of technique but also because of changes in training methods. The early twentieth century interpretation of the term "amateur athlete" seems to have been associated with lack of training and a light-hearted concentration on the competition itself, with a little "conditioning" beforehand. The development of training methods for discus may be classified as follows:

1. Acceptance, especially in the last 20 years, of systematic strength training in the form of weight training. Before the advent of this type of training, throwers were content solely with skill training and general conditioning.

2. Training throughout the winter, with perhaps a month or two of rest at the end of the competitive season.

3. Intensity of throwing in training. This aspect has been subject to changed thinking on more than one occasion. Following the early days of very limited training of any kind and until the time of the 1960 Olympics, it was considered necessary to throw virtually until one dropped. It was not uncommon for discus throwers to do more than 100 throws in a single training session. The drawback to this approach is that as one continues to throw, muscular and mental fatigue set in. These lead to lack of concentration and inability to sustain the good features of technique that exist to start with. In fact, continued throwing in such a tired state can do more harm than good, by establishing the poor features of technique that have developed through fatigue.

Far better results may be obtained from training sessions of 30–40 throws at three-fourths to full effort, with maximum concentration throughout. Such a session may be rounded off with three or four "competition" throws at maximum effort.

Further justification for this approach is provided by the fact that too much easy throwing can develop the wrong timing in the throw, and as described in the section on technique, correct timing is as important to good discus throwing as correct body position. The emphasis has moved from quantity to quality.

It is of utmost importance for the thrower to obtain regular attention from a well-qualified coach. Only the coach will be able to analyze the thrower's technique accurately and make any alterations he thinks necessary.

Unfortunately, as most throwers learn to throw by trial and error and by imitation, faults are very difficult to eradicate once they have been formed. Because of this, any alterations geared to the development and improvement of the thrower's technique may take months, or even years, to correct.

The value of being filmed by the coach and having a loop made cannot be overemphasized. This is best done toward the end of the competitive season so that coach and athlete may analyze the thrower's technique and decide what aspects of technique will require special attention during the coming off-season.

A discus thrower's training schedule should be geared to the development of the following:

1. Technique
2. Strength
3. Mobility
4. General Fitness.

Technique. This has already been dealt with at length. The important features are the acquisition of a coach, filming of technique, study of films of better throwers, and throwing sessions as indicated.

Strength. Weight training for the development of strength is essential. Although weight training must not be regarded as the "open-sesame" to athletic success, many would-be throwers suffer from a lack of strength, which can be overcome by systematized weight training. Increased strength, as well as increasing speed and power in the actual performance of technique, will enable the thrower to handle and utilize stronger positions within the execution of the turn.

The weight training exercises recommended for discus throwing are these:

1. Deep knees bend or squat (going down to a position where the thighs are parallel with the ground).
2. Bench press (preferably inclined, with hands somewhat wider than shoulder width apart).
3. Lateral raise, seated (dumbbells).
4. Lateral raise, lying (dumbbells).
5. Power clean.
6. Snatch.

The power clean and snatch are particularly valuable as they develop explosive action, especially of the legs. If available, pulley weights can be used to similate actual discus throwing actions with increased resistance, in the form of weights attached to the other end of the pulley wire. Such exercises can be valuable in strengthening the trunk rotators, muscles which are used in discus throwing, but which, at the same time are almost impossible to strengthen with normal weight training exercises.

The value of isometric muscle contraction as a means of strength training also has gained recognition in recent years, and may be conveniently used by athletes not having access to weight training equipment. Its success as a strength training method compared with weight training has not been fully determined. Isometric training may be done as partner resistance exercise, or as contraction of muscle groups against the resistance of one's own body or an immoveable object, or even during weight training when a near-maximum has been reached and the athlete can merely exert force against the weight without being able to move it.

Mobility. General mobility or range of joint movement is recognized as valuable to all track and field athletics. Intensified weight training of the type necessary for successful discus throwing may be accompanied by a restriction of joint mobility because of the muscular development. Weight training should therefore be accompanied by mobilizing exercises, especially paying attention to the shoulder and hip joint complexes. As good a time as any for such stretching exercises as arm circling, hurdle stretching, etc., is preceding a throwing session when such exercising can prove a valuable part of the general warm-up.

General Fitness. General fitness is necessary to enable the thrower to endure training sessions of any kind without loss of energy. Throwing sessions at the track should be preceded by a steady jog of at least a mile and sprints of 30 yards, aiming at explosive effort and speed off the mark. Participation in other events, such as hurdling or triple jumping, can have the dual effect of increasing fitness, mobility, and leg strength, as well as alleviating boredom from throwing over a sustained period. Participation in other games during the winter, such as basketball, volleyball, handball, etc., can have a similar desirable effect.

A typical mid-winter week's training program for a discus thrower follows:

Monday	Weight training	1½ hours.
Tuesday	Track session	Warm-up run (1½ miles).
		Mobilizing exercises.
		Throwing—30–40 throws, concentrating on particular points of technique, as necessary. Finish with three throws for distance.
		Triple jumping from 3-stride approach.
Wednesday	Weight training	1½ hours.
Thursday	Track session	Warm-up run (1½ miles).
		Mobilizing exercises.
		Sprint starts (10 x 30 yards from alternate feet).
		Throwing—same as Tuesday.
Friday	Weight training	1½ hours.
	Game of basketball	1 hour.
Saturday	Track session	Warm-up run (1½ miles).
		Mobilizing exercises.
		Hurdling over three barriers.
		Throwing—same as Tuesday and Thursday.
Sunday	Rest	

As the competitive season approaches, the number of throwing sessions per week should be stepped up. As far as weight training is concerned, some throwers continue throughout the competitive season, trying to increase their poundages. Others, once the competitive season starts, are content to maintain the strength they have acquired in the winter, and therefore may cut the number of weights sessions down to two or even one per week, making no effort to increase poundages.

General Training Points

Work with 3–6 disc in training sessions. The more disc the thrower has, the better. The short break in throwing while the thrower collects the disc is a worthwhile respite from throwing, especially if the thrower is working at nearly full effort. Also, in colder winter climates, if the thrower runs or sprints to collect, it can prevent him from getting cold, which can also affect his throwing.

Depending on individual differences of temperament, there is often an advantage in throwers of similar ability working together, by virtue of the ever-present competitive atmosphere. If this is not possible, the thrower should indulge in some target throwing during the early competitive-season training sessions. If he has a good winter's training behind him, he can set a marker at a distance a few feet beyond his reach to provide a helpful psychological spur.

Chapter 19

TEACHING THE BEGINNING JAVELIN THROWER

by Dick Held

The javelin throw is a straight-line event, so begin by drawing a line lengthwise down the center of the throwing area or use a chalk line on the football field.

Grip

Hold the throwing hand next to the ear, palm up, thinking of it as a launching platform. Cup the hand slightly and place the javelin grip in the "valley" of the bent hand with the point extending forward from the heel of the hand and the tail extending out between the thumb and first finger. Wrap the middle finger, the strongest one, around the rear edge of the grip, like a hook. The finger should be between the grip cord and the shaft. Allow the first finger to rest along the shaft behind the grip and the thumb to press against the shaft at the rear of the binding. The other two fingers curl around the grip and hold it in the palm of the hand. Sometimes the first finger is placed on the same side of the shaft as the thumb. This is a matter of preference.

The Standing Throw

Stand with the feet about one yard apart, the right foot on the line and pointed about 60 degrees to the right, and the left foot slightly to the left of the line and parallel to it. A line drawn through the shoulders would be parallel to the chalk mark. Grip the javelin, holding it palm upward next to the ear, with the point up slightly. Withdraw the javelin backward along a straight line until the arm is extended, but the elbow is not locked. The javelin is now parallel to the chalk line, point high and close to the right eye. The head is turned in the throwing direction, and the left arm is wrapped loosely across the chest.

Throw directly along the chalk line with the hand traveling straight along the line of the shaft. The hand passes close to the head at about the level of the top of the ear and continues straight out and up until after the release. The elbow gives the impression of folding up and then extending during the throw. It must not remain extended as is possible when throwing a baseball. This would impart an arc to the travel of the hand. Circular application of power will cause undesirable rotation of the implement about its minor axis.

The elbow remains outside the vertical plane of the javelin during the throw. Never use a sidearm motion, allowing the javelin to pass outside the elbow. Repeat throwing several times, adding a pronounced lean to the rear and a forward sway at release.

Keep the javelin aligned in the direction of the throw at all times. When the tip strikes the ground, the tail should point directly back at the thrower. If it does not, then the force was not applied along the length of the shaft.

Transition to the Run

Take a baseball and, using a short run, throw it directly overhand as far as possible. Do this several times noting the position of the right foot as it is planted, preparatory to driving off during the throw. Did it pass in front of and about three feet beyond the left foot? If so, skip the next drill, as that was a perfect execution of the crossover. If the right foot just came up to the left and stopped, or if it passed behind the heel of the left foot, there is work to do. Run the length of the field, traveling along the chalk line, right arm withdrawn in the throwing position, shoulders parallel to the line, hips at a 45-degree angle, and the right foot passing in front of and well beyond the left toe. Use this drill at the start of each practice until it is natural to throw with the crossover.

Return to the javelin. Using the proper grip, carry it comfortably over the shoulder and begin to run. Raise the point until the throwing angle of about 30 degrees is reached. Withdraw the javelin in a straight line, keeping the palm up at all times, elbow outside the vertical plane of the throw and very slightly flexed. The hips are at 45 degrees and the shoulders parallel to the direction of the run, with left arm held loosely across the chest.

The run is now similar to the crossover drill practiced earlier. Pause and throw, watching the flight as before for signs of misdirection of force. Does the point drop too fast? Does it remain high? Does it swing out to one side? If so, the force was not applied in a straight line along the length of the shaft. Repeat this frequently, gradually eliminating the pause and developing a rearward lean at the beginning of the throw.

Technique

Some of the following pointers are either frequently overlooked or inadequately stressed. Concentrate on getting the body weight as low as possible, consistent with maintaining forward momentum at the beginning of the throw.

During the throw, the left leg, which has bent to allow the body mass to pass over without loss of forward speed, straightens explosively to drive the whole body upward along the intended path of the javelin. The impression should be one of trying to drive the body in the direction of the flight. The right leg kicks powerfully to provide the forward portion of this upward and outward motion. This kick also begins the throw and triggers the forward turn of the hips, which is followed by the drive of the shoulder and finally the arm strike. These all blend into one long, continuous application of power with the legs and hips doing the slow heavy, early work of starting the javelin, and the shoulder and finally the arm providing the speed.

After the thrower has advanced beyond the beginner stage, check marks should be used—one at the beginning of the run and another to be hit by the right foot two to four strides before it is planted for the throw.

The point of the javelin can be elevated about two degrees above the line of force application to increase lift at higher speeds. Care must be taken not to raise the point too high or a stall will result, with air resistance shortening the flight.

Chapter 20

THE JAVELIN THROW

by Wilf Paisch

It might appear that the technique of the javelin throw has changed little since the 11th century B.C. Certainly, the poses captured by the artists on ancient Greek pottery illustrate throwers in poses similar to those taken by photographers of today. To a large extent this is true, since the javelin throw was often performed as a running, straight-line throw for distance. However, to the student of javelin throwing, the technique has continued to change.

With the changes in technique, there often is a change in the records achieved, but every change in the record book need not necessarily be associated with a new technique. Many improved standards in track and field athletics must now be linked with our better understanding of training methods. Such understanding helps us to produce a faster, fitter, stronger and more mobile athlete who is capable of handling the advanced techniques of today.

Superficial studies of most field events indicate a fairly uniform pattern of movement among the world's top performers. This is not wholly true with the javelin event. In this event the individual differences in technique between athletes are greater than in the other throwing events. This is possibly why there seems to be a divergence of opinion about technique among certain coaches. One has only to read the articles on javelin throwing in the world's coaching journals for this situation to be made apparent.

The controversies over differences in javelin technique appear to be fairly recent, and possibly can be associated with the introduction of the aerodynamic javelin, particularly the Held javelin. Very little is known about the aerodynamics of javelin flight, as it differs considerably from anything on which extensive research work has been done.

Although there exists a difference of opinion on certain aspects of technique, there are many other aspects which are common to all good throwers. In the main, these aspects are supported by sound mechanical principles; they have stood the test of time, hence they can be accepted as factors contributing to good technique. These points will be emphasized throughout this chapter.

Significant differences of technique will be mentioned, too, along with reasons for accepting some and rejecting others.

The main aim of javelin throwing is to get the spear to travel the maximum possible horizontal distance. This is affected by three main factors:

1. The speed of release
2. The angle of release
3. Flight stability and associated aerodynamic factors.

The Speed of Release

Speed of release is determined by the magnitude of the forces acting on the javelin at the point of release. The forces are, of course, produced by the powerful muscles of the whole body coordinating together for maximum efficiency. Hence the timing of the movements is of paramount importance so that all of the forces generated in the various muscles combine together to produce the greatest result. This will be so if the forces are applied over the maximum possible range and directed in a straight line. Here the athlete is concerned with the physical principle of WORK.

$$\text{(Work} = \text{Force} \times \text{Distance.)}$$

In this case, the force is that produced by the coordinating muscles, and the distance is represented by the range through which the point of application (the grip) is moved. If the athlete can increase the force or the range of application, it will be to his advantage. For example, the force exerted by the muscles could be improved by a carefully planned strength training schedule, and the range of movement improved by mobility training and the adoption of a suitable technique. It is, however, of little value to the athlete if one of these aspects is improved to the detriment of the other, as the total effect would be nullified.

The range of action is, in the main, dependent upon the mobility of the athlete, but it can also be affected by the speed of the approach run and the body position on landing from the "cross-over" stride. The straight-line action is one of prime importance for an efficient throw. Many throwers "come 'round the corner," as it is often expressed in coaching circles. That is, the elbow leads the direction of the throw at some distance away from the body. This type of throw usually results in excessive elbow pain because of the pressure exerted on the joint.

The straight-line movement is determined by the center of gravity of the athlete. The pull and release should be closely in line above this. Possibly this is one of the reasons that top-class throwers turn the head away from the throwing shoulder, so that the arm can follow a movement more closely in line with the center of gravity.

Angle of Release

The theoretical optimum angle of release for a projectile, whose point of release and landing are the same height above the ground, is 45 degrees. In this case, horizontal and vertical components are equal. This is, of course, a theoretical angle and does not allow for the fact that the javelin is not released at the same level as its landing, and neither are the aerodynamic factors affecting flight taken into consideration. Careful loop film analysis of top European throwers illustrates a release angle of between 30 and 40 degrees. The finalists in the 1966 European Championships indicated a mean angle of release of 34 dégrees 42 minutes.

Ignoring, for the moment, the properties of the javelin, one realizes there are three things which affect the angle of release:
1. The direction of force by the levers of the body
2. The point of release relative to the front foot
3. The position of the javelin after alignment.
The latter however affects mainly the angle of attack, which should not be confused with the angle of release. (See Fig. 225.)

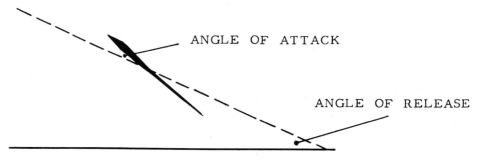

ANGLE OF ATTACK

ANGLE OF RELEASE

(THE ANGLE OF ATTACK IS THAT BETWEEN
AEROFOIL AND AIRFLOW)

Figure 225.

Aerodynamic Factors

The design of a javelin could well be considered a compromise. In order for the javelin to go a long way, the athlete requires two things:
1. Maximum lift
2. Minimum drag.
Lift and drag are two of the forces acting on a javelin during flight. (See Fig. 226.) It is unlikely that at the speeds of release possible in javelin throwing much extra lift, other than that given by its initial release, can be obtained through design. Thus, the main concern should be directed to reducing the drag force. Here, the thrower and the manufacturer can do much to minimize the effect of this retarding force.

At this stage, it might be wise to make a brief study of the forces likely to act on a javelin in flight. They can be divided into two components: those aiding

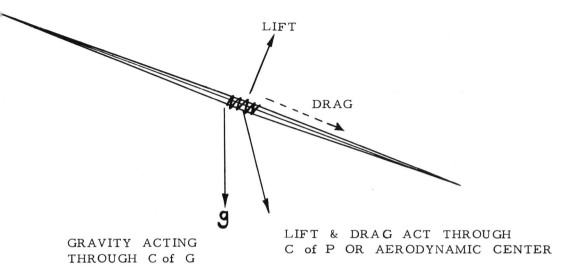

LIFT

DRAG

GRAVITY ACTING
THROUGH C of G

LIFT & DRAG ACT THROUGH
C of P OR AERODYNAMIC CENTER

Figure 226.

motion and those opposing motion. The important overall effect of the forces is that the airflow about the javelin must be kept laminar (the flow of air which closely follows the shape of a streamlined surface without turbulence). If the laminar flow breaks down, the drag force becomes excessive.

Forces aiding motion (Lift). There are two forces that aid motion—the lift given by the initial speed of release that offsets the effect of gravity and the spinning effect imparted by the athlete. For the most part, the latter is a force that reduces drag rather than increasing lift, although in theory it is possible to obtain what is known as a magnus effect due to rotation about the long axis of the javelin. However, this is unlikely at the speeds of rotation possible in javelin throwing.

Forces restricting motion (Drag). The forces that restrict motion are air resistance, rotation about the short axis, and vibration about the long axis. When a javelin is moving through the air and its major axis is also its line of flight, the projectile is symmetrical. The effect of the air's viscosity is solely that of causing deceleration resulting from a force opposing motion. By virtue of the shape of the javelin and the material of construction, it has a very low coefficient of drag, the protrusion of the binding being the only aspect likely to upset the air flow. Hence, provided the javelin does not present its side to the air flow, the effect of the air resistance is minimal on a good javelin.

However, if rotation occurs during flight, the javelin will present its side to the air flow, experiencing a greater resistive force, and thus shortening its range. Rotation about the minor axis can be caused by a poor release, but this should not be the case with an experienced thrower. It can, on the other hand, be caused by poor javelin design, over which the athlete has no control. A javelin has a center of gravity through which its weight acts, but it has also an aerodynamic center, or center of pressure (C of P) through which lift and drag act. If a javelin were constructed such that these two centers were one point, irrespective of attitude, no rotation will occur, provided the javelin is gripped at the center of gravity.

To comply with the rules a certain amount of rotation must take place. A javelin launched "nose up" must land point first. In order for this to happen, the aerodynamic center must be behind the center of gravity. If the aerodynamic center is too far behind the center of gravity, the rotation in the air will be excessive, thus causing the javelin to land steeply, forcing it to present a side to the air flow, and consequently causing a decreased range of flight. Ideally the javelin should land as flat as possible. Also the greater the range of flight, the slower must be the rotation in the air. Thus there are distance-rated javelins where the C of P is located carefully relative to the C of G.

The action of throwing the implement is such that the javelin tends to flex longitudinally in flight. This process results in a greatly increased air resistance and a secondary effect upon rotation about the short axis. This is often shown on poor javelins by what is known as tail quiver. The effect can be greatly minimized by using a carefully manufactured javelin.

To take full advantage of the aerodynamic aspects of javelin flight, the implement must be designed with several points in mind. It has been found that:

1. Lift is greater if the javelin diameter is greater.

2. Vibration about the long axis is less if the mass of the javelin is more concentrated about the grip.

3. Within certain limits, the stability of a javelin increases as the C of G is moved closer to the tail.

4. The lower the C of G in the cord grip the more stable the flight is likely to be.

5. For the javelin to land correctly and still make the best use of the angle of attack, the C of P must be behind the C of G.

6. The closer the C of P to the C of G, the less the rotation about the short axis.

7. The less a javelin rotates about the short axis, the longer the effect of lift is maintained.

If one studies the aerodynamic javelin carefully, he can see that the diameter is as wide as the rule permits, especially about the grip. The center of gravity is as far to the tail as the rules permit, and the C of G is as low in the binding as possible. The center of pressure is also very carefully located with respect to the center of gravity, so that it will rotate sufficiently for the spear to nose down at the correct attitude. Therefore, it is not by coincidence that most of the record throws are achieved with an aerodynamic javelin.

The manufacturers have given the athletes the best possible implements, within the rules. To take full advantage of these javelins, the athlete can produce a spin, thus stabilizing flight by using the correct grip. By pulling the javelin correctly in a straight line, vibration about the long axis can be minimized. However, the most important factor is to make sure that the initial angle of attack is not too steep. This should be somewhere between 0–10 degrees, there being very little difference in range between these limits. If the angle is too steep, the drag forces will be increased, causing the javelin to stall earlier. The javelin must be held down firmly to the palm, and the hand should be held high.

TECHNIQUE OF JAVELIN THROWING

The javelin thrower's only concern is to release the javelin at the maximum possible speed, in such a way that its flight is stable, and at such an angle that full use is made of the release speed. Other things being equal, the faster the athlete can release the javelin the farther it will go. To do this, the athlete must take a firm grip on the javelin, run up toward the foul line, and get into a powerful throwing position to release the javelin at a safe follow-through distance from the foul line.

For these conditions to be observed, careful thought must be given to the individual aspects of the throw.

The Grip

Most texts indicate that there are three possible grips for the athlete to use. These are:
1. The first and second finger, often known as the "horseshoe" or "V" grip.
2. Thumb and first finger.
3. Thumb and second finger.

There are two very important factors which must be present in the grip, and these factors will influence the one chosen. They are:
1. The grip must be firm behind the ledge provided by the binding.
2. The palm of the hand must be underneath the javelin in such a way that it lies directly down the palm and not across it. This makes it easier for the athlete to exert a straight-line pull down the length of the javelin, and it places the elbow in an efficient, safe throwing position. Because of this very important factor, it is suggested that there are only two grips worth considering. The "V" grip permits a very secure grip behind the binding, with the javelin positioned along the length of the palm. Some athletes find it uncomfortable to splay the fingers wide enough to hold the diameter of the javelin using the "V" grip, hence their preference for one of the other grips.

Probably the most natural of the three grips is the use of the thumb and first finger, although it is often not recommended. With this grip the javelin tends to position itself across the palm, making it easy for the athlete to drop the elbow and throw in a round arm fashion.

There is one other very important factor which arises from the grip, and that is the positioning of the fingers not secured behind the binding. These must fold over the top of the javelin in order to keep it stable and flat on the launching palm. If this does not happen, the javelin's angle of attack could be sadly affected. Also, experiments seem to indicate that these fingers, positioned as they are to one side of the javelin, impart the spin about the long axis that is so essential for flight stability.

The Carry

The foundations for a good throw are set by a controlled, accelerating approach run. As the speed of approach is an important consideration, the carry should be such that it will not impede the smooth running action. For this to be so, the javelin can only be carried over the shoulder. It matters little if the point of the javelin is slightly up or down. A horizontal position slightly above the level of the ear is probably best.

As in normal running, the arms move in coordination with the legs, so the throwing arm follows a slightly modified cycle in this position above the shoulder.

It follows a horizontal path of about eight inches on either side of the ear, with the free arm following a similar cycle below the shoulder.

The Approach Run

The main aim of the approach run is to enable the thrower to arrive in a safe, powerful throwing position as close to the throwing arc as the follow-through will permit. Certainly the most difficult aspect of the throw is to blend together all of the movements which place the athlete in the final throwing position. During the complete phase the body must be accelerated to the maximum possible controlled speed at release. Also, the javelin must be taken from the position of carry into a carefully aligned position, as far behind the body as possible, without any slowing or breaking of the running rhythm. For coaching purposes it is wise to split the run-up into parts, although it must be emphasized that when performing the skill, it is not a series of parts but one complete rhythmical movement that flows from one stage to the next. The parts are:

1. The preliminary run-up.
2. The transition, which includes the withdrawal phase and the cross-over stride.
3. The throwing stride.
4. The recovery phase.

The Competition Run-up (See Fig. 227)

It is difficult to lay down any hard and fast rules as to the length of run-up, speed of run-up, or position of check marks. The essential thing is that the

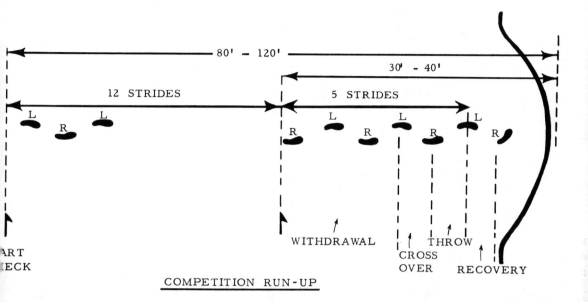

COMPETITION RUN-UP

Figure 227.

run-up enable the individual athlete to obtain maximum controlled speed at release. Many throwers take a run-up which is too long; therefore, instead of accelerating into the throw, they slow down. Observation of world class throwers reveals that they use a run-up distance of approximately 80–100 feet.

The Preliminary Run-up

Most athletes take twelve strides in the preliminary run-up. Toeing a check mark with both feet together, the athlete begins the run-up with his left foot moving forward first. The twelve-stride pattern fits in ideally with the five-stride withdrawal mark, giving a total of 17 strides. Athletes who do not like starting their run from a static position may take a few walking or slow jogging paces to the beginning check mark. The method used must be practiced often to make sure that it is accurate in leading up to the withdrawal mark.

This phase of the run-up should be a smooth, gradual buildup of speed, hitting the withdrawal check mark with the right foot. During the run the javelin is carried over the shoulder, and the hips and shoulders are square to the front in a good natural running position.

The Transition Phase

This phase should occupy five strides, although some throwers take seven.

During it, the javelin is withdrawn and the body is placed in the strong position for the final throwing effort.

The withdrawal phase. This is one of the most important aspects of the run, since a poor throw will certainly result if the body is off balance, or if the javelin is incorrectly aligned. With most throwers the phase starts as the right foot comes to the ground at the check mark (Fig. 227) and usually takes three strides to complete. The important thing is that it is fully withdrawn as the left foot strikes the ground before the right cross-over stride. As the left foot comes to the ground (the first stride after the check mark), the javelin starts on its movement to the rear. The javelin is withdrawn with a straight pull back with the throwing hand passing backward directly over the shoulder. A number of world class throwers swing the javelin forward or to the side before finally taking it to the rear. The important thing is that the javelin ultimately get to a position of perfect alignment without disrupting the run-up.

As the arm goes to the rear, the shoulders must turn to the side and the free arm should start to wrap across the chest to relax the muscles of the shoulder girdle. There should be little, if any, checking of the forward speed. During this phase the hips should be kept to the front, as much as is possible, and there should be a slight, gradual lowering of the horizontal plane of the hips.

It is important not to delay the withdrawal any later than the first stride after the check mark. This is a common fault with inexperienced and poorly coached athletes who withdraw later and find that they have to take the javelin back and bring it forward again, all in the space of two very quick strides. The result usually is that neither is done correctly, and a poor throw must result.

Once the javelin is to the rear, it is important to keep the hand high and the javelin flat on the palm. If either is allowed to drop, it will affect the angle of release or angle of attack, probably resulting in a poor throw. The javelin should be kept close to an "athletically" straight arm with the palm serving as a level, stable platform of support.

Cross-over stride. This is a very difficult phase of the movement to describe. It is called a cross-over stride because it is difficult to think of a better name, especially since the term "cross-step" does not really describe the action. Years ago it was common for javelin throwers to completely turn the shoulders and hips to a side position during this phase of the run-up. Associated with the turning of the hips was a definite, slowing cross-step. The right leg was picked up fairly straight with heel leading, and on landing the right foot was at 90 degrees to the line of throw, resulting in a deceleration of the forward speed of the body. This action, known as the "cross-step," is very seldom seen today.

One of the main aims of the cross-over stride is to obtain body lean so that the powerful muscles of the trunk can help in the throw. To prevent slowing of the body momentum, a short, fast cross-over should be completed in the air. The hips and feet remain facing in the direction of the throw. It is a fast pickup of the right knee, causing the legs to be split in the air, with the left leg trailing. The left leg must then be pulled through very quickly into a fairly long last stride.

Although the stride is completed in the air, very little time must be spent with both feet out of contact with the ground. Hence there is an attempt to get the right foot down to the ground very quickly. Here it is essential for the heel of the right foot to come down first, since landing on the toe would certainly produce poor throwing. As the right heel strikes, there is a further settling over the foot which helps to keep the body lean. Also there is a more noticeable lowering of the hips.

At this stage, it might be wise to study the technique of several world class performers during this very important phase of the throw. The study was made by careful film loop analysis of film taken during a top international competition.

1. *Placement of right foot on landing from cross-over.* The angle was measured between a line drawn through the center of the right foot and the line of throw. The range of the throwers was between 0 degrees (foot directly on line of throw) and 50 degrees. The mean angle of foot placement was 23 degrees. The lower angle is favored, since there will be less slowing of the forward speed, and the right leg will be in a better position to drive the hips forward and upward.

2. *Body lean back at the moment the right foot contacts the ground.* The angle was measured between a line drawn approximately down the length of the body and the vertical. The range was from 5 to 20 degrees, with a mean of approximately 15 degrees.

3. *Angle of hips to line of throw at moment of right foot contact.* The angle was measured between a line drawn horizontally through the top of the shorts and the line of throw. For example, 90 degrees would mean hips perfectly to the front; 0 degrees would mean hips fully to the side. The range was between 75 and 30 degrees, with a mean of 65 degrees. Probably the hips should be as far to the front as mobility will allow at this stage.

Also, the films showed that the mean alignment of the javelin to the horizontal was 28 degrees, and all athletes showed a good lowering of the hips which was impossible to measure in terms of distance, but could be expressed in terms of abstract units. The drop between the top of the shorts at the highest point and lowest point during this phase was 3–9 units.

The Throwing Stride

There seem to be two schools of thought on the throwing stride—those supporting a bent front leg and those who support a straight front leg. The latter group has been influenced by a principle known as the "Hinged Moment theory." There is little reference to this theory in standard works on physics and body movements, apart from the excellent book by Geoffrey Dyson, *The Mechanics of Athletics.*

If one can visualize the body as a straight rigid lever moving forward at speed, and if the base of this lever is suddenly stopped, there is a tremendous rotational effect in all parts of the body above this point. This rotational effect is much increased with the length of the lever, and toward the top (i.e. the throwing arm) there would be a greatly increased angular velocity. Careful film loop analysis suggests that none of the top class performers makes use of this principle. Of course, the body moving forward at speed offers too great a resistance for the knee joint to hold back in a rigid position. Hence the stress on this joint would be too great to accept it without the bending of the joint. Any attempt to do otherwise would certainly result in a permanent injury to the joint. But this theory could affect what happens from here on.

If the left leg does not bend, then valuable forward speed will be lost at this very critical stage. If an attempt is made to lock this front leg, energy which could be valuably used in accelerating the spear is wasted in raising the body over this long lever.

The action performed by most throwers is what appears to be correct. On landing from the cross-over, the left leg is pulled through quickly into a fairly long last stride of about 5–6 feet. As there is a reaching out of the left leg, it strikes the ground straight with the heel contacting first, but as it receives the body weight, it bends. The degree of bend must not be excessive or the body will collapse over it. Because the left leg has moved quickly away from the right leg, the hips will open up, introducing an important aspect of technique. The right leg must drive the right hip forward and upward very quickly. This is, in fact, a rotation which will often cause the right heel to turn outward. Some coaches emphasize this as a fast turn out of the right heel or as a fast drive of the hips, forward and upward, by the right leg and trunk. Certainly the right leg will have started this action and almost have completed it by the time the left foot contact is made. The toe of the right foot then drags the ground until the javelin is released.

Once the hips have been driven to the front, aided by the right leg and trunk, the arm must start to strike very quickly. The speed at which the arm strikes is responsible for a very large proportion of the throw. The striking of the arm must be led by a turning of the head. This, in turn, brings with it, at an increased speed, the right shoulder. The right shoulder pulls forward and upward bringing with it the elbow, which is bent slightly. With the rotation of the shoulder, the elbow is rotated slightly outward, which puts it above the level of the hand. This is essential for a fast arm movement, as it permits the flail-like action of the forearm about the elbow joint, giving an increased speed to the releasing hand.

The path of the throwing arm is directly over the shoulder. The path of the elbow is slightly to the outside. As the javelin is coming over the shoulder, the left leg, which has remained bent, must straighten under the javelin; this will give a release over or slightly in front of the left foot.

The release point is quite critical. With the bending and then straightening of the left leg, it is possible to get the release in front of the left foot and still be working up on the javelin, thus increasing the range of action. The release must not be too late, or there will be a pulling down on the javelin, which will make it fly flatter and produce tail quiver. From this type of action, where the timing is so precise, it could lead to erratic throwing, especially when throwers are going for the "big ones."

Recovery Stride

At the time of release the thrower still has quite a lot of forward speed to control. Because of this, most throwers release the javelin some feet before the arc so that they have a distance left to recover from the throw without fouling. There are several methods acceptable for recovery, but the most natural, and probably the most effective, is known as the reverse. Once the spear has been dispatched over or slightly in front of the left leg, the right leg is brought forward into a running stride. The weight is quickly transferred onto the right leg, which bends at the knee joint to absorb the forward speed. The left foot must remain in firm contact with the ground until the javelin has been released and the right knee has passed the left in the recovery stride. It is essential to release the javelin as close to the throwing arc as possible, and only experience can tell a coach or athlete how far this will be.

IMPORTANT POINTS TO WATCH FOR DURING THE VARIOUS STAGES OF THE THROW

The throwing of the javelin demands certain fundamental aspects of technique, some of which follow:

The Run

1. That it is relaxed and that it builds up in speed.
2. That the javelin is carried in a comfortable position over the shoulder.
3. That the stride pattern is consistent.
4. That a good running action, with the shoulders, hips and feet to the front, be used during this early part of the throw.

The Withdrawal

1. That it is straight back over the shoulder with the palm uppermost and with the javelin close to the arm and parallel with it. At this stage of the throw, particularly for mature throwers, it is not essential for the palm to be twisted to the top. This tends to put the shoulder muscles under tension earlier than necessary. But it is essential for the palm to be in this position before the arm action takes place. Therefore, if the palm is up early, there is less for the athlete to think about and perform during the very quick final moments.
2. That once the javelin is withdrawn, it remains in a firm grip without any deviation of point or tail.
3. That the speed of the approach run is maintained.

4. That the shoulders turn to the side, with the left arm relaxed across the chest, and the hips are to the front in a good running action.

The Cross-over Stride

1. That the hips are kept as far as possible to the front with the feet pointing in the direction of the throw.
2. That the stride is not a long bound.
3. That the movement of the right leg be led by the right knee in a good running action.
4. That the right leg get down to the ground quickly with the weight being taken first on the right heel.
5. That there is a lowering of the hips.
6. That the throwing arm is not allowed to drop.

The Throwing Stride

1. That the left leg move quickly into a fairly long last stride.
2. That the right leg drive the right hip forward and upward very quickly.
3. That the left leg is not kept rigidly straight once the drive has started.
4. That the body is fairly low.

The Arm and Upper Body Movement

1. That the head turn to the left.
2. That the arm movement is very fast.
3. That it is not brought into action before the legs and trunk have contributed their power.
4. That the right shoulder lead the arm movement.
5. That the pull is over the shoulder with the palm passing directly over it, and the elbow is slightly to the side at a higher level than the palm.

The Recovery

That the release is sufficiently behind·the throwing arc, permitting a recovery action to prevent fouling.

JAVELIN TECHNIQUE ANALYSIS

Figures 228 and 229.

The thrower is in the important withdrawal phase. His weight is well balanced on the right leg, five strides from throwing. As the left foot comes to the ground, the javelin continues on its movement to the rear.

Figure 228.

Figure 229.

Figure 230.

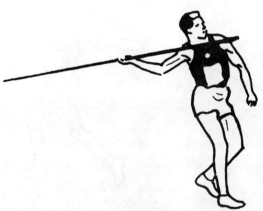

Figure 231.

Figure 232.   Figure 233.

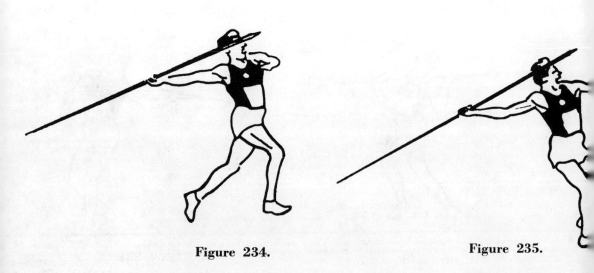

Figure 234.   Figure 235.

Figure 236.   Figure 237.

Figure 238.   Figure 239.

Figure 240.

Figure 241.

Figure 242.

Figure 230.

This shows an almost perfect position—that of a good running action, modified only by the controlled backward movement of the javelin. As in a good running action, the left arm is forward as the right leg is forward. The backward movement of the throwing arm is in sympathy with the leg movement, thus giving balance and control. (Hence the importance of starting the withdrawal at the correct position in order to obtain the balance required at this critical stage.) The javelin is being withdrawn almost straight over the shoulder, thus helping to obtain perfect alignment.

Figure 231.

This is the completion of the stride from the previous frame. The javelin is almost completely to the rear, the palm is high and the javelin is close to the body. The shoulder muscles are kept relaxed by delaying the pronation of the throwing hand.

Figures 232 and 233.

This is the third stride after the start of the withdrawal. The javelin is fully to the rear, the throwing arm being reasonably straight. The javelin is perfectly aligned close to the arm and body. The excellent running action is maintained, with the hips to the front and the feet pointing in the direction of the run. The lowering of the hips is apparent.

Figure 234.

It would be hard to better the position illustrated here. It is the middle of the right cross-over phase. The hips are to the front and the feet are in the direction of a good straight-line running action. The emphasis on the knee leading this action is apparent. The left arm is starting to wrap across the chest as the shoulders go fully to the "side-on" position. The javelin is well aligned, with the hand still high and just starting to turn the palm upward.

Figure 235.

A perfect landing from the "cross-over." The weight is on the heel of the right foot, pointing directly in the throwing direction. The settling over this foot to aid body lean is well illustrated. The palm is now fully to the top and the alignment is perfect. (The importance of landing on the right heel and NOT on the toes of this foot must be emphasized.)

Figure 236.

The driving out stage for the final throwing stride. The left foot reaching forward has caused the hips to open out. The right leg is in a perfect position to drive the right hips forward and upward.

Figure 237.

An excellent position just prior to the arm strike. The rotation, about the vertical axis, is almost complete. The right leg having driven the hips fully to the front is now trailing the ground. The head is leading the throwing arm into a striking position, with the throwing shoulder almost square to the front. The left leg is bent and the javelin is well aligned. (Note how the arm action is delayed until the slower moving parts of the body have contributed their power.)

Figure 238.

Rotation of the various parts of the body to the fore is complete and the arm action is taking place. The head has turned well to the left and the left leg is well bent. The rotation, having caused the right elbow to lift up and out, is leading the throwing hand forward. The right heel has turned out, aiding a fast right hip.

Figure 239.

The final action before release. The elbow is fully to the front enabling the "whip-lash" effect of the trailing forearm. The left leg is straightening and is perfectly timed with the javelin coming over the shoulder.

Figure 240.

The javelin has been released and the action of recovery, one of a continued running action, is about to start. (Note the left foot is in firm contact with the ground as the right knee passes the left. This means that at release there was a firm base for throwing.)

Figures 241 and 242.

The completion of the recovery stride with room to stop before the throwing arc.

COACHING THE JAVELIN THROW

Coaching is 90 percent encouragement. This is essential to accept if a good coaching partnership is to be formed. The coach should not inflict his personality on the athlete with a series of "Do's and Don't's." Rather, the coach should work with the athlete, letting him know why certain things are being done and at all times encouraging the athlete to think for himself. The success of a good coaching partnership is measured in terms of how the athlete conducts himself when the coach is absent. The coach should pass over so much knowledge and confidence to the athlete that the coach is only required when something goes wrong and when encouragement is needed.

It is important that the coach observe several throws, from different angles, before giving advice to the athlete. When observing an athlete for the first time, watch carefully from the observation points listed below, and make notes on what you observe.

Observation Positions

1. To the open side of the thrower, about ten yards back. From here the coach can observe the stride pattern of the run, the action of the legs during the throw, and the accuracy of the run with respect to check marks and throwing arc.

2. Behind the thrower. Here the coach can observe the straight-line movement, especially that of the throwing arm.

3. To the closed side of the thrower, about 20 yards in front of the arc. Here the coach can see the rotational aspect of the throw, the turning of the head and hips, and the opening of the chest.

4. To the front of the thrower, beyond his maximum range of throw. Here the coach can get an excellent picture of the complete movement. For safety reasons, this position should only be used with experienced throwers.

When observing a javelin thrower for the first time, always put out one marker in the position of an approximate withdrawal mark, 35 feet back from the throwing arc. Then observe the stride pattern carefully, counting the strides from withdrawal to the position of throw, relative to the foul line. Watch the thrower from the rear to observe the direction of the arm movement. From these two positions, the true quality of a thrower can be noted. A good run-up, a controlled withdrawal (both of which enable the athlete to get into a good throwing position), and a good arm action are the essential features of a throw.

The coach should make full use of all coaching aids, of which the tape measure and stopwatch are important. However, once the technique becomes good and fast, the vital tool of the trade is the movie camera and analyzing projector. This is the only possible way to observe what is actually happening. Plain visual impressions, although helpful, can often be very misleading.

Above all else, a good coach must realize that a sound technique can only be molded onto a fit, strong, supple body. There is no shortcut to success. All aspects of the throw can only be built up, over a period of years, by diligent practice.

Training for Javelin Throwers

To reach a good level of competition, the javelin thrower must be very fit, strong and mobile. Ideally he should be the complete all-around athlete, who includes other events in his training which will help to make him faster, stronger and more controlled for his specialist event.

To encourage athletes to adopt a wider and more systematic approach to their training, introduce them to the "unit plan," a very simple method of putting the various aspects of training in true perspective. It is systematic and flexible, and it can accommodate an athlete's strengths as well as his weaknesses.

A total of TEN units is allotted per week to the "S" factors, which cover all of the essential aspects of any athletic event. In the case of the young thrower, one unit could equal 30 minutes, meaning he trains for a total of five hours per week, but with the experienced thrower the time value per unit should be more than an hour.

Unit Plan

"S" factors	No. of units	Method of training
Speed	2	Sprinting, short hill running, jumping, bounding, etc.
Strength	3	Weight training, throwing shot.
Stamina	1	Fartlek, cross-country, Circuit training.
Suppleness	2	Partner stretching exercises, etc.
Skill	2	Throwing from short run-up, concentrating on certain aspects of technique, full effort throwing.

Competition is not included in the above scheme, but will come as extra sessions during the season.

Ideally, the pattern should change monthly to allow for the buildup to the competitive season. For example, the emphasis might shift from strength during the winter months to skill during the pre-season period.

Along with the conventional running and throwing programs, the javelin thrower should interest himself in a variety of activities which are likely to promote POWER. Above all, he should practice other events, such as hurdling, long jumping, sprinting, etc., to add variety and stimulate interest.

Other Activities

Activity	Average	Good	Very good	Excellent
		Grading		
1. Standing long jump	Own height	+1'3"	+2'	+2'6"
2. Standing triple jump	22'	24'	26'	28'
3. Standing two hops, step and jump	30'	33'	36'	39'

4. Standing two hops, two steps and one jump	39'	41'	43'	45'
5. Standing two hops, two steps and two jumps	42'	45'	48'	51'
6. 5 x two-foot bounds	38'	41'	43'	46'
7. Timed 25 yards hop	4.5 secs.	4.0	3.5	3.0

8. Throwing the 6-pound and the 8-pound 13-ounce shot, using a standing javelin throw technique, and later using a three-stride run. A strong thrower can use the 10-pound shot quite successfully.
9. Throwing a 16-pound shot over the head, backwards, using a double hand-hold. This is good for mobilizing and strengthening the back muscles.

Mobility

WORK is the product of the force and the distance, through which the point of application of the force is moved ($W = f \times d$). The javelin thrower should aim to get the value of W (work) as large as possible, and this can be done by increasing either, or both, of the other quantities. In the past, most athletes have concentrated on increasing the value of the force through selected weight training exercises, but little attempt has been made to increase the "range of movement." A number of Eastern European countries have realized the need for this kind of work, and most of their athletes include specific mobility work in their programs. Such exercises are probably more essential for the javelin thrower than for any other specialist track and field performer.

Through childhood most are gifted with natural flexibility of joints, but unless systematized exercises are performed, this innate mobility is lost with maturity. The ballet dancer is a classic example of a person who has retained mobility through exercise of a specific nature. But the majority of athletes come to their specialist event with a restricted range of movement. Once this stage has been reached, the only way to improve this important quality is to perform exercises of a stretching nature.

Mobility Exercises

These can be done with or without resistance, working the joints carefully and gradually through an increased range. The resistance can be in the form of weights, springs, and the like. If resistance is used, great care should be taken not to stretch the joint beyond the elastic limit, or injury will result.

As well as the general mobility exercises, the javelin thrower must also perform more specific exercises, taking the joints through movements similar to those of the throw itself. These can best be performed with medicine balls, hand weights and pulley weights.

The Training Schedule

Too many athletes read the training methods of the current champions and follow them blindly. Much of what is printed on how the champions train is really how they would LIKE to train. But even if they were correct, training schedules are personal things and should only be worked out after the coach has had the chance to observe the athlete in competition and training.

The beginner will follow a different schedule from that of the mature, experienced athlete. However, there are certain common elements which will serve as a guide to athlete and coach:

1. A schedule should aim at all-around development of speed, strength, stamina and suppleness.

2. A schedule should include throwing the year around. It is a mistake to concentrate on just strength training during the off-season. An increase in strength will almost certainly mean a slight modification in style to accommodate it. If strength is developed considerably, we could arrive at the stage where a complete re-education of skill is necessary. Strength, skill, mobility, etc., must all be brought along "hand in glove" so that only slight modifications in style are required.

3. Any proposed change in style must be made during the off-season so that it does not interfere with competition.

4. Any training scheme should be progressive in its buildup. There is no shortcut to success. One does not acquire the strength overnight to press 200 pounds or throw the javelin 250 feet. They are qualities developed over a period of years.

5. Training time is valuable; do not waste it.

To give an idea of the pattern of training, listed below are two fairly typical schedules for a thrower at two different times of the year.

14-day cycle, October–February (Off-season)

Day   1.   Work at gymnasium. Extra activities, weights, mobility.
Day   2.   Work on track. 8 x 60 yds. sprints. 4 x 25 yds. hopping. Throwing weight.
Day   3.   Work at gymnasium. Circuit training, weight training, mobility work.
Day   4.   Fartlek run for 30 mins. Weight training.
Day   5.   Rest.
Day   6.   Major game or pentathlon competition.
Day   7.   Mobility work. Technique work from the short run-up. Six full-effort throws, 3 x 80 yds. sprinting.
Day   8.   Same as day 1.
Day   9.   Interval training on track. Mobility work.
Day 10.   Gymnastics, rope work, extra activities, basketball, etc.
Day 11.   Quality weight training, working on Olympic lifts, maximum poundage.
Day 12.   Rest.

Day 13. Major game or pentathlon competition.
Day 14. Mobility work. Technique work using short run-up. 6 x 4 hurdles fast.

Each session should start with a gradual warm-up in the sweat suit. Warming up may or may not have physiological effects, but it certainly has psychological ones.

For the winter months, work with a 14-day cycle, but for the pre-season and competitive periods, it is better to use a weekly cycle. This gives more scope for modifying schedules should early competitions or quality throwing sessions indicate a weakness. During the off-season it is sufficient for the athlete and coach to meet just once every two weeks, although ideally a more frequent meeting would be better. But during the pre-season period, it is essential to meet at least once a week.

7-day cycle, March–April (Pre-season)

Day 1. Weight training and mobility work.
Day 2. 8 x 60 yds. sprinting. Mobility work, throwing the shot, extra activities.
Day 3. Quality throwing. Hurdling at speed.
Day 4. Throwing from short run-up, long jumping, shot putting.
Day 5. Rest.
Day 6. Competition or throwing training.
Day 7. Pentathlon competition.

Competition Season

Athletes are made in the winter and merely blossom in the spring. So all of the hard work must be done before the season begins. Training during the competitive season will, to a large extent, be determined by the frequency of competition. The following is suggested:

1. Keep one good quality weight training session.
2. Have at least one pentathlon a week and score against personal bests.
3. Mobility work must be increased.
4. Include one throwing session per week from the short run-up. If there is no competition in the week, a quality throwing session should be done.
5. One quality sprinting or hurdling session.
6. One day of complete rest prior to competition to prepare for the mental and physical effort.

Many of the ideas on training are empirical ones and are not really supported by sound evidence. For the future success of coaching this might be a good thing. Athletes are individuals and do not all react in the same way to the same training stimuli. Hence the good coach must continually modify and adopt his methods to suit individuals and to keep them in line with current trends.

Following are aspects of training which should be emphasized:

1. A sound technique can only be molded onto a sound physique. The athlete needs to be strong enough and mobile enough to accept the technique. If difficulty is experienced in forming a technique, consider carefully the reason; it could be lack of strength, mobility or motor educability. Thus it might be wiser to accept a slight deviation from what the coach believes to be correct to allow for what might be an innate deficiency.

2. Strength is very important, but not to the exclusion of everything else. Strength is specific to the activity; the javelin thrower does not need or want the type of strength of the Olympic lifter. There is a level of static strength beyond which further developments will not improve the standard of throwing.

3. Training must be regarded as an investment. You can only take out what you put in!

Chapter 21

TEACHING THE BEGINNING HAMMER THROWER

by Orlando Guaita

1. Necessary equipment is a 5–7 pound bag of some soft material, with handle and rope attached to the bag, totaling three feet in length. Hold arms straight out, parallel to the ground, and walk on the spot while turning left. Make two complete turns in this manner.

2. Teach the grip. Put the left hand through the handle, then the right hand over the left. Do not cross thumbs.

3. Hold arms straight out, parallel to the ground, with hands properly on the handle. Hammer-bag is just slightly off the ground. Now walk on the spot, turning left. Centrifugal force causes the bag to swing about knee high. Make three complete turns, slowly. Rest briefly. Repeat twice.

4. Repeat No. 3 but *run* on the spot while turning left, and lift the hammer-bag to above head height and swoop it downward with each complete turn. Make three turns. Rest, and repeat twice.

5. Repeat No. 4 but after getting the hammer-bag moving, release it over the left shoulder while on the uplift. Repeat this at least three times. Introduce a limited competition here, if possible.

6. The preliminary swing. Stand with feet about shoulder width apart. Grip the handle in the right hand *only*. Put the hammer-bag behind the right leg, as far to your rear as possible. Swoop the hammer-bag off the ground, as far in front as possible, and then back toward the point where it was originally resting. Bend the elbow of the right arm to bring the bag back overhead. Note that the bag is moving in a circle, mostly on your right side. Learn to move your hips in the opposite direction to the hammer-bag. Swing the bag slowly, smoothly, keeping a "tight hammer wire." Keep the left hand on the left hip.

7. While swinging the bag as in No. 6, put the left hand over the right hand and continue to swing the bag.

8. Take a proper grip on the handle and swing the bag as in No. 7.

9. Transition. Take two preliminary swings as in No. 8, and when the bag

gets directly in front, freeze your arms in front of you at arm's length. With arms in front and hammer-bag still in front, run on the spot while turning left as in No. 4. Rest after three turns, and repeat at least three times.

10.   Repeat No. 9 but deliver the hammer as in No. 5. Repeat at least five times. Introduce competition here, if possible.

11.   Turns. Walk several steps on the right toe and left heel. This procedure is simply to get the sensation of what is to follow.

12.   Stand on a line with the left foot. The line runs the length of this foot. The right foot is shoulder width from the left foot and parallel to it. Rise slightly on the right toe, and lift the left toe, bearing the weight of the foot on the left heel. Hands on hips. Turn left 180 degrees and place the left toes again on the line. Now rise on the left toes and walk away. Stop after two or three steps. Take the same position again. Continue to "turn and walk away." Repeat this at least ten times.

13.   Turn on a line as in No. 12, but when the left toe is placed on the line after having turned 180 degrees, lift the left heel and continue turning to make a 360-degree turn with the left foot. After the right toe leaves the ground, it makes a complete 360-degree circle *in the air*, to land again parallel to the left foot, but two foot-lengths behind its original starting point. The hands remain on the hips throughout. Take one turn at a time. Make these turns with the left foot always on a line. Repeat this at least 15 times.

14.   Use a proper hammer. Put the right arm through the handle and hold the ball of the hammer in the right hand. Repeat No. 12 but do two turns without stopping between. After repeating this at least ten times, try three turns without stopping. Keep the left hand on the left hip. Turn slowly. If you like, lift the hammer-ball outward to help keep your balance as you turn. In other words, "lean" on the hammer-ball to help maintain balance.

15.   Hold the handle of the hammer in the right hand (only) and roll it around you at arm's length, turning left. Take several turns without stopping in this way. Repeat at least five times.

16.   While turning as in No. 15, place the left hand on the right lower arm and gradually extend this grip to the right wrist and then the right hand on the hammer.

17.   Take a correct grip on the hammer and repeat turns while rolling the hammer. As you go faster, lift the hammer slightly off the ground. As you continue, you will gradually be doing turns, with the hammer about knee high.

18.   Take two preliminary swings, transition, and turns with hammer about knee high. Repeat often.

19.   Take two preliminary swings, transition, one turn, and delivery.

20.   Take two preliminary swings, transition, two turns, and delivery.

21.   Take two preliminary swings, transition, three turns, and delivery.

Chapter 22

THE HAMMER THROW

by Sam Felton, Jr.

What are the major factors which permit an athlete to throw the hammer more than 240 feet?

Speed. Blinding hammer-head speed at the release. Blinding, yet controlled.

Strength. The hammer builds up about 650 pounds of centrifugal force at release if it is to travel 240 feet.

Coordination. Agility. Highly-developed *reflexes.* A keen sense of *rhythm.* All are essential.

A thorough *understanding* of and an *ability to apply* the basic *physical principles* governing rotating forces. They are tricky, and not as straightforward as one might think.

Good coaching.

Hard work. Years of it. Self-discipline. Determination. Desire to succeed. Desire to learn . . . open-mindedness.

Will reading this chapter transform the reader into a 240-foot thrower? Probably not, but it should help minimize many of the trial and error aspects of learning this fascinating event. With some luck and ability, combined with hard work, putting the principles discussed in this chapter to work should add 10–20 percent in one season to the distance an average thrower can throw.

I have seen several athletes with the speed and strength to throw 240 feet, but have watched them struggle to hit 170–180 feet. I have even seen a few turn as fast as Connolly and Zsivotzky, but end up with no more than 180 or 190 feet for their efforts. Successfully applying the more important principles in this chapter should substantially narrow this unnecessary gap.

How can a thrower turn as fast as Connolly or Zsivotzky and only throw 180 or 190 feet? Table 1 shows how three throwers of equal ability can generate the same *turning speed* at the instant the hammer is released, yet throw 180, 200, and 220 feet.

Table 1

Thrower	Turning Speed (rev./sec.)	Length of Hammer Radius	Angle of Release	Distance Thrown
A	2.2	5'8"	35°	180'
B	2.2	5'8"	42°	200'
C	2.2	6'0"	42°	220'

Thrower C used good form . . . the principles advocated in this chapter. Thrower B, a super-strong weight lifter, pulled the hammer in with his arms during the release, thereby reducing the hammer's effective radius from 6'0" to 5'8" as he fell away from the hammer. This loss of 4 inches in effective radius cost 20 feet in distance thrown. Thrower A made the same mistake, but also threw the hammer too low. Another 20 feet lost.

Let us go back to the point on loss of hammer radius, and state it positively. A four inch increase in effective hammer radius can produce up to 20 feet more in distance thrown, provided the thrower's *turning speed* (revolutions per second) remains constant. The physical principles behind this point are covered later in the section called Physical Concepts. Bringing about this increase in effective radius is relatively easy, as Figure 243 suggests.

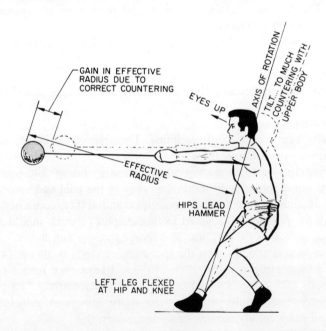

Figure 243.   As the hammer rises, relax the arms and shoulders and let them be pulled forward in the direction of the hammer. Keep your left knee flexed as you do this.

All top European throwers take full advantage of this seemingly small but immensely productive point. From the very beginning they are taught to maximize the hammer's *peripheral velocity* by combining *turning speed* with the longest hammer *radius* they can control. They know that the faster the hammer-head is moving at release, the farther it will go, provided the release angle is around 42–44 degrees. They know that true hammer-head speed (peripheral velocity) is a function of both turning speed and the distance the hammer-head is from its axis of rotation.

This chapter covers many points, like this one on effective radius, in an effort to break the event into specific things to do to improve performance.

Overall Concepts

1. *Constantly strive to make the hammer go faster. The faster it is moving at release, the farther it will go. But be sure it is moving its fastest at the instant of release, not before.*

Bill Gilligan puts it this way: "You must work hard on speed. The more at the finish, the better. But it must be controlled speed. Unfortunately lots of beginners hit maximum speed somewhere between the second and third turn, then peter out during the release. Always work on *acceleration* so the hammer is moving its fastest at release, even if you have to take something off it during the earlier turns."

Speed. Lots of it. Continually analyze your actions in the circle to be sure each contributes in some specific way toward making the hammer go faster, through a wide radius. Do as Dennis Cullum exhorts: "Concentrate on quick and early feet. The feet set the pace, and the hammer follows." Eliminate any movement which does not contribute to the hammer's peripheral speed. Keep the event simple.

2. *Increase the hammer's peripheral speed by combining high turning speed with a long hammer radius.* Rolfgünter Jabs has frequently stressed: "It is the hammer's peripheral velocity which counts, not just turning speed." The hammer's peripheral velocity is a function of both turning speed and length of hammer radius. "Each one inch increase in effective hammer radius can lead to an extra 5 to 7 feet in distance thrown," adds Jabs, "provided turning speed, angle of release, balance, etc., remain constant."

Figure 244 shows, in somewhat exaggerated fashion, why peripheral velocity increases with radius, even when turning speed (angular velocity) remains constant. The longer the radius, the greater the distance the hammer-head travels during the same period of time: therefore the faster it is moving.

Gabor Simonyi adds that it takes great patience and perseverance to achieve a longer hammer radius without sacrificing turning speed. As you try to increase the hammer's radius by letting your upper body relax and bend forward in the direction of the hammer, you may have to slightly reduce your turning speed temporarily to adjust to the increase in the hammer's centrifugal force. Then you can gradually build up your turning speed as your trunk muscles adjust

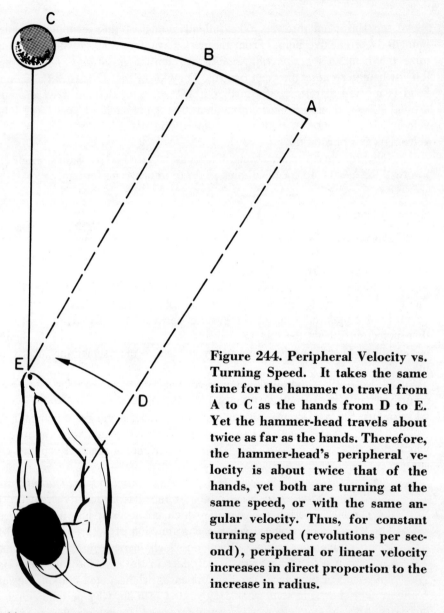

Figure 244. Peripheral Velocity vs. Turning Speed. It takes the same time for the hammer to travel from A to C as the hands from D to E. Yet the hammer-head travels about twice as far as the hands. Therefore, the hammer-head's peripheral velocity is about twice that of the hands, yet both are turning at the same speed, or with the same angular velocity. Thus, for constant turning speed (revolutions per second), peripheral or linear velocity increases in direct proportion to the increase in radius.

to this new strain, with a net gain, and a substantial one, in the hammer's peripheral velocity and centrifugal force.

3. *During the turns, increase the hammer's effective radius by countering its pull with your lower body, not your arms and shoulders.* Do this by letting your arms and shoulders relax and be pulled forward slightly by the hammer's pull during the 10° to 270° portion of each turn, but *without letting the hammer get ahead of you.* (See Figure 245 to tie degrees mentioned in this chapter into hammer position.)

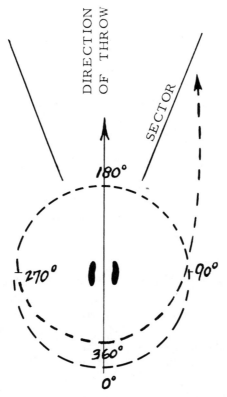

Dotted line represents path of hammerhead.

Degrees indicate where hammerhead is relative to thrower and direction of the throw.

Figure 245.

Combine this "stretching with the hammer" with a sufficiently deep sitting effect to maintain balance and to develop a *strong leg-lifting* action between each turn.

Regarding countering, Jabs adds the following: "Proper countering increases the hammer's radius and peripheral velocity without having to increase turning speed. If one can also increase turning speed, so much the better. Increased peripheral speed means more hammer-head centrifugal force and distance thrown.

"To counter effectively with the hips, sit back from the hammer's pull while both feet are on the ground, and hang from it when the right foot is off the ground. Naturally the longer both feet are on the ground, the more power you can generate between the turns. Sit and hang."

Figure 243 shows a good sitting position—tail down, upper body pulled forward slightly. Figure 282 shows the natural transfer of this sitting position into the start of a good "hang" from the hammer's pull. Figure 285 shows the result of a good "hang" at the completion of a turn, with legs "under the throw," arms stretched and relaxed, hammer way to the thrower's right, legs and hips way ahead of the hammer, etc.

Increasing the hammer's effective radius by proper countering makes the event look deceptively easy. Throwers who do this correctly seem to turn easily, almost slowly, yet achieve excellent distance. England's Ron Bowen described this phenomenon when he commented on what he saw while watching Zsivotzky train.

"The Hungarians played soccer for a while to warm up. Shortly Zsivotzky wandered over to the throwing circle and started to throw easily. His first throw was something to behold. Two easy winds, three relaxed turns, and a seemingly effortless release. The hammer rose and rose, way up, before dropping out at 212 feet. I have never seen an easier effort at this distance. Then he added a little more speed for the next six or eight throws and consistently dropped the hammer out in the 220'–224' range.

"With each throw, he turned with a relaxed, rhythmical, easy motion, and worked for the *widest range of movement possible*, rather than sheer speed. In fact, his turns appeared to be relatively slow, but it was apparent, because of the great radius, that the hammer-head was really moving. In addition, he accelerated beautifully throughout each effort."

This critically important *"wide range of movement"* is the result of countering the hammer's pull correctly with the lower body, not the arms and shoulders. Many potentially fine hammer throwers who have done a fair amount of weight training find this difficult to do. Often their arms and shoulders are too strong, and they use this great strength to force the hammer, particularly between the turns. As they complete each turn, they almost reflexively pull the hammer, thereby causing it to accelerate too much and overtake them. Once it does, the throw is lost. Instead they should complete each turn as indicated in Figure 246, with arms stretched and relaxed. They should then use their *legs* to press into the next turn. If this is done correctly, the relaxed arms will stretch even farther as the hammer's centrifugal force mounts. Figure 246 illustrates perfect "sitting and stretching."

Then, as the hammer starts to rise, continue to drive the legs and hips ahead of the hammer, but also let the upper body relax and stretch with the hammer a little. As you do this, the hammer will tend to seek a wide radius and help you achieve a "wide range of movement."

4. *Develop a keen "feel" for the event.* There is a rhythm to hammer throwing which must be learned. Either you develop this rhythm or "feel" or you cannot come close to achieving your maximum potential. Tom Gage describes it well: "I search for the position which produces the most speed and angle on the ball (angle between hammer-head and legs). Once I *feel* it, I try to keep hitting it until a muscular-neuro pattern is set up. At this

point, you must continue to search for an even better *feel* to throw farther. I look most for a *constant hang* on my shoulders *that is transmitted to my legs*, and through a flexed back (which is much in the position for a good squat or dead lift). With each turn, I try to *feel my hips gain on my shoulders* which remain *as relaxed as possible*."

Tom's advice is extremely well put, and is worth committing to memory. All top throwers I have talked to have stressed all the points Tom brings out in his statement. They all *feel a constant or increasing "hang" or "pull"* as they turn, and have *learned to respond to it reflexively* in a natural manner which increases its intensity. In effect, they have set up a self-feeding system.

The more the hammer pulls away from them, or the tighter the wire becomes, the more they sit or hang in direct response to this sensation. The more they do, the more centrifugal force is imparted to the hammer-head, and the more it pulls away in a straight line from the thrower's left shoulder straight out to the hammer-head. The more it pulls, the more they respond until the tension they build up is so great that the hammer literally rips from their grasp during the release.

If a thrower learns to respond to this pull reflexively, he should be able to *pick up speed almost at will* by sitting or hanging from the hammer's pull at the right time with a little more force, or by completing each turn a little faster, a little farther ahead of the hammer, or by stretching his legs with a little more "umph" between the turns. Each of these actions increases the hammer's centrifugal force, or pull, which in turn causes the thrower to react with even more force . . . relaxed force.

While a *feel* for the hammer's increasing pull is essential, there is a companion tension or sensation which must be felt simultaneously. As you *feel* the hammer pull away, you must let this tension be transmitted through *relaxed arms* to your legs between the turns (Figure 246), and your *legs must press with a greater force*. If they don't, the hammer will gain on you. You can't just match the hammer's pull. Your legs must add even *more force, enough force to insure that your legs and hips will drive into the next turn with sufficient force to gain substantially on the hammer and permit you to complete the next turn way ahead of the hammer.* As your legs press you into each turn, you will *feel* considerable pressure in your thighs and considerable pull through your back muscles, particularly the trapezius and latissimus dorsi groups. While there is tension in your arms, you should *feel* more of a pulling-away sensation, a stretching sensation. But this tension is clearly less pronounced than that developed through your thighs and back.

All of this is possible only if your arms are relatively relaxed and somewhat passive during the turns. The instant your arms pull the hammer with more force than your legs and back exert between the turns (particularly in the position shown in Figure 246), two serious errors will strike. Either the hammer will gain on you, or, if you pull the hammer too hard, it will pull you forward. In either event, the throw will be lost.

Figure 246. Legs "under the throw." This is a key position: legs in strong lifting position before hammer passes its low point; weight firmly on left foot; and arms stretched and relaxed.

But how can one relax and still control the mounting centrifugal force involved? "Relax" isn't quite the right word, but is almost correct. How does a top pro golfer smash a 250–300-yard drive with a "smooth, relaxed, almost effortless" swing? Or a top tennis player smash an incredibly powerful serve in the same manner. None of these actions can be performed with the optimum or maximum result unless the athlete combines *relaxation* with *rhythm* and *explosive power*, and acts on reflex action, not thought-initiated action. Throw hard . . . easily . . . within yourself. Don't rush the throw. Take time to work the hammer through a wide radius. Develop a feel for the event. Develop rhythm. Accelerate.

5. *View the throw as a single, powerful, continuous, rapidly accelerating action.* While the throw can be broken into parts for discussion purposes (winds, turns, final sweep), it cannot be viewed in parts while actually throwing. The entire action, from the start of the winds through the release, must be one continuous, powerful action. Each phase must flow smoothly, but powerfully, into the next. There can be no pauses. The entire action is dynamic. You must constantly and relentlessly increase the hammer's centrifugal force.

Each part of the throw is dependent on correct execution of the preceding part. A powerful final sweep depends on achieving the strong position shown in Figures 274–276.

Achieving this position, and the tremendous hammer-head speed indicated, depends on completing each turn well ahead of the hammer (Figures 274, 269 and 264), with both feet in position on the ground and the body weight concentrated predominately on the left foot, BEFORE THE HAMMER PASSES ITS LOW POINT (Figure 246).

Hitting this position depends on (a) producing an increasing lead-angle on the hammer-head throughout the turns (angle between hips and hammer); and (b) countering, sitting, and hanging properly from the hammer's pull at the right instant.

Both these points depend on a perfectly executed sweep (transition) into the first turn, which, in turn, is dependent upon perfectly executed preliminary winds. Unless they are executed correctly, way to the thrower's right, the rest of the throw will be out of whack, and below one's potential.

So, don't overlook perfecting each part of the throw, including the winds. But blend each part into one continuous, rhythmic, powerful action, one where the hammer gains speed from turn to turn. Lots of speed!

6. *Use your legs as your primary source of turning and throwing power.*

Coach Gilligan hits this point well: "As you start winding the hammer, remember that this is primarily a leg and body event. The arms only implement what the legs and body have done.

"The leg position–this is one thing you must really do right during the turns. They must be in a lifting position while the hammer moves through most of its power arc, or from around 270° through 10°. During this arc, sit on your thighs, in a good, deep flex. It is easy to lose some of this flex as the turns progress and as the hammer tries to lift you from the ground as it sweeps up to its high point . . . so, SIT. The top throwers try to increase the amount of flex from turn to turn so, just before that all-important explosive finish, their legs are really under the hammer, in a powerful lifting position.

"The hammer accelerates most immediately after the ball of the right foot hits the ground at the completion of each turn. The earlier it hits, the more you can accelerate the hammer, provided, of course, your legs are deeply flexed. The instant your right foot feathers in, let your weight settle hard on your bent left leg . . . quickly shift most of your body weight onto your left heel, toward its rear outer edge. Go down on it in a grinding, twisting motion.

"It starts with your feet. Your legs, hips and trunk all pull, while your arms stretch as the hammer pulls with increasing force from you. All this is done from a lifting position, from bent legs (Figure 246) . . . deeply bent legs. Sure, the arms work on the hammer during this power arc, but not the way the legs and body do. The latter do the real work, AHEAD of the hammer. As a result, the lagging hammer should almost pull your arms from their sockets as you fly into the next turn.

"Start into the next turn before the hammer passes your right knee. Press leftward with the right foot. As the hammer passes its low point, continue to drive ahead of it, but keep your arms out of it. Move your body and leave the arms and hammer behind. Let the hammer lag from relaxed arms. Counter the hammer's pull, of course, but let it sweep as far to your left as possible, *without letting it get ahead of you*. As the hammer sweeps from 270° to about 10°, the legs straighten somewhat, but not all the way, and they do it *ahead of the hammer*. Then as the hammer rises to its high point, flex the knees again so you can hang down from its pull and settle on your left foot as the right foot feathers in again, well ahead of the hammer (Figure 283). As the hammer descends from its high point, let the legs flex as much as possible, AHEAD OF THE HAMMER."

Connolly adds the following regarding the legs during the final sweep: "At the completion of the last turn, my body weight is greatly inclined toward my left foot, but there is also a significant amount of weight on my right foot. Both knees are bent considerably (even more than in Figure 275), and both legs are used in a strong upward and around thrust to initiate the power during the delivery. This causes a follow-through on the left foot which, in my case, leads to an extra recovery spin immediately after the hammer is released. During a good delivery, I can really feel my legs add great velocity to the hammer-head."

7. *During the entire throw, use your head as a rudder to help set or lead the action. Also use it as a stabilizer to help maintain balance.* The head acts like a rudder and tends to determine where the shoulders will be relative to your hips and legs. Turn your head too far left during the turns, and the chances are that your shoulders will also turn left. Bear in mind that it is imperative to try to increase the lead-angle between your legs/hips and shoulders/arms from turn to turn. So don't turn your head so far left that it causes you to lose some of this important lead-angle.

Let's break the throw into its parts and comment on correct head position.

a. *During the preliminary winds, keep your head and eyes facing well to your right to help enable you to hold your shoulders and the hammer's low point way to your right.* During the winds, do not turn your eyes, head, or shoulders leftward with the hammer as it sweeps to the 0° point until you sweep into the first turn. During the winds, look out in a 280–290° direction.

b. *During the transition into the first turn, don't turn your head too far or too
fast to the left of the hammer.*

Simonyi describes the action as follows: "Don't turn the eyes too quickly to
the left during the transition. Doing so will cause you to drag the hammer and
shorten its radius. Turn the head at the same speed as the hammer, and concentrate on sweeping the hammer through the widest possible arc. Turn the head
ahead of the hammer, with the hips. Just think of *turning the head and hips
together, and leave the hammer behind,* lagging from stretched, relaxed arms."

Connolly adds: "As you sweep into the first turn, keep your head up. Don't
lift the hammer up, however, and don't bury your head." Figure 282 shows an
excellent transition into the first turn, with eyes up, head and hips together,
lagging arms stretched and relaxed, and with a good lead-angle on the hammer.

c. *Throughout the turns, turn your hips and head together, ahead of the
hammer, and leave the arms and hammer behind—farther behind with
each turn.*

Simonyi continues: "From the moment the turn commences on the outer edge
of the left heel, the head should start turning to the left of the hammer slightly
(Figure 261), and gradually become part of the axis on the left side. The head
should lead the hammer together with the hips and the legs from the moment the
hands pass the right knee during the transition. My experience indicates it is a
lot easier to 'leave the arms and shoulders behind' if the head leads. Leading
with the head also makes it easier to hang from the hammer. So, turn the head
and hips together, as a unit, and leave the hammer behind. With each turn, try
to leave it farther behind."

How much head-lead depends on the individual, and how proficient he is.
Some lead is essential. Too much can reduce what should be a power-laden
lead-angle on the hammer. And beginners might do well to minimize the amount
of head-lead, then let it increase slightly as they become more proficient.

d. *Don't turn your head way left in preparation for or anticipation of the
final sweep.* Note the head position in Figures 272–276. Many lesser
throwers anticipate the final sweep by "gathering themselves" and turning
their heads way left as they fly into the last turn. In committing this
serious error, the essential lead-angle is lost just when it is needed most. As
a result, the right foot lands late, and probably hard, or just as the hammer
passes its low point. The result is a very weak finish. By contrast, Figures
274–275 show perfect position prior to the final sweep. Notice how the
head and hips still turn together, almost 90° ahead of the hammer!

e. *During the final sweep, use your head to initiate a powerful, almost violent,
lifting action.*

Simonyi's comments are again helpful: "During the 'sling'—'delivery' sounds
sluggish—the head should be thrown up and back just before the hammer
reaches its low point, which must be to the right of the right foot (Figure 246
shows excellent position just as the head is being thrown up and back). Again
the head and hips work together. As the hips are thrown forward, the head is
thrown up and back."

f. *Throughout the entire throw, keep your eyes and head up. Don't look down.* During the turns, it is important to keep the eyes up. If you look down, your center of gravity will shift forward and you will probably be

Figure 247.   Stretch. Arms and shoulders stretch with hammer's pull— head helps resist hammer's pull as body weight settles firmly on left foot.

Figure 248.   Drive the Legs and Hips. "If there is a secret to the event, it is the ability to work with the upper body relaxed and relatively passive, and the lower body active and generating great drive and power." Throughout the turns, drive the legs and hips well ahead of the hammer.

pulled off balance. You can use your head to counter the hammer's pull, provided you do not overdo it. Doing this correctly requires a proper "feel" for the hammer's pull. Figure 247 shows how this is done. Notice how the head seems to act as a brace or anchor to help prevent the hammer from pulling the thrower's arms from their sockets. As suggested earlier, this can be overdone, and lead to countering with the shoulders. Be careful. As with most points of form, there is a happy medium between the extremes which invariably lead to trouble.

8. *During the entire throw, keep the hammer's low point well to your right.* During the winds and turns, the hammer's low point will creep leftward. This must be controlled, and the low point must not pass the 330° point by the time of the start of the final sweep. Table 2 sets forth a framework you should stay within.

Table 2

	Progression of Low Point Leftward Location of Low Point
End first wind	270°–280°
Start into 1st turn	280 –300
Completion 1st turn	300 –310
Completion 2nd turn	310 –320
Completion 3rd turn	320 –330

Hauling the hammer with the arms, or turning the head too far left during the turns are two of the most frequent reasons for a straying low point. Beware.

9. *"If there is a secret to the event, it is the ability to work with the upper body relaxed and relatively passive, and the lower body active and generating great drive and power" (Figure 248).* This is another of Gilligan's key points. How true it is. Too many beginners try to bull or force the hammer with their arms and shoulders, particularly if they are strong weight lifters. Don't get me wrong. I am not against a sensible amount of weight training. You must be strong, very strong, and must be able to apply your strength quickly if you are to throw over 200 feet. Weight training is essential. But when it becomes an end in itself, throwing performance will suffer.

Top throwers know how to relax their arms and shoulders in response to the mounting tension in the hammer wire during the turns. Doing this correctly increases the hammer's effective radius and facilitates more effective sitting and hanging from the hammer's pull. They combine this extra radius with increased turning speed generated by driving the legs and hips ahead of the hammer at the start of each turn. This blending of increased radius with increased turning speed produces a tremendous pickup in the hammer's peripheral velocity and centrifugal force.

The Parts Which Make Up The Throw

10. *The preliminary swings or winds.*

a. *Throughout the winds, keep the hammer's low point way to your right, or around 270–280°.* As has been stressed frequently in this chapter, it is imperative to maintain a substantial (and as the turns progress, an increasing) lead-angle between the hips/legs and the shoulders/hammer. Unless you maintain this desirable lead-angle during the winds, you probably won't be able to during the subsequent turns. Simonyi develops this point well:

"During the winds, the head should be kept facing the same direction, to the thrower's right. If he does this, the shoulders cannot rotate too far left. Sometimes I stand a few yards in front of the thrower, to his right, off at about 280–300°, and insist he look me in the eye all throughout the winds. This prevents him from turning his head to follow the hammer leftward. It is O.K. if he turns his head a little to the right so the left shoulder points out to 0° as the hammer descends. This permits the hammer's lowest point to remain around 270°, or where it should be. Don't let it creep leftward." Some throwers place a towel out where Simonyi stands and keep their eyes on it in an effort to hold their eyes and shoulders to the right during the winds.

b. *Sweep the hammer through the widest possible radius while accelerating it strongly with your entire body, not just your arms.*

Connolly stresses, "My winds are done with the body, with my arms as passive as possible." Cullum states: "The body initiates the movement of the hammer; the arms guide its correct path." The action during the winds is whip-like, with the hips initiating a strong, countering force, constantly moving in the opposite direction from the hammer's pull. When done properly, you feel a stretching and pulling sensation up and down your back, side and stomach muscles, as they stretch with the hammer and accelerate it. Simultaneously you should feel your relaxed arms and shoulders stretch forward with the hammer's pull as it rises in front of you. Note how the thrower bends forward at the waist in Figures 256–258, thereby adding substantially to the hammer's effective radius. As he bends, his hips automatically move in the opposite direction, thereby setting up an effective lower-body counter.

During the winds, keep the feet comfortably spread, a little wider then shoulder width apart. Also keep your legs comfortably bent at the knees and hip. This is essential, if you are to counter effectively. *Sit* as the hammer descends to its low point (Figures 256–258).

Note how the thrower's weight shifts from foot to foot, *ahead* of the hammer. In Figure 249, his weight is almost entirely on his left foot, while the hammer is way to his right. In Figure 253 almost all his weight has shifted onto his right foot, when the hammer is way to his left. Left heel is up. Then again in Figure 257 his weight is firmly on his left foot, well before the hammer passes his right knee. This strong shifting action, ahead of the hammer, is vigorous and positive,

Figure 249.   Figure 250.

Figure 251.   Figure 252.

Figure 253.   Figure 254.

Figure 255.   Figure 256.

Figure 257.   Figure 258.

Figure 259.   Figure 260.

Figure 261.   Figure 262.

Figure 263.   Figure 264.

Figure 265. Figure 266.

Figure 267. Figure 268.

Figure 269.   Figure 270.

Figure 271.   Figure 272.

Figure 273.   **Figure 274.**

Figure 275.   **Figure 276.**

Figure 277.   Figure 278.

Figure 279.   Figure 280.

and emanates from the hips. Feel that the action is to the left with each swing so you will set the proper rhythm for the transition into the first turn.

Note how the left shoulder dips while the weight is still on the left foot (Figures 250–251), then turns sharply to the right as the weight shifts quickly to the right foot before the hammer reaches its high point (Figures 252–253).

During the winds, keep the knees bent comfortably, as in Figures 250, 251 and 255.

In summary, work the hammer with your body, particularly the hips which move in opposition to the hammer. Don't force the hammer with your arms. Let them stretch and permit the hammer to sweep through a very wide radius. Concentrate on *moving your hands through the widest possible orbit*.

11. *The Sweep/Transition into the First Turn (Figures 255–261)*. Sweep into the first turn with a smooth, wide-ranging, powerful action. Do this by sitting back from the hammer's pull as the hammer descends from the last wind (Figures 254–258). Simultaneously bend forward at the waist, with the hammer's pull, to achieve a long radius as the hammer sweeps through its low point (Figures 258 and 281). As you do this, let the arms stretch and relax—don't force the hammer!

In Figures 256–261 the hips counter the hammer's pull nicely as the thrower sits into a fairly deep squat. Without this "sitting" effect, it is virtually impossible to develop a smooth, powerful transition into the first turn. Figure 281 shows particularly good position, with the arms and thighs almost parallel. Note that the full sitting position is achieved *before the hammer passes its low point*, with the body weight concentrated primarily on the left foot. As the hammer approaches its low point (Figures 258 and 281), the throwers in both illustrations start pushing or pressing into the turn. The hips and legs turn ahead of the hammer, and, with the aid of a pushing effort by the right foot, they start to turn faster than the hammer. This right foot push is important. It cannot be a jerky effort. It is smooth and firm. It is like a short-stroke piston. It does not result in the right foot being picked way up as the turn unfolds. It pushes, then skims in close to the left heel so it will alight quickly, ahead of the hammer. This push helps insure that the thrower sweeps both himself and the hammer as far to his left as possible as he drives into the first turn. It also helps provide much of the "oomph" or momentum required to (a) insure that the hammer does not move ahead of the thrower, and (b) insure that the legs and hips will complete the turn well ahead of the hammer, as in Figure 264.

During the transition, the legs and hips lead the hammer. They lead by about 45° as the press into the turn starts in Figure 258. By Figure 262 the lead is still about 45°, and as the thrower completes the turn, with legs "under the throw" in Figure 264, the lead is 90°.

Correct head action is important during the transition. Drive the head and hips together, ahead of the arms and hammer. Unfortunately many strong beginners use their head to lead or even initiate the action into the first turn, and let the hips and hammer lag. Don't. Do as is shown in Figures 258–262. The head and hips lead the hammer as the transition starts in Figure 258. Then the

Figure 281.   Sit into the First Turn. Arms and thighs are almost parallel as the hammer sweeps through its lowest point during transition into first turn.

head and hips turn together and lead the hammer by about 45° in Figure 262. Excellent! Remember Simonyi's advice. "Drive the head and hips together and leave the arms and hammer behind."

During the transition, let the hammer rise naturally to its high point. Don't force it with the arms. The pressing leftward effect, a slight straightening of the legs ahead of the hammer, and a slight straightening effect of the back as you sit back against the hammer's pull will all combine to lift the hammer on a reasonably steep plane, or one inclined about 35–40° to the ground, provided the arms are stretched and relaxed.

During the transition, the hammer must sweep way to your left, without getting ahead of you, as is shown in Figures 261, 262 and 282.

Figure 282. Way to Your Left. . . . Let the hammer sweep as far to your left as possible as you enter each turn. Shoulders stretch with hammer. Hips and head turn together, ahead of arms and hammer.

Thrower Ed Burke adds the following: "The hammer must pull up and away from the thrower during the transition as he turns on his left foot into the first turn." Once again, this involves a feel for the hammer's pull, and it must be felt early in the transition. You should feel the hammer pull away as it sweeps through its low point. As it does, continue to sit back from this pull from relaxed arms, but sit back quickly enough and with enough force so your body remains ahead of the hammer.

12. *The Turns*

a. *Throughout the turns, constantly increase the amount of torque between your lower body, that is, your legs and hips, and the hammer. With each turn, your legs and hips must gain on the hammer, and can do so only if your arms are stretched and relaxed.* All top throwers and coaches stress this critical point, as the following representative comments indicate.

"Lead the hammer, but don't drag it. The body must always be in advance of the hammer . . . and that must start from the moment you start winding and continue through the turns."—Connolly.

"During the turns, feel your hips gain on your shoulders, which must remain as relaxed as possible. Gain more and more on the hammer with each succeeding turn, until immediately before the final sweep, when you must be way ahead of the hammer (as in Figures 274 and 275), and are in the strong position required to unleash the tremendous torque generated to that point."—Gage.

"You must constantly increase the amount of lead-angle on the hammer as the turns progress."—Frenn.

After carefully analyzing the top throwers at the Tokyo Olympics, Dennis Cullum observed that the leaders "maintained a high degree of torque throughout the turns, so that the hips always led the shoulders, both when the hammer was rising and when it was coming down. The amount of torque varied during the turns, but in the better throws, was at its greatest when the right foot alighted for the last time prior to delivery, whereupon a vigorous 'unwind' took place."

A note of caution. The more torque you develop, the more you must (a) relax your arms and shoulders, and (b) hit the position in Figures 246 and 283 with *deeply flexed legs.* If you do not combine high torque with relaxed arms all throughout the turns, and deeply bent legs between the turns, the hammer will pull you off balance.

b. *Between the turns, use your legs and back as the primary source of power to substantially accelerate the hammer. Do this by completing each turn with both legs deeply flexed, in a strong lifting position, before the hammer passes its low point. Then use your legs and back muscles to stretch the hammer through its low point.*

Figure 246 illustrates perfect position between the turns. The flexed legs are in a strong lifting position well ahead of the hammer, *body weight is concentrated strongly on the left foot,* arms and shoulders are stretched and relaxed, and head and hips are in position together, way ahead of the hammer.

All top throwers hit this position turn after turn, almost automatically. With each turn, they feel the increasing strain of this position. With each turn, their

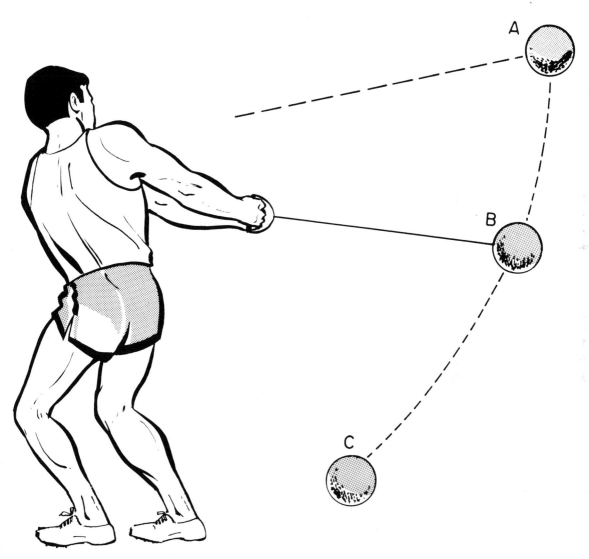

Figure 283. Way Ahead of Hammer. . . . A. Ball of right foot alights. Knee bent. B—C. With weight predominately on left foot: (1) unwind and (2) stretch legs ahead of hammer. Hit strong lifting position before hammer passes its lowest point.

thighs must press harder to resist and overcome the hammer's mounting pull. At times this tension becomes so great during the final sweep that their legs almost buckle under it.

There are several things you must do to hit this key position correctly.

The ball of the right foot must alight before the hammer passes 270°.

In addition, at the completion of the second and third turns, the ball of the right foot should alight before the hammer falls below shoulder level, as shown in Figures 269 and 274.

As it alights, the legs and hips must lead the hammer by 90°, as indicated in Figures 263–264, 269–270, and especially 274–275. Doing this is referred to as "crossing the X."

"The experienced thrower knows that the ability to maintain a great counter in the back half of the turn is a factor largely responsible for producing 220-plus throws. In the process of all the turns, the thrower must be careful to keep the hammer well back, that is, with legs and hips facing one way, and his chest, shoulders and arms facing at right angles to his lower body. 'Cross the X' is what the Europeans say."—George Frenn.

Figure 274 illustrates "crossing the X" perfectly. Commit it to memory.

As the ball of the right foot alights, both legs are flexed substantially at the hip and knee.

The real key to hitting the position in Figure 246, with both legs under the throw, lies in your ability to hang effectively from the hammer's pull as it sweeps through its high point and starts to fall.

To hang effectively, you must let your left knee bend or "give" quickly as the hammer sweeps through its high point. Note the amount of increase in bend in the left knee in Figures 262 vs. 263, 267 vs. 269 and 272 vs. 274. As the left knee "gives" or, as Jabs puts it, "collapses," the hammer's strong pull will tend to support or suspend you. The more you hang from its pull, the more you will accelerate the hammer as it descends, provided your body leads it. The more you let your left knee "give," and the quicker you do it, the more you will be able to hang or sink down from the hammer's pull. And the more the left knee bends, the more both legs will be flexed as you complete each turn.

To hang effectively, you must also let the hammer sweep as far as possible to your left at the start of each turn, as is suggested in Figure 282. The farther it sweeps to your left, the more you will have to hang from its pull to prevent being pulled out of the circle. Also, the farther left it sweeps, the more you will increase the hammer's effective radius. The more you do this without reducing your turning speed, the more you will increase the hammer's peripheral velocity and centrifugal force. The greater its centrifugal force, the harder you can hang—and so we are back to the self-feeding system referred to earlier.

Simonyi covers this important element of good form well: "I do not try to teach 'hanging from the hammer's pull' directly. Hanging is a by-product of a correct action, like the reverse in the shot. If the thrower lets the hammer sweep way to his left, and lets it pull his shoulders forward somewhat as it approaches its highest point, then he must hang correctly or be pulled out of the circle. True, the left knee sags quickly as the hammer moves through its highest point, but this is a response required to maintain balance. If it isn't a required response, the thrower probably hasn't let the hammer sweep left far enough.

"Teach letting the hammer sweep through the widest circle possible. Teach letting the shoulders be pulled forward as the hammer rises, but don't let the hammer lead the thrower. Hanging will follow, as will effective countering with the hips."

Gilligan adds: "It's funny, in a way, as most throwers believe the hammer moves way to their left, when in fact it doesn't. Experiment. See how far left you can let it pull you *without letting it get ahead of you*. Don't be timid. Get it out there!"

But as the hammer sweeps way to your left during the start of each turn, be sure to keep the left leg flexed both at the hip and knee, particularly as the hammer sweeps up to its high point in the second and third turns. If you do not, the chances are you are countering the hammer's pull too much with your shoulders. This will cause you to complete the turn off balance by landing hard on your right foot with a telltale thump. This in turn will let the hammer get ahead of you, thereby ruining the throw. A heavy, noisy right foot is for oafs. Beware. Watch that important "hip-angle," as Simonyi aptly calls it (Figure 284), and don't lose it during the turns.

    c. *Start each turn before the hammer passes your right knee, and use your legs to press into the turn.* The transition into the first turn has already been covered. Figures 264–265 and 270–271 show the start into the second and third turns. Note how quickly the thrower sits back from the hammer's pull, heavily against the left foot. During this "sitting back" you unwind somewhat as you partially "uncross the X" and as a result translate part of the torque developed to that point into increased hammer-head velocity.

Unwind before the hammer passes its low point and augment the action with a powerful stretching effort from your legs. If the legs are in a strong lifting position, ahead of the hammer (Figure 246), you can use them to *"stretch the hammer through its low point."* As you do, the hammer will pick up tremendous additional speed, provided your arms remain stretched and relatively relaxed. If they are, and if you stretch your legs with sufficient speed and force, your left arm should be pulled across your chest as you sweep into the next turn (Figure 246).

While it is important to straighten your legs somewhat ahead of the hammer between the turns, it is most important that you do not straighten them all the way. Remember Simonyi's important "hip-angle." Don't lose it, particularly as the hammer sweeps up to its high point during the last turn. This is when the hammer's pull will almost be strong enough to lift you off the ground. Don't let it. Maintain contact with the ground with your left foot always, and don't let your left leg straighten all the way.

While it is important to sit back from the hammer's pull between the turns, don't exaggerate this action by countering with your shoulders. As you sit, feel the pressure primarily in your thighs and back, and don't pull your shoulders back.

Powerful leg action between the turns depends on getting the legs "under the

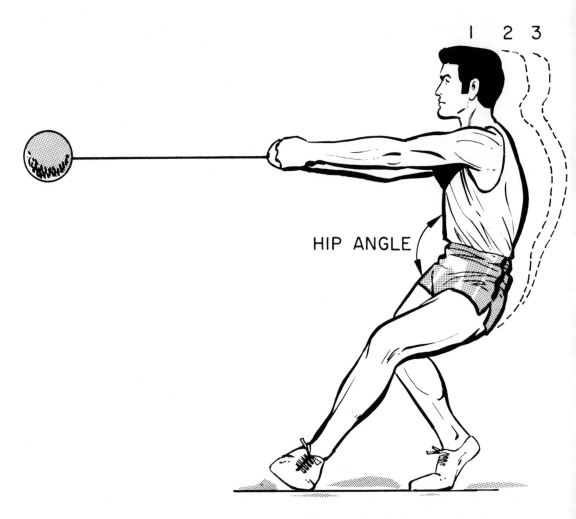

Figure 284. Hip Angle. Remain flexed at the hip. Don't lose the important "hip-angle" during the second and third turns, even though your upper body will have to counter the hammer's mounting pull with more force. Don't counter too much!

throw," as shown in Figures 246 and 270–271, then—and the action is almost simultaneous—sitting, unwinding, and stretching the legs. A word of caution, however. Do not let the left leg bend any more as the ball of the right foot alights, and, of course, do not straighten it before the right foot lands.

By how much should you lead the hammer at the start or completion of a turn? Just as much as you can without (a) forcing the hammer with your arms, (b) being pulled hard on your right foot at the completion of any turn, or (c) letting the left foot break from the ground at any point during the turns. "Lead the hammer, but do not haul it."

d. *Throughout the turns and final sweep, keep both feet on the ground as long as possible, and never—I repeat, NEVER—let your left foot be pulled from the ground until after the hammer has ripped from your hands.* The greatest increases in torque and the hammer's peripheral velocity are generated when both feet are on the ground, pressing against it. Torque and hammer peripheral velocity are quickly lost when both feet are off the ground. The left foot is the key, and must not leave the ground, even for an instant. If, during practice, you feel your left foot break from the ground, I suggest you stop turning by banging the hammer on the ground immediately as it descends, and start the throw over again, after collecting your bearings.

The Left Foot

During the turns, roll along the outer edge of your left foot as you track down the circle in a straight line (Figures 260–262, 265–268, etc.). This "outer-edge roll," as Simonyi calls it, is important. He continues, "The turn on the left foot does not start with the big toe being raised high. There is no time for that. Rather, the turn starts on the outer edge of the heel and proceeds quickly along the outer edge of the central portion of the foot. It is then completed on the ball of the foot. The entire action is quick, active and flowing. It is unbroken and smooth, being *one* fast rolling motion. The tempo is not 'one-two'. It is 'zip' and it is done."

The Right Foot

Once the right foot leaves the ground (Figure 282), get it back down as quickly as possible. To do this, it must travel the shortest distance possible. Therefore, once it leaves the ground, keep it close to both the ground and the left heel. Don't pick it way up or let it fly way out. Instead, keep it in tight.

Most beginners and many more experienced throwers lift the right foot off the ground too early at the start of each turn, and also carry it too high during the back half of each turn. This causes the right foot to land late and too hard, often after the hammer has passed its low point. When this happens, it is impossible to catch up to the hammer, and the throw is lost. Get the right foot back down before the hammer passes 270°!

Gilligan adds: "That right foot must feather in at the completion of each turn, well ahead of the hammer. By feather in, I mean it comes in softly (but firmly), on the ball of the foot; but it reacts quickly, with power to help push you into the next turn. Don't bang it in hard. As it feathers in, keep your weight firmly on your left foot, and keep pressing leftward. Start into the next turn before the hammer passes your right knee.

"If the right foot comes in heavy, it is because you are off balance. One way to eliminate this fault is to *let the hammer ride way* OUT TO YOUR LEFT as you sweep into each turn (without letting it get ahead of you, as that too will cause you to complete the turn heavily on the right foot). The farther you let the hammer pull you left, while staying ahead of it, the easier it will be to complete the turn with your weight firmly on your left foot so you can pull down to the hammer's low point. And the easier it will be to simultaneously let that right foot feather in quickly, just ahead of the hammer, and in time to help press left.

"If you do not let the hammer ride way out to your left at the start, you are bound to come in hard on the right foot. If you do, you will check your turning speed, but the hammer will maintain its speed and probably pull you into the next turn. When that happens, the throw is lost."

Work for quick, tight turns. Keep the right foot in close. Get it back down quickly.

(Note how the thrower completes each turn on the ball of his right foot in Figures 263–264, 269–270, and 274–275.) His right heel does not touch the ground at all during the turns. Some throwers improperly complete their turns by landing heel first, thereby braking the turning action and reducing turning speed. When this brake is applied, the hammer maintains its speed, and gets ahead of the thrower.

The right foot must help push left and into each turn. In watching the top throwers, it appears that the ball of their right foot barely touches the ground between the turns. The action is that quick. The right foot acts like a powerful short-stroke piston, or like a cat's paw quickly scuffing the ground. The ball of the right foot reacts the instant it touches the ground at the completion of each turn by pushing and pressing. After it has helped push you into the next turn, it is carried close to the ground and the left heel. Press/push. Relax. Press/push. Relax . . . quick . . . quick. Simonyi describes the power-stroke portion of the turn as a "turning press." If you visualize it in this manner, your right foot should not be lifted too early.

At times picking the right foot up too early is the symptom of another bad error, pulling the hammer in with the arms or shoulders at the start of each turn. The two go hand in hand. Do as Gilligan, Simonyi, and most top coaches advocate. Press left at the start of each turn and let the hammer sweep as far to your left as you can control. Maintain some "hip-angle" and let the arms and shoulders be pulled forward slightly as the hammer sweeps to its high point, but do not let the hammer get ahead of you. Keep working on that important lead-angle. Drive the legs and hips around hard, and leave the arms and hammer behind.

13. *The Final Sweep*

Complete the last turn with both deeply bent legs in a strong lifting position before the hammer passes its lowest point (Figures 274–276), and explode with all your strength to whip the hammer on its way (Figures 275–280).

Fly into the last turn just as you would any turn, that is, do not "gather yourself" or anticipate the final sweep by turning your head way left, by tightening your arms and shoulders, or by straightening your legs too early.

Get the ball of your right foot back down early, before the hammer passes

270° and before it drops below shoulder height (Figures 274 and 285) . . .
weight firmly on your left foot . . . left shoulder dipped . . . X crossed . . . arms
stretched . . . legs flexed deeply at knees and hip.

Immediately as the ball of the right foot alights, execute a powerful "shovel-
pitch" release by sweeping the hammer way around your left leg. Let's break
this point down.

**Figure 285.   Start of Final Sweep. Ball of right foot in place before
hammer drops below shoulders—legs flexed—weight predominately on
left foot—legs and hips way ahead of shoulders—arms stretched and
relatively relaxed, in spite of tremendous pull.**

The final sweep is somewhat like shoveling and pitching snow or dirt with an exaggerated wide sweeping motion. Try it right now without the hammer. Reach way to your right as if you had a shovel in your hands . . . knees bent, strong lifting position . . . left arm across your chest, left shoulder dipped . . . shoulders and hips forming an X . . . eyes to the right, but a little ahead of the shovel. Now pivot on the ball of your left foot and sweep the shovel counterclockwise letting your hands rise to slightly higher than eye level, and no higher, as you pitch its "contents" out in the 180° direction. Pivot leftward on the balls of both feet so you end up in a cross-legged position. Don't straighten your left knee until just after the shovel passes the 0° point (note correct left leg action in Figures 276 and 277—imitate it).

This wide sweeping action is most important if you are to come close to achieving your potential, and for this reason I may seem to be belaboring the point. But you must learn to *work the hammer through the longest practical arc during the final sweep, and do it in the shortest interval of time.* Unfortunately many throwers, more than half I have seen, concentrate on getting rid of the hammer quickly and as a result whip it through too short an arc during the final sweep. The left leg is just as important in the hammer as it is in the other throwing events, and the final sweep must be made around it, as is shown in Figures 274 through 280.

As an adjunct to the "shovel and pitch" motion described above, practice the final sweep with a short hammer, one which is about one foot long overall. Merely replace the hammer wire by a sturdy nylon cord. Try this exercise with a "wrist-grip" (left hand on handle as usual, right hand holding the left wrist, thumb up). First swing the hammer to your left to gain momentum, then sweep it to your right, way behind you, pointing back at 180°. As you sweep it back, dip your left shoulder so it is almost pointing straight down when the hammer is all the way back . . . look back at the hammer in this position . . . knees flexed deeply, almost in a full squat position . . . left heel raised, almost all your weight on your right foot. Then rotate leftward while shifting most of your weight onto your left foot and shovel-pitch it through a very wide arc, in the manner shown in Figures 274–280. Be sure to keep your left foot firmly on the ground until AFTER releasing the hammer.

The points covered in the three preceding paragraphs apply to the final sweep with the regulation hammer, except the action is much quicker and involves tremendous power, balance and reflexes to do correctly.

Bill Gilligan summarizes a good release this way:

> "What is a good release, and how do we get it? A good release is the result of successively tighter turns, taken progressively faster, where control is maintained to the very end. When you complete the third turn, with the right foot in well ahead of the hammer, with your body in good balance (settled primarily on left foot), with legs *well flexed* at knees and hips, and the hammer way behind—to your right—you are in a strong lifting position and are ready for a powerful release.

"As the right foot feathers in, and the hammer starts to sweep to its low point, continue to lean down and away from the hammer with extended, stretched arms [Figures 274–275]. The instant it reaches its low point (or an instant before), drive with your strong lifting muscles—stretch with your legs and throw your back and shoulders back, as if you were tearing something out of a hole and pitching it straight up, to your left. This lift supplements the tremendous momentum the hammer has. It is so explosive that the hammer rips from your fingers at the last instant, when it is about shoulder high."

He adds the following caution:

"What are some of the pitfalls during the release? A late right foot is perhaps the worst error. The earlier it lands (i.e., the farther ahead of the hammer it is), the more work you can do on it during the release. So as you whip around in the last turn, don't let that right foot fly out. If it does, it will land late. Keep it in tight, and get it in early.

"Also avoid straightening the back and shoulders too abruptly or leaning back for too long as the hammer passes in front and to your left. Doing this will cause the center of gravity to shift back toward the right side of the body thereby making it difficult or impossible to get sufficient weight on the left leg to continue into a proper release. Keep your hips and torso turning in the direction of the throw. Keep your left foot firmly on the ground until after the hammer has left your hands.

"Then as the violent force of the rotary motion brings the body around to the left after the release, you can help keep the body in the circle by doing the following. One, swing the left leg quickly back toward the center of the circle after the hammer is released; and two, then drop the hips into a sitting position, thereby moving the center of gravity back four to eight inches toward the center of the circle. This will help avoid fouls at the front of the circle."

One of Connolly's greatest assets was his ability to use his great leg strength to really lift the hammer during the release. He stated: "When I am really throwing well, I feel as if I am going straight down into the ground in the last turn. Then suddenly I pull out of it just as the hammer sweeps through its low point, and I throw straight up in the air. It feels straight up, although my release angle is what it should be, or around 42–45°. I definitely feel both legs come into the throw. I come down, then both legs start extending immediately, and I drive way up on both toes and throw straight up. Not out—up."

Burke summarizes the final sweep this way: "I would stress the importance of the 'throw' (final sweep). Done right, this can add 10 to 25 feet in distance thrown.

"(a) As the hammer rises in the third turn, *let the arms and shoulders be pulled farther out, in the direction of the hammer*. This keeps your weight on your left foot and also adds to the hammer's momentum as turning speed and radius increase.

"(b) Hit the right foot early, but slightly *over-complete* your turn. This frees your hips for rotation on the 'throw' [Figures 275–276].

"(c) Accelerate the hammer by pushing to the left with your right foot, knee, and hip. This will allow the ball to swing way over to the left [Figures 275–278].

"(d) As the ball reaches its lowest point, the bent left leg [Figures 275–278] is *violently straightened*. The head goes back and chin points toward the throw. Arms remain relatively passive until the left leg is straightened. Then the X is uncrossed as a violent pull with the left hand is executed."

Look carefully at Figures 276, 277 and 278. It is hard to picture a more powerful finish position. The left leg is still bent in Figure 276, but is straight in Figure 278. Just that quick. Also note how much the hips rise from Figure 275 through 279. Tremendous power.

Do likewise!

PHYSICAL CONCEPTS

There are several physical principles which materially affect the distance one can throw the hammer. Most of us know that a hammer in flight behaves like a projectile, and that once released gravity will eventually bring it back down. We know that a projectile will travel the maximum distance if it is propelled initially at a 45° release angle. All of us know that the faster the hammer-head is moving when released, the farther it will go, provided the release angle is about 45°. But few of us really understand how the thrower's *turning speed* and the hammer's *effective radius* combine to make up true, *linear hammer-head velocity*. For example, few realize that *a 10% increase in effective hammer radius can produce up to 40 feet in distance thrown, given exactly the same turning speeds and a 45° release angle.*

If you think I am going to suggest that proper application of certain physical principles can improve distances thrown by as much as 40 feet, you are right. Furthermore, relatively simple adaptations of form can lead to this happy result, adaptations which are well within the capabilities of most average throwers.

There are two basic written sources for the data, as well as some of the ideas, in this important section.

1. Toni Nett's *Die Technique beim Stop und Wurf*. His Nomograph showing the relationship between distance thrown, release velocities, angle of release, and hammer flight time is shown as Figure 286.
2. Geoffrey Dyson's *The Mechanics of Athletics*.

Let's start with a slight modification of a statement made above.

> *The faster the hammer-head is moving, in terms of true, linear velocity, at the instant of release, the farther it will travel, provided it is released within a 42–44° range.*

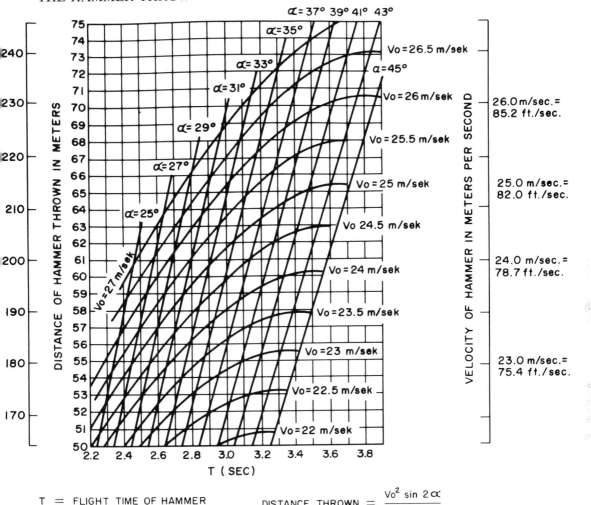

Figure 286.   **Relationship between Distance Thrown, Release Velocity, Angle of Release and Flight Time of Hammer.**

Importance of Linear Velocity

Table 3 highlights the tremendous importance of hammer-head linear or peripheral velocity. It shows, for example, that a 10 percent increase in hammer-head linear velocity at the instant of release can produce up to 40 feet more in distance thrown, provided the release angle is 42–44°.

Table 3

| IMPORTANCE OF HAMMER VELOCITY | | |
Hammer-head velocity[1] (feet/second)	Turning speed[1] (revolutions/second)	Distance thrown[3] (feet)
75	2.0	180
79	2.1	200
83	2.2	220
87[2]	2.3	240

(1) At instant of release
(2) 88 feet/second is the same as 60 miles per hour
(3) Based on 44° angle of release

Variables Making up Linear Velocity

In hammer throwing, we must deal with two kinds of velocity: *turning* or angular velocity, and *linear* or peripheral velocity.

Consider the following experiment. Make up two, four pound hammers, using lead fishing weights as hammer-heads. One hammer should be the regulation length, four feet—the other three feet. Then take both and execute three normal turns, and release them simultaneously. The longer contraption will travel much farther than the the shorter one, perhaps 60 feet farther, yet both were released while turning at exactly the same *turning speed*. Obviously the longer hammer was moving at a higher *linear velocity* (it traveled a longer path during the same amount of time) than the shorter implement.

Let's now turn to the formula for *linear velocity*. It is—

$$v = \omega r$$

v = velocity in feet per second.
ω = turning speed in radians per second. A radian equals about 57.3°. (2π radians = 360°).
r = hammer's effective radius (distance in feet from near center of hammer-head to axis of rotation of turning system—note Figure 243).

From this formula, it is clear that linear velocity is a function of *both turning speed and the effective radius*. Hold turning speed constant and increase the hammer's effective radius, and the hammer-head's linear velocity will increase proportionally. Better still, increase both.

Importance of Long Effective Hammer Radius

For some strange reason, the importance of a long hammer radius is often overlooked in the Eastern United States. Frequently the emphasis is on *turning faster*, rather than on *"turning as fast as you can while sweeping the hammer through the widest radius you can control."*

Table 4 shows that a six-inch increase in the hammer's effective radius can produce 30–40 feet more in distance thrown, provided turning speed and release angle remain constant! Figure 243 shows how many throwers can easily add three to six inches to their effective radius by letting their upper body relax and stretch in the direction of the hammer during the turns, particularly as the hammer rises into each turn.

Table 4

IMPORTANCE OF A LONG EFFECTIVE HAMMER RADIUS			
Thrower's turning speed (revolutions/second) vs different lengths in hammer's effective radius			
Turning speed at instant of release (revolutions/sec.)	Distance thrown[1] based on effective hammer radius[2] of—		
	6'0"	5'9"	5'6"
2.0	180'	166'	151'
2.1	200	186	168
2.2	220	203	185
2.3	240	221	203
(1) Based on 44° angle of release.			
(2) Distance from axis of rotation to about center of hammer-head.			

Let's examine Table 4 carefully. Take a thrower who is turning at a respectable, but not spectacular, rate of 2.2 revolutions per second at the instant the hammer is released. Assume he counters the hammer's pull too much with his upper body, and as a result sweeps the hammer through a 5'6" radius. This combination of turning speed and radius would produce sufficient linear velocity to throw the hammer 185 feet provided the release angle was 44° (next to last line, Table 4).

Now assume the same thrower relaxed his upper body somewhat, and let it stretch forward with the hammer, thereby permitting the hammer to sweep through a six-inch wider radius, *while maintaining the same turning speed* of 2.2 revolutions per second. This combination of the same turning speed and extra radius would produce sufficient linear velocity to propel the hammer 35 feet farther, provided the release angle remained at the same 44°.

We now know why throwers like Zsivotzky and Klim can easily outdistance many of their competitors while turning through what might appear to be slower turns. *A wider radius—a wider range of movement*—is a significant part of the answer.

Of course it takes tremendous strength and flexibility, especially through the back and midsection, to be able to let the hammer sweep through the extra inches of radius Zsivotzky and Klim do. It also takes a higher developed "feel" for the amount and direction of the hammer's pull, and the ability to counter this pull with enough force to increase turning speed, but not with so much force that there is a disproportionate loss in hammer radius. For example, during the final sweep, the hammer's radius will be decreased as the legs and body pull the hammer inward somewhat, but the great pickup in hammer velocity (stemming from the feet pressing against the ground with tremendous force) will more than offset this loss.

Centrifugal Force

It is easy to say "to throw your best, *turn as fast as you can while sweeping the hammer through the widest radius you can control.*" As indicated above, doing this requires a great deal of strength, plus the ability to use this strength quickly. A rotating object exerts a pull directly away from its center of rotation. Given a constant radius, the faster it revolves, the more it will pull out. This pull is called centrifugal force. It is always matched by an equal force pulling into the center called centripetal force.

Let's look at the formula for centrifugal force (F) so we can understand the relative importance of the variables which make it up, and can appreciate the amount of force which is involved.

$$F = mr\omega^2$$

m = hammer's mass, 16 pounds, divided by gravitational
         constant 32.

r = hammer's effective radius.

ω = angular or turning velocity in radians per second.

From this formula, we can see that turning speed is clearly the most important variable, but radius still retains the importance accorded it earlier. *Turn fast, but sweep the hammer through a wide radius.*

Table 5 shows how much centrifugal force is involved to throw certain distances between 180 and 260 feet.

Table 5

RADIUS VS. CENTRIFUGAL FORCE VS. DISTANCE THROWN			
	Linear Velocity	Approximate Centrifugal Force Required with—	
Distance Thrown	at Release	6.0' radius	5.75' radius
180'	75'/second	460 pounds	490 pounds
200	79	520	540
220	83	575	600
240	87	630	660
260	91	690	715
Angle of Release = 44°			

Table 5 shows, for example, that it takes about 575 pounds of centrifugal force to produce a release velocity of 83 feet/second, which is required to throw 220 feet, if the hammer's effective radius is 6.0 feet, and the release angle

44°. If the effective radius were reduced three inches to 5.75 feet, it would take 25 pounds more centrifugal force to produce the required release velocity of 83 feet/sec. needed to throw 220 feet.

Angle of Release

It is well established that a projectile will travel the maximum distance horizontally when it is released at a 45° angle. This assumes that the release and landing points are level. In the case of the hammer the release point is about five feet higher than the landing point. Accordingly, the optimum angle of release for the hammer is 42–44°.

Release angles falling outside this optimum range will result in shorter distances thrown, as Nett's Nomograph (Fig. 286) shows. Table 6 summarizes the distances to be gained in shifting from a 30° release angle to the optimum 42–44° range.

Table 6			
IMPORTANCE OF 42–44° ANGLE OF RELEASE			
Hammer-head velocity at release (feet/second)	Distance thrown based on release angle of:		Difference
	30°	42–44°	
75	161′	180	19′
79	179	200	21
83	195	220	25
87	213	240	27

Some throwers, particularly the strong weight-lifter type, have difficulty exceeding a 30–35° release angle. This is because they overcounter the hammer's pull with their arms and shoulders. This error usually flattens the plane on which the hammer travels.

Instead you must keep your arms and shoulders relatively relaxed during the winds and turns, and passively *guide* the hammer up to its high point during each turn. Note the hands in Figures 262, 268 and 273.

The word "guide" is stressed because forcing or lifting the hammer artificially to its high point will destroy the essential rhythm of the turns, and will reduce the hammer's effective radius, with a resulting loss in linear velocity. Instead, guide it up naturally while simultaneously stretching forward at the waist in the direction of the hammer. Guide the hands up to about eye level during each turn, and the release angle will automatically be 42–44°, provided you do not pull the hammer in sharply during the final sweep.

WHAT TO WATCH FOR—A CHECKLIST

The following are the main points coaches watch for.
1. Note the overall tempo of the throw. It must be one smooth, rapidly

accelerating, continuous action, from start through release. Each turn must be faster than the preceding one. There must be a pronounced, continuous buildup in hammer-head speed. There can be no pauses.

2. In evaluating speed, pay more attention to hammer-head speed than to the thrower's turning speed.

3. Sense that the thrower gains on the hammer with each turn, that is, increases his lead-angle on the hammer with each turn. Make sure the thrower stays ahead of the hammer during the turns.

4. Watch the hammer wire. Sense that it picks up great speed from turn to turn. Sense that it gets tighter and tighter. It must not become slack at any time, particularly during the back portion of any wind or turn.

5. Watch for a smooth, but dramatic and pronounced, pickup in hammer-head speed as the ball of the right foot alights at the completion of each turn.

6. Stand off at the 270° point and watch where the hammer is at the instant the ball of the right foot alights at the completion of each turn. It must alight ahead of the hammer, before it passes 270° (e.g., Figure 264)— and it should alight farther ahead with each succeeding turn. In addition, it should alight before the hammer drops below shoulder height at the completion of the second and third turns (Figures 269 and 272).

7. Watch the right foot. It should not be lifted too early at the start of each turn, and it must not be lifted way up, or fly too far out. The right foot should travel the shortest route possible and alight quickly so the thrower can bring both legs to bear on the hammer to make it go faster.

8. Watch the right foot as it completes each turn. Only the ball of the right foot should be in contact with the ground between the turns. Make sure the heel does not hit first—if it does, it will brake the turning momentum.

9. Watch the right foot during the turns. It should appear to push the thrower leftward, into each turn.

10. Listen for the right foot as it alights. It should be silent. A thump means the thrower is off balance, or the hammer is ahead of him.

11. Watch the left foot. It must not leave the ground during the winds or turns, even for an instant, until after the hammer is released.

12. Watch the left foot track down the circle. It should do so in a straight line across the circle. Make sure none of the turns are undercompleted; each must be a full 360°, and the last can be a little overcompleted.

13. Watch the sweep into the first turn. Make sure the thrower shifts his weight firmly onto his left foot just before the hammer passes its low point (Figure 281), and holds it there throughout the transition. Make sure he presses way left and turns "outside his left foot" with a well-executed outer-edge roll.

14. Watch the left foot for a good "outer-edge rolling action" throughout the turns.

15. Watch the hammer's lowest point. With each wind and turn, it will creep to the thrower's left, but should remain within the bounds indicated in

Table 2. In particular, watch the low point during the sweep into the first turn (280–300°), and at the start of the final sweep (320–330°).

16. Watch the width of the hammer's radius during the winds and turns. When thrown correctly, one is impressed with the extremely wide radius the hammer sweeps through.

17. Watch the shoulders during the turns. They should not be pulled back as indicated by the dotted lines in Figure 243. Sense that they are relatively relaxed and are pulled forward slightly in the direction of the hammer from the instant the hammer passes 10° until the right foot alights, particularly during the first two turns. (Note Figure 282.)

18. Watch the left shoulder at the completion of each turn to see if the hammer's pull makes it dip naturally a bit more with each turn (e.g., Figure 270 vs. 274). This is a sign that the thrower is completing the turns farther ahead of the hammer with each turn.

19. During the back portion of each turn, watch the left knee to see if it "gives" or bends quickly, ahead of the hammer, immediately after it passes its highest point, and before the right foot alights (e.g., contrast Figures 268 and 269).

20. Watch the legs between the turns. They must be flexed deeply, in a strong lifting position before the hammer passes its lowest point. The thrower must get his legs "under the hammer," so to speak, before the start of each turn (Figure 246).

21. It is difficult to see where the thrower actually starts each turn, but it should start before the hammer passes the right knee.

22. Watch the head position relative to the hips. They should turn together, square to each other. The eyes should not turn ahead of the hips by an appreciable amount during the turns, particularly during the back portion of the last turn.

23. While watching to see if the hips and head are turning together, watch the arms and hammer. With each turn, they must lag the head and hips/legs by an increasing amount.

24. Also watch the eyes. They must not look down, particularly at the completion of each turn . . .

25. . . . and watch the eyes and head during the winds. The head should remain facing the same direction, to the thrower's right (about 280°), all throughout the winds. The head must not turn to the front as the hammer comes forward except during the sweep into the first turn.

26. Watch for the "hip-angle" (Figure 284). It must not disappear, particularly during the last turn.

27. Watch the hands during the winds. They must pass through a very wide radius.

28. Watch how high the hands are as the hammer sweeps through its highest point. In the first turn, they should naturally rise to shoulder height, and in the succeeding turns, a little more, to about eye level. If this is done correctly, the hammer will travel on a properly inclined plane, and the

release angle will be an optimum 42–44°. Watch the thrower from the side to make sure this is true.

29. Watch how far the hands are from the thrower's body. They must stretch way out, particularly as the hammer sweeps up to its high point (e.g., Figure 282).

30. Watch the back portion of the last turn. The thrower must not "gather himself," or turn his head way left in anticipation of the final sweep.

31. Also watch to make sure the thrower does not pull his arms in during the final sweep.

32. Watch the left foot during the release. It must not break from the ground until after the hammer is released (Figures 279–280).

33. Watch where the hammer lands. It should land a little to the right of the center line bisecting the foul sectors, as you look out in the direction of the throw.